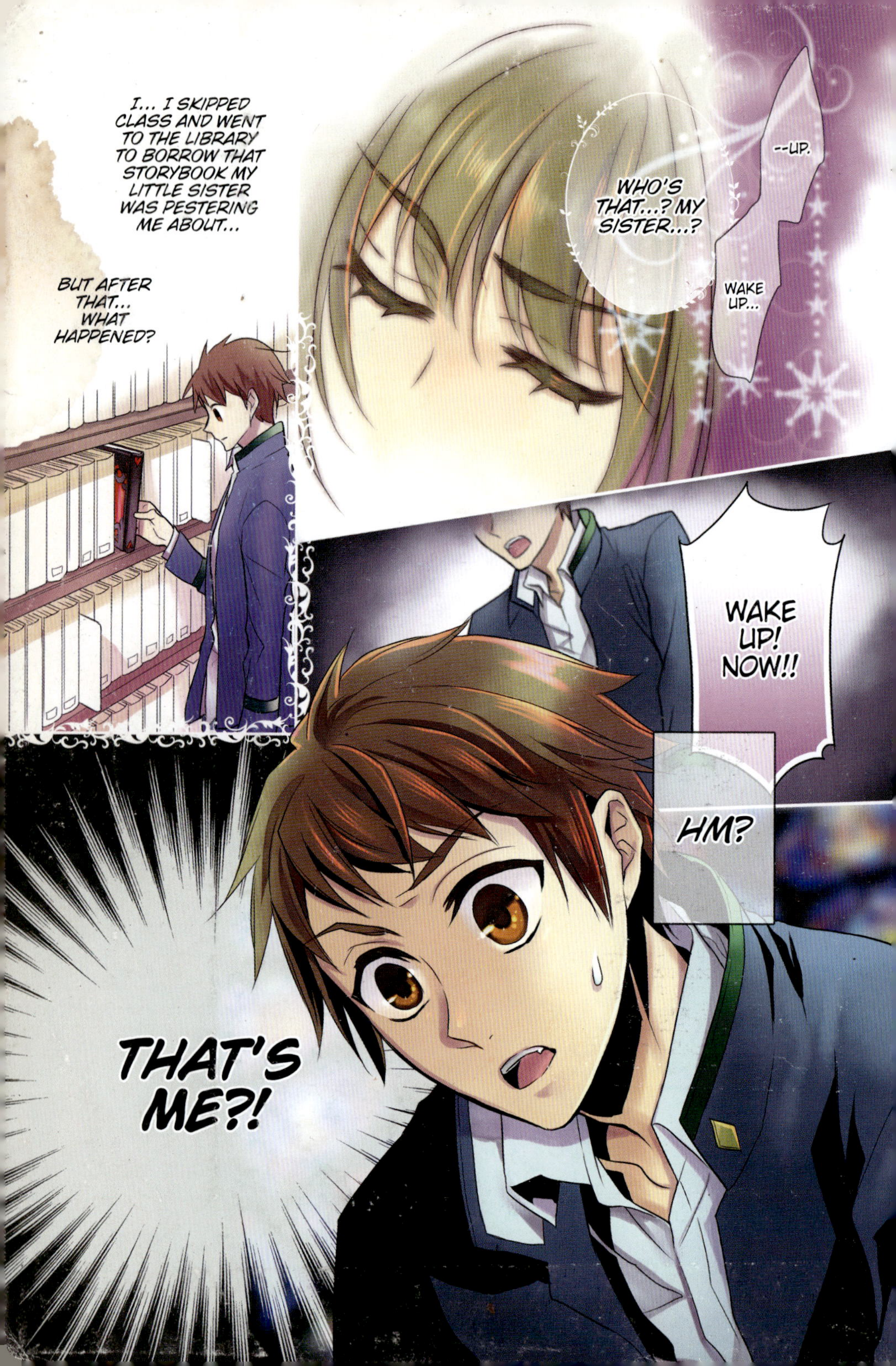
--UP.
WAKE UP...
WHO'S THAT...? MY SISTER...?
I... I SKIPPED CLASS AND WENT TO THE LIBRARY TO BORROW THAT STORYBOOK MY LITTLE SISTER WAS PESTERING ME ABOUT...
BUT AFTER THAT... WHAT HAPPENED?
WAKE UP! NOW!!
HM?
THAT'S ME?!

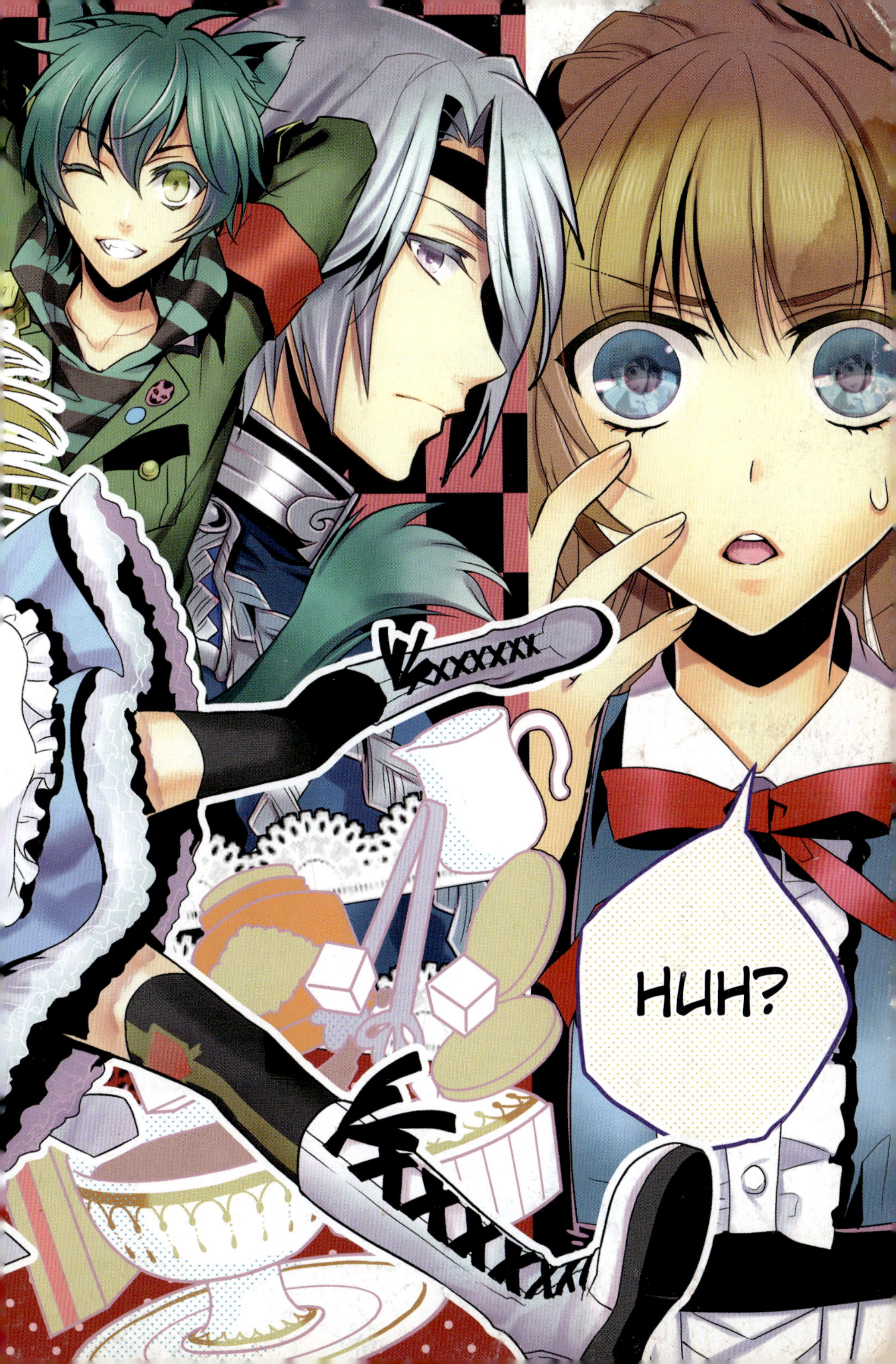
HUH?

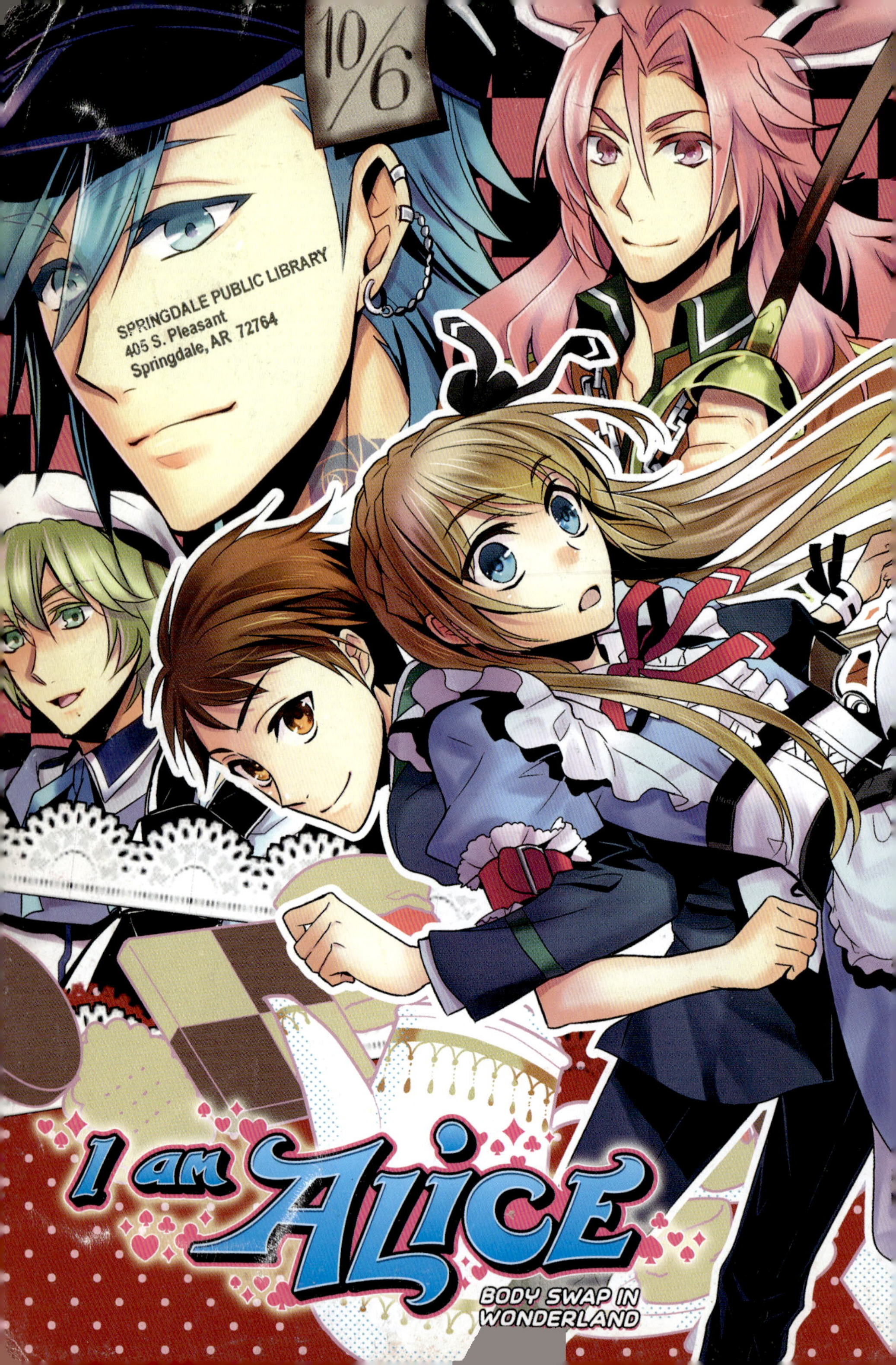
10/6
I am Alice
BODY SWAP IN WONDERLAND

CHARACTERS

I AM ALICE

Body swap?!

Alice

The girl who is now in Makoto's body. Strong, likeable, and obsessed with weapons.

Makoto

The protagonist, dragged into Wonderland--and into a girl's body. Essentially good-natured.

The White Rabbit

Captain in the King of Hearts' army. A responsible, brotherly type, he keeps the more chaotic elements in line.

The Hatter

Soldier in the King of Hearts' army. Sharp-tongued and sadistic, he shouldn't be trusted too far.

The Cheshire Cat

Palace cat who gradually transformed into a human boy. A playboy with a heart of gold.

The Dormouse

A beautiful gentleman who left the army to indulge his love of naps. Far more dangerous than he appears.

Dum (Tweedledum)

Formerly under the direct supervision of the king, he is now the leader of the rebel army. Taciturn and serious.

Access BLobby right here to play the social game *I Am Alice!*

Make friends with the Wonderland characters, train them, and try to escape from Wonderland!

Click on *I Am Alice* under "Games" on the top page. Price: Free! ※Charges may apply for some items. http://blby.jp/?m=comic001

The King of Hearts

The ruler of Wonderland. A ruthless, ambitious leader for whom the ends may very well justify any means...

The King of Heart's valet

Loyal retainer trusted completely by the king.

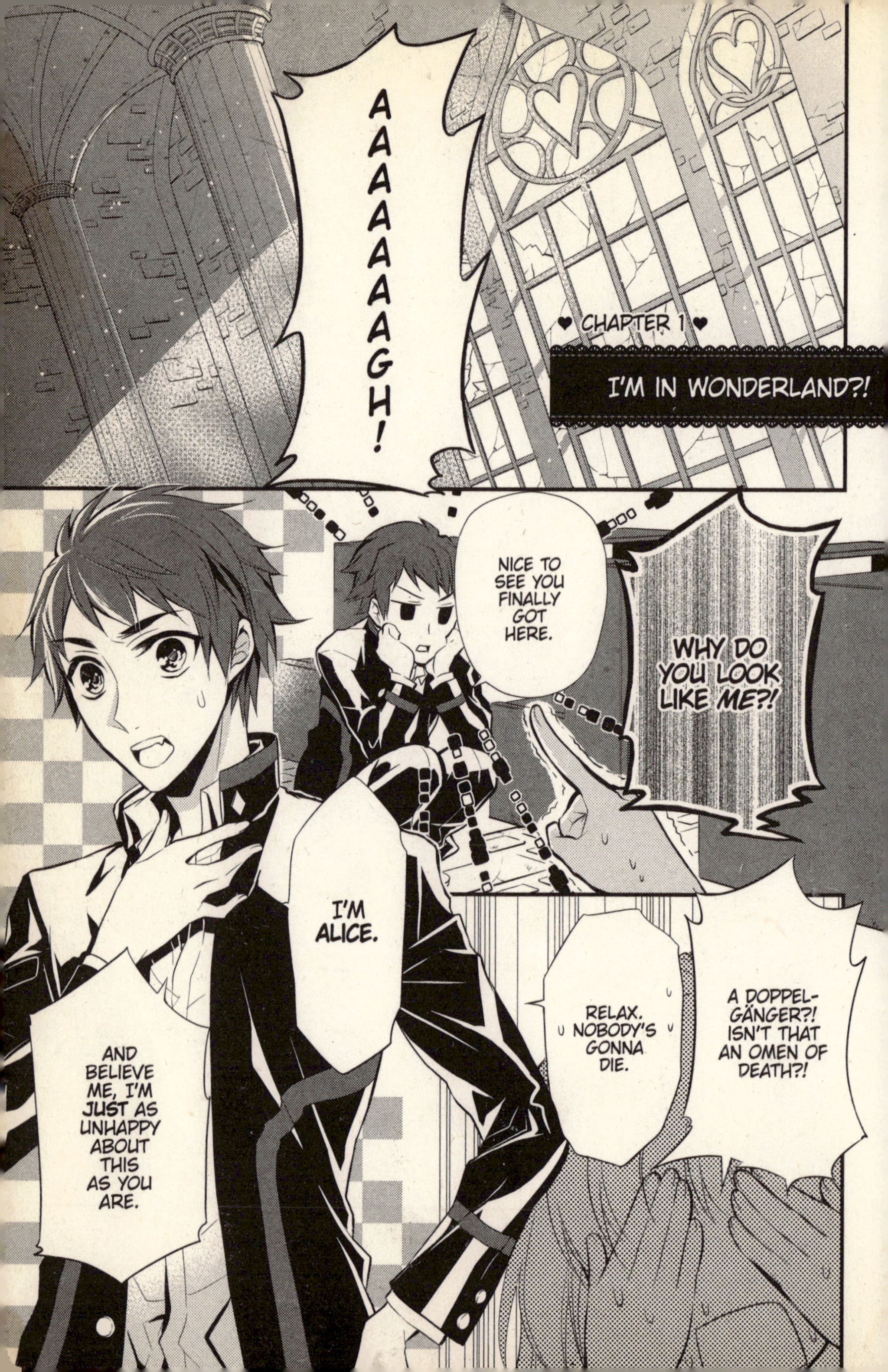
CHAPTER 1
I'M IN WONDERLAND?!
AAAAAAAGH!
NICE TO SEE YOU FINALLY GOT HERE.
WHY DO YOU LOOK LIKE ME?!
A DOPPELGÄNGER?! ISN'T THAT AN OMEN OF DEATH?!
RELAX. NOBODY'S GONNA DIE.
I'M ALICE.
AND BELIEVE ME, I'M JUST AS UNHAPPY ABOUT THIS AS YOU ARE.

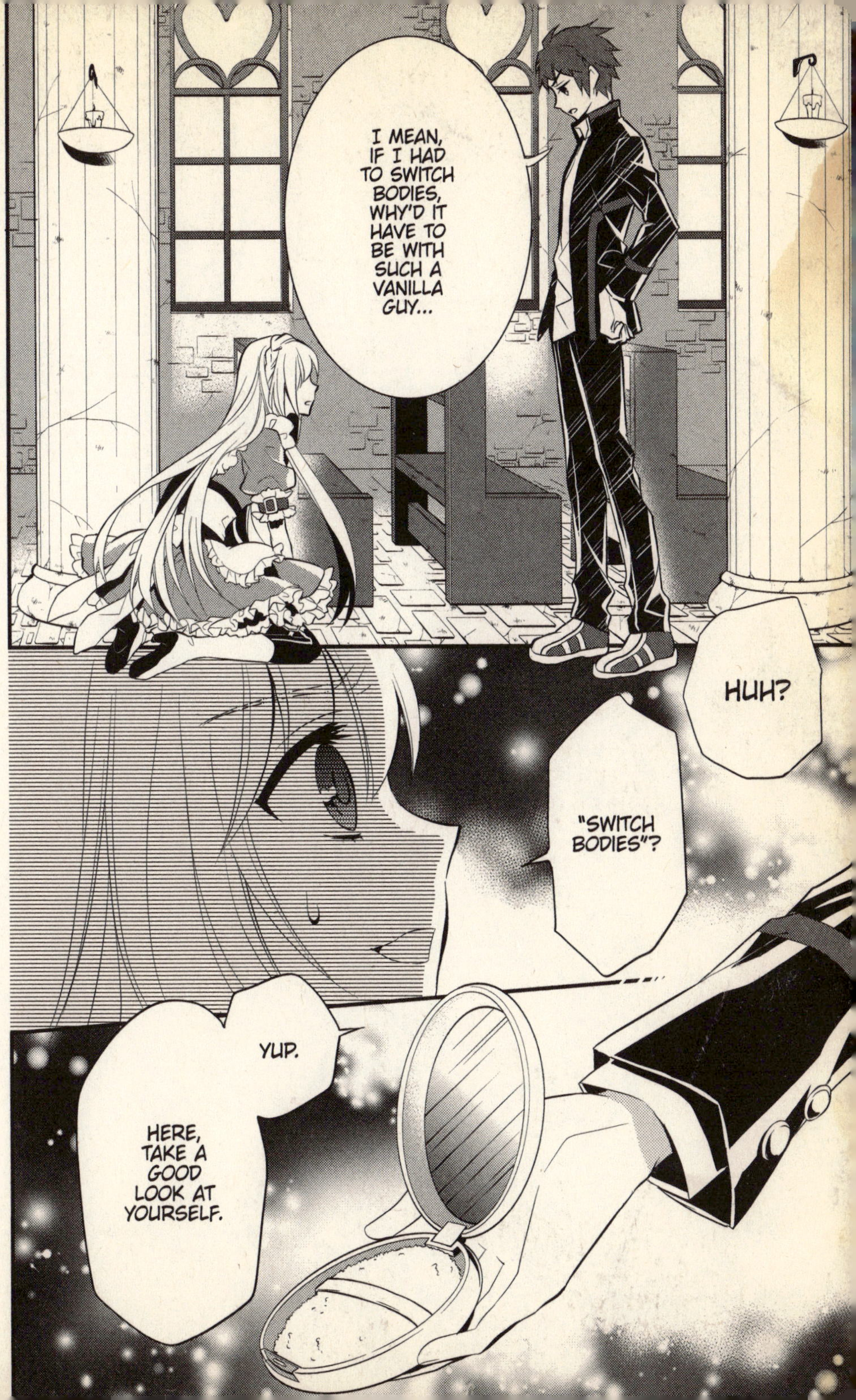
I MEAN, IF I HAD TO SWITCH BODIES, WHY'D IT HAVE TO BE WITH SUCH A VANILLA GUY...
HUH?
"SWITCH BODIES"?
YUP.
HERE, TAKE A GOOD LOOK AT YOURSELF.

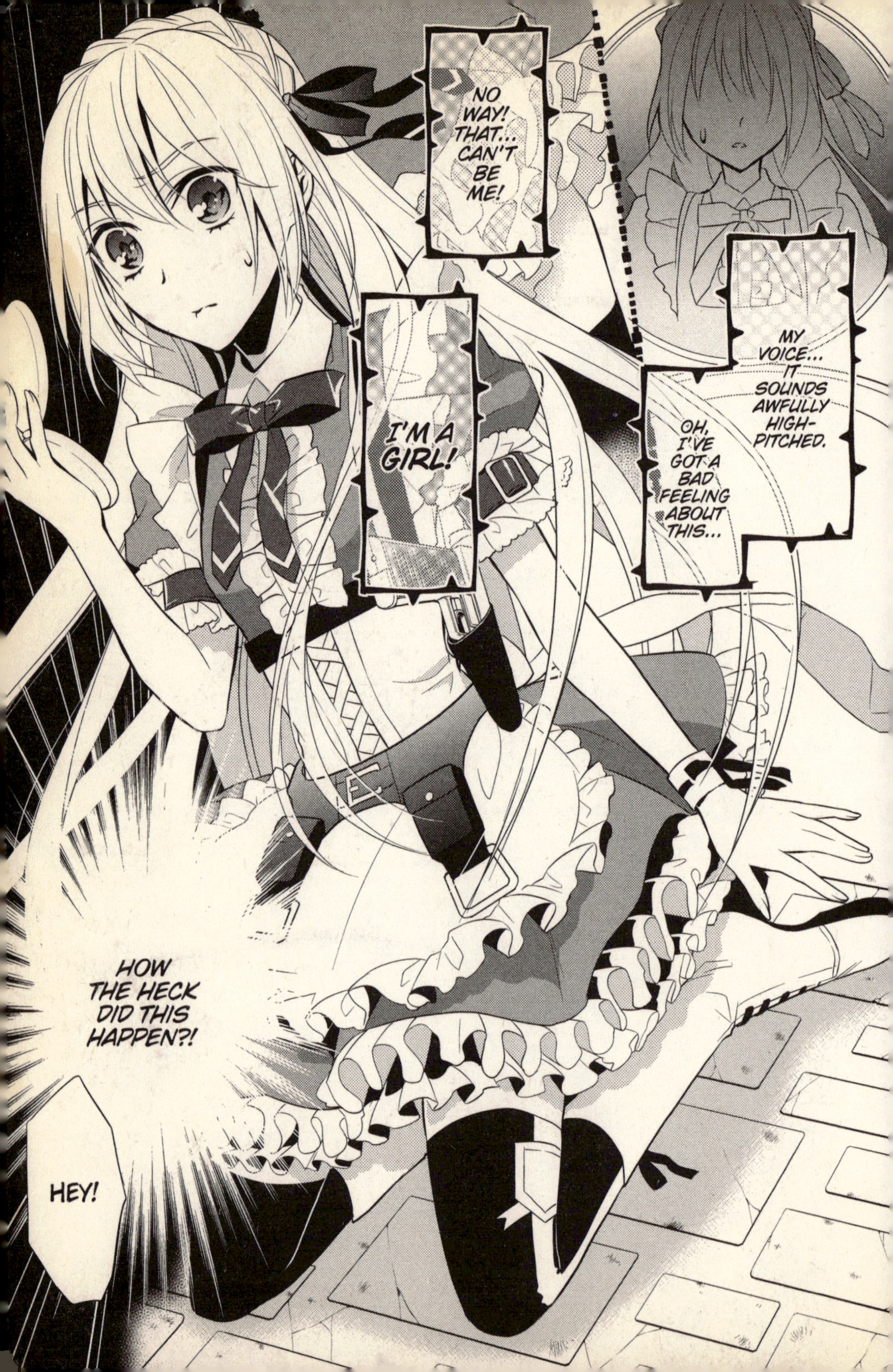
MY VOICE... IT SOUNDS AWFULLY HIGH-PITCHED.
OH, I'VE GOT A BAD FEELING ABOUT THIS...
NO WAY! THAT... CAN'T BE ME!
I'M A GIRL!
HOW THE HECK DID THIS HAPPEN?!
HEY!

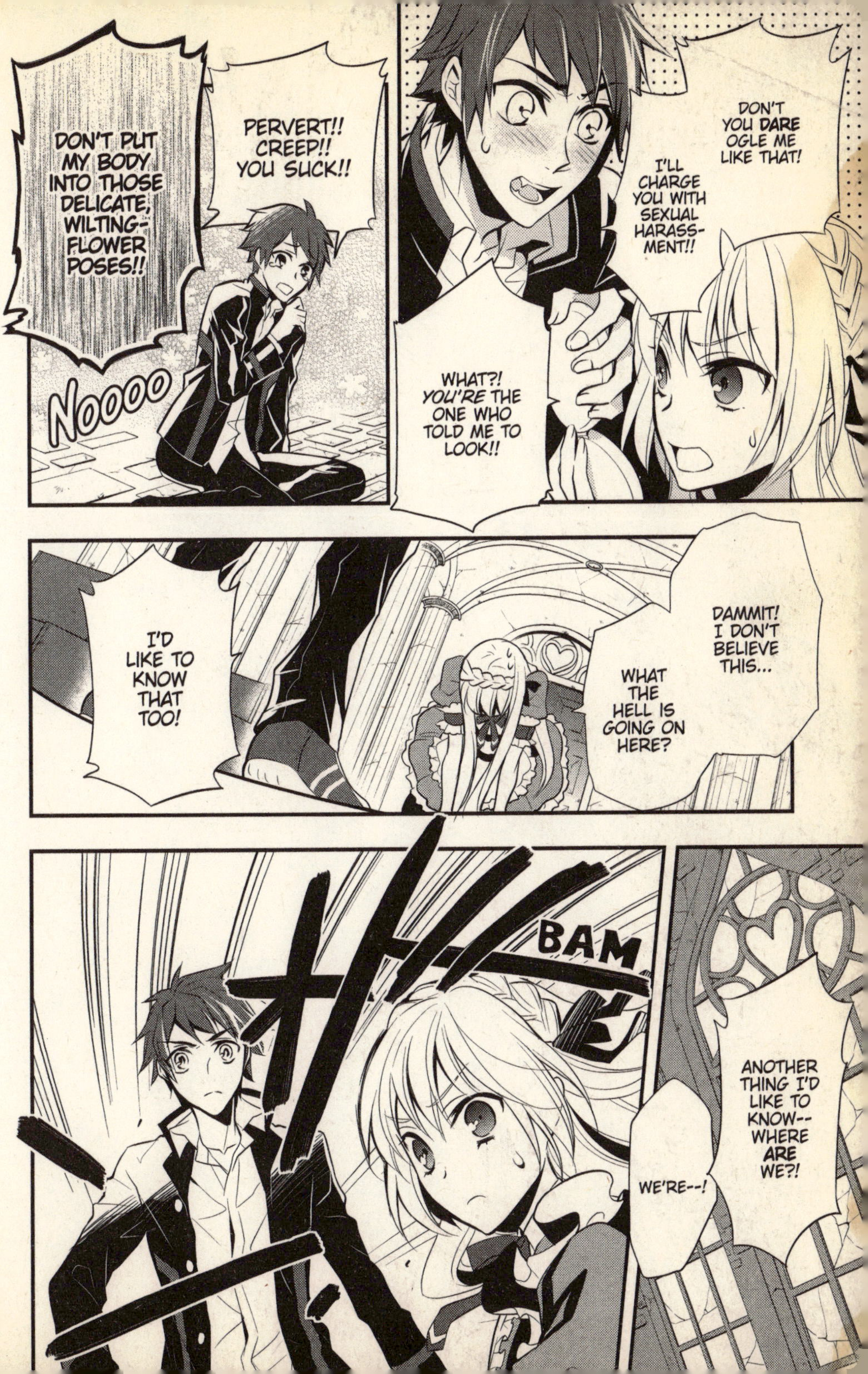
DON'T YOU DARE OGLE ME LIKE THAT!
I'LL CHARGE YOU WITH SEXUAL HARASS-MENT!!
WHAT?! *YOU'RE* THE ONE WHO TOLD ME TO LOOK!!
PERVERT!! CREEP!! YOU SUCK!!
DON'T PUT MY BODY INTO THOSE DELICATE, WILTING-FLOWER POSES!!
Noooo
DAMMIT! I DON'T BELIEVE THIS...
WHAT THE HELL IS GOING ON HERE?
I'D LIKE TO KNOW THAT TOO!
ANOTHER THING I'D LIKE TO KNOW--WHERE ARE WE?!
WE'RE--!
BAM

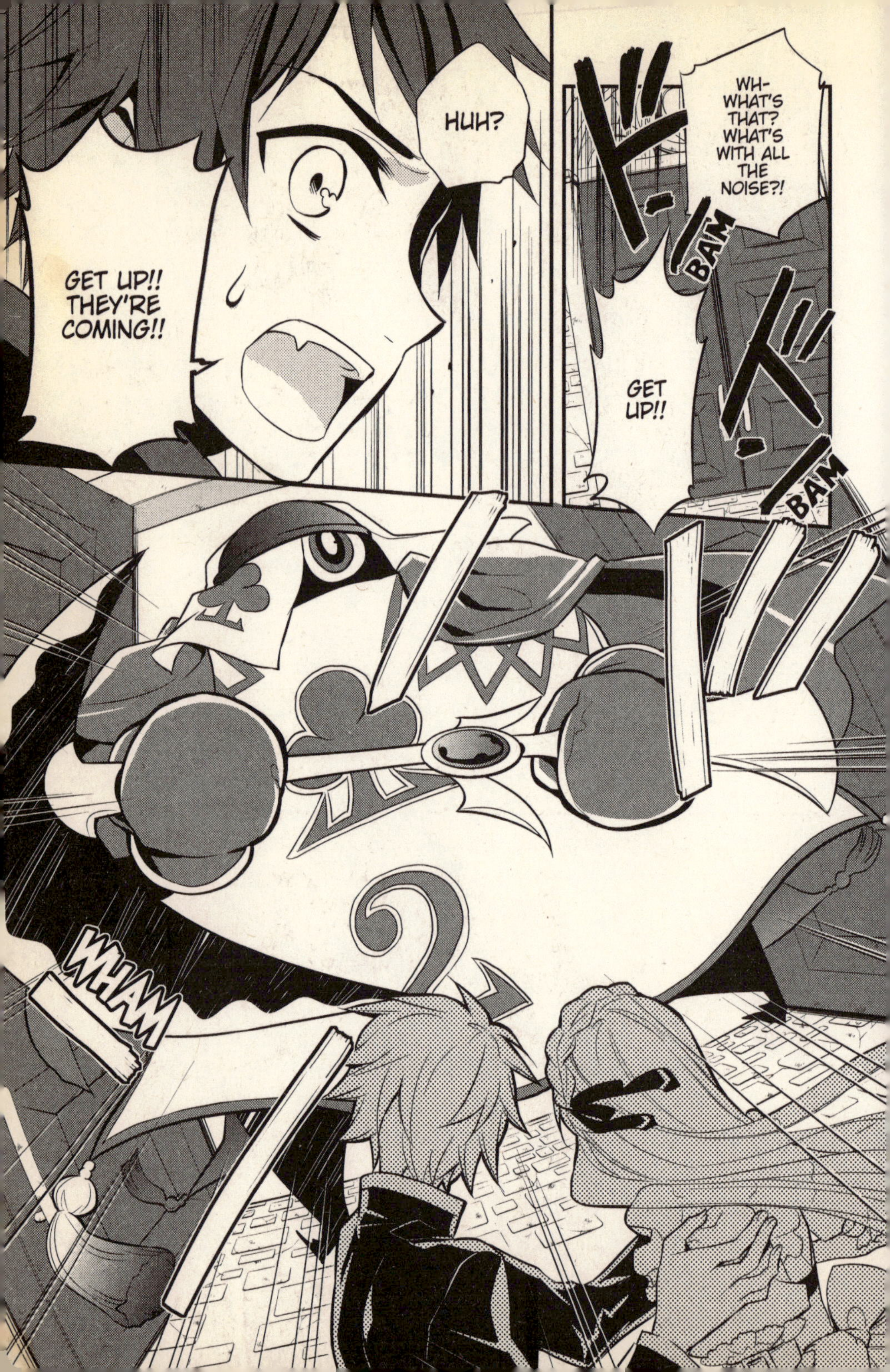
WH-WHAT'S THAT? WHAT'S WITH ALL THE NOISE?!
BAM
GET UP!!
BAM
HUH?
GET UP!! THEY'RE COMING!!
WHAM

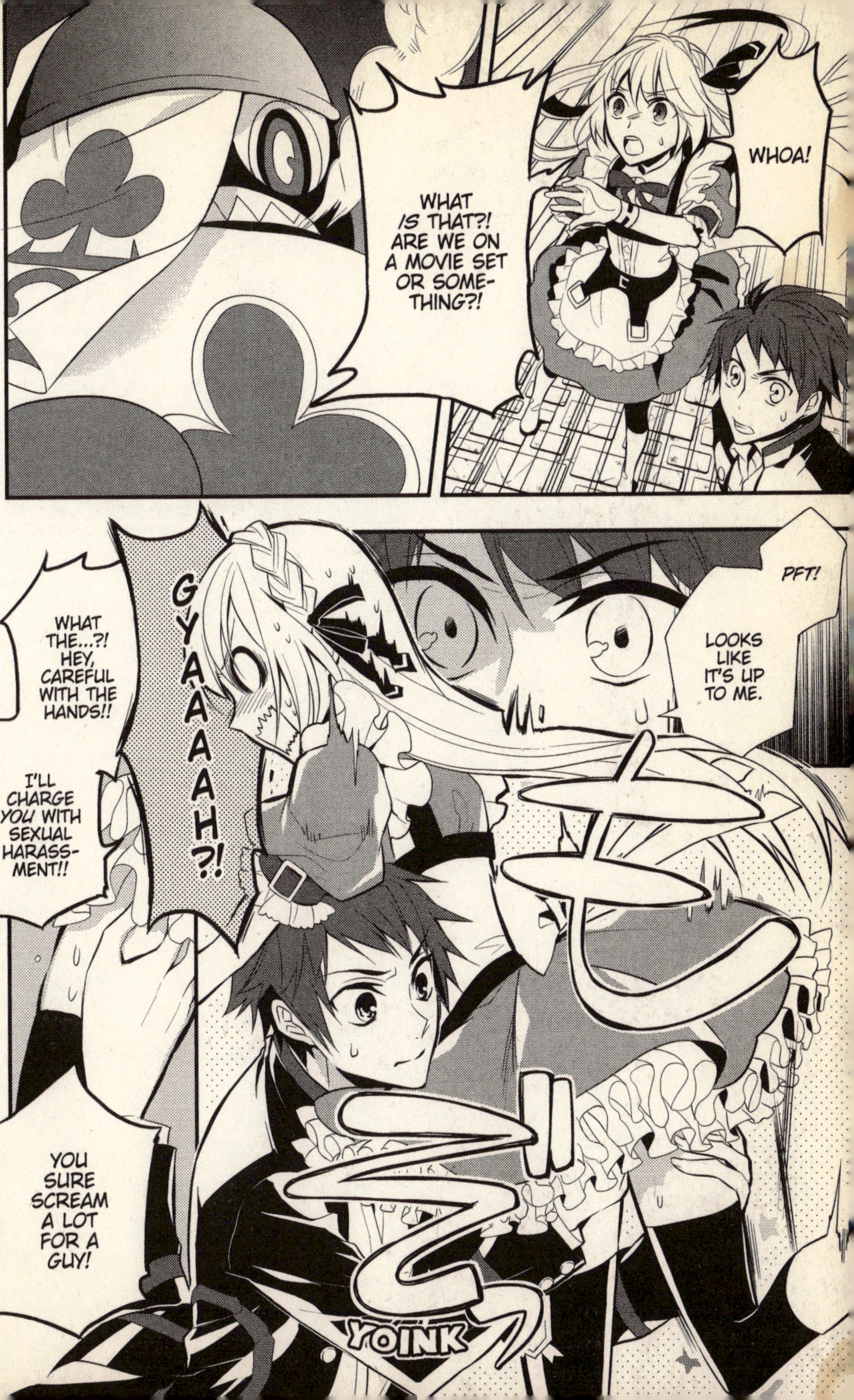
WHOA!
WHAT *IS* THAT?! ARE WE ON A MOVIE SET OR SOME-THING?!
PFT!
LOOKS LIKE IT'S UP TO ME.
GYAAAAH?!
WHAT THE...?! HEY, CAREFUL WITH THE HANDS!!
I'LL CHARGE *YOU* WITH SEXUAL HARASS-MENT!!
YOINK
YOU SURE SCREAM A LOT FOR A GUY!

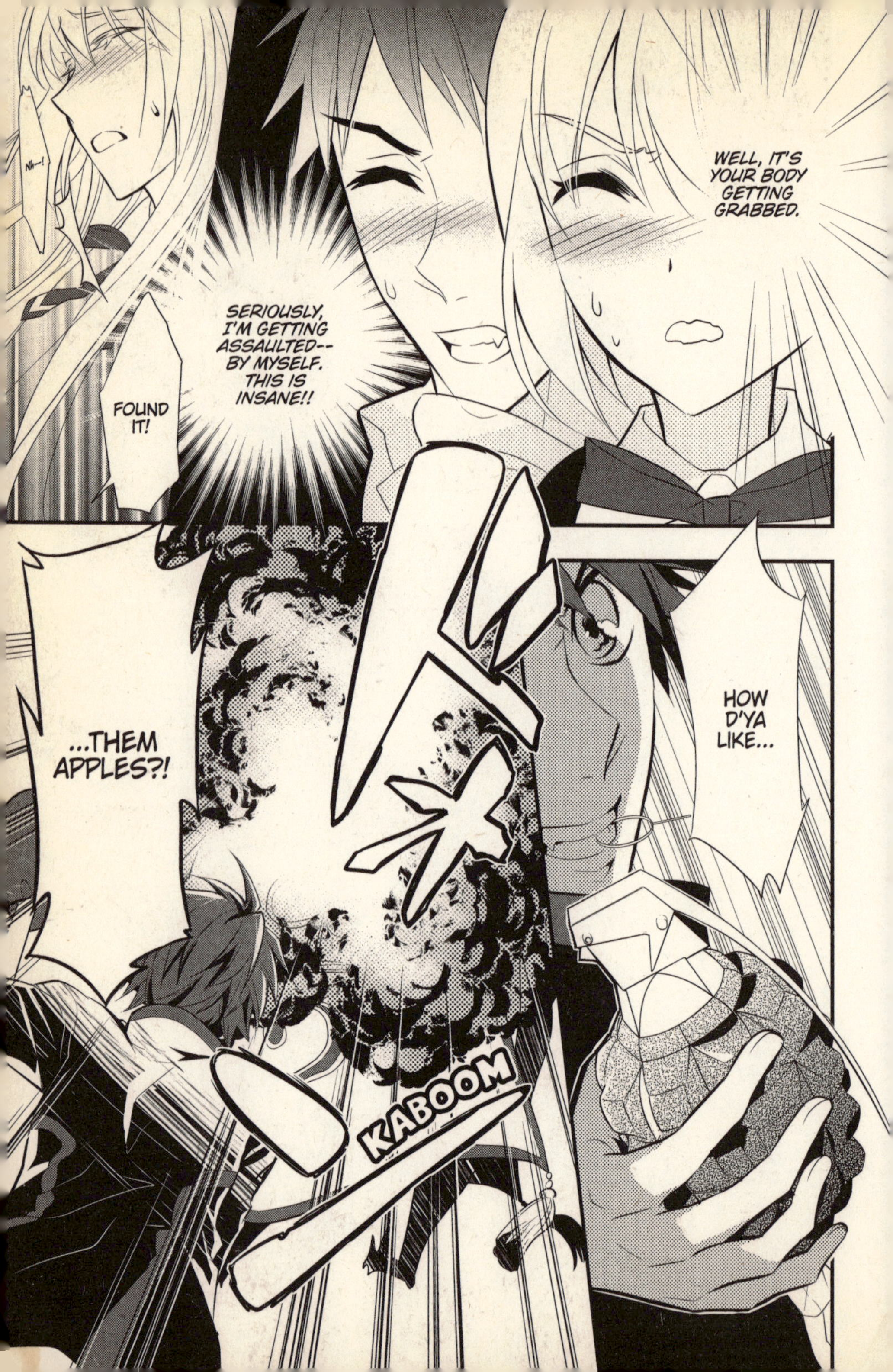
WELL, IT'S YOUR BODY GETTING GRABBED.
SERIOUSLY, I'M GETTING ASSAULTED-- BY MYSELF. THIS IS INSANE!!
FOUND IT!
Nh--!
HOW D'YA LIKE...
...THEM APPLES?!
KABOOM

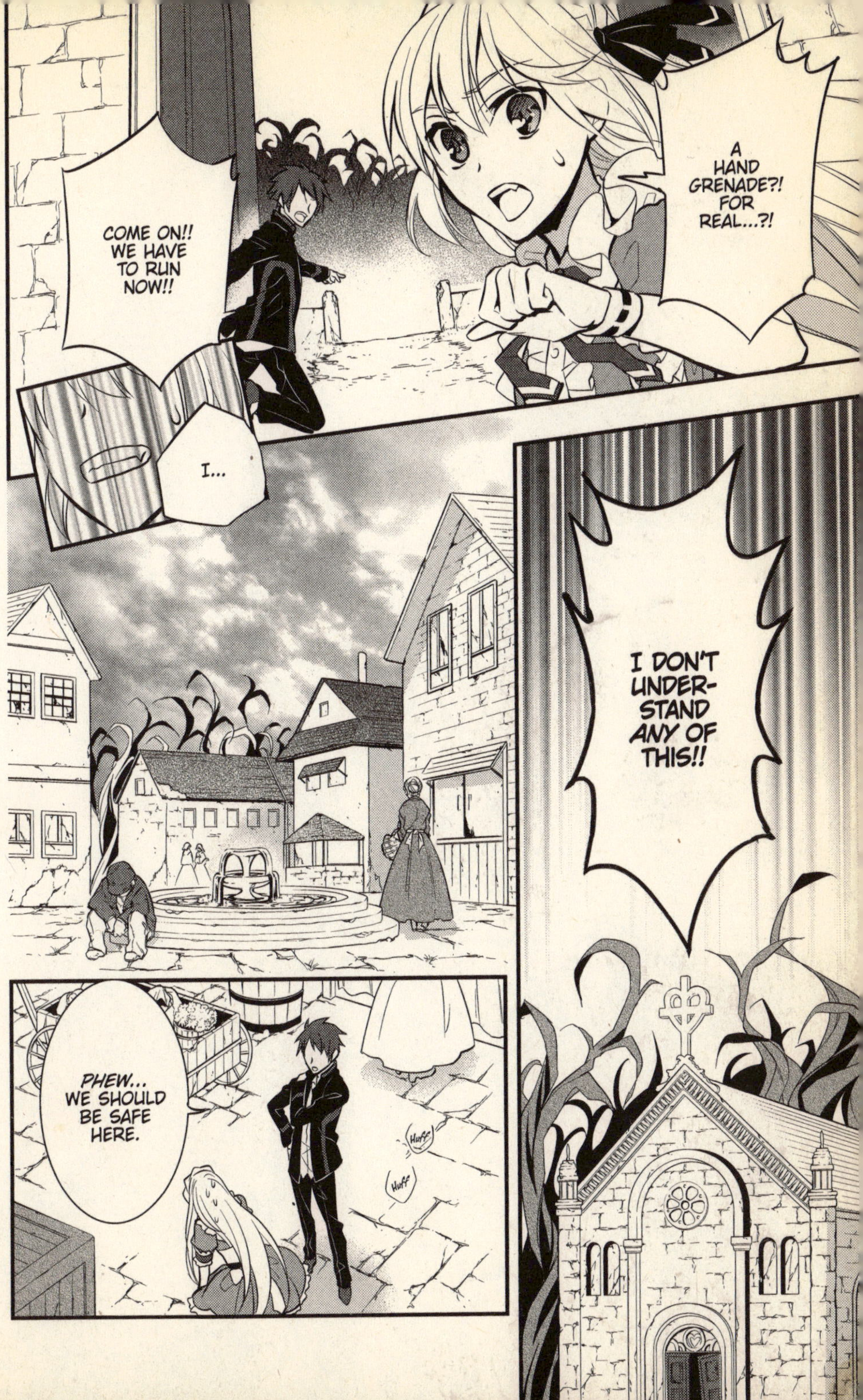
A HAND GRENADE?! FOR REAL...?!
COME ON!! WE HAVE TO RUN NOW!!
I...
I DON'T UNDERSTAND ANY OF THIS!!
PHEW... WE SHOULD BE SAFE HERE.
Huff
Huff

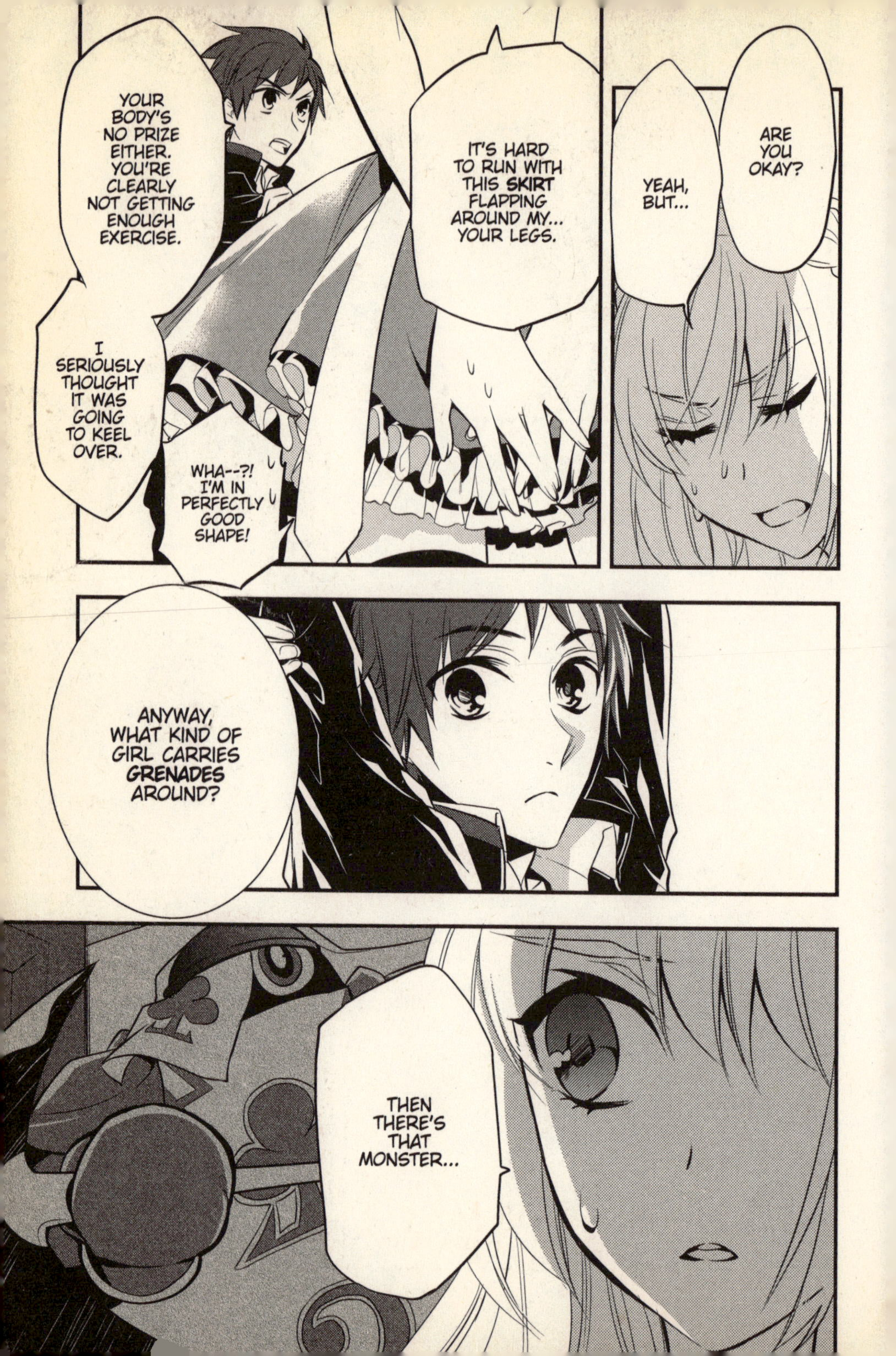
ARE YOU OKAY?
YEAH, BUT...
IT'S HARD TO RUN WITH THIS **SKIRT** FLAPPING AROUND MY... YOUR LEGS.
YOUR BODY'S NO PRIZE EITHER. YOU'RE CLEARLY NOT GETTING ENOUGH EXERCISE.
I SERIOUSLY THOUGHT IT WAS GOING TO KEEL OVER.
WHA--?! I'M IN PERFECTLY GOOD SHAPE!
ANYWAY, WHAT KIND OF GIRL CARRIES **GRENADES** AROUND?
THEN THERE'S THAT MONSTER...

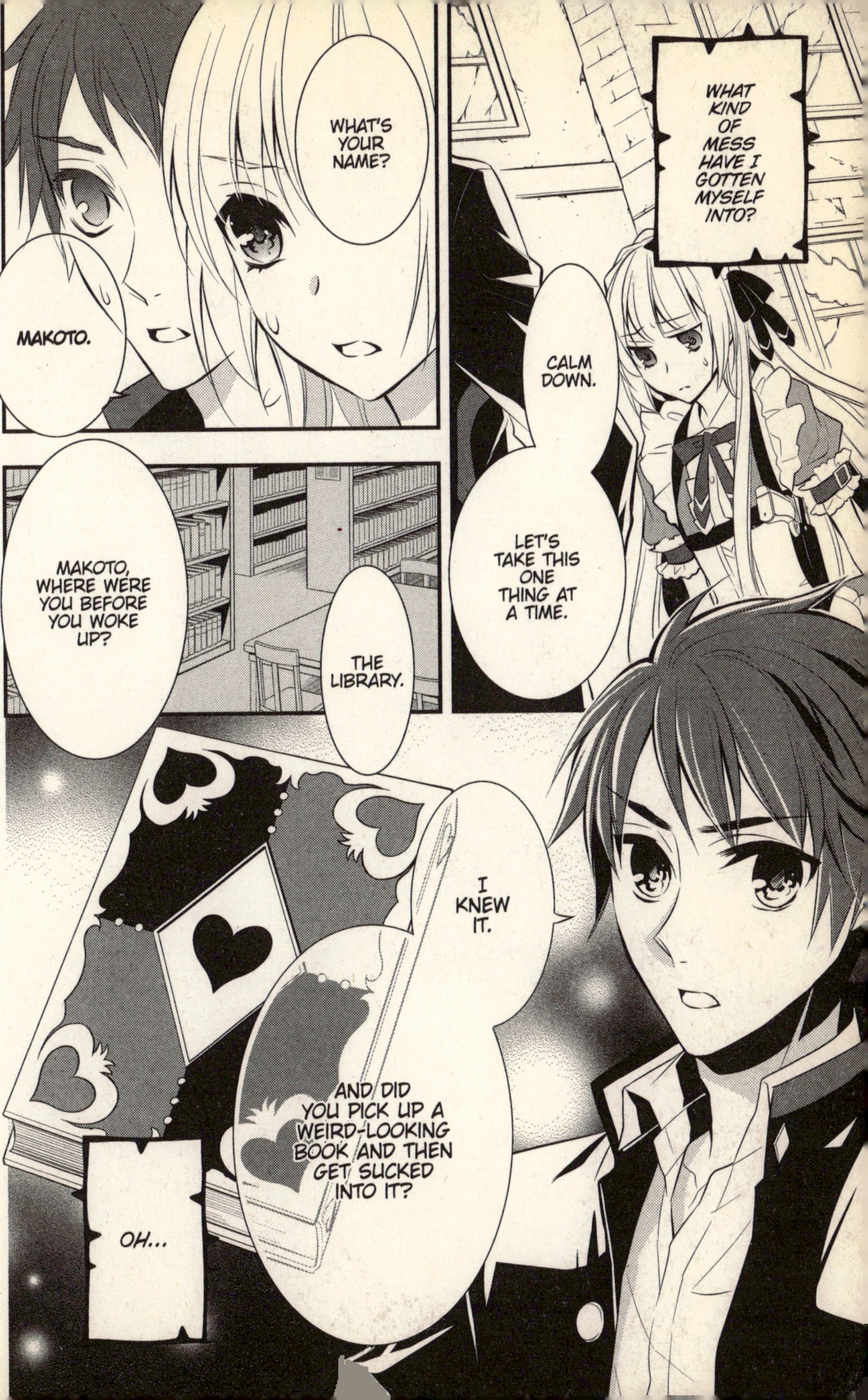
WHAT KIND OF MESS HAVE I GOTTEN MYSELF INTO?
CALM DOWN.
LET'S TAKE THIS ONE THING AT A TIME.
WHAT'S YOUR NAME?
MAKOTO.
MAKOTO, WHERE WERE YOU BEFORE YOU WOKE UP?
THE LIBRARY.
I KNEW IT.
AND DID YOU PICK UP A WEIRD-LOOKING BOOK AND THEN GET SUCKED INTO IT?
OH...

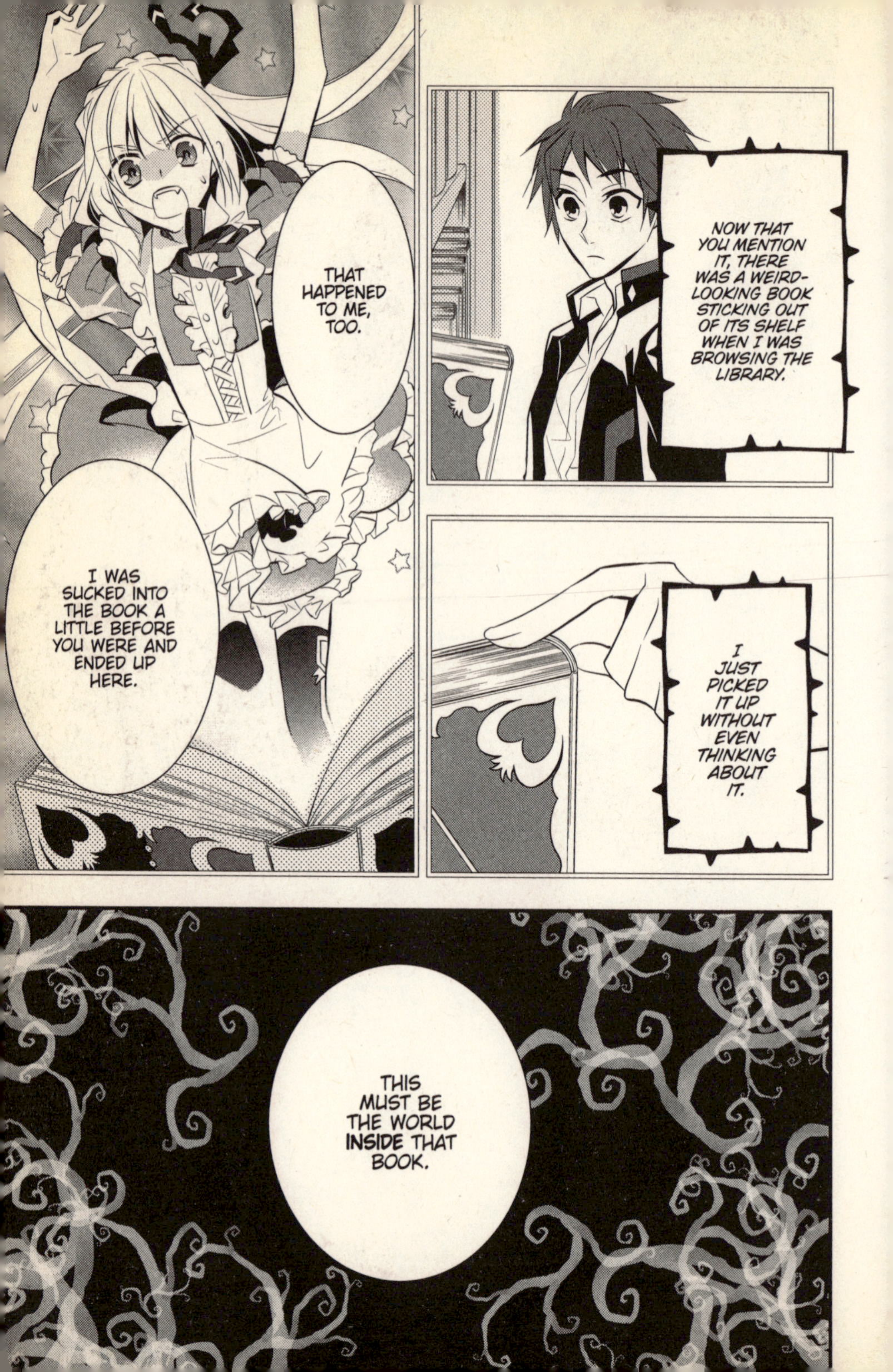
NOW THAT YOU MENTION IT, THERE WAS A WEIRD-LOOKING BOOK STICKING OUT OF ITS SHELF WHEN I WAS BROWSING THE LIBRARY.
I JUST PICKED IT UP WITHOUT EVEN THINKING ABOUT IT.
THAT HAPPENED TO ME, TOO.
I WAS SUCKED INTO THE BOOK A LITTLE BEFORE YOU WERE AND ENDED UP HERE.
THIS MUST BE THE WORLD INSIDE THAT BOOK.

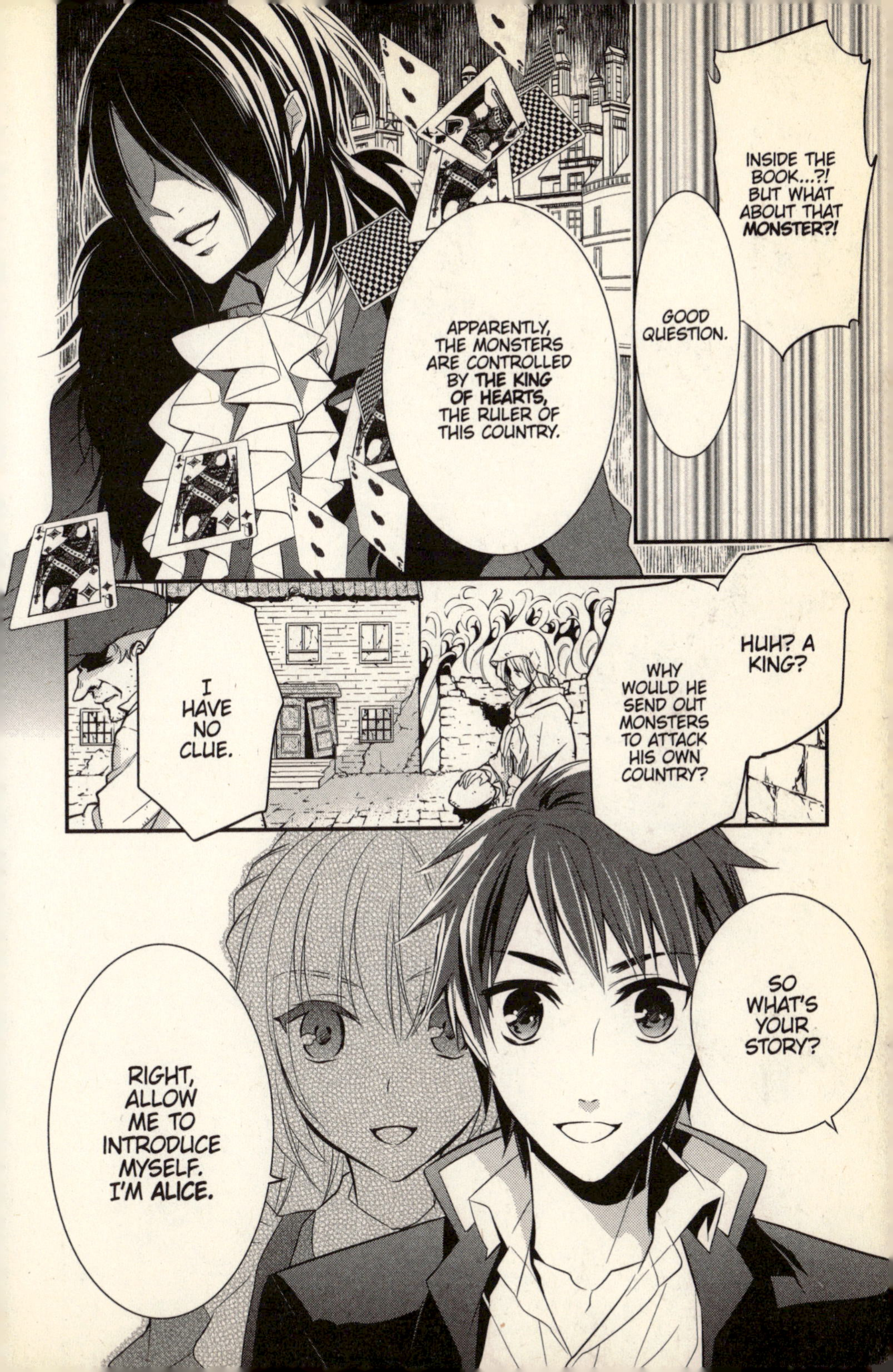
INSIDE THE BOOK...?! BUT WHAT ABOUT THAT **MONSTER?!**
GOOD QUESTION.
APPARENTLY, THE MONSTERS ARE CONTROLLED BY **THE KING OF HEARTS,** THE RULER OF THIS COUNTRY.
HUH? A KING?
WHY WOULD HE SEND OUT MONSTERS TO ATTACK HIS OWN COUNTRY?
I HAVE NO CLUE.
SO WHAT'S YOUR STORY?
RIGHT, ALLOW ME TO INTRODUCE MYSELF. I'M **ALICE.**

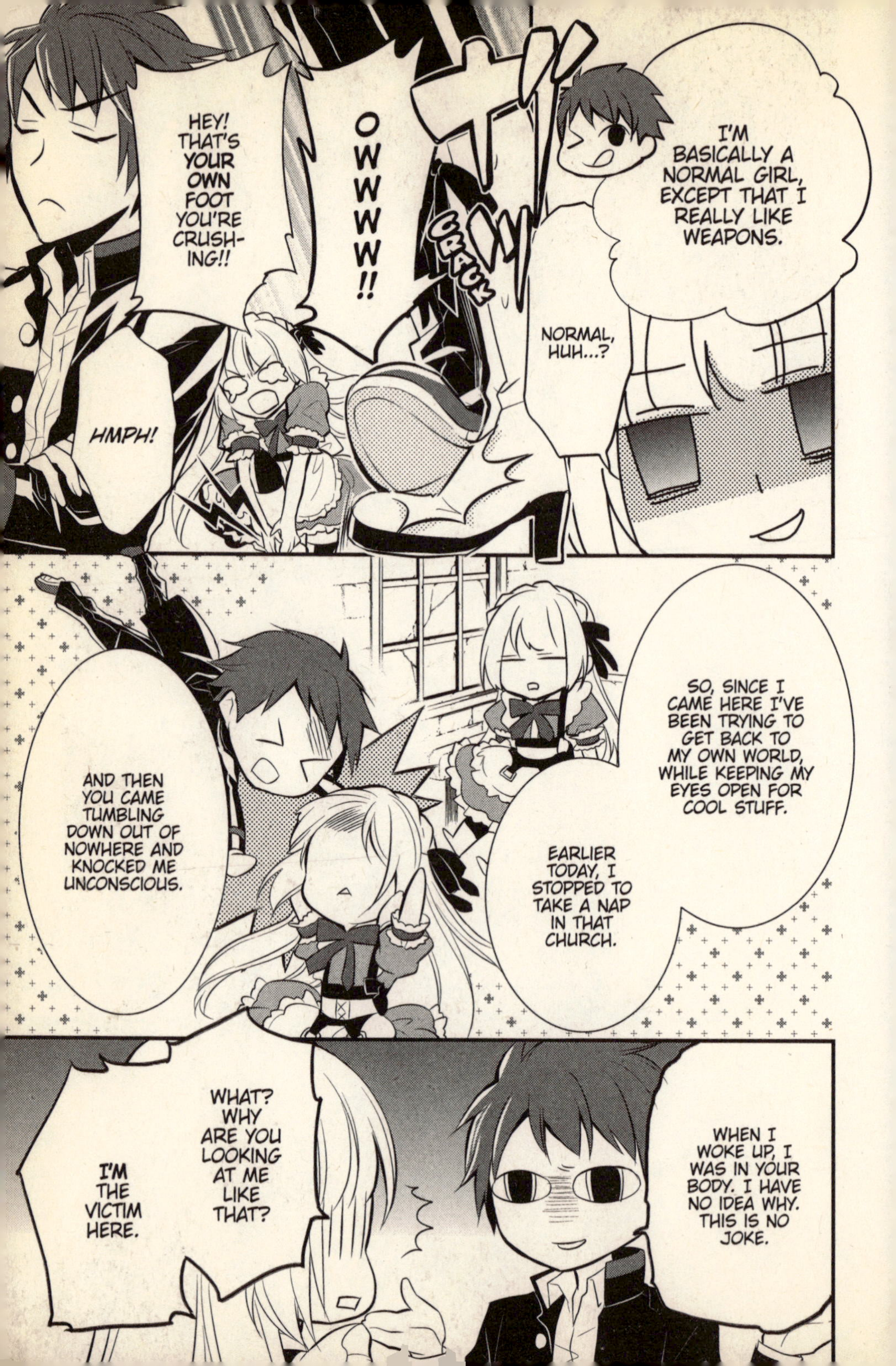
I'M BASICALLY A NORMAL GIRL, EXCEPT THAT I REALLY LIKE WEAPONS.
NORMAL, HUH...?
CRACK
OWWWWW!!
HEY! THAT'S YOUR OWN FOOT YOU'RE CRUSH-ING!!
HMPH!
SO, SINCE I CAME HERE I'VE BEEN TRYING TO GET BACK TO MY OWN WORLD, WHILE KEEPING MY EYES OPEN FOR COOL STUFF.
EARLIER TODAY, I STOPPED TO TAKE A NAP IN THAT CHURCH.
AND THEN YOU CAME TUMBLING DOWN OUT OF NOWHERE AND KNOCKED ME UNCONSCIOUS.
WHEN I WOKE UP, I WAS IN YOUR BODY. I HAVE NO IDEA WHY. THIS IS NO JOKE.
WHAT? WHY ARE YOU LOOKING AT ME LIKE THAT?
I'M THE VICTIM HERE.

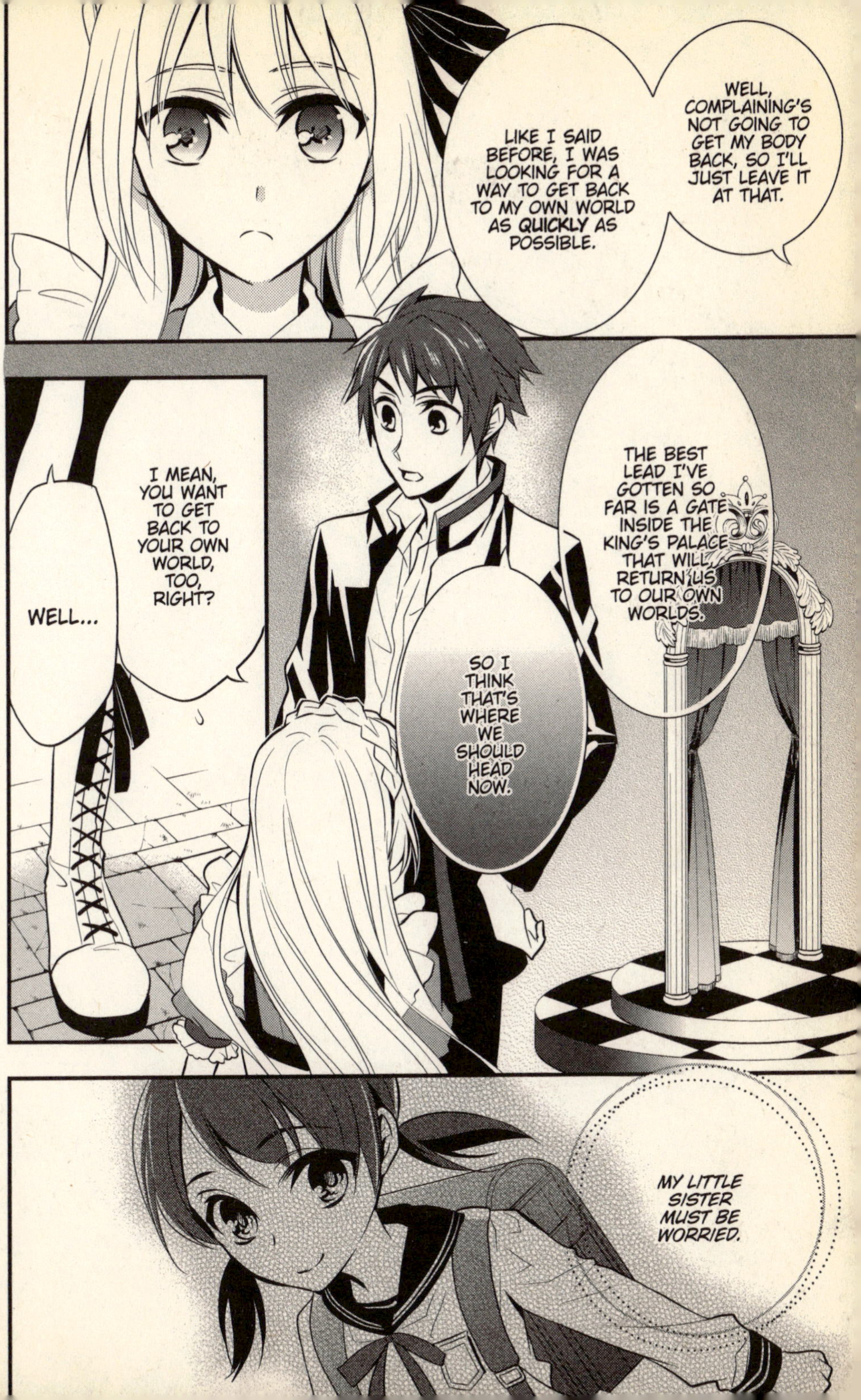
WELL, COMPLAINING'S NOT GOING TO GET MY BODY BACK, SO I'LL JUST LEAVE IT AT THAT.
LIKE I SAID BEFORE, I WAS LOOKING FOR A WAY TO GET BACK TO MY OWN WORLD AS **QUICKLY** AS POSSIBLE.
THE BEST LEAD I'VE GOTTEN SO FAR IS A GATE INSIDE THE KING'S PALACE THAT WILL RETURN US TO OUR OWN WORLDS.
SO I THINK THAT'S WHERE WE SHOULD HEAD NOW.
I MEAN, YOU WANT TO GET BACK TO YOUR OWN WORLD, TOO, RIGHT?
WELL...
MY LITTLE SISTER MUST BE WORRIED.

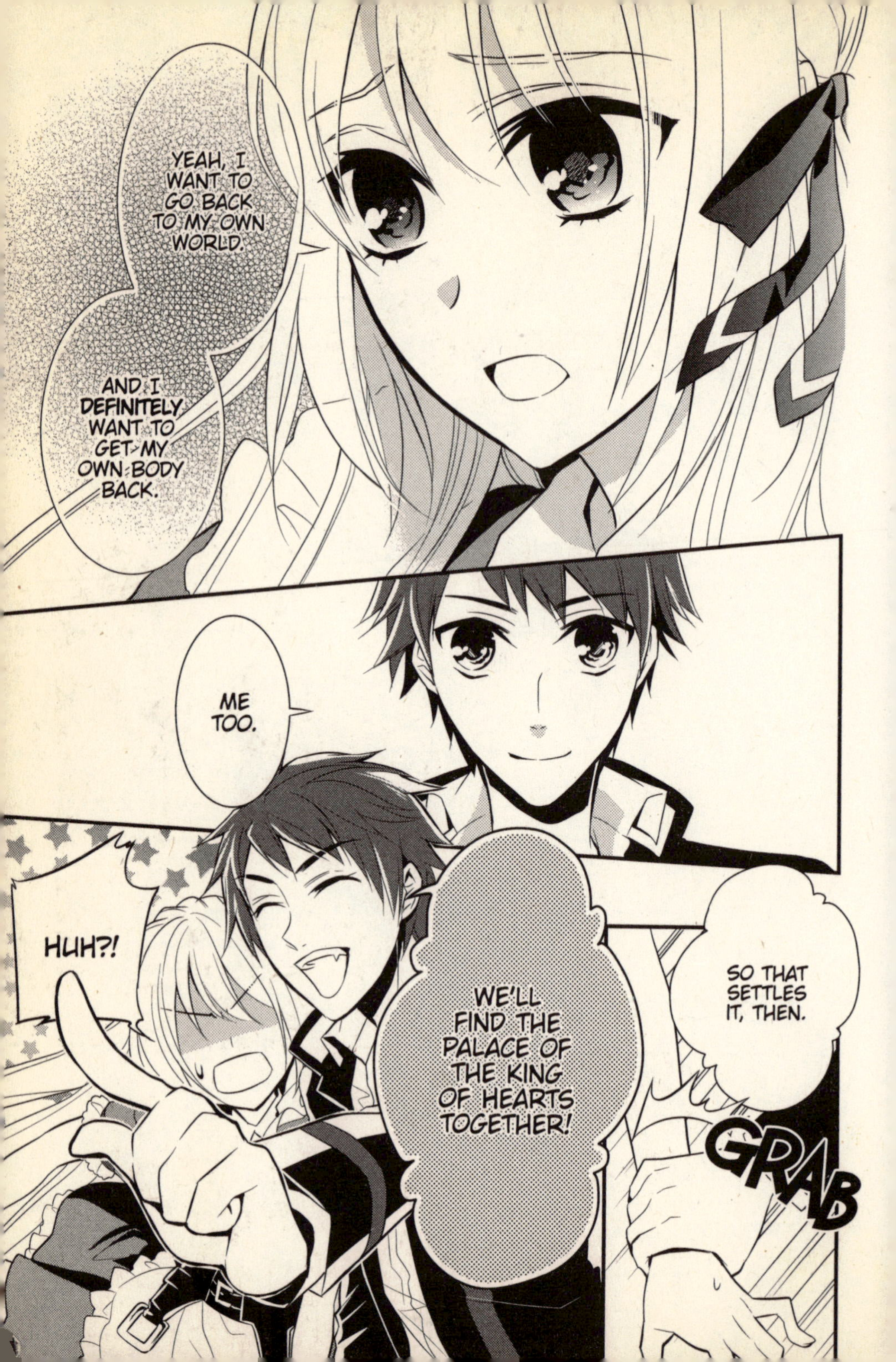
YEAH, I WANT TO GO BACK TO MY OWN WORLD.
AND I DEFINITELY WANT TO GET MY OWN BODY BACK.
ME TOO.
SO THAT SETTLES IT, THEN.
WE'LL FIND THE PALACE OF THE KING OF HEARTS TOGETHER!
GRAB
HUH?!

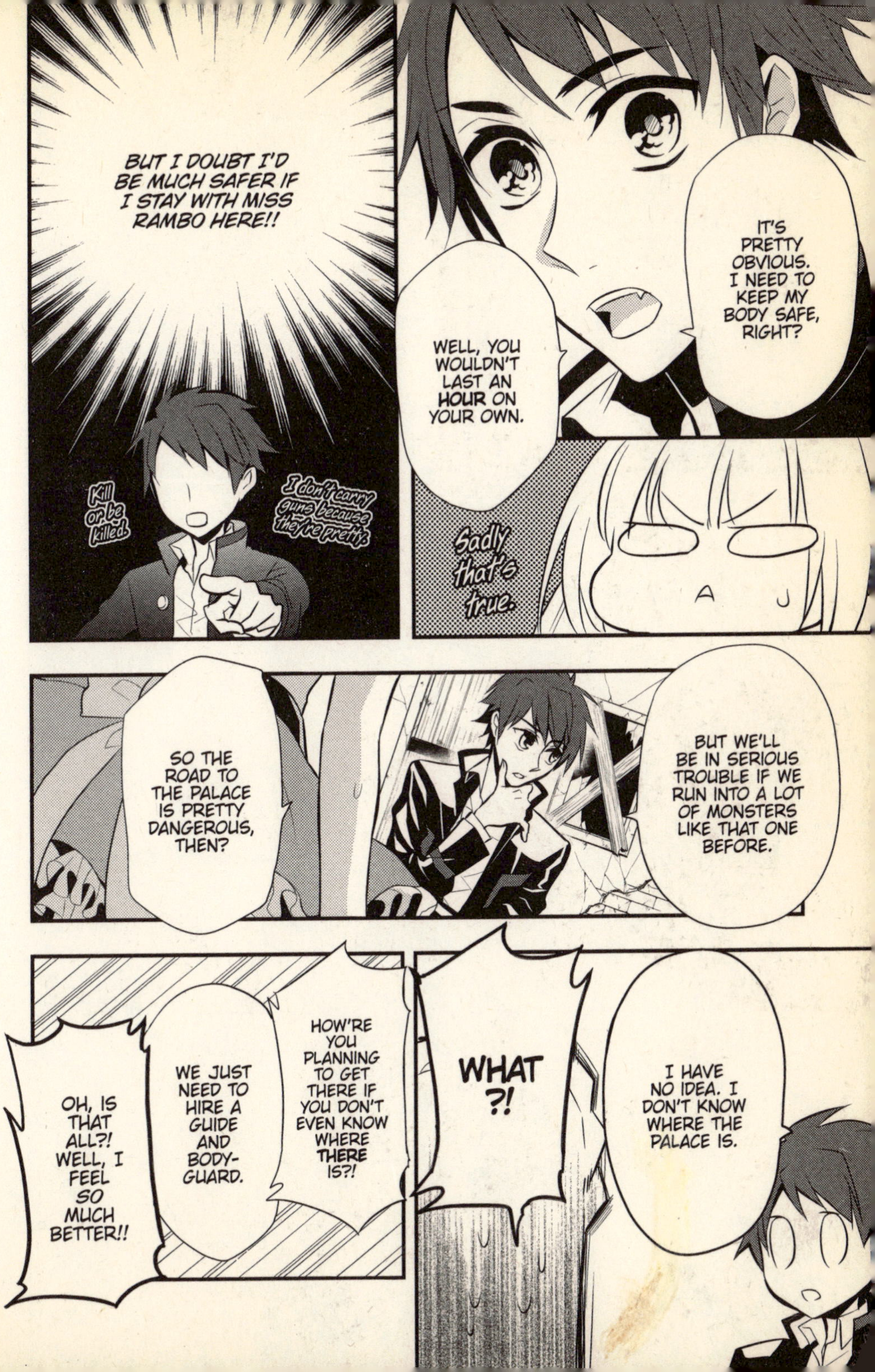
IT'S PRETTY OBVIOUS. I NEED TO KEEP MY BODY SAFE, RIGHT?
WELL, YOU WOULDN'T LAST AN **HOUR** ON YOUR OWN.
Sadly that's true.
BUT I DOUBT I'D BE MUCH SAFER IF I STAY WITH MISS RAMBO HERE!!
I don't carry guns because they're pretty.
Kill or be killed.
BUT WE'LL BE IN SERIOUS TROUBLE IF WE RUN INTO A LOT OF MONSTERS LIKE THAT ONE BEFORE.
SO THE ROAD TO THE PALACE IS PRETTY DANGEROUS, THEN?
I HAVE NO IDEA. I DON'T KNOW WHERE THE PALACE IS.
WHAT?!
HOW'RE YOU PLANNING TO GET THERE IF YOU DON'T EVEN KNOW WHERE **THERE** IS?!
WE JUST NEED TO HIRE A GUIDE AND BODY-GUARD.
OH, IS THAT ALL?! WELL, I FEEL SO MUCH BETTER!!

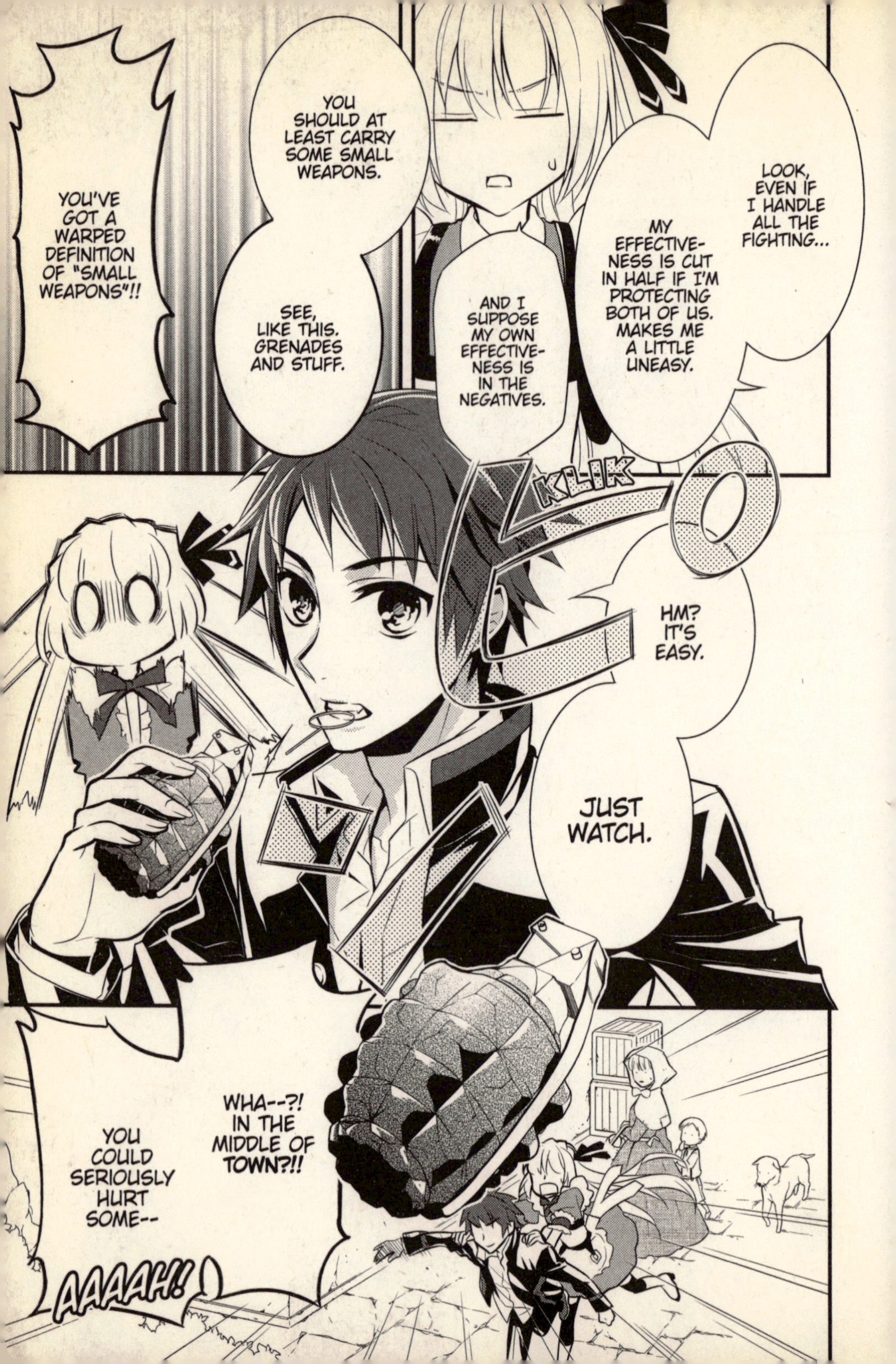
LOOK, EVEN IF I HANDLE ALL THE FIGHTING...
MY EFFECTIVENESS IS CUT IN HALF IF I'M PROTECTING BOTH OF US. MAKES ME A LITTLE UNEASY.
AND I SUPPOSE MY OWN EFFECTIVENESS IS IN THE NEGATIVES.
YOU SHOULD AT LEAST CARRY SOME SMALL WEAPONS.
SEE, LIKE THIS. GRENADES AND STUFF.
YOU'VE GOT A WARPED DEFINITION OF "SMALL WEAPONS"!!
KLIK
HM? IT'S EASY.
JUST WATCH.
WHA--?! IN THE MIDDLE OF TOWN?!!
YOU COULD SERIOUSLY HURT SOME--
AAAAH!

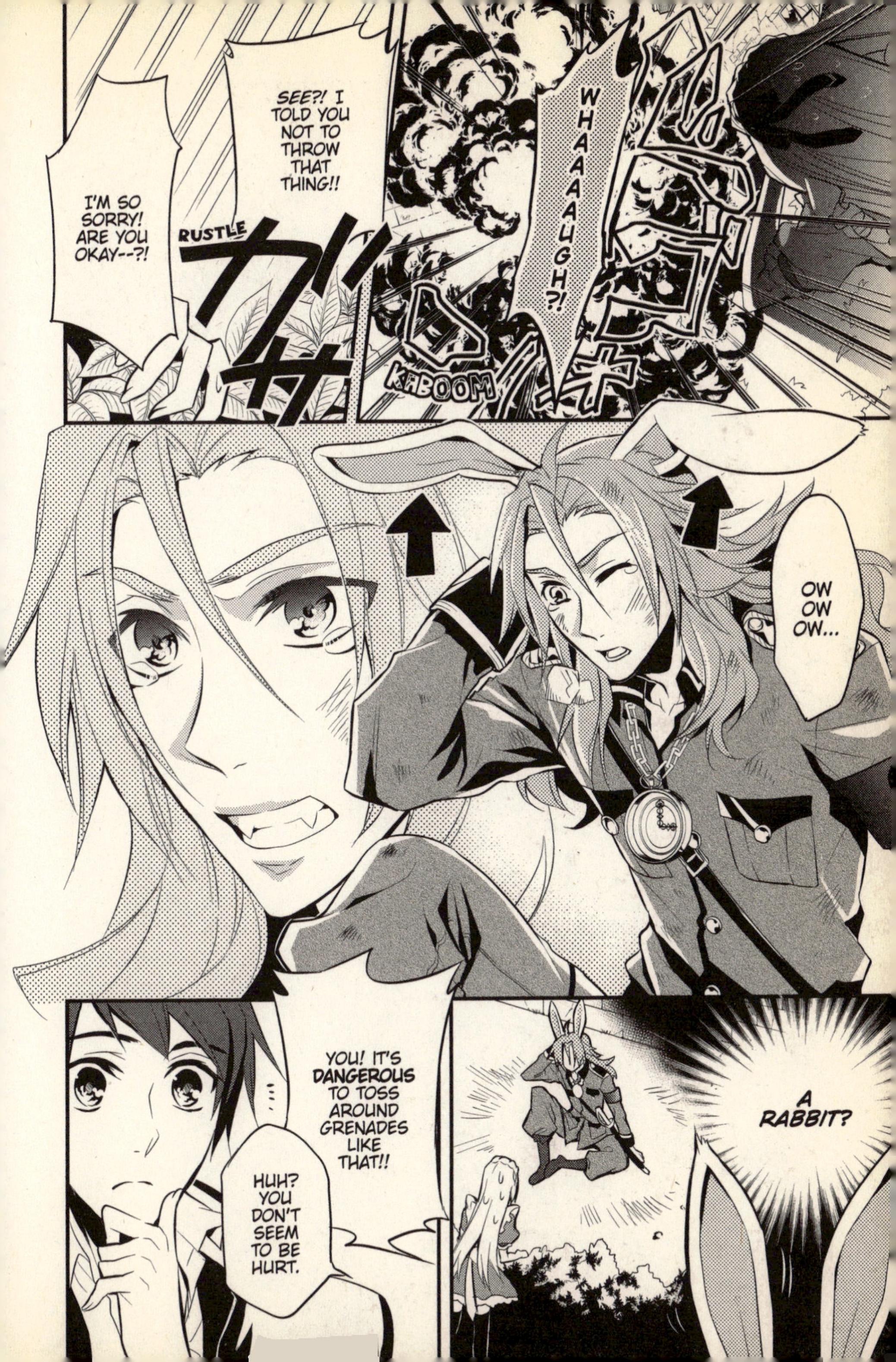
WHAAAAUGH?!
KABOOM
SEE?! I TOLD YOU NOT TO THROW THAT THING!!
I'M SO SORRY! ARE YOU OKAY--?!
RUSTLE
OW OW OW...
A RABBIT?
YOU! IT'S DANGEROUS TO TOSS AROUND GRENADES LIKE THAT!!
HUH? YOU DON'T SEEM TO BE HURT.

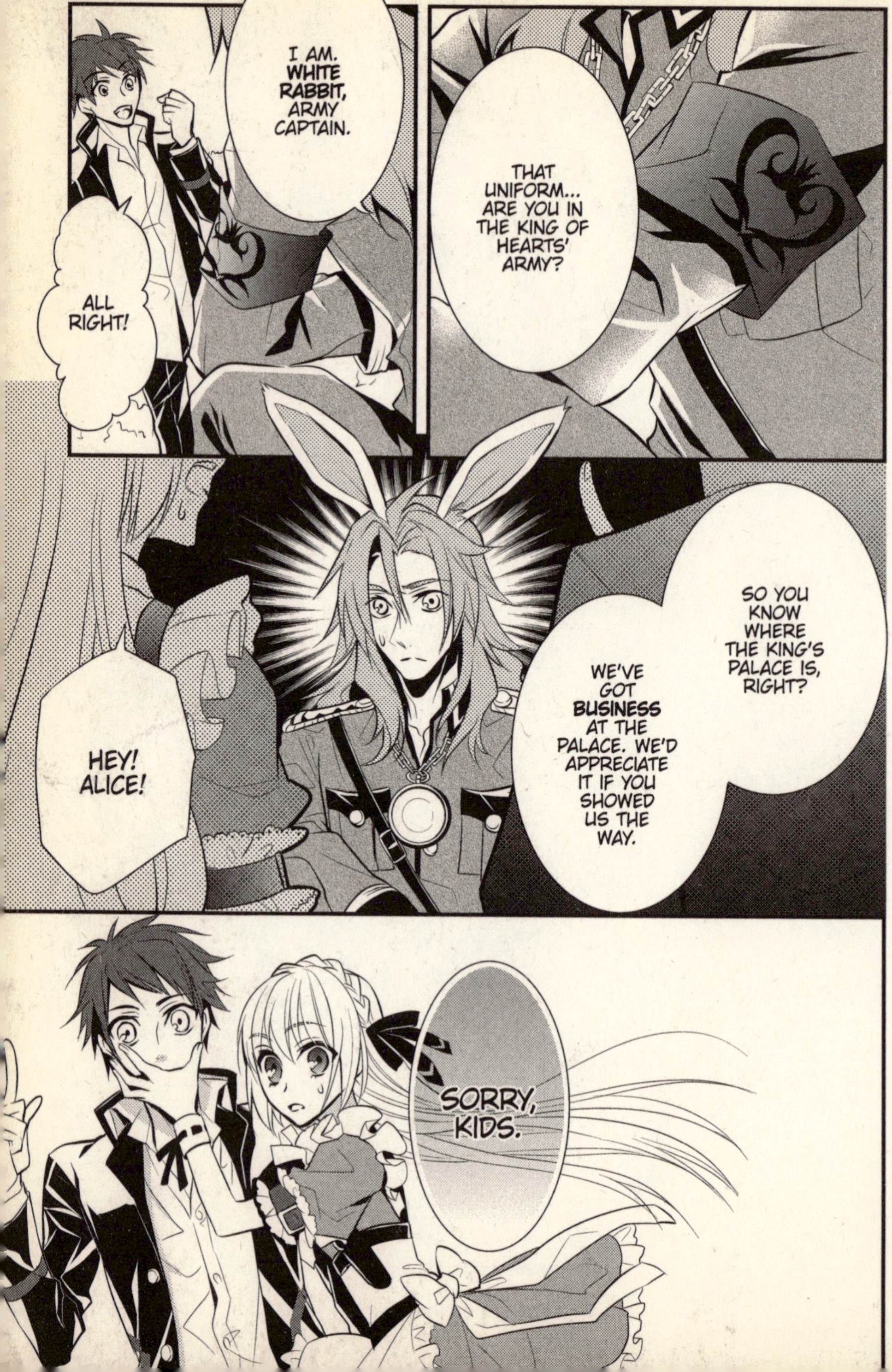
THAT UNIFORM... ARE YOU IN THE KING OF HEARTS' ARMY?
I AM. WHITE RABBIT, ARMY CAPTAIN.
ALL RIGHT!
SO YOU KNOW WHERE THE KING'S PALACE IS, RIGHT?
WE'VE GOT BUSINESS AT THE PALACE. WE'D APPRECIATE IT IF YOU SHOWED US THE WAY.
HEY! ALICE!
SORRY, KIDS.

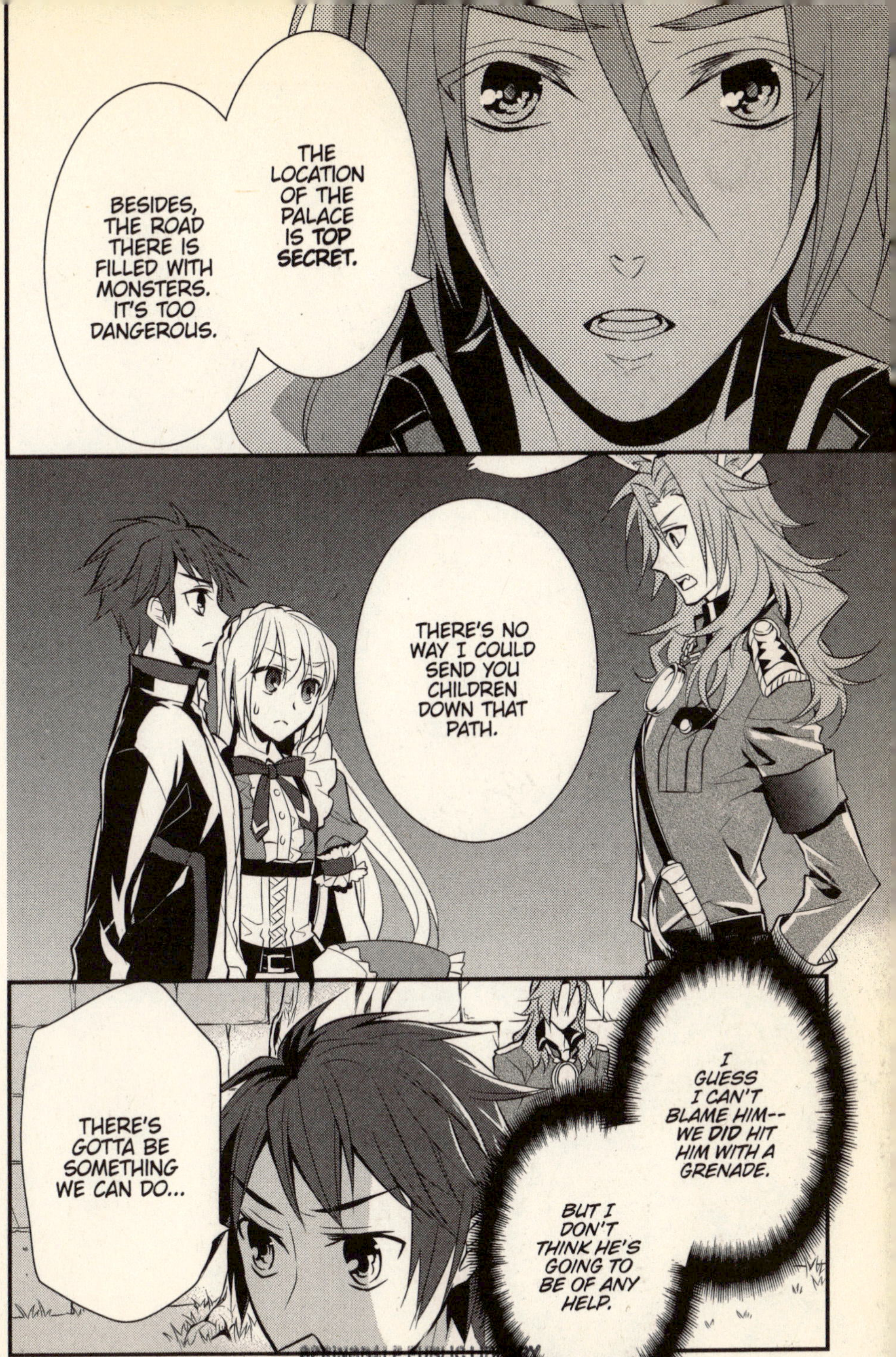
THE LOCATION OF THE PALACE IS TOP SECRET.
BESIDES, THE ROAD THERE IS FILLED WITH MONSTERS. IT'S TOO DANGEROUS.
THERE'S NO WAY I COULD SEND YOU CHILDREN DOWN THAT PATH.
I GUESS I CAN'T BLAME HIM--WE DID HIT HIM WITH A GRENADE.
BUT I DON'T THINK HE'S GOING TO BE OF ANY HELP.
THERE'S GOTTA BE SOMETHING WE CAN DO...

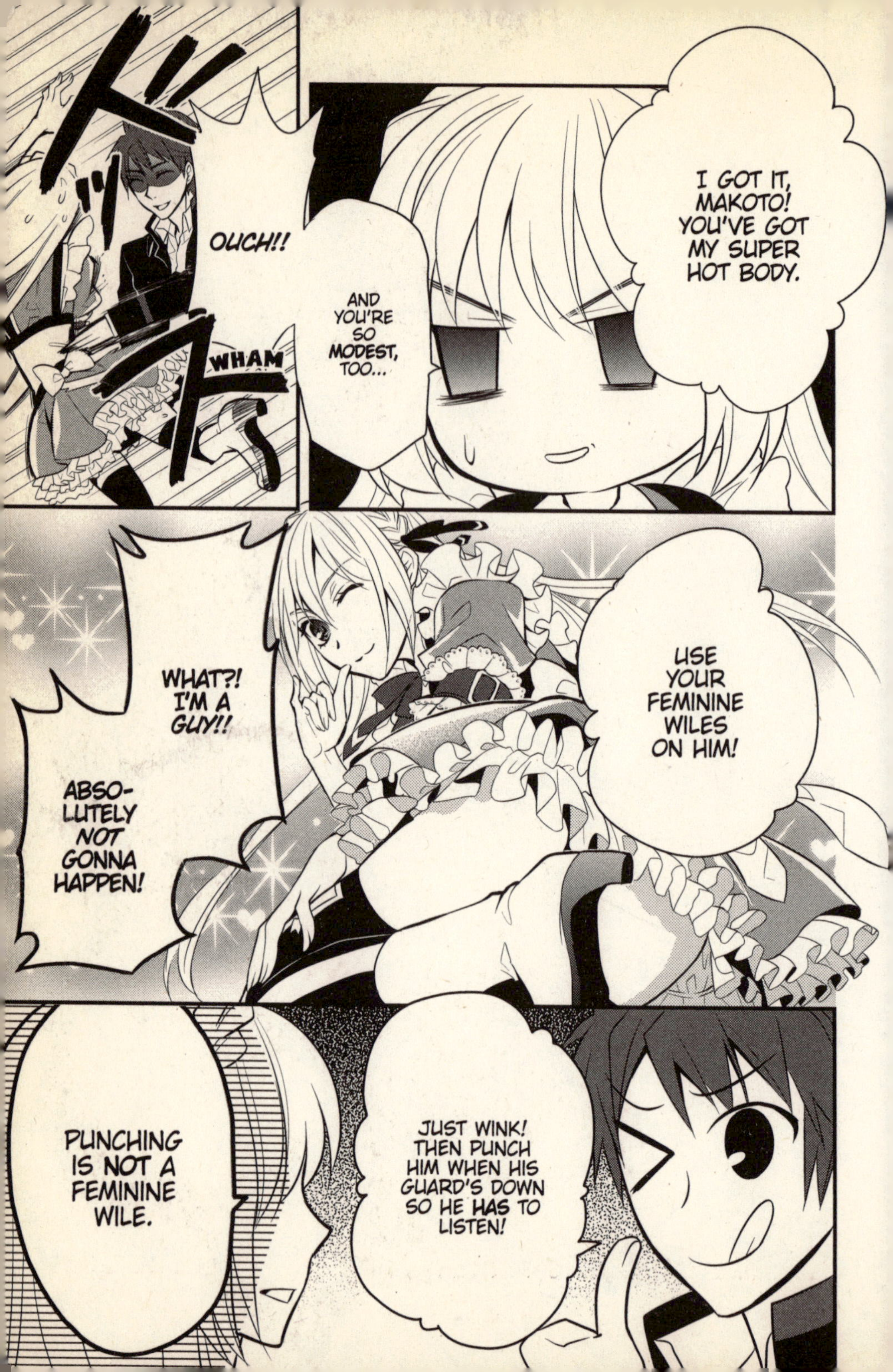

I GOT IT, MAKOTO! YOU'VE GOT MY SUPER HOT BODY.
AND YOU'RE SO MODEST, TOO...
OUCH!!
WHAM
USE YOUR FEMININE WILES ON HIM!
WHAT?! I'M A GUY!!
ABSO-LUTELY NOT GONNA HAPPEN!
JUST WINK! THEN PUNCH HIM WHEN HIS GUARD'S DOWN SO HE HAS TO LISTEN!
PUNCHING IS NOT A FEMININE WILE.

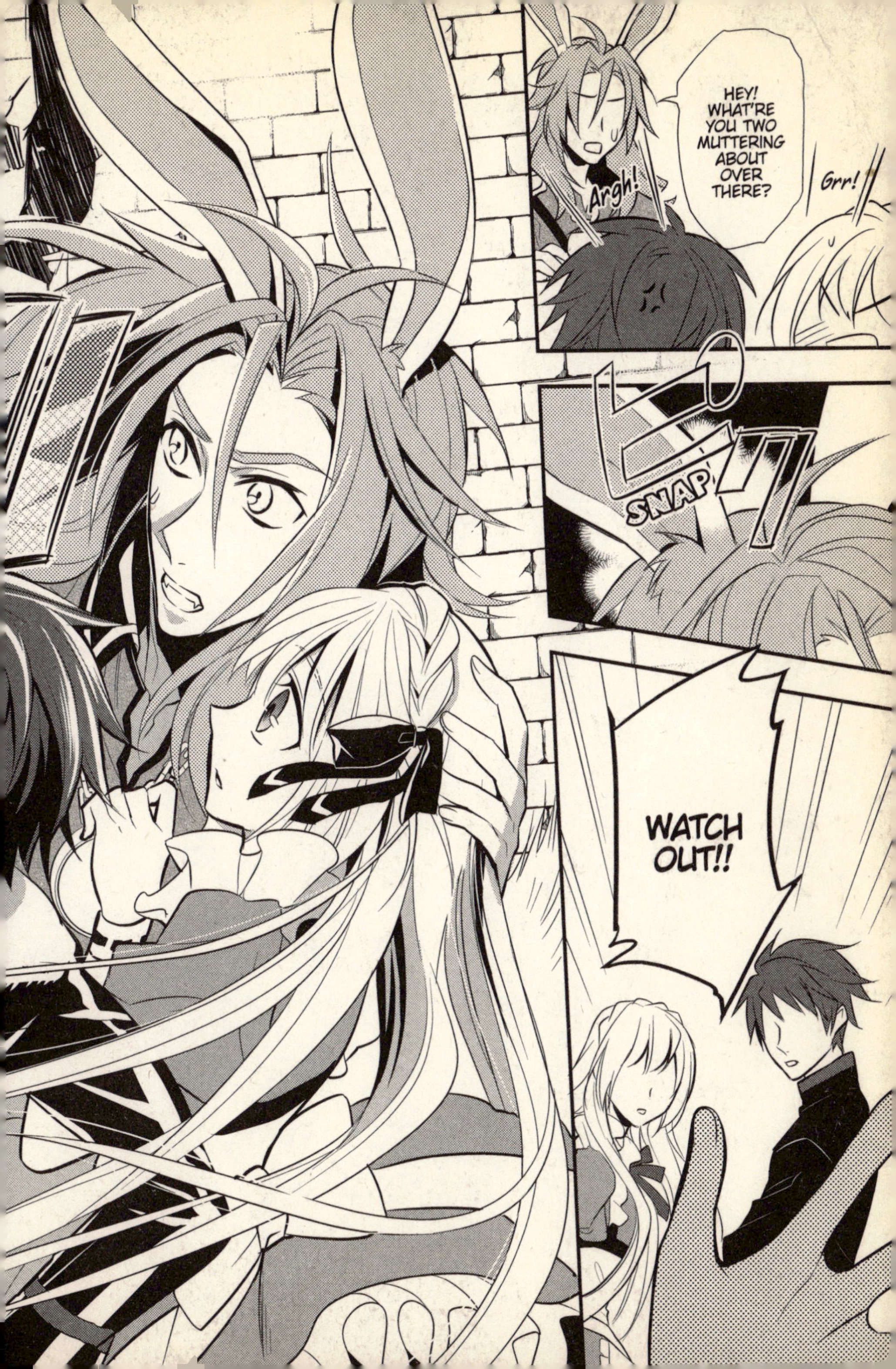
HEY! WHAT'RE YOU TWO MUTTERING ABOUT OVER THERE?
Grr!
Argh!
SNAP
WATCH OUT!!

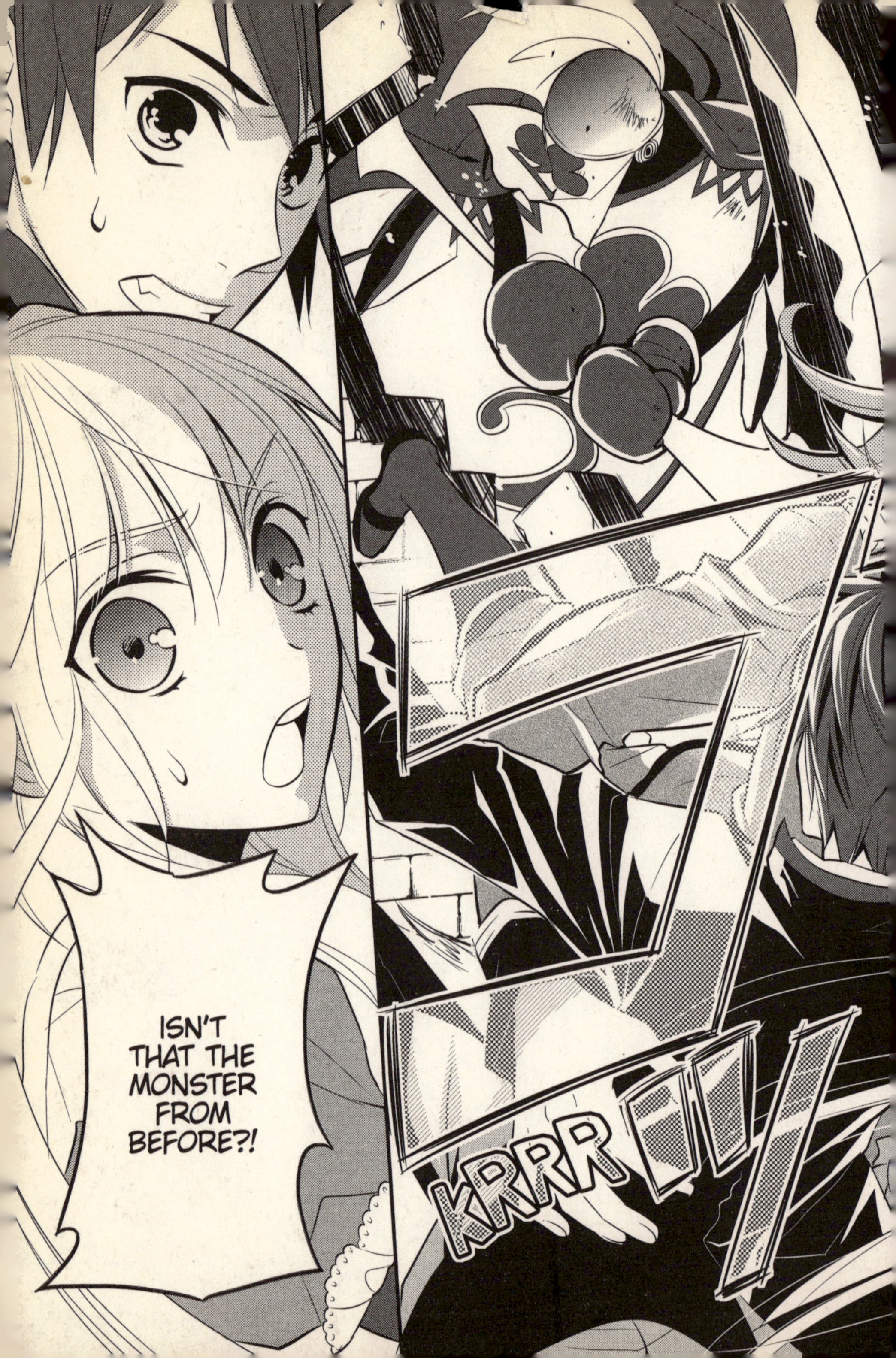
ISN'T THAT THE MONSTER FROM BEFORE?!
KRRR

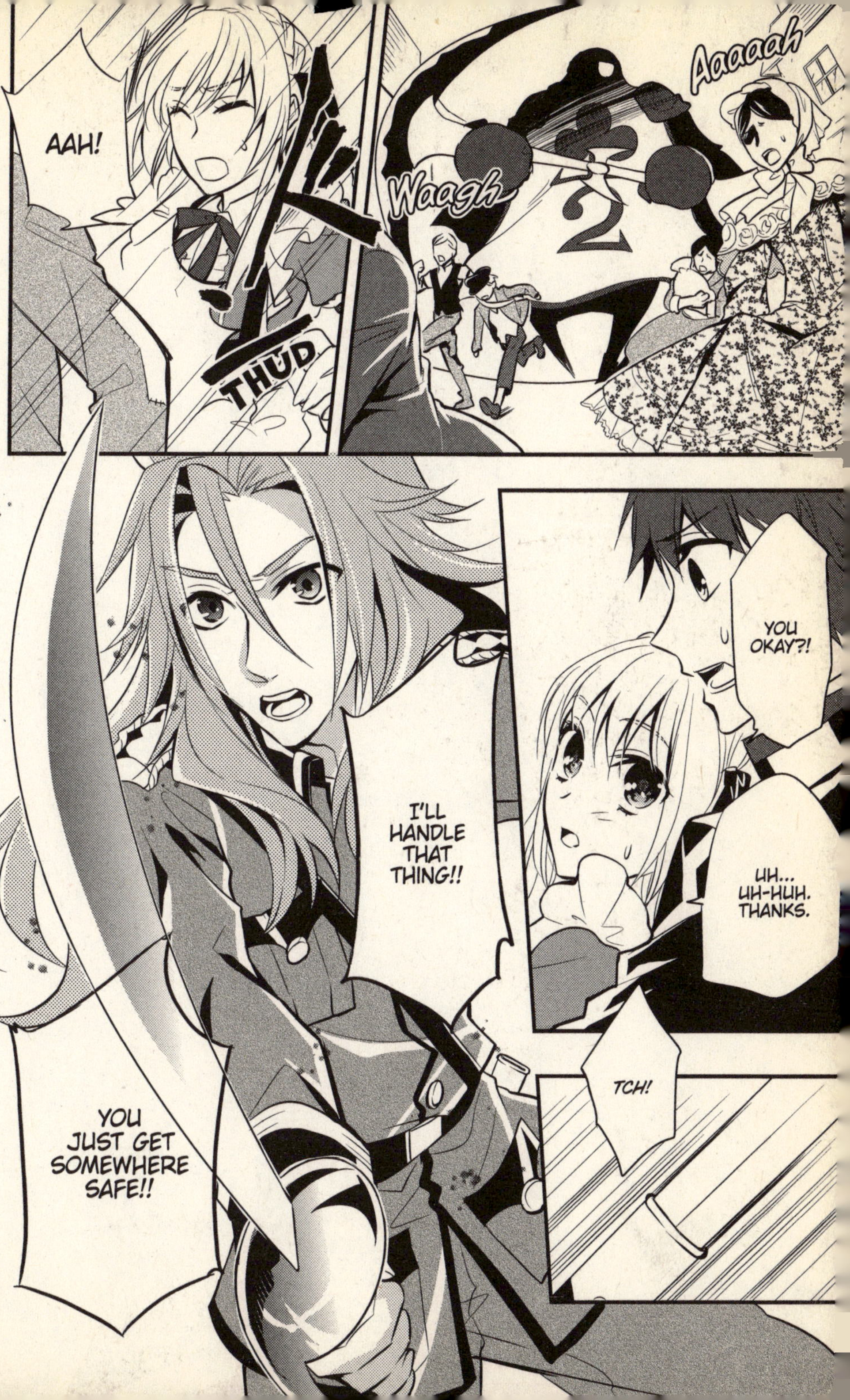
Aaaaah
Waagh
AAH!
THUD
YOU OKAY?!
UH... UH-HUH. THANKS.
TCH!
I'LL HANDLE THAT THING!!
YOU JUST GET SOMEWHERE SAFE!!

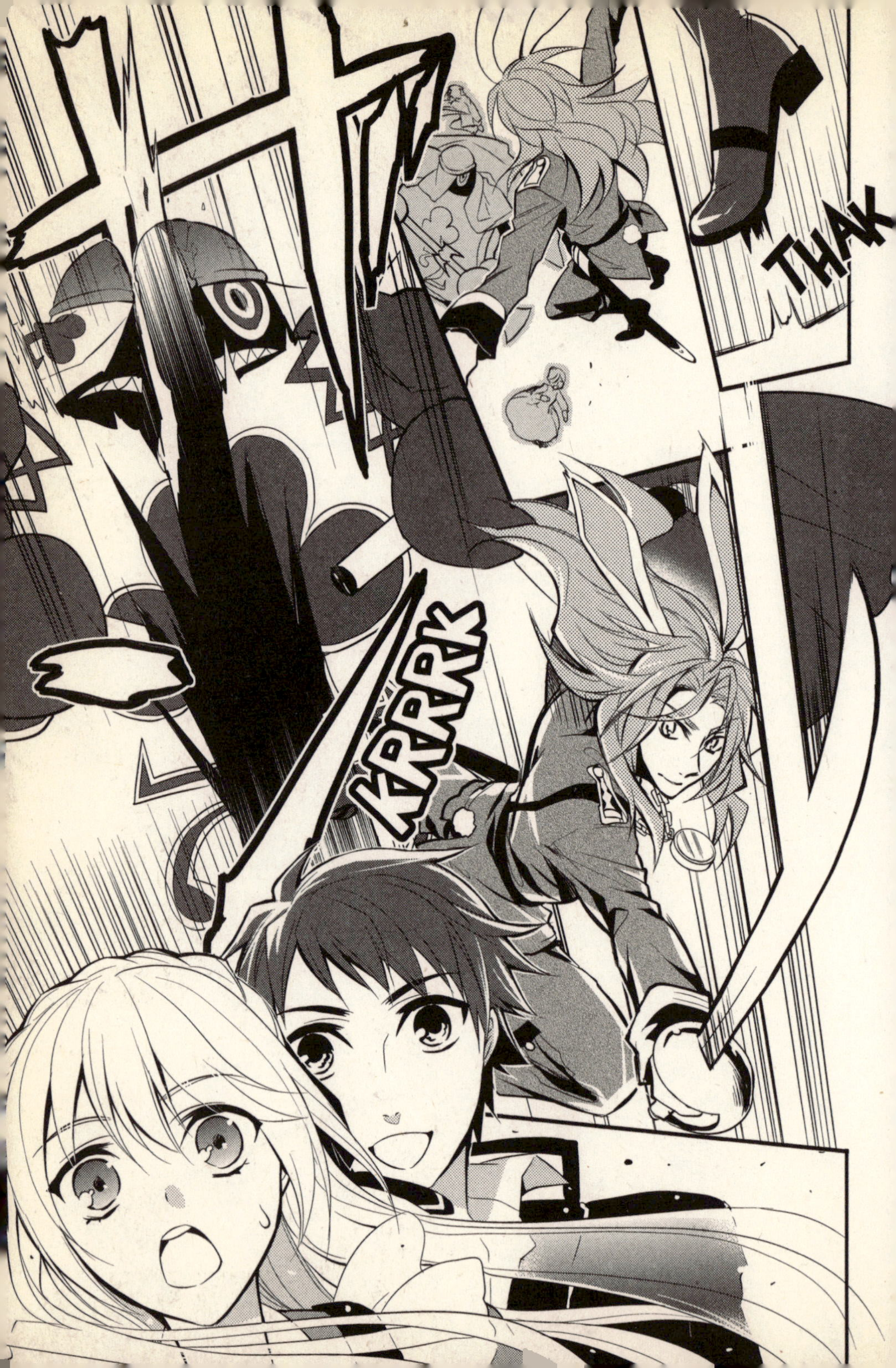
THAK
KRRRK

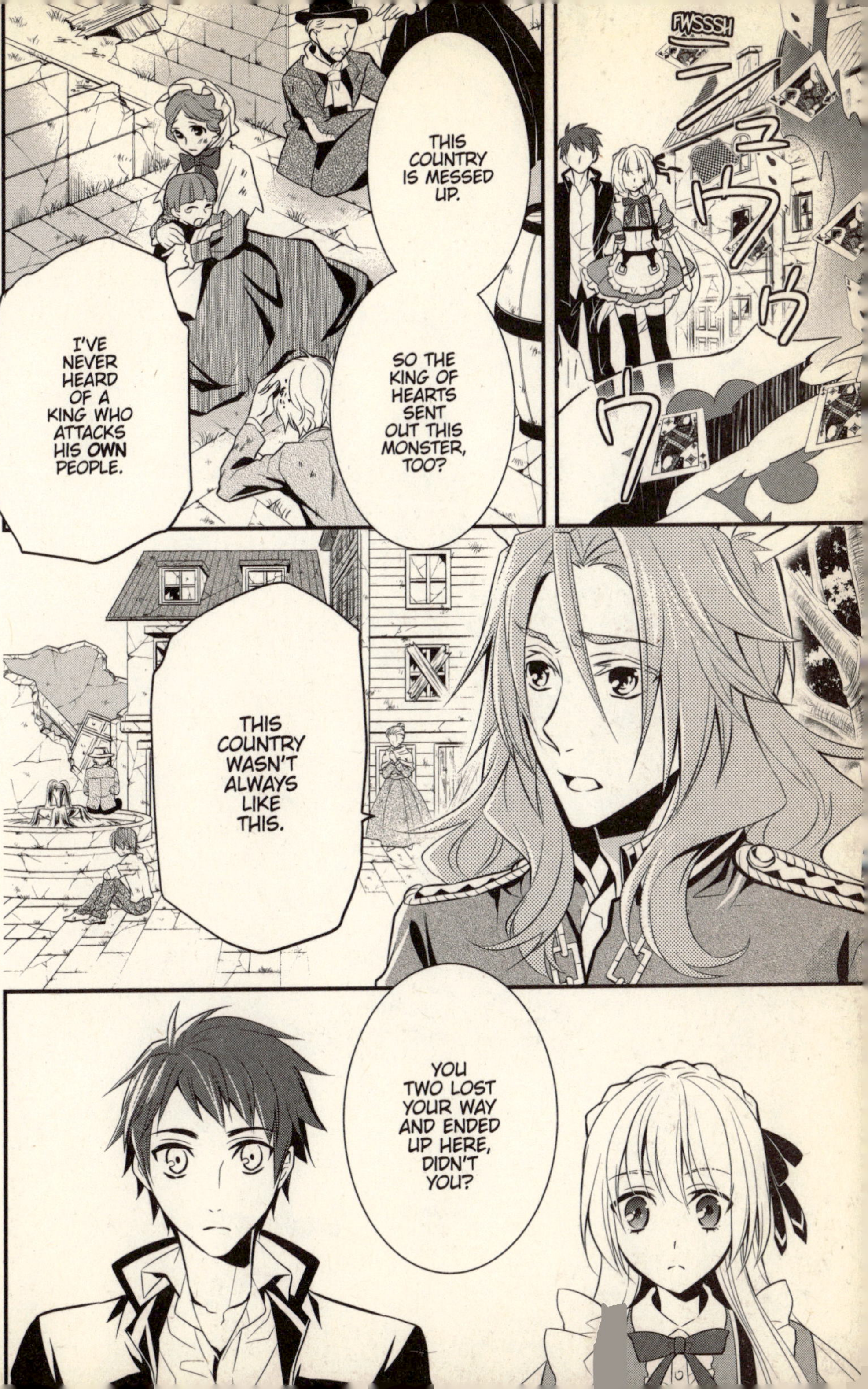

FWSSSH
シュウウウウ
THIS COUNTRY IS MESSED UP.
SO THE KING OF HEARTS SENT OUT THIS MONSTER, TOO?
I'VE NEVER HEARD OF A KING WHO ATTACKS HIS **OWN** PEOPLE.
THIS COUNTRY WASN'T ALWAYS LIKE THIS.
YOU TWO LOST YOUR WAY AND ENDED UP HERE, DIDN'T YOU?

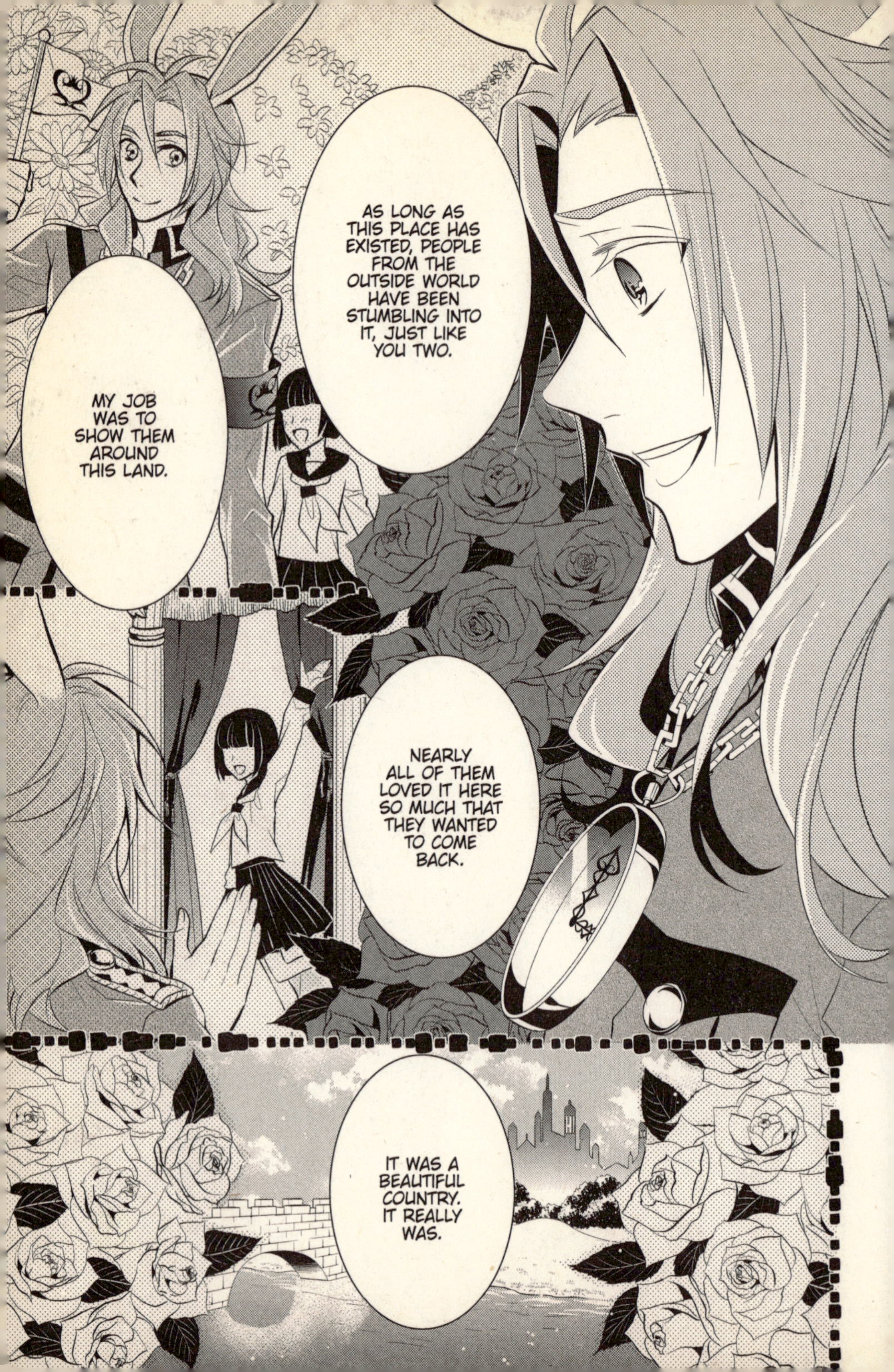
AS LONG AS THIS PLACE HAS EXISTED, PEOPLE FROM THE OUTSIDE WORLD HAVE BEEN STUMBLING INTO IT, JUST LIKE YOU TWO.
MY JOB WAS TO SHOW THEM AROUND THIS LAND.
NEARLY ALL OF THEM LOVED IT HERE SO MUCH THAT THEY WANTED TO COME BACK.
IT WAS A BEAUTIFUL COUNTRY. IT REALLY WAS.

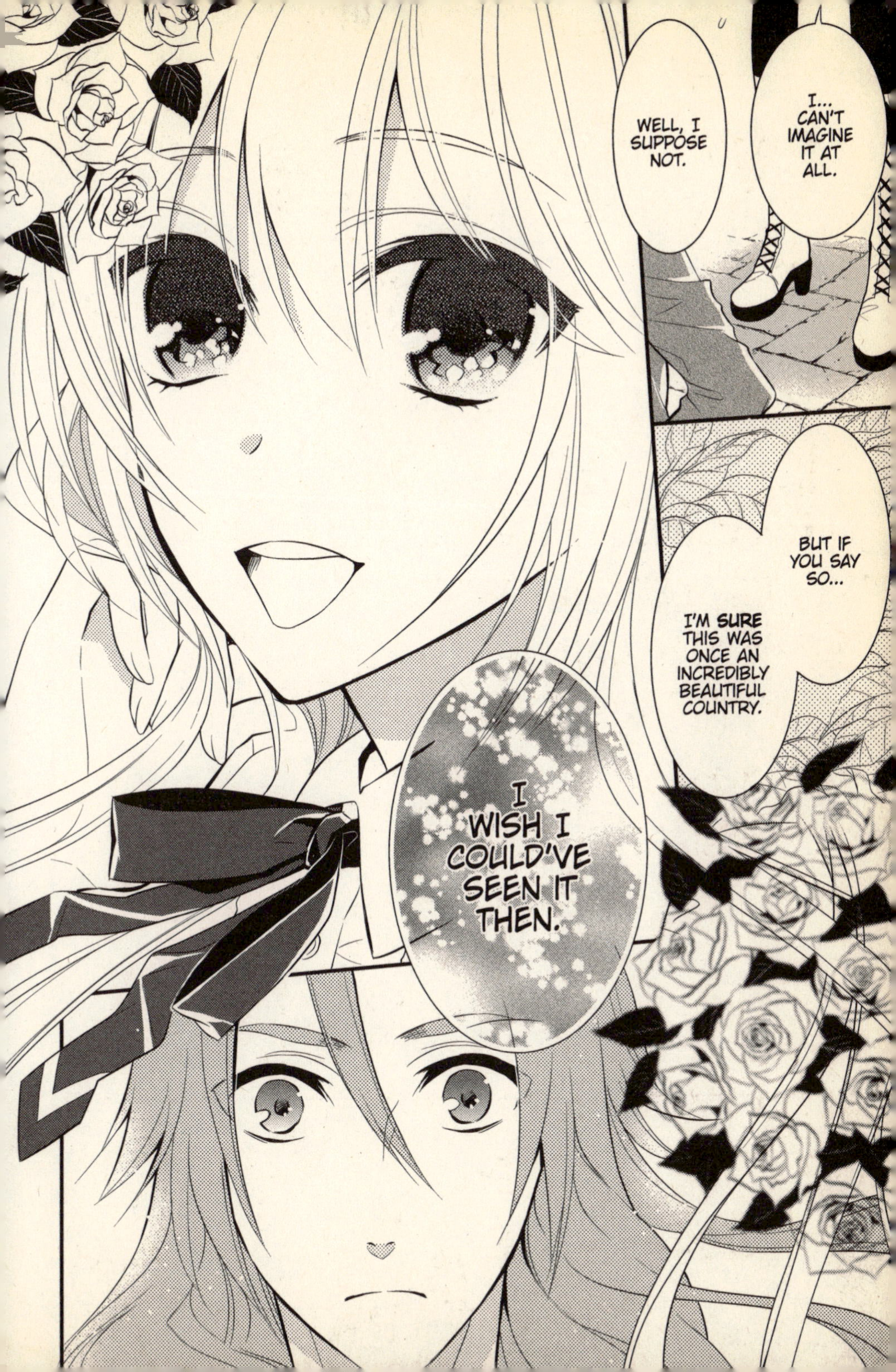
I... CAN'T IMAGINE IT AT ALL.
WELL, I SUPPOSE NOT.
BUT IF YOU SAY SO...
I'M SURE THIS WAS ONCE AN INCREDIBLY BEAUTIFUL COUNTRY.
I WISH I COULD'VE SEEN IT THEN.

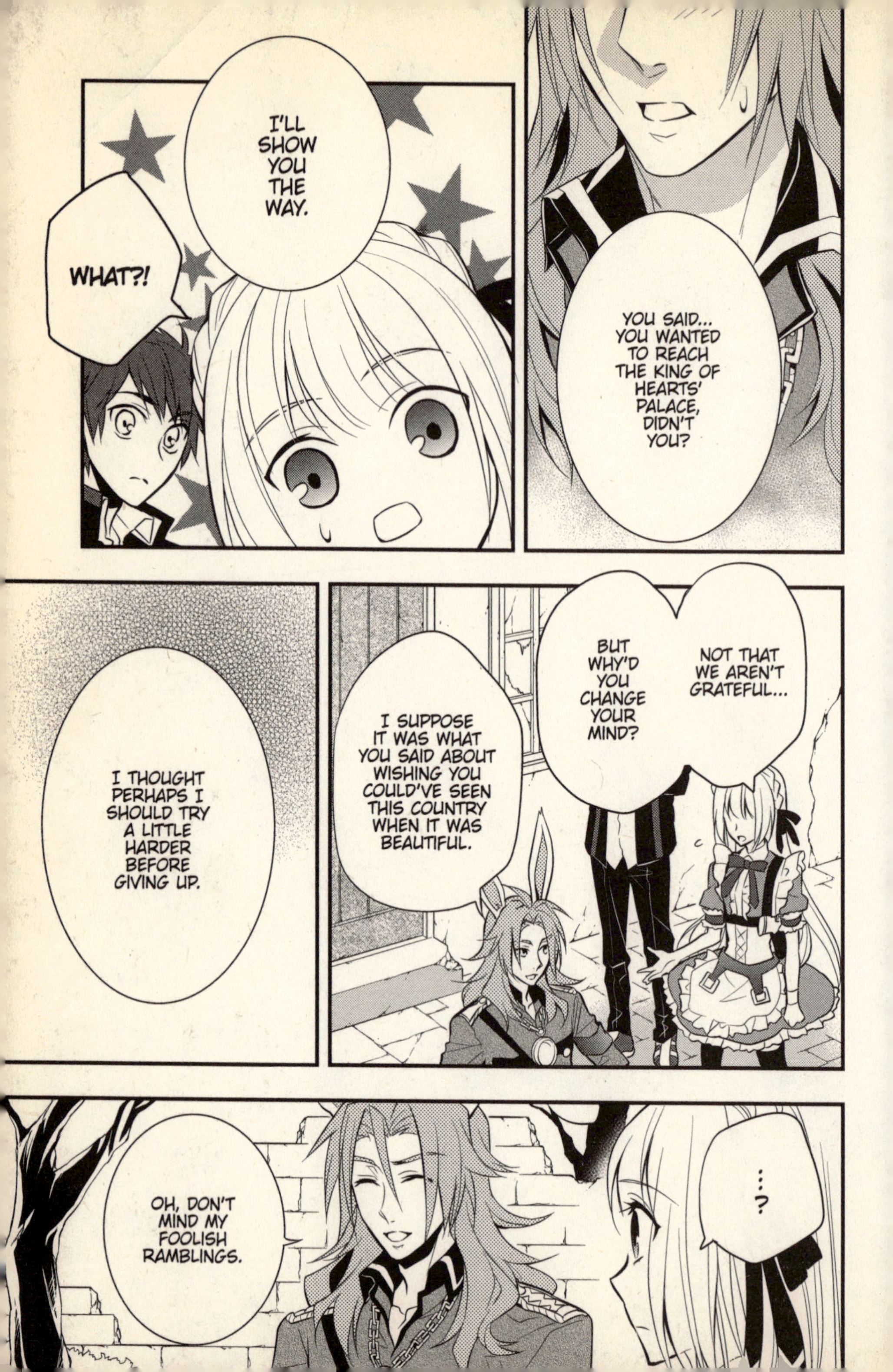
YOU SAID... YOU WANTED TO REACH THE KING OF HEARTS' PALACE, DIDN'T YOU?
I'LL SHOW YOU THE WAY.
WHAT?!
NOT THAT WE AREN'T GRATEFUL...
BUT WHY'D YOU CHANGE YOUR MIND?
I SUPPOSE IT WAS WHAT YOU SAID ABOUT WISHING YOU COULD'VE SEEN THIS COUNTRY WHEN IT WAS BEAUTIFUL.
I THOUGHT PERHAPS I SHOULD TRY A LITTLE HARDER BEFORE GIVING UP.
...?
OH, DON'T MIND MY FOOLISH RAMBLINGS.

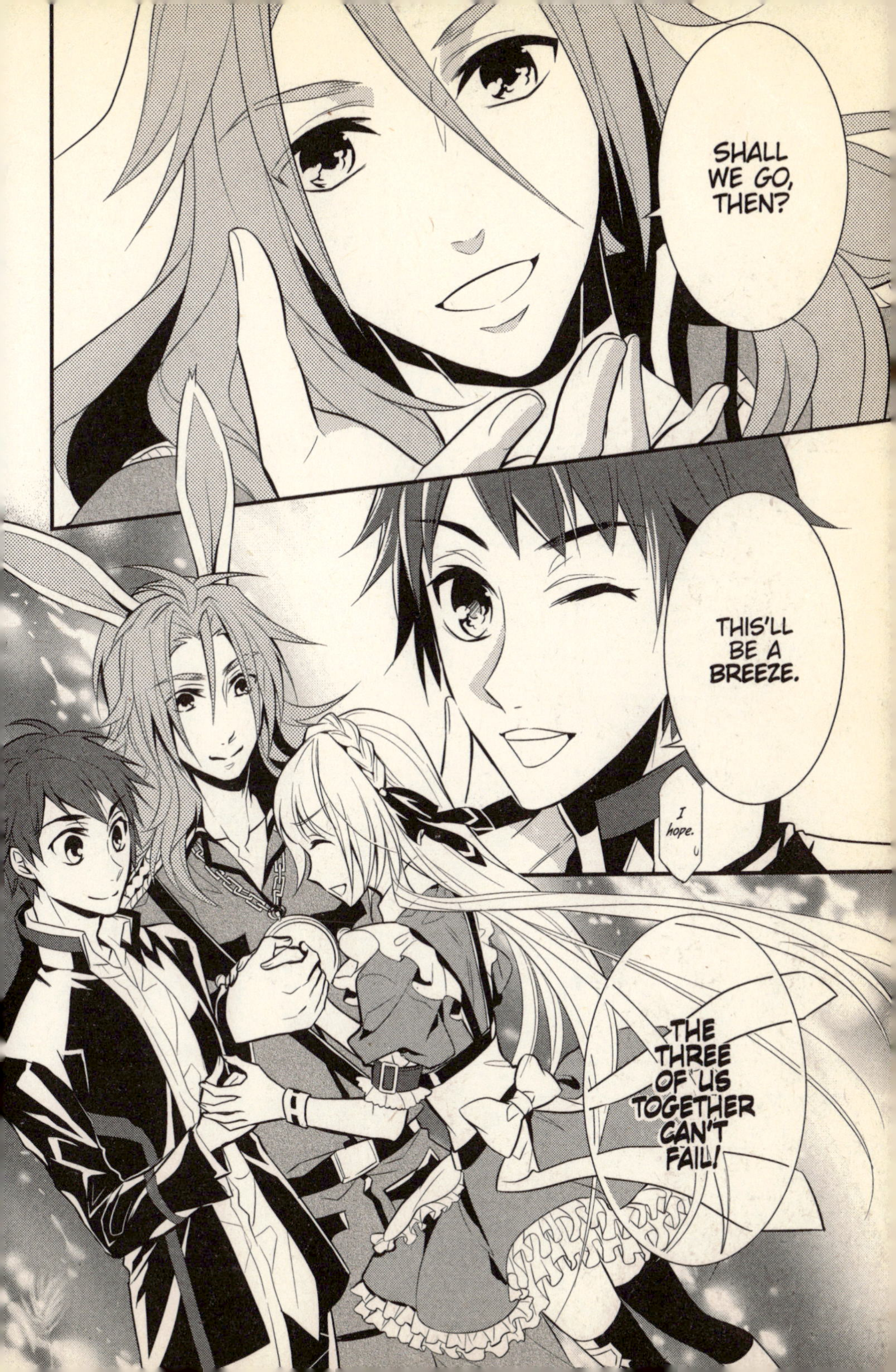
SHALL WE GO, THEN?
THIS'LL BE A BREEZE.
I hope.
THE THREE OF US TOGETHER CAN'T FAIL!

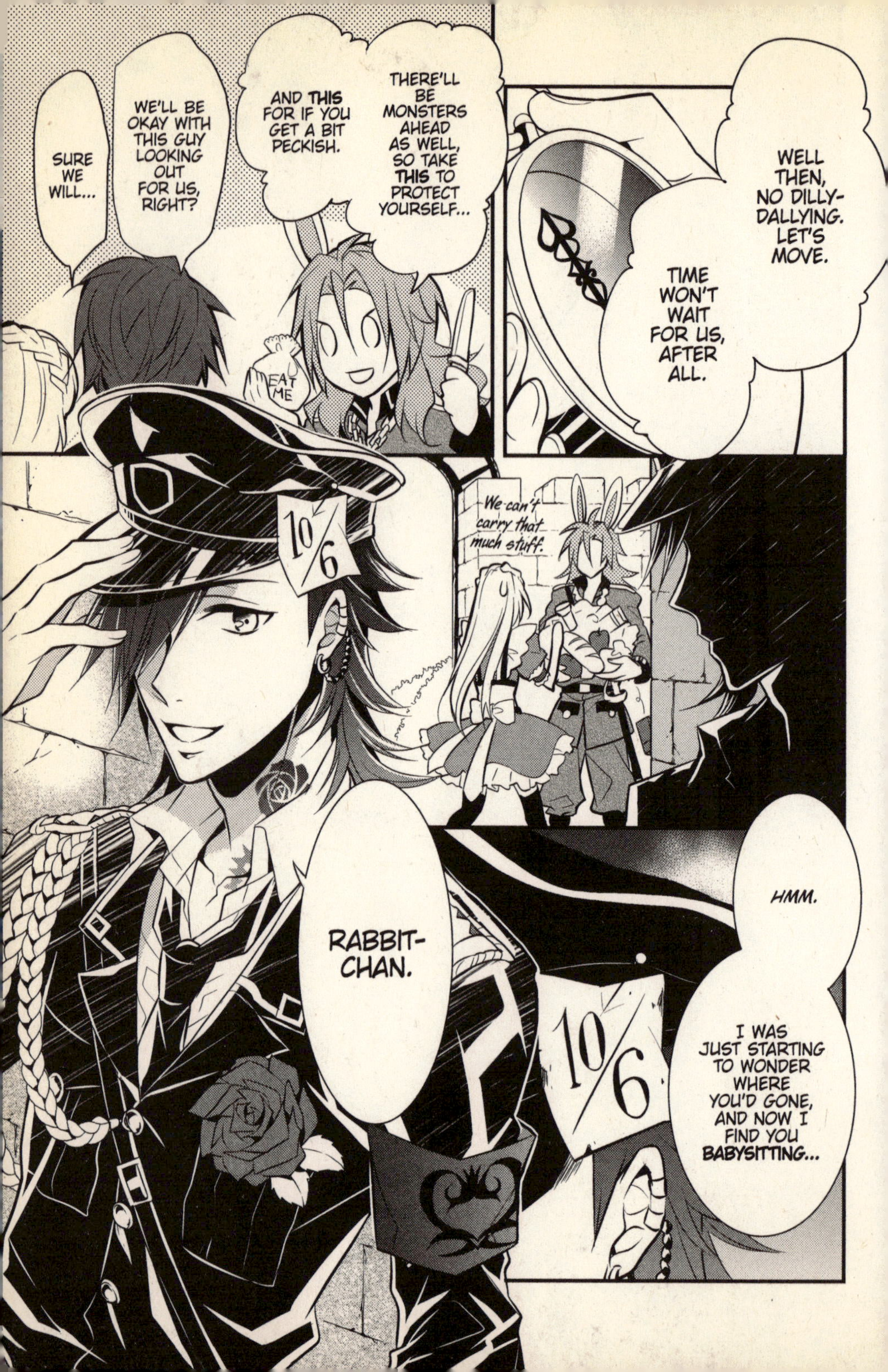
WELL THEN, NO DILLY-DALLYING. LET'S MOVE.
TIME WON'T WAIT FOR US, AFTER ALL.
THERE'LL BE MONSTERS AHEAD AS WELL, SO TAKE **THIS** TO PROTECT YOURSELF...
AND **THIS** FOR IF YOU GET A BIT PECKISH.
EAT ME
WE'LL BE OKAY WITH THIS GUY LOOKING OUT FOR US, RIGHT?
SURE WE WILL...
We can't carry that much stuff.
HMM.
I WAS JUST STARTING TO WONDER WHERE YOU'D GONE, AND NOW I FIND YOU **BABYSITTING...**
RABBIT-CHAN.

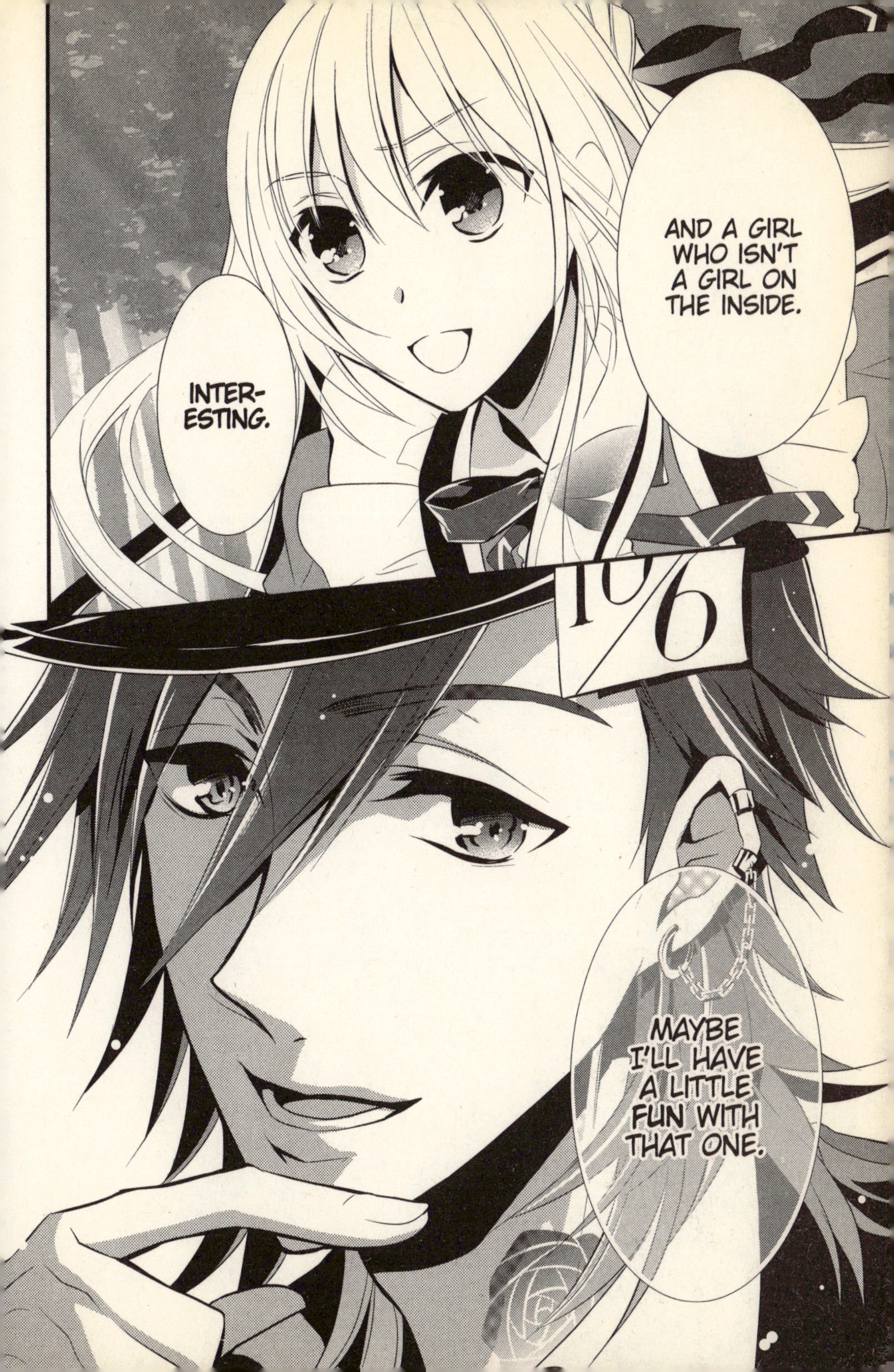
AND A GIRL WHO ISN'T A GIRL ON THE INSIDE.
INTER-ESTING.
MAYBE I'LL HAVE A LITTLE FUN WITH THAT ONE.

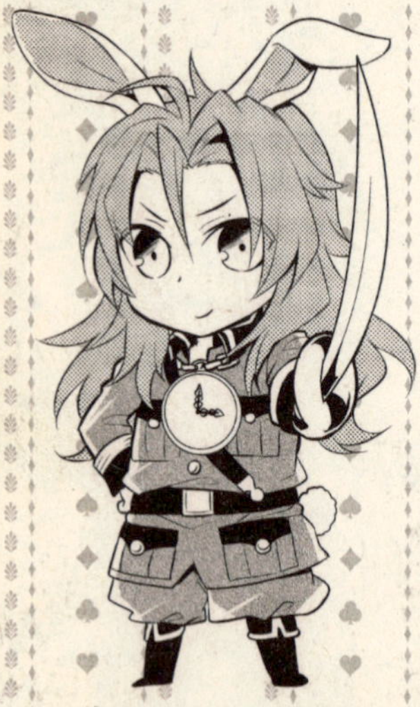

I AM ALICE

I AM ALICE

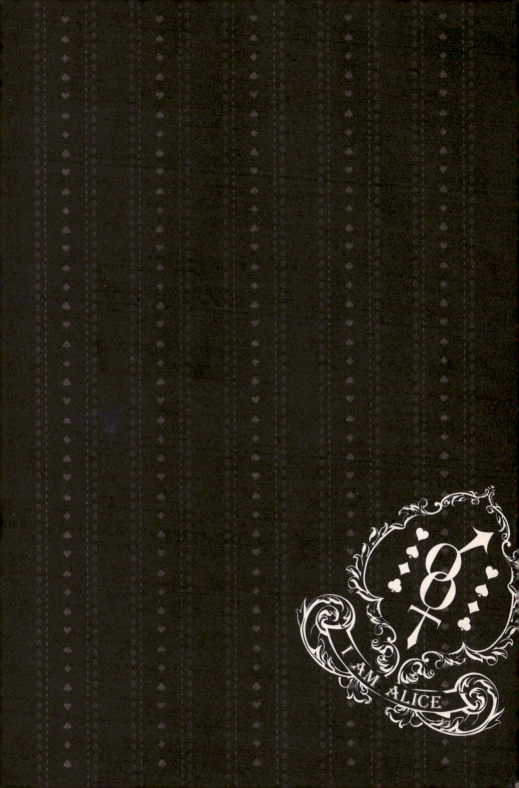

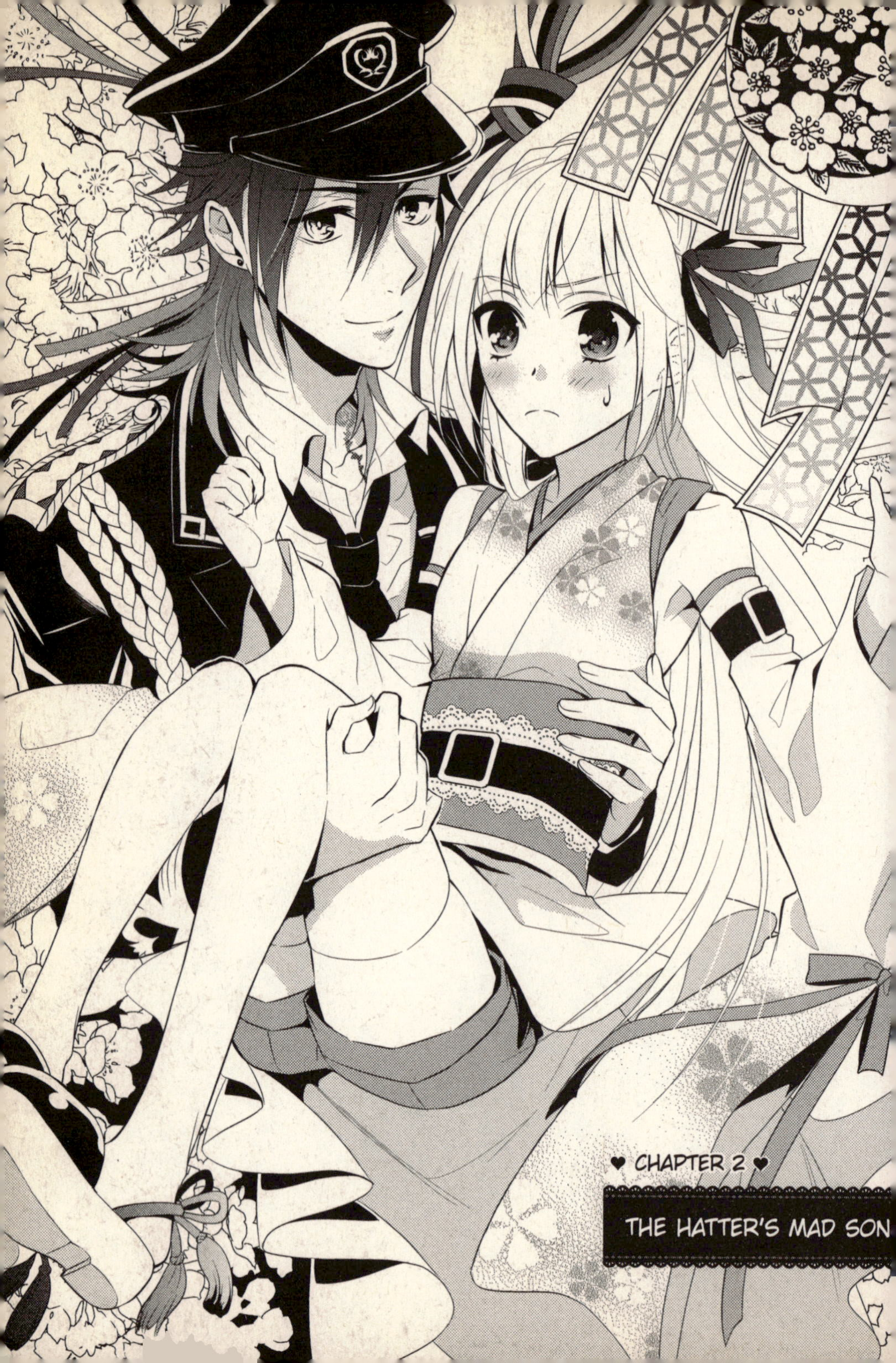
♥ CHAPTER 2 ♥
THE HATTER'S MAD SON

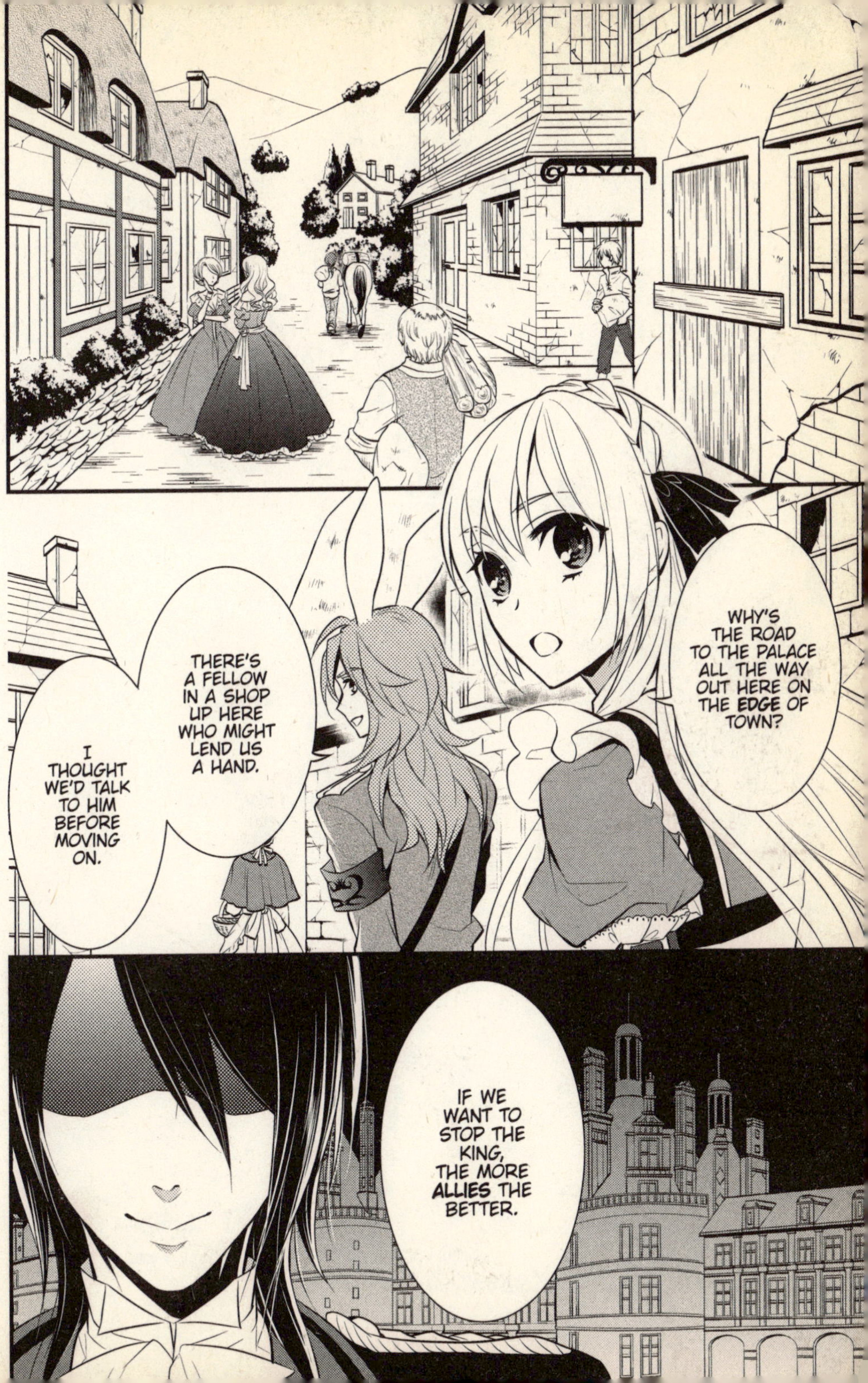
WHY'S THE ROAD TO THE PALACE ALL THE WAY OUT HERE ON THE EDGE OF TOWN?
THERE'S A FELLOW IN A SHOP UP HERE WHO MIGHT LEND US A HAND.
I THOUGHT WE'D TALK TO HIM BEFORE MOVING ON.
IF WE WANT TO STOP THE KING, THE MORE ALLIES THE BETTER.

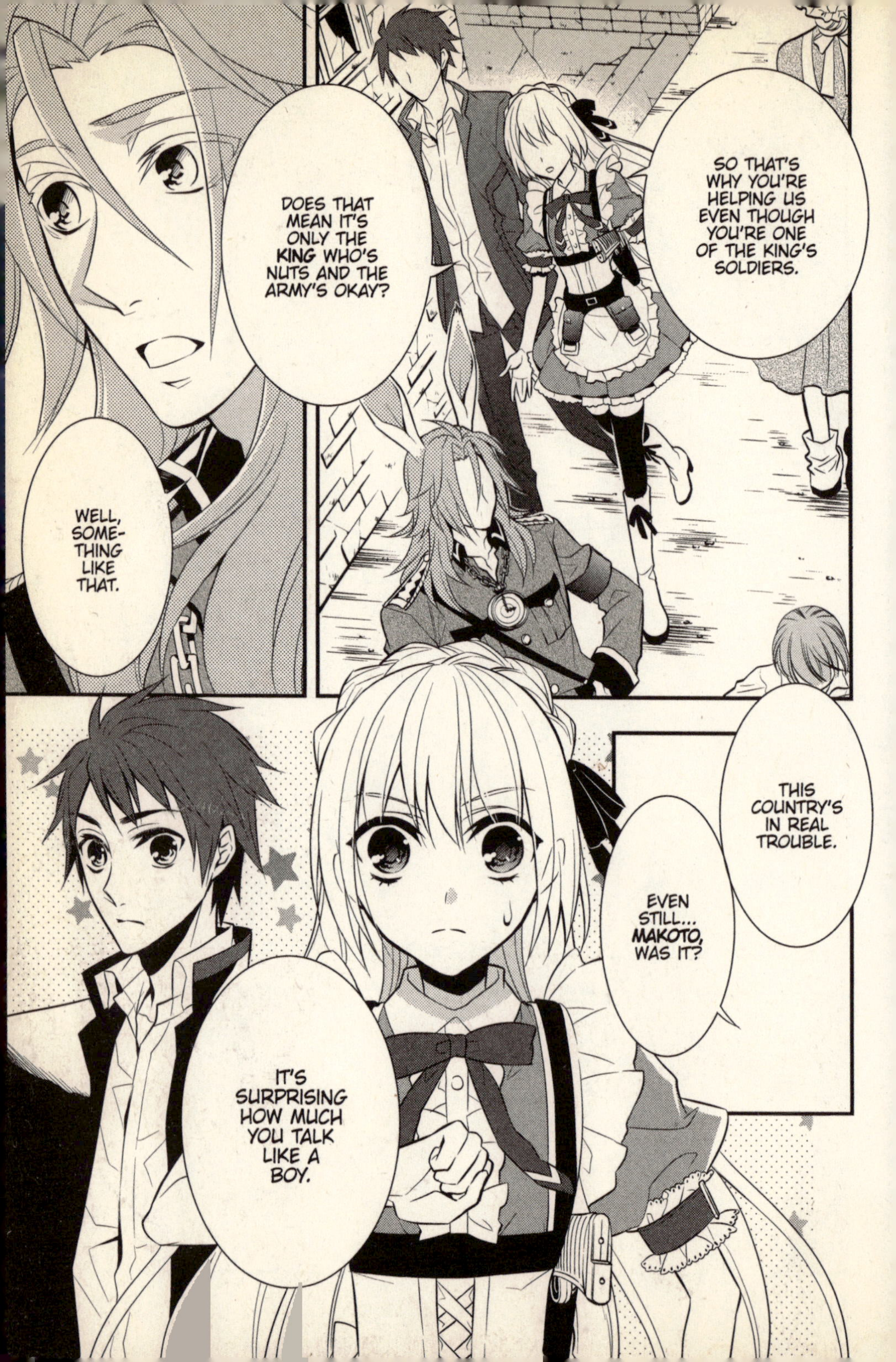
SO THAT'S WHY YOU'RE HELPING US EVEN THOUGH YOU'RE ONE OF THE KING'S SOLDIERS.
DOES THAT MEAN IT'S ONLY THE **KING** WHO'S NUTS AND THE ARMY'S OKAY?
WELL, SOME-THING LIKE THAT.
THIS COUNTRY'S IN REAL TROUBLE.
EVEN STILL... **MAKOTO**, WAS IT?
IT'S SURPRISING HOW MUCH YOU TALK LIKE A BOY.

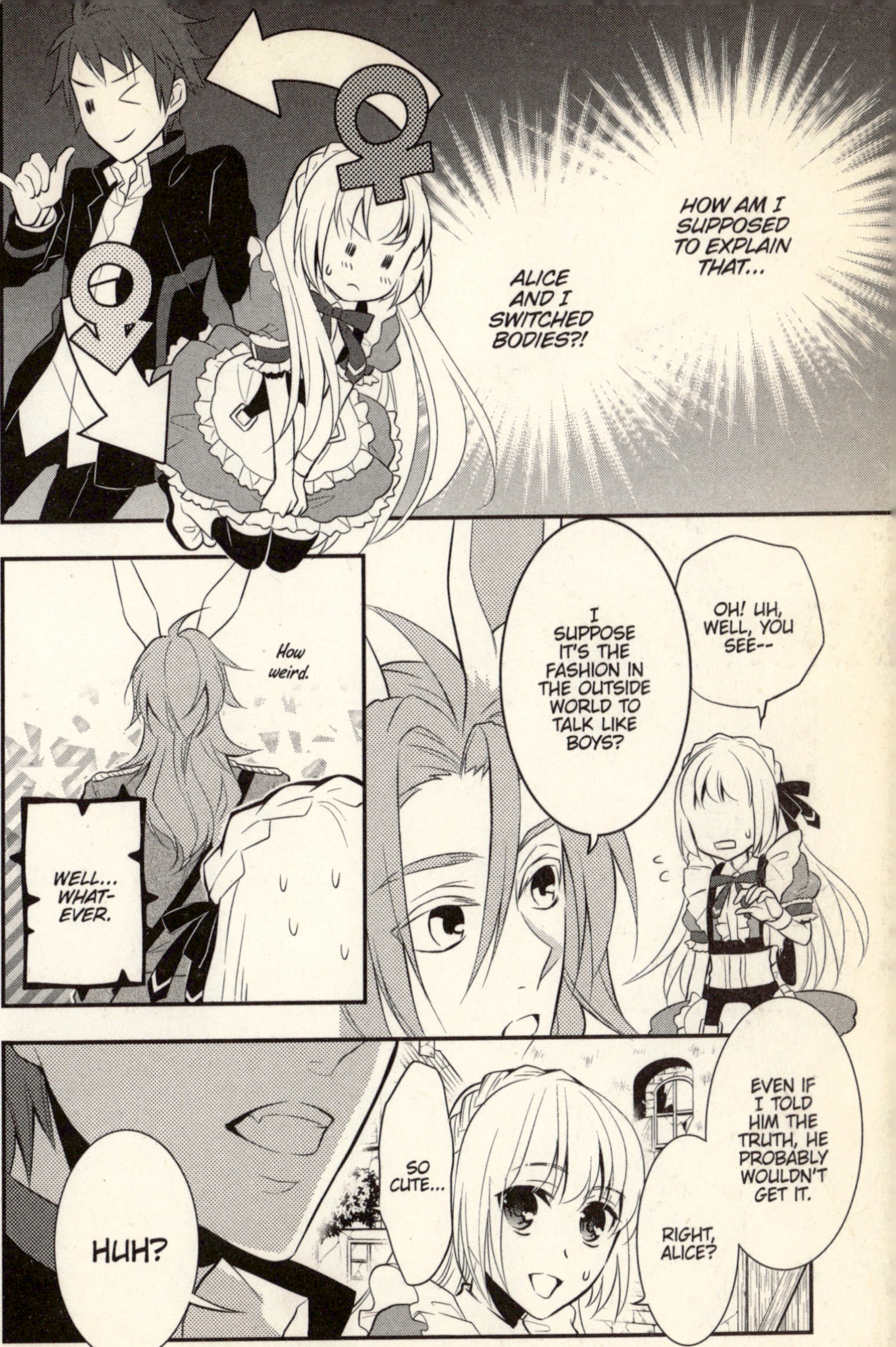
HOW AM I SUPPOSED TO EXPLAIN THAT...
ALICE AND I SWITCHED BODIES?!
OH! UH, WELL, YOU SEE--
I SUPPOSE IT'S THE FASHION IN THE OUTSIDE WORLD TO TALK LIKE BOYS?
How weird.
WELL... WHATEVER.
EVEN IF I TOLD HIM THE TRUTH, HE PROBABLY WOULDN'T GET IT.
RIGHT, ALICE?
SO CUTE...
HUH?

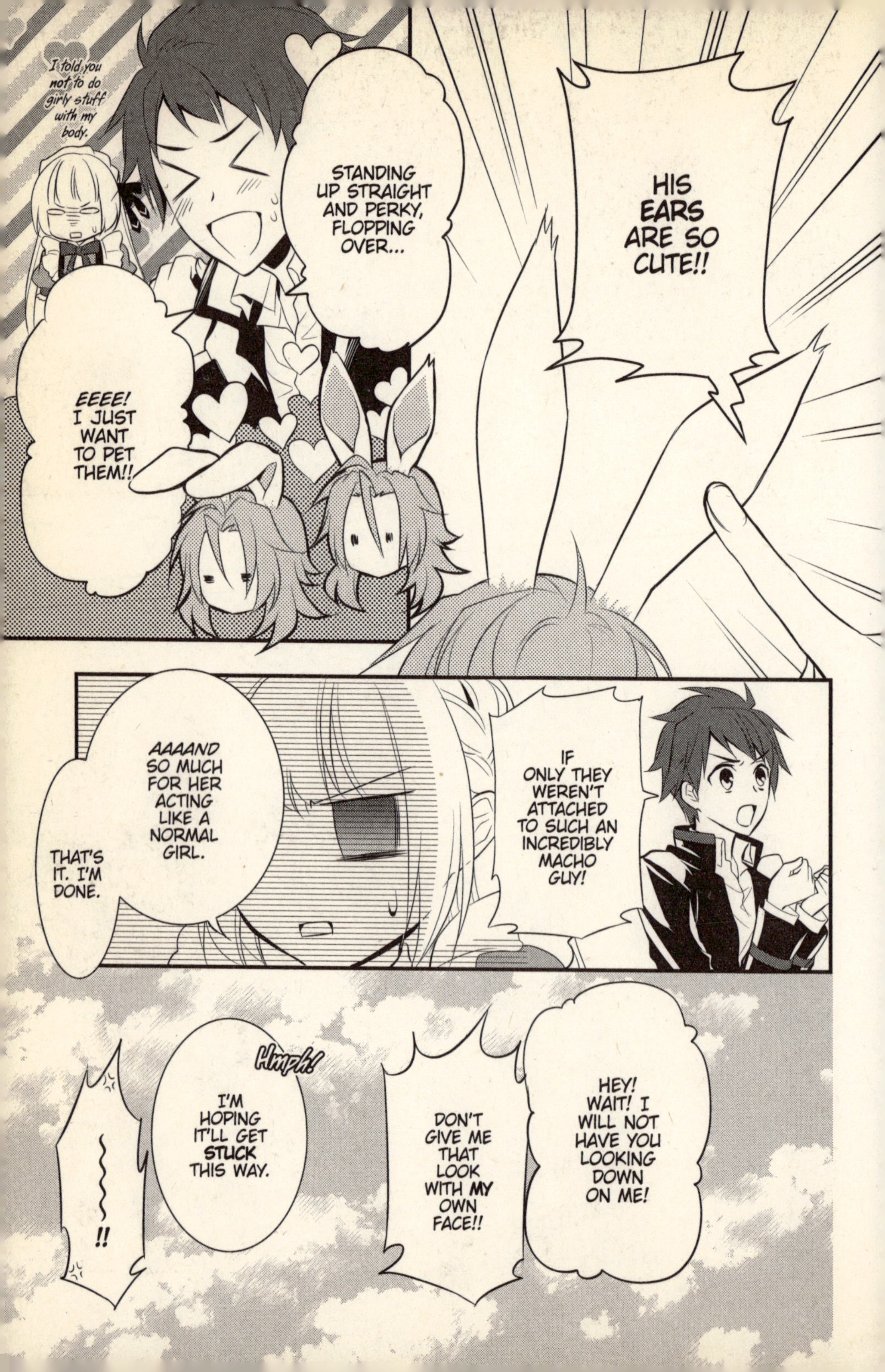
HIS EARS ARE SO CUTE!!
STANDING UP STRAIGHT AND PERKY, FLOPPING OVER...
I told you not to do girly stuff with my body.
EEEE! I JUST WANT TO PET THEM!!
IF ONLY THEY WEREN'T ATTACHED TO SUCH AN INCREDIBLY MACHO GUY!
AAAAND SO MUCH FOR HER ACTING LIKE A NORMAL GIRL.
THAT'S IT. I'M DONE.
HEY! WAIT! I WILL NOT HAVE YOU LOOKING DOWN ON ME!
DON'T GIVE ME THAT LOOK WITH **MY** OWN FACE!!
Hmph!
I'M HOPING IT'LL GET **STUCK** THIS WAY.
!!

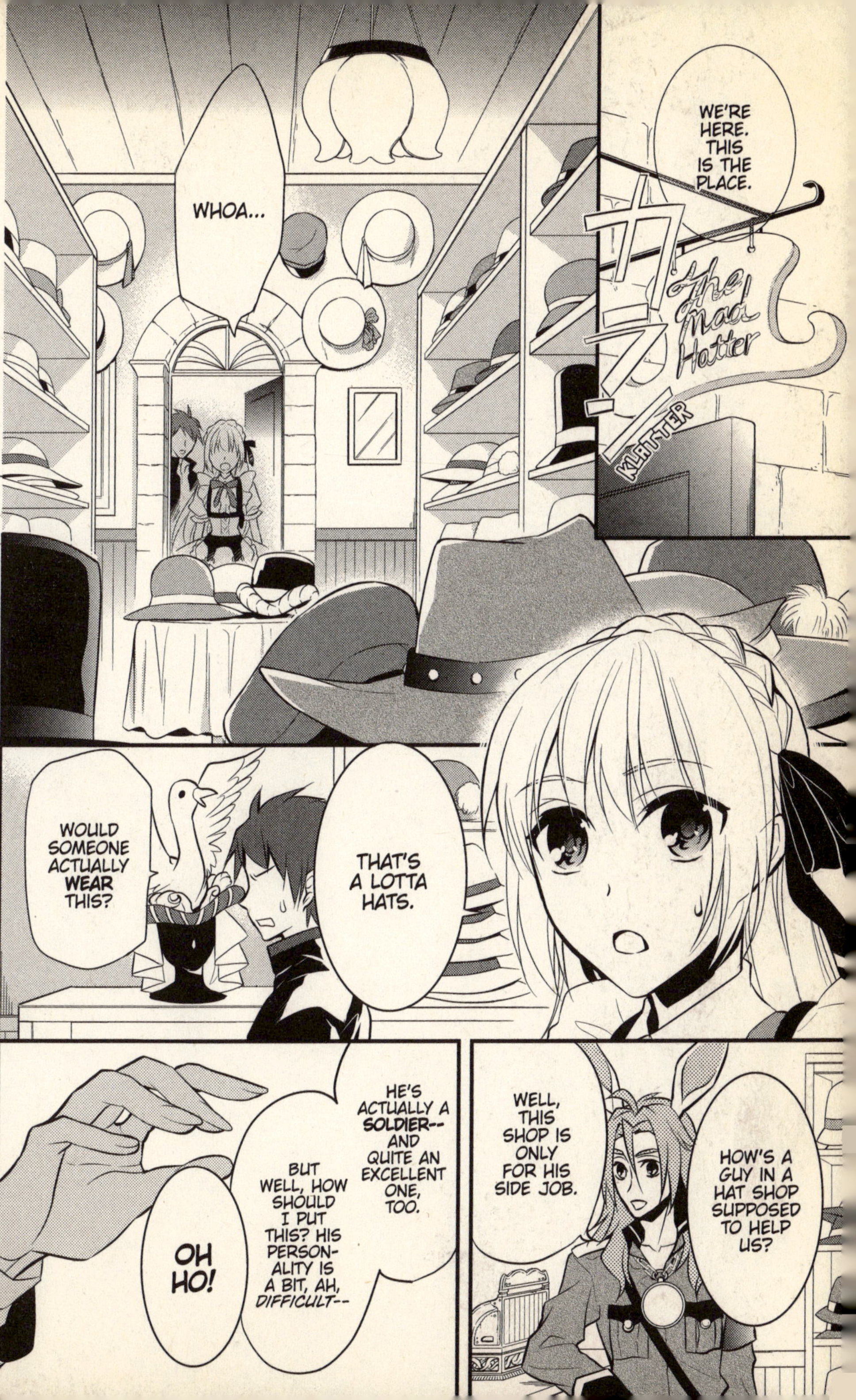

WE'RE HERE. THIS IS THE PLACE.
the mad Hatter
KLATTER
WHOA...
THAT'S A LOTTA HATS.
WOULD SOMEONE ACTUALLY **WEAR** THIS?
HOW'S A GUY IN A HAT SHOP SUPPOSED TO HELP US?
WELL, THIS SHOP IS ONLY FOR HIS SIDE JOB.
HE'S ACTUALLY A **SOLDIER**-- AND QUITE AN EXCELLENT ONE, TOO.
BUT WELL, HOW SHOULD I PUT THIS? HIS PERSONALITY IS A BIT, AH, *DIFFICULT*--
OH HO!

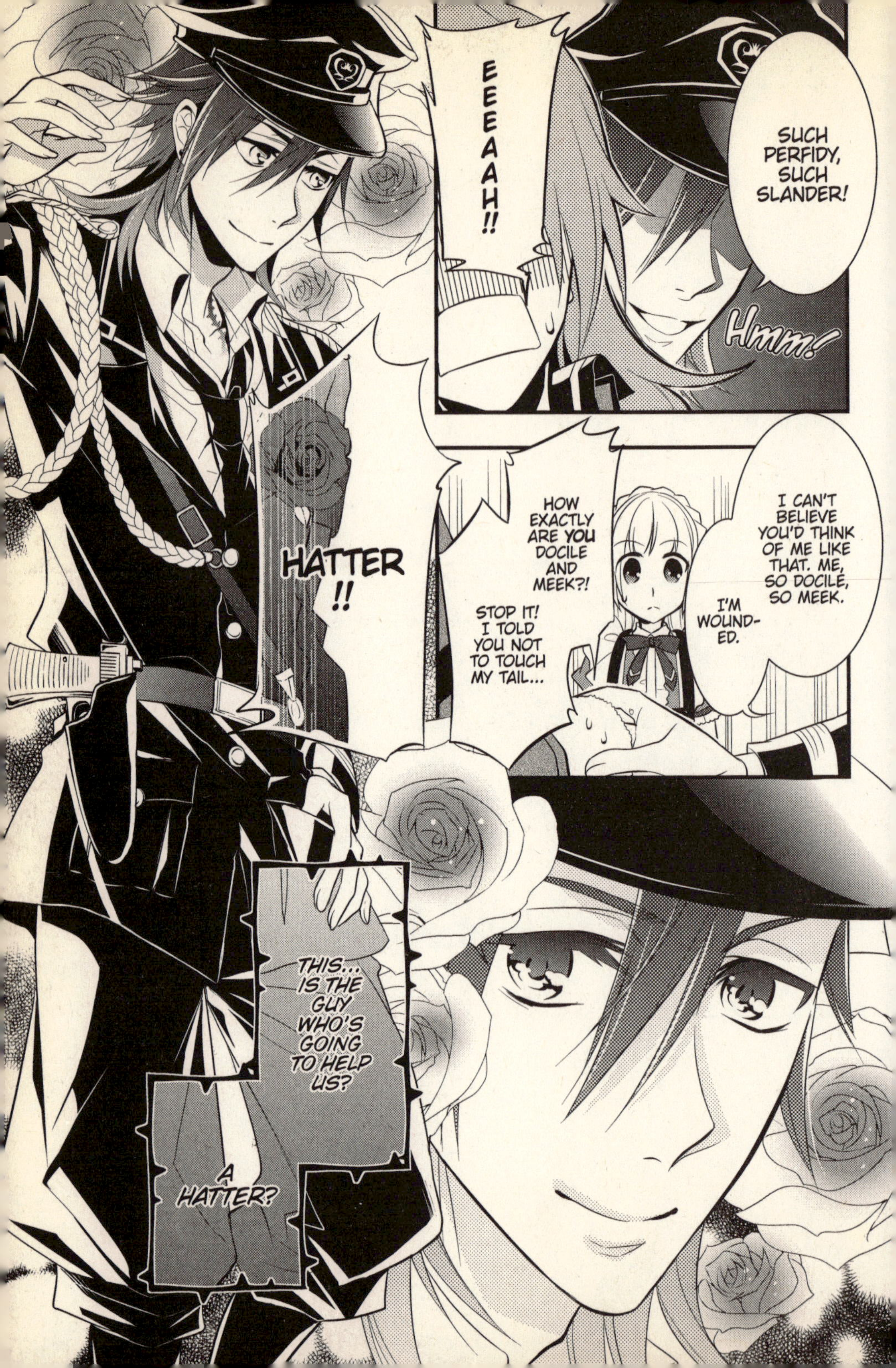
SUCH PERFIDY, SUCH SLANDER!
Hmm!
I CAN'T BELIEVE YOU'D THINK OF ME LIKE THAT. ME, SO DOCILE, SO MEEK.
I'M WOUND-ED.
HOW EXACTLY ARE YOU DOCILE AND MEEK?!
STOP IT! I TOLD YOU NOT TO TOUCH MY TAIL...
EEEEAAAH!!
HATTER!!
THIS... IS THE GUY WHO'S GOING TO HELP US?
A HATTER?

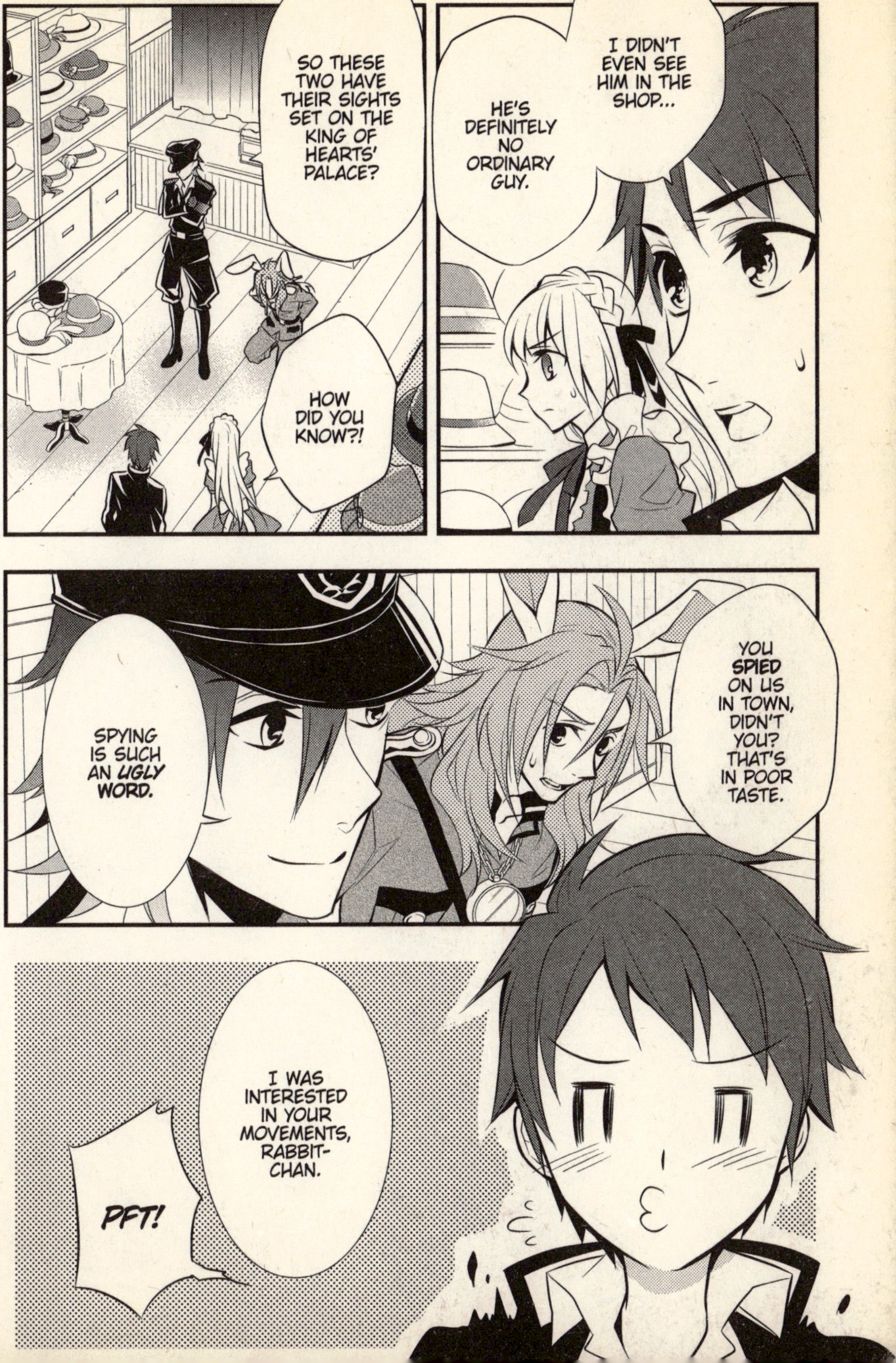
I DIDN'T EVEN SEE HIM IN THE SHOP...
HE'S DEFINITELY NO ORDINARY GUY.
SO THESE TWO HAVE THEIR SIGHTS SET ON THE KING OF HEARTS' PALACE?
HOW DID YOU KNOW?!
YOU **SPIED** ON US IN TOWN, DIDN'T YOU? THAT'S IN POOR TASTE.
SPYING IS SUCH AN *UGLY* WORD.
I WAS INTERESTED IN YOUR MOVEMENTS, RABBIT-CHAN.
PFT!

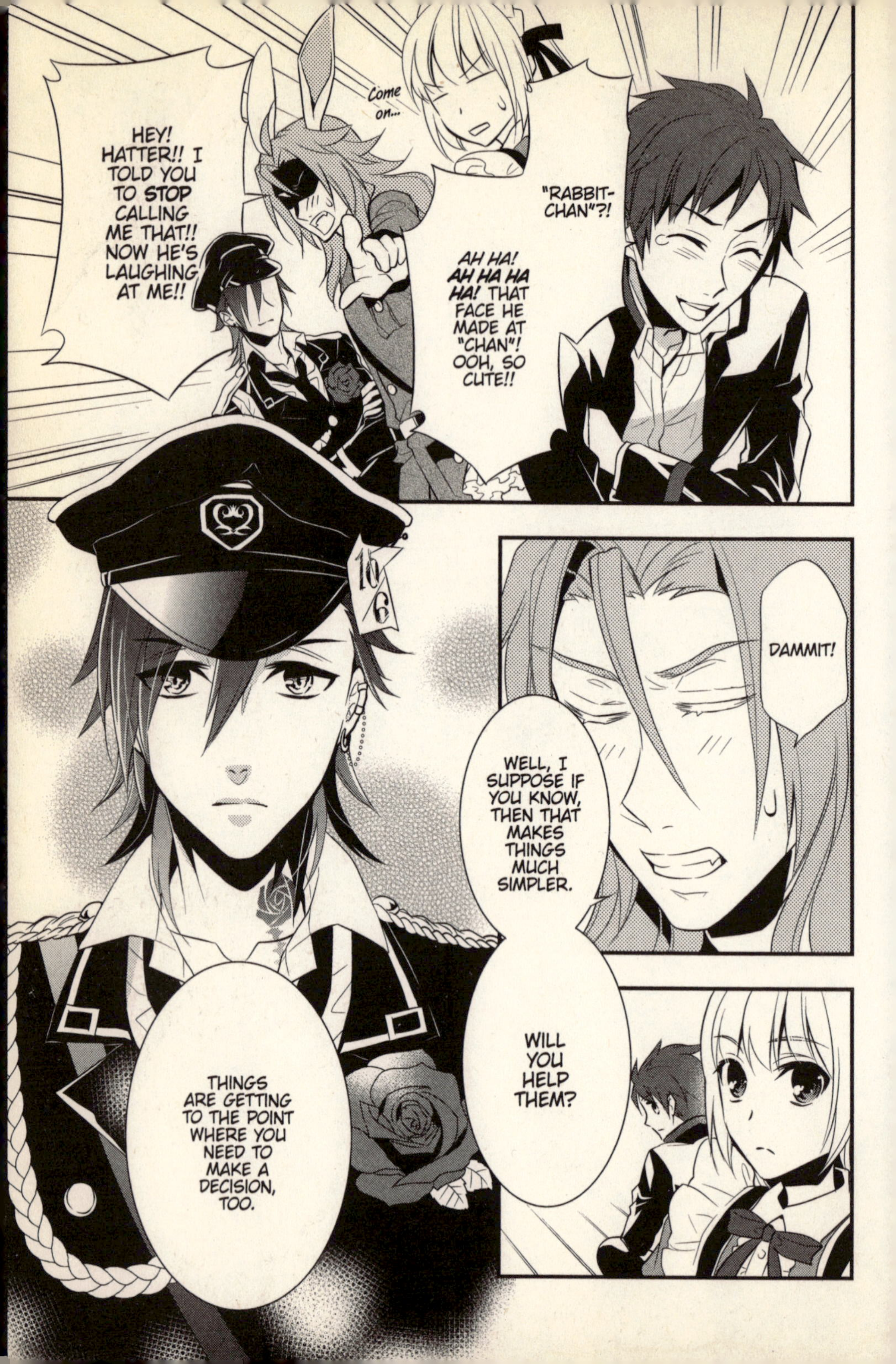
"RABBIT-CHAN"?!
AH HA! AH HA HA HA! THAT FACE HE MADE AT "CHAN"! OOH, SO CUTE!!
Come on...
HEY! HATTER!! I TOLD YOU TO STOP CALLING ME THAT!! NOW HE'S LAUGHING AT ME!!
DAMMIT!
WELL, I SUPPOSE IF YOU KNOW, THEN THAT MAKES THINGS MUCH SIMPLER.
WILL YOU HELP THEM?
THINGS ARE GETTING TO THE POINT WHERE YOU NEED TO MAKE A DECISION, TOO.

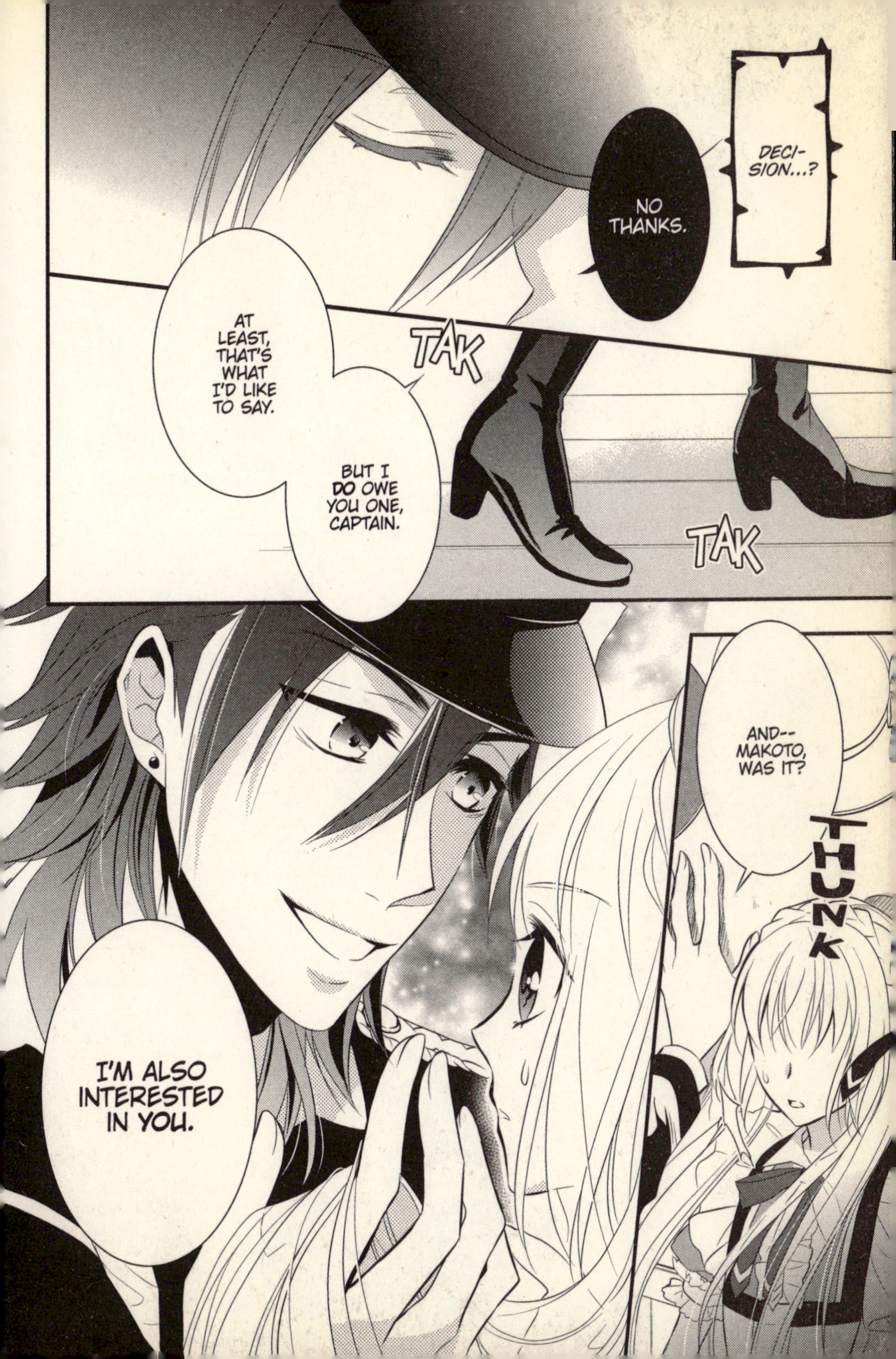
DECI-
SION...?
NO THANKS.
TAK
AT LEAST, THAT'S WHAT I'D LIKE TO SAY.
BUT I DO OWE YOU ONE, CAPTAIN.
TAK
AND-- MAKOTO, WAS IT?
THUNK
I'M ALSO INTERESTED IN YOU.

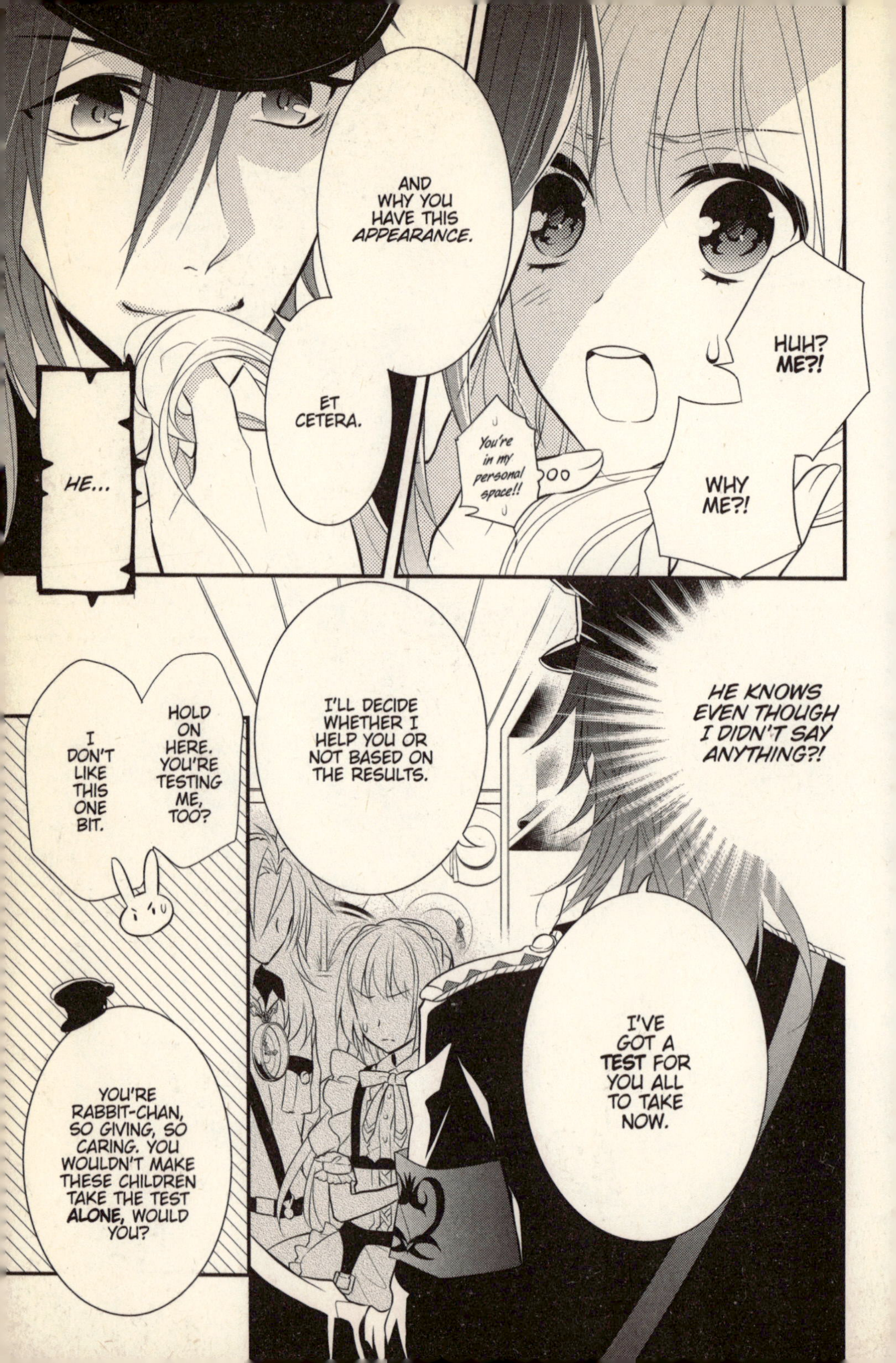
HUH? ME?!
WHY ME?!
You're in my personal space!!
AND WHY YOU HAVE THIS APPEARANCE.
ET CETERA.
HE...
HE KNOWS EVEN THOUGH I DIDN'T SAY ANYTHING?!
I'VE GOT A TEST FOR YOU ALL TO TAKE NOW.
I'LL DECIDE WHETHER I HELP YOU OR NOT BASED ON THE RESULTS.
HOLD ON HERE. YOU'RE TESTING ME, TOO?
I DON'T LIKE THIS ONE BIT.
YOU'RE RABBIT-CHAN, SO GIVING, SO CARING. YOU WOULDN'T MAKE THESE CHILDREN TAKE THE TEST ALONE, WOULD YOU?

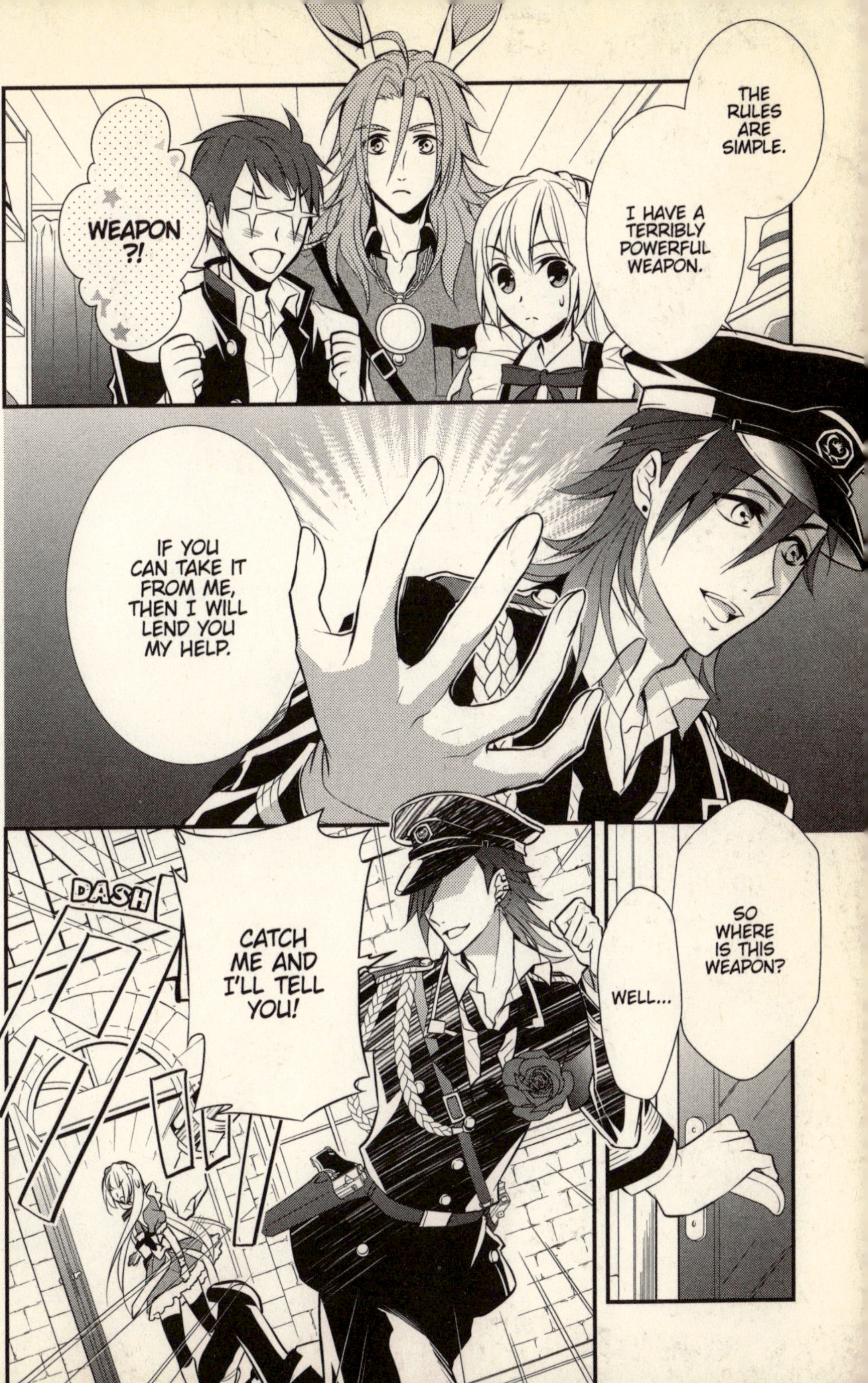
THE RULES ARE SIMPLE.
I HAVE A TERRIBLY POWERFUL WEAPON.
WEAPON ?!
IF YOU CAN TAKE IT FROM ME, THEN I WILL LEND YOU MY HELP.
SO WHERE IS THIS WEAPON?
WELL...
CATCH ME AND I'LL TELL YOU!
DASH

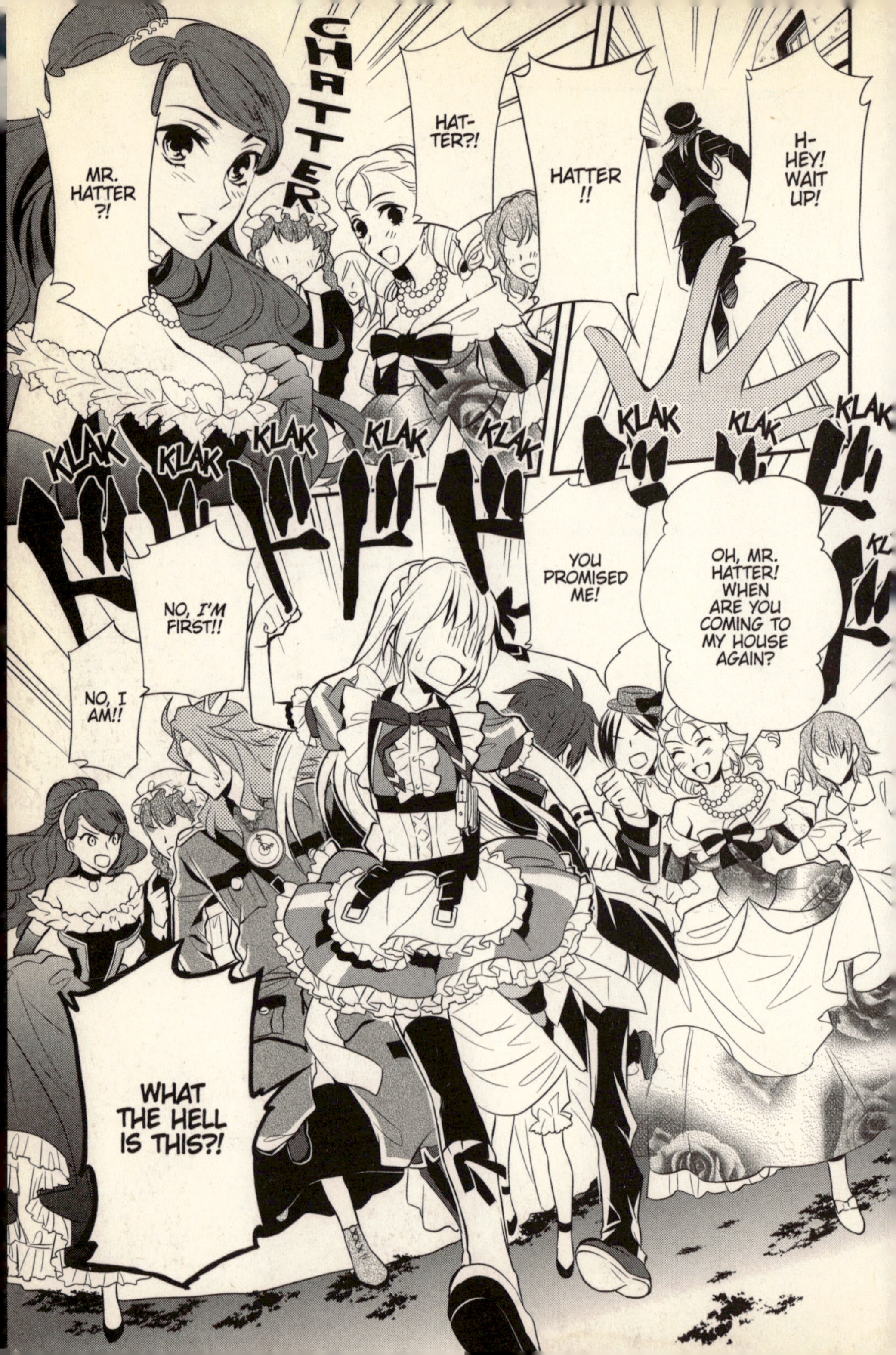
H-HEY! WAIT UP!
HATTER!!
HATTER?!
CHATTER
MR. HATTER?!
KLAK
KLAK
KLAK
KLAK
KLAK
KLAK
KLAK
KLAK
OH, MR. HATTER! WHEN ARE YOU COMING TO MY HOUSE AGAIN?
YOU PROMISED ME!
NO, I'M FIRST!!
NO, I AM!!
WHAT THE HELL IS THIS?!

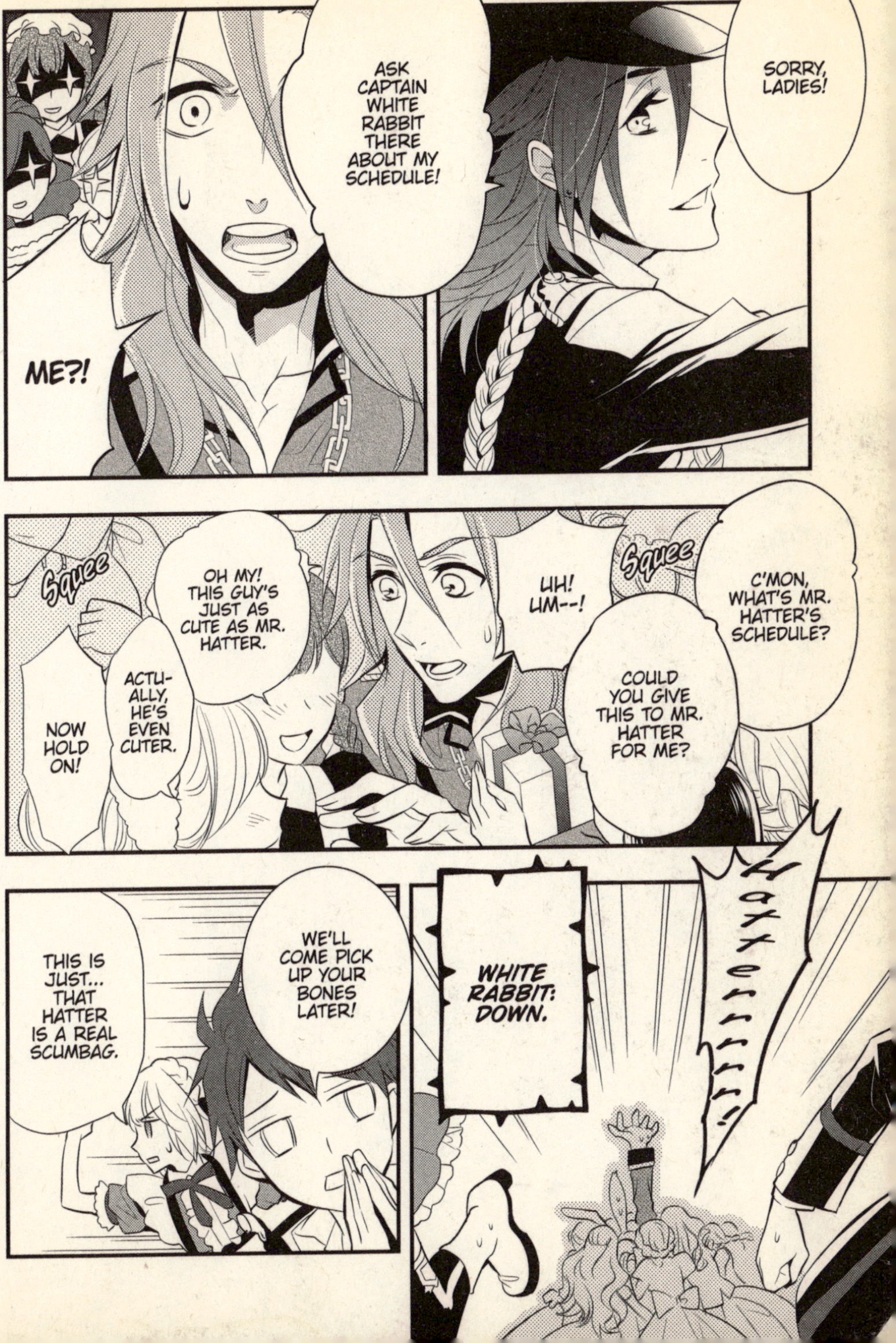
SORRY, LADIES!
ASK CAPTAIN WHITE RABBIT THERE ABOUT MY SCHEDULE!
ME?!
C'MON, WHAT'S MR. HATTER'S SCHEDULE?
Squee
COULD YOU GIVE THIS TO MR. HATTER FOR ME?
UH! UM--!
OH MY! THIS GUY'S JUST AS CUTE AS MR. HATTER.
Squee
ACTU-ALLY, HE'S EVEN CUTER.
NOW HOLD ON!
Hatterrrrrr!
WHITE RABBIT: DOWN.
WE'LL COME PICK UP YOUR BONES LATER!
THIS IS JUST... THAT HATTER IS A REAL SCUMBAG.

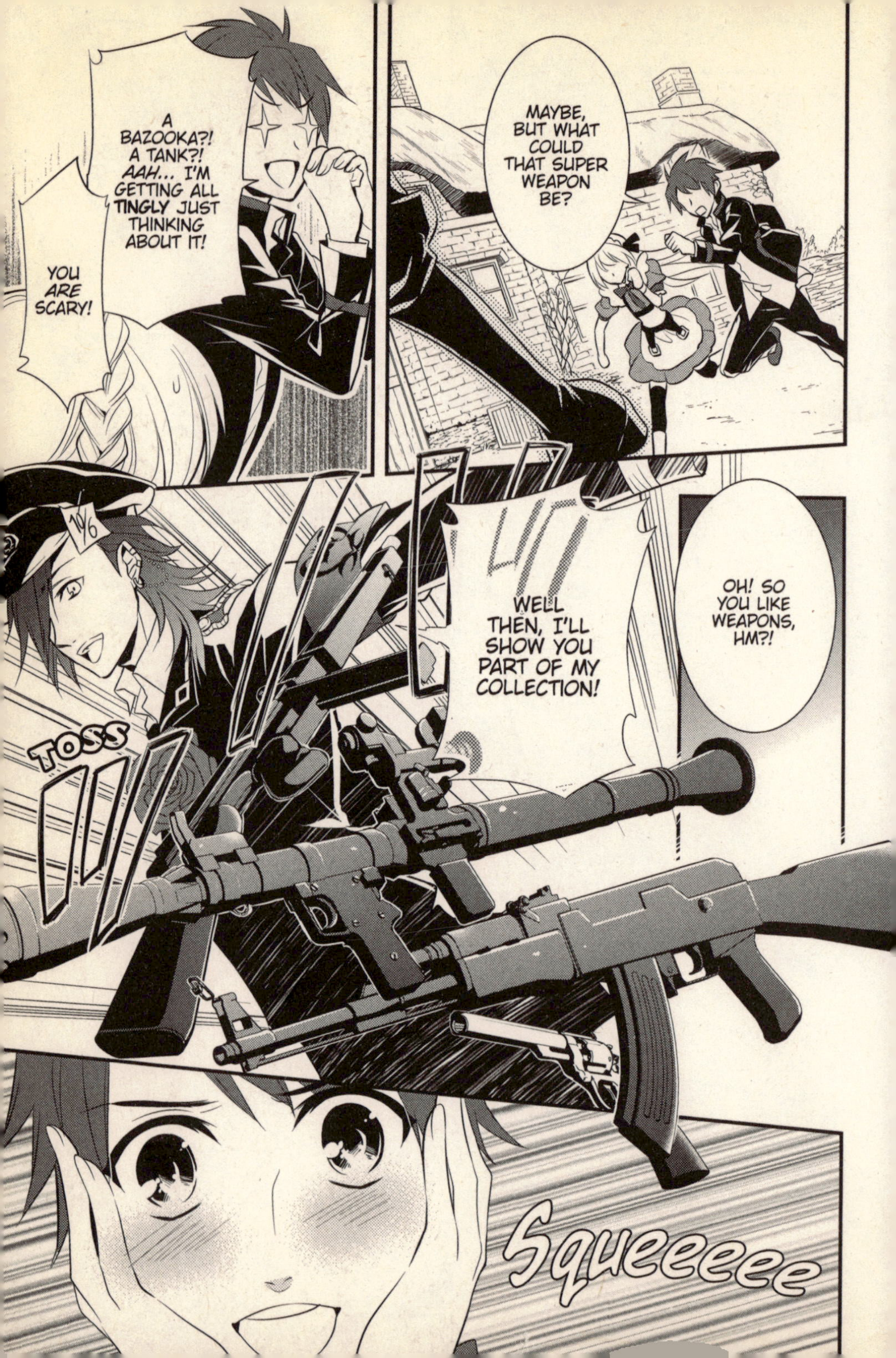
MAYBE, BUT WHAT COULD THAT SUPER WEAPON BE?
A BAZOOKA?! A TANK?! AAH... I'M GETTING ALL TINGLY JUST THINKING ABOUT IT!
YOU ARE SCARY!
OH! SO YOU LIKE WEAPONS, HM?!
WELL THEN, I'LL SHOW YOU PART OF MY COLLECTION!
TOSS
Squeeeeee

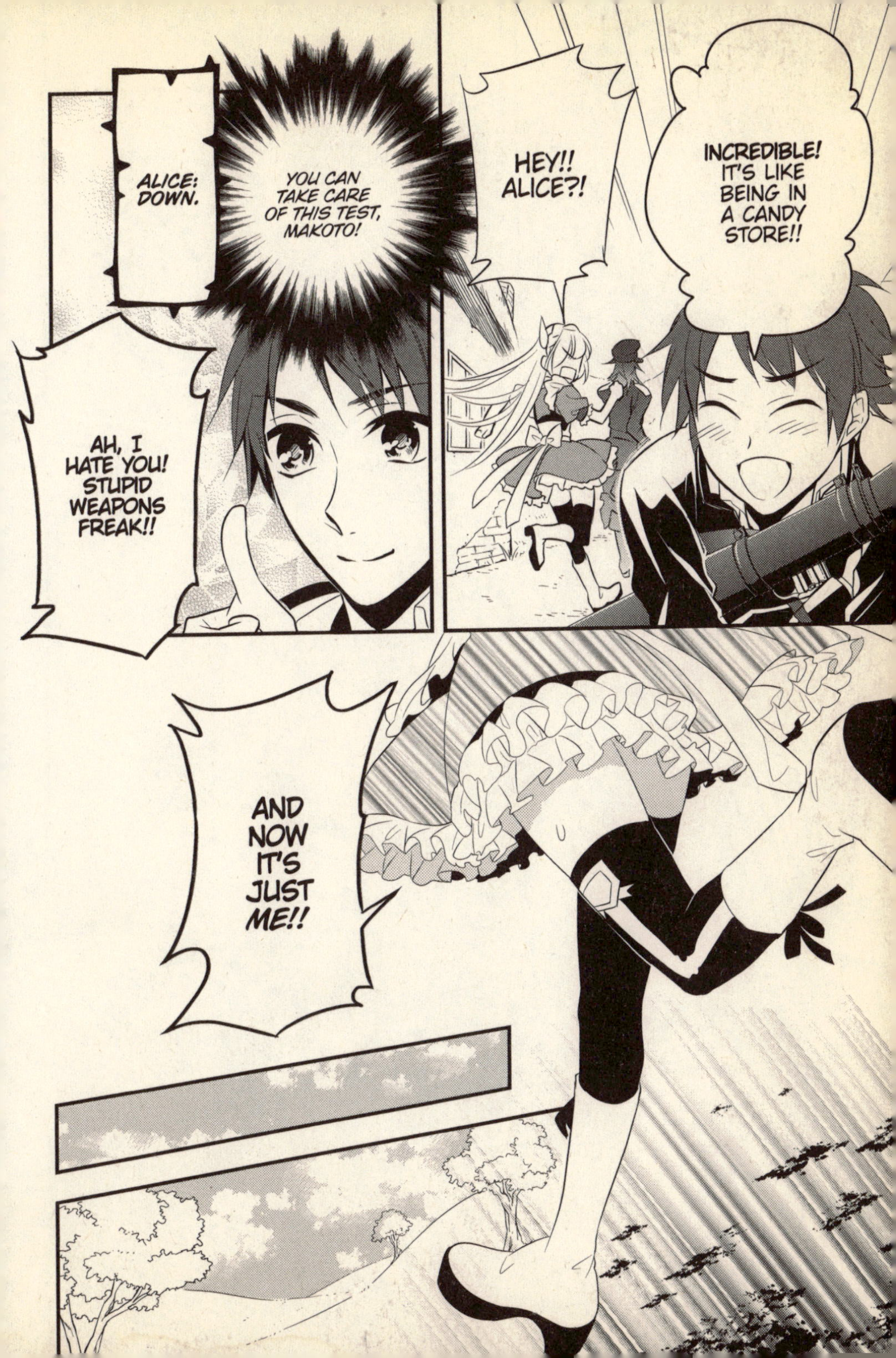
INCREDIBLE! IT'S LIKE BEING IN A CANDY STORE!!
HEY!! ALICE?!
YOU CAN TAKE CARE OF THIS TEST, MAKOTO!
ALICE: DOWN.
AH, I HATE YOU! STUPID WEAPONS FREAK!!
AND NOW IT'S JUST ME!!

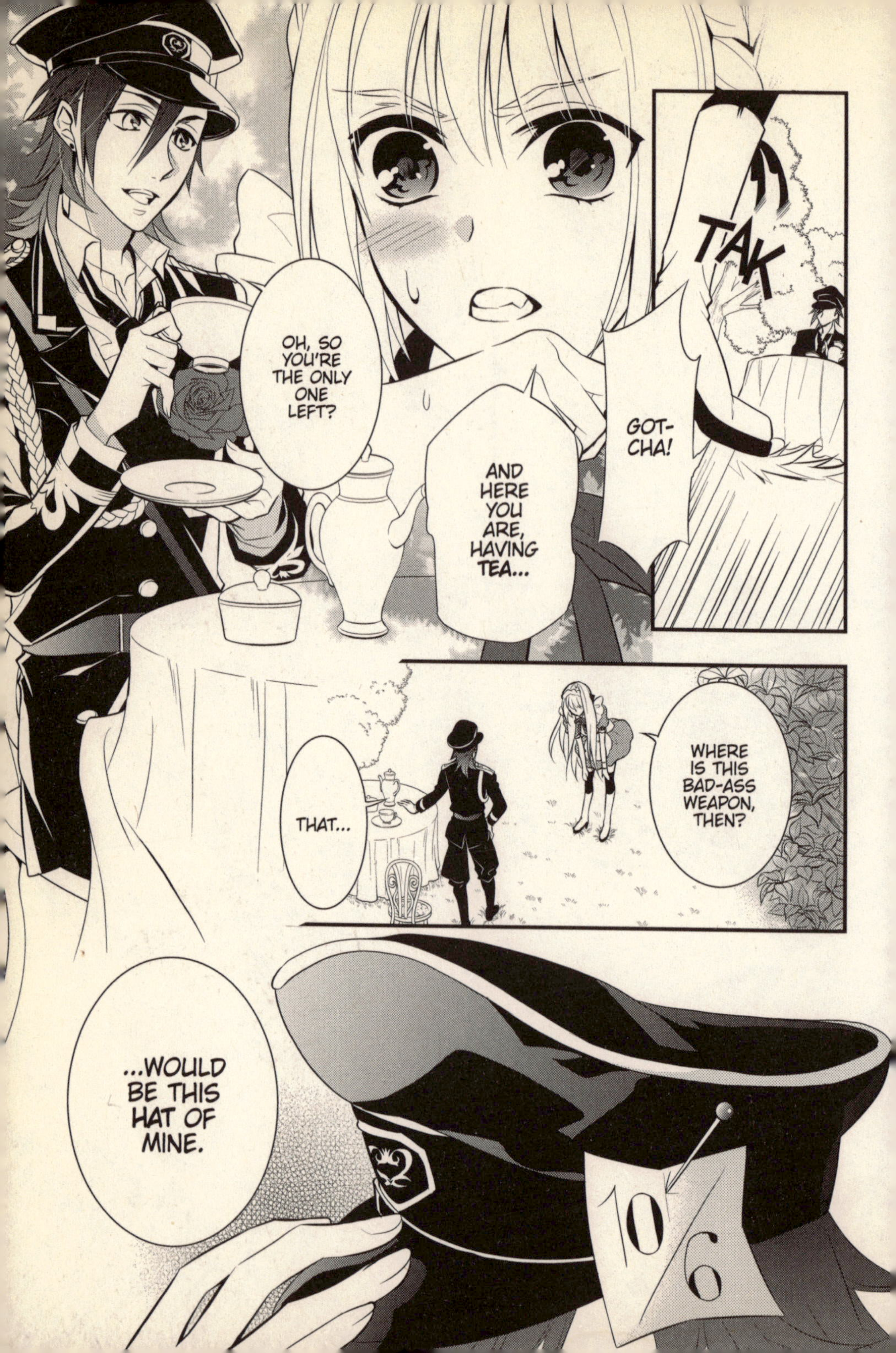
TAK
GOT-CHA!
OH, SO YOU'RE THE ONLY ONE LEFT?
AND HERE YOU ARE, HAVING TEA...
WHERE IS THIS BAD-ASS WEAPON, THEN?
THAT...
...WOULD BE THIS HAT OF MINE.
10/6

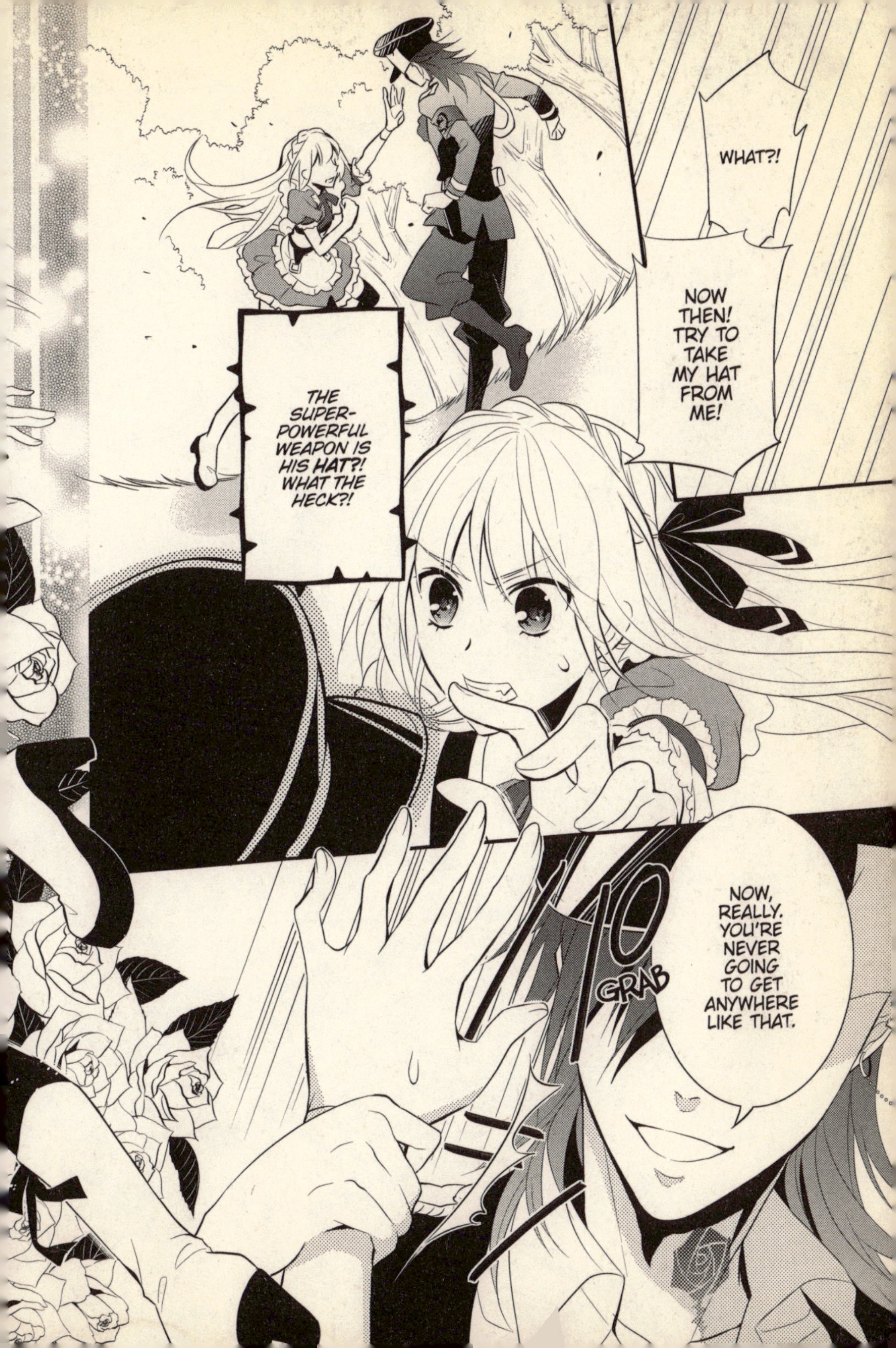
WHAT?!
NOW THEN! TRY TO TAKE MY HAT FROM ME!
THE SUPER-POWERFUL WEAPON IS HIS HAT?! WHAT THE HECK?!
NOW, REALLY. YOU'RE NEVER GOING TO GET ANYWHERE LIKE THAT.
GRAB

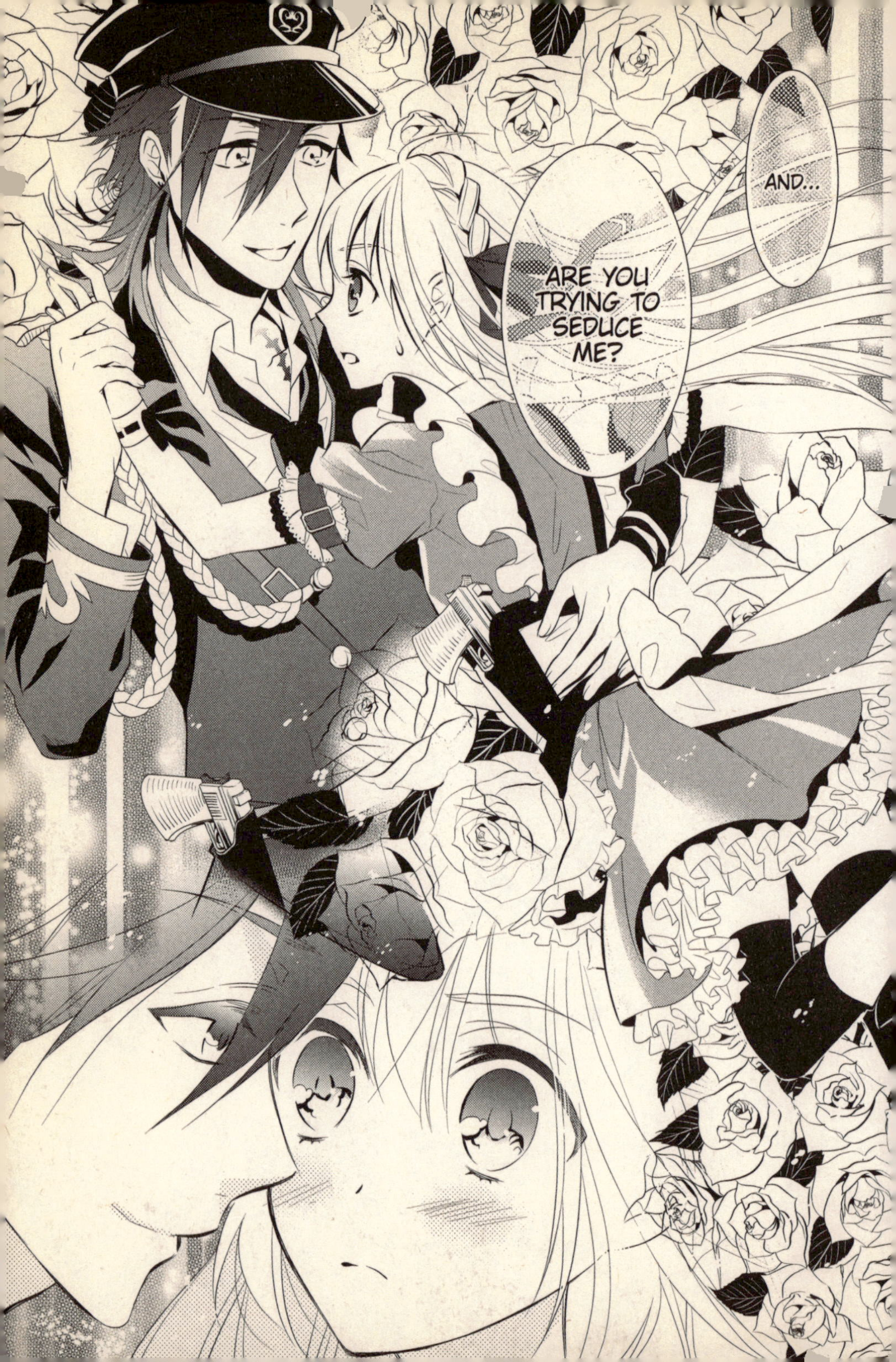
AND...
ARE YOU TRYING TO SEDUCE ME?

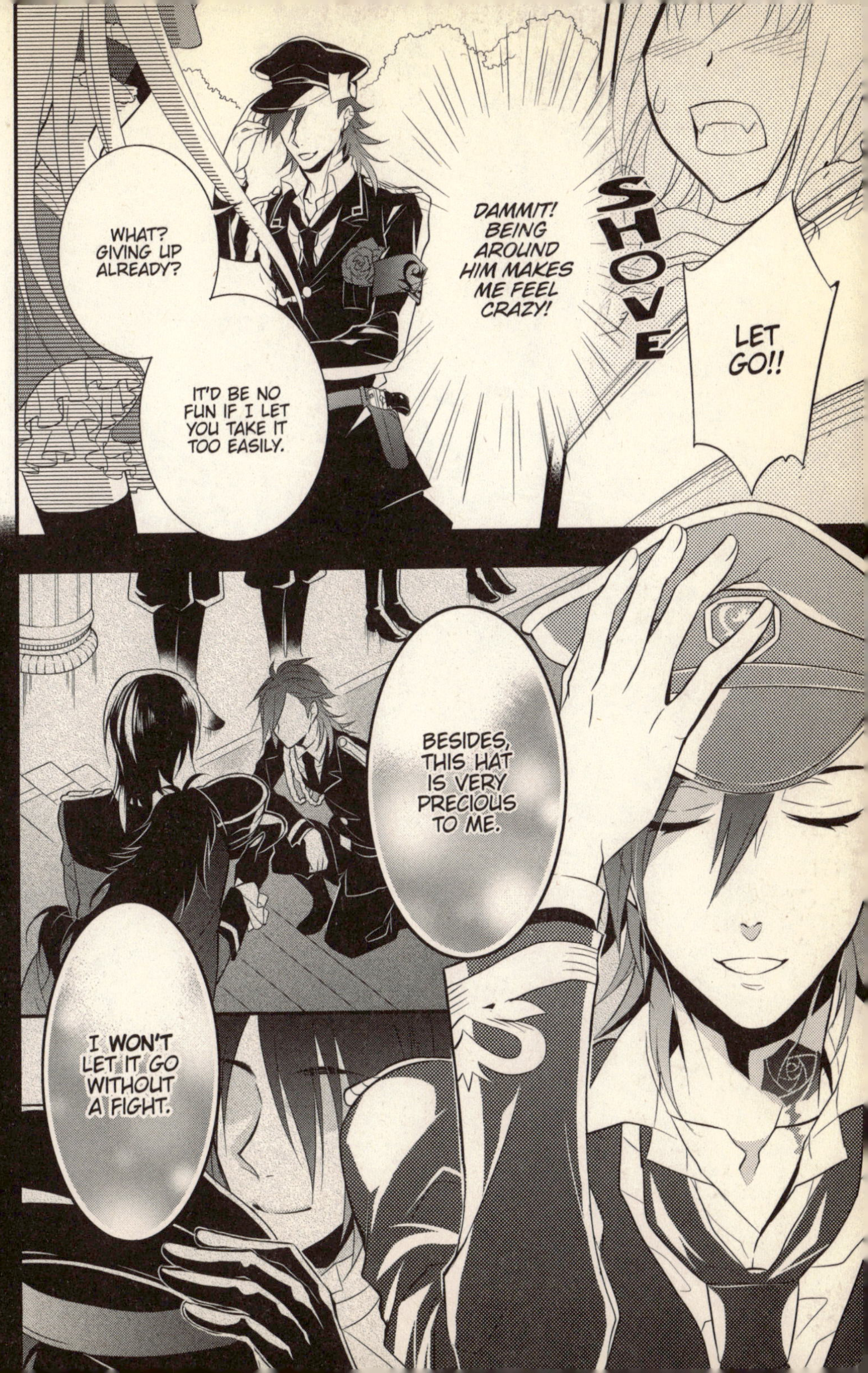
LET GO!!
SHOVE
DAMMIT! BEING AROUND HIM MAKES ME FEEL CRAZY!
WHAT? GIVING UP ALREADY?
IT'D BE NO FUN IF I LET YOU TAKE IT TOO EASILY.
BESIDES, THIS HAT IS VERY PRECIOUS TO ME.
I WON'T LET IT GO WITHOUT A FIGHT.

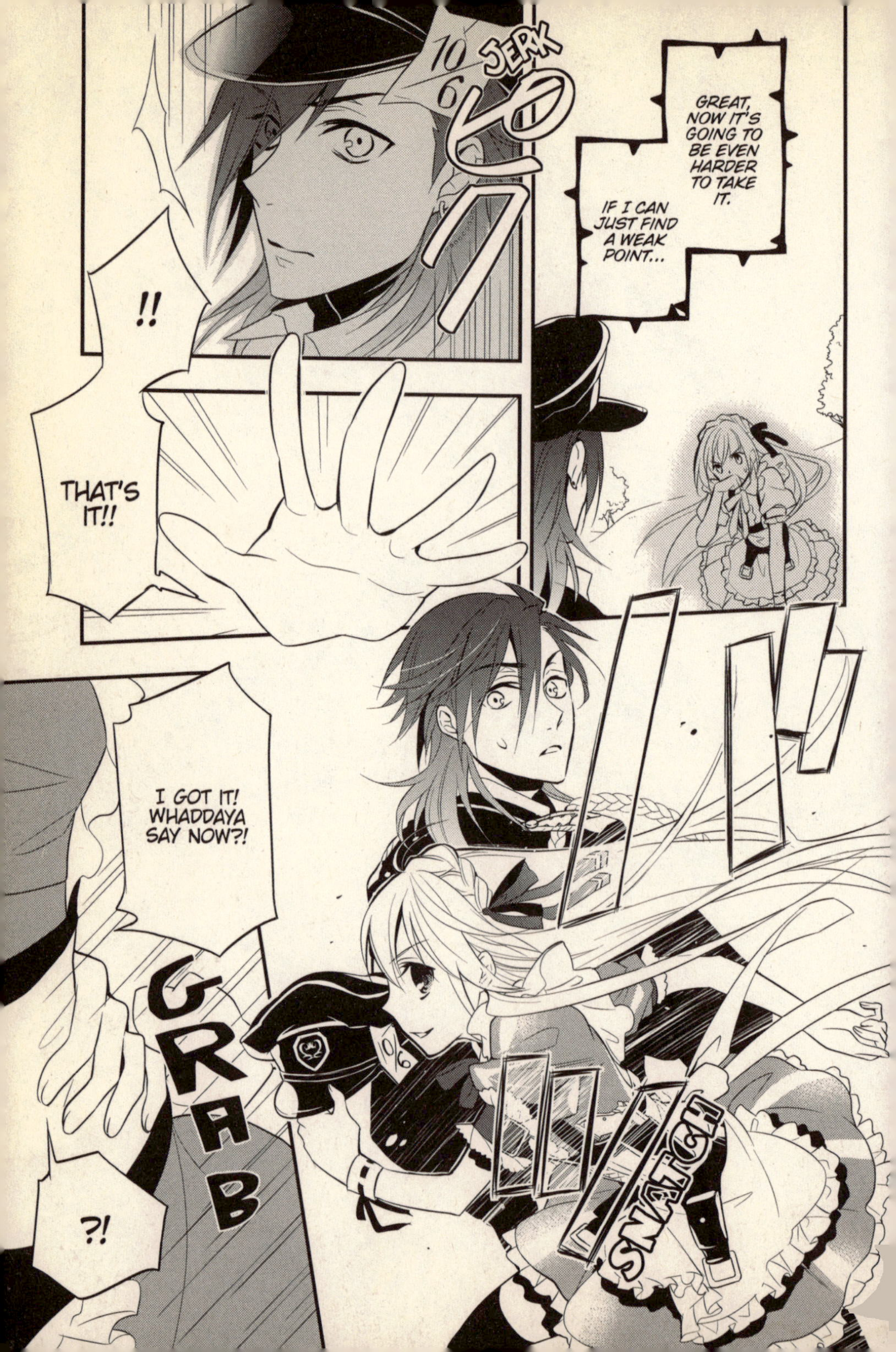
GREAT, NOW IT'S GOING TO BE EVEN HARDER TO TAKE IT.
IF I CAN JUST FIND A WEAK POINT...
JERK
!!
THAT'S IT!!
I GOT IT! WHADDAYA SAY NOW?!
SNATCH
GRAB
?!

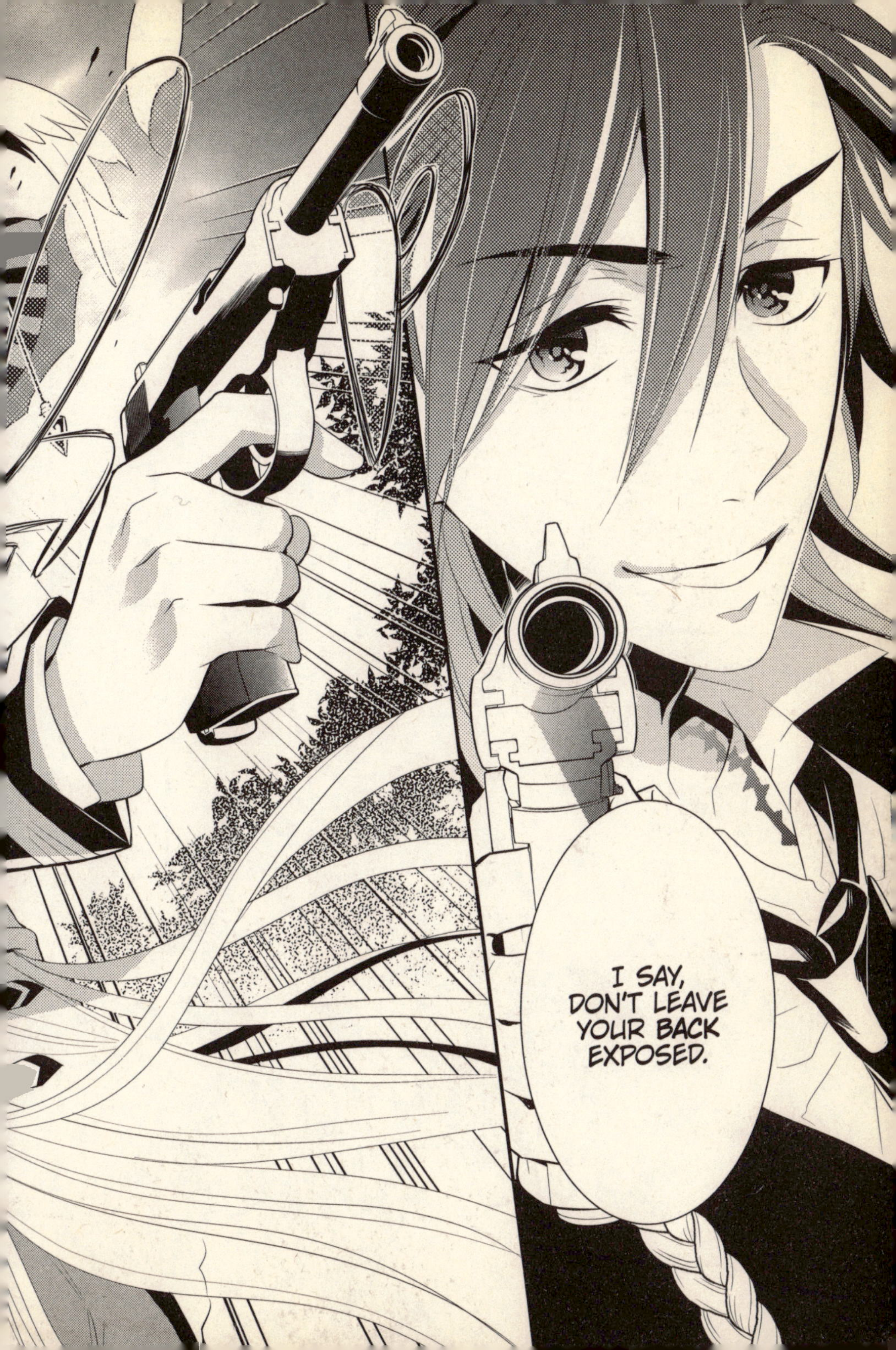
I SAY, DON'T LEAVE YOUR BACK EXPOSED.

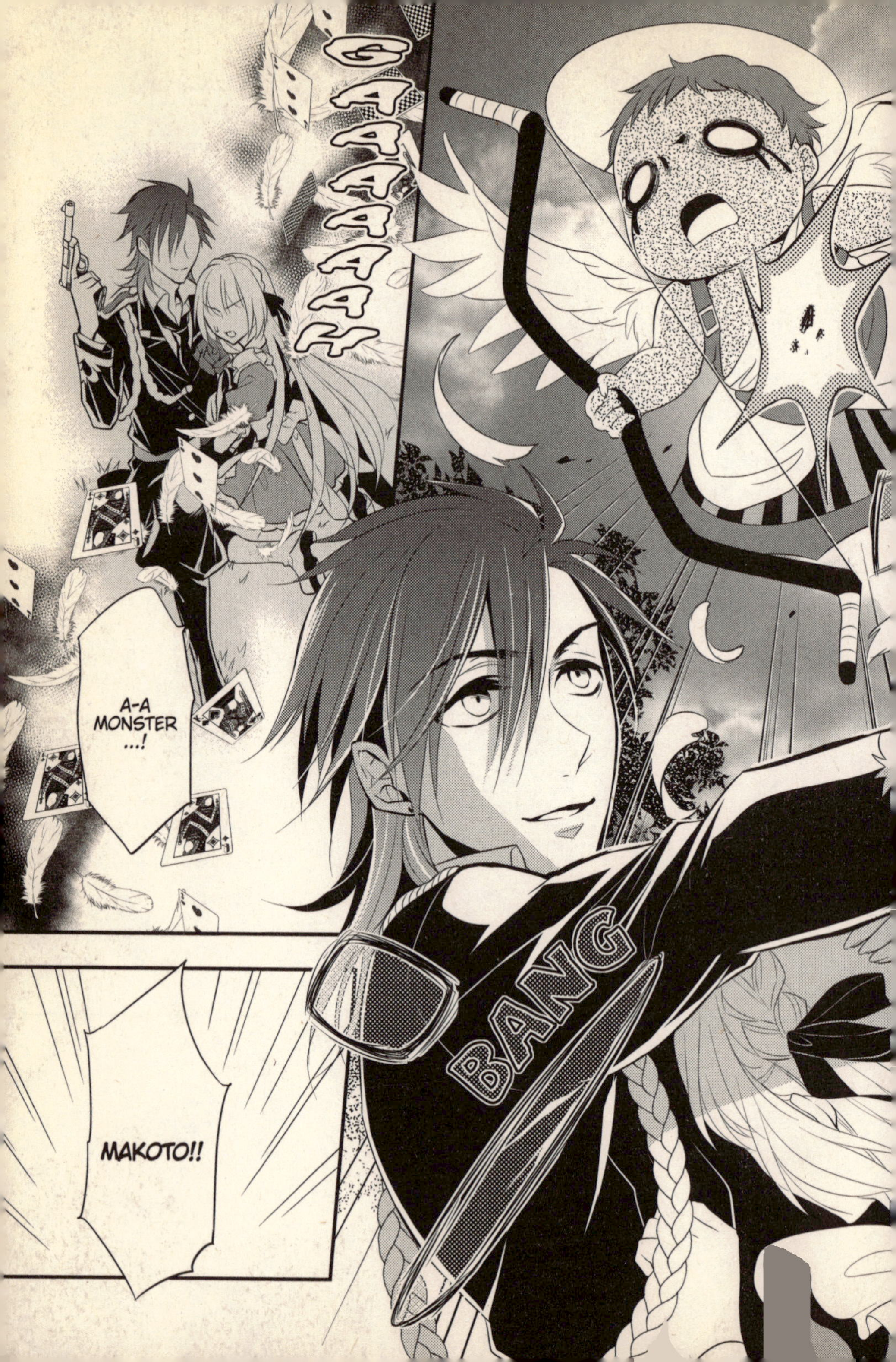
BANG
GAAAAAH
A-A MONSTER ...!
MAKOTO!!

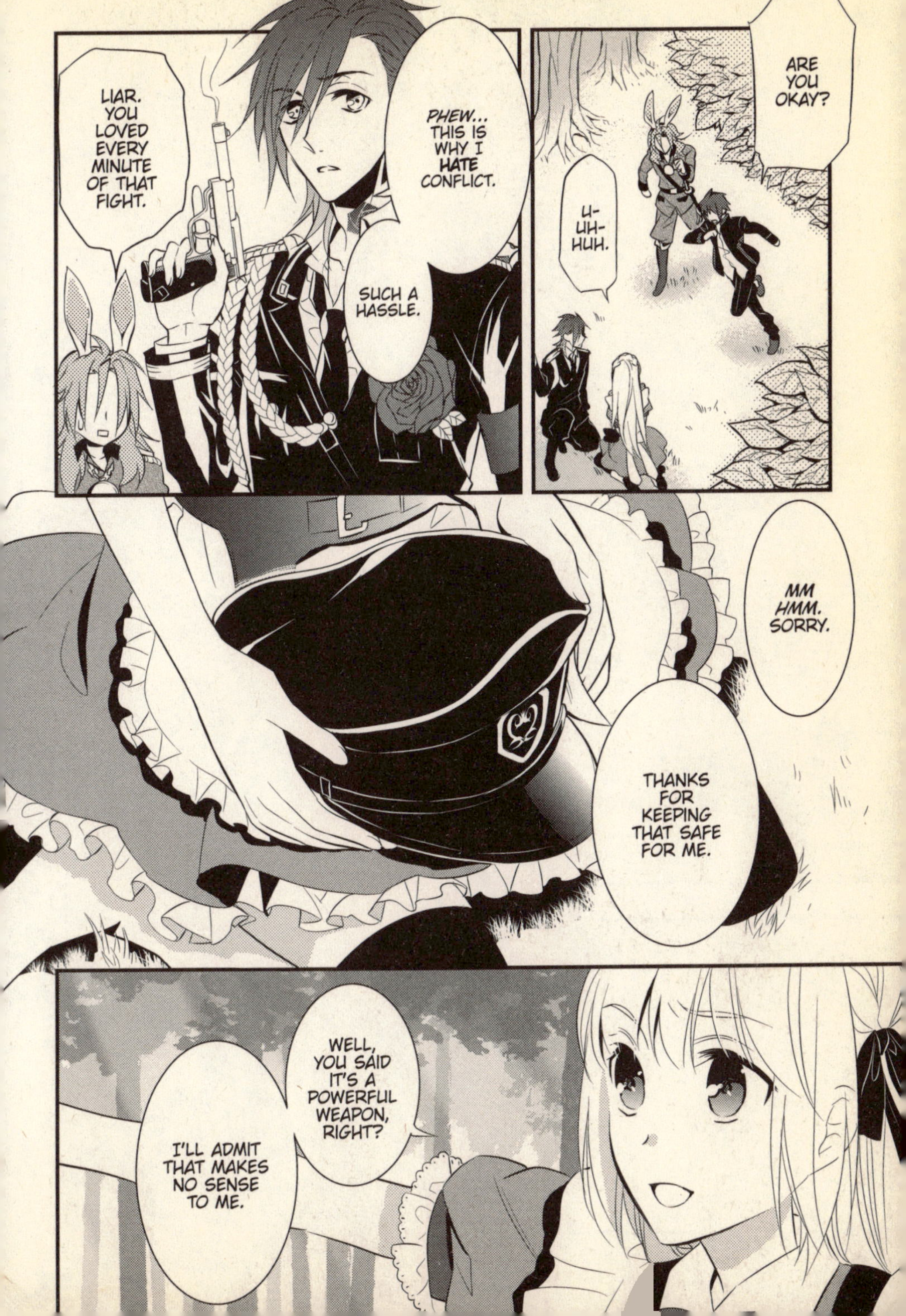
ARE YOU OKAY?
U-UH-HUH.
PHEW... THIS IS WHY I **HATE** CONFLICT.
SUCH A HASSLE.
LIAR. YOU LOVED EVERY MINUTE OF THAT FIGHT.
MM HMM. SORRY.
THANKS FOR KEEPING THAT SAFE FOR ME.
WELL, YOU SAID IT'S A POWERFUL WEAPON, RIGHT?
I'LL ADMIT THAT MAKES NO SENSE TO ME.

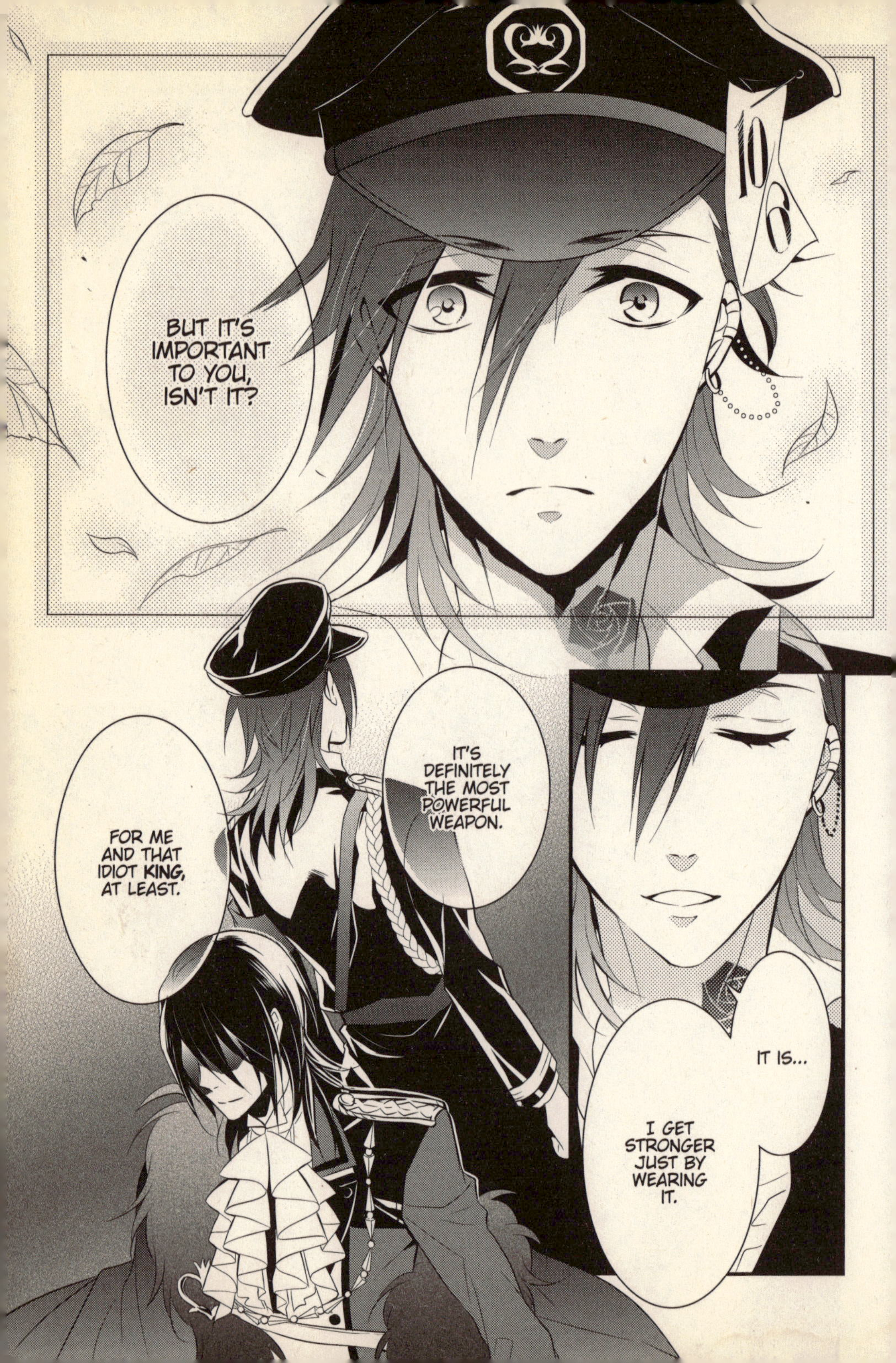
BUT IT'S IMPORTANT TO YOU, ISN'T IT?
IT IS...
I GET STRONGER JUST BY WEARING IT.
IT'S DEFINITELY THE MOST POWERFUL WEAPON.
FOR ME AND THAT IDIOT KING, AT LEAST.

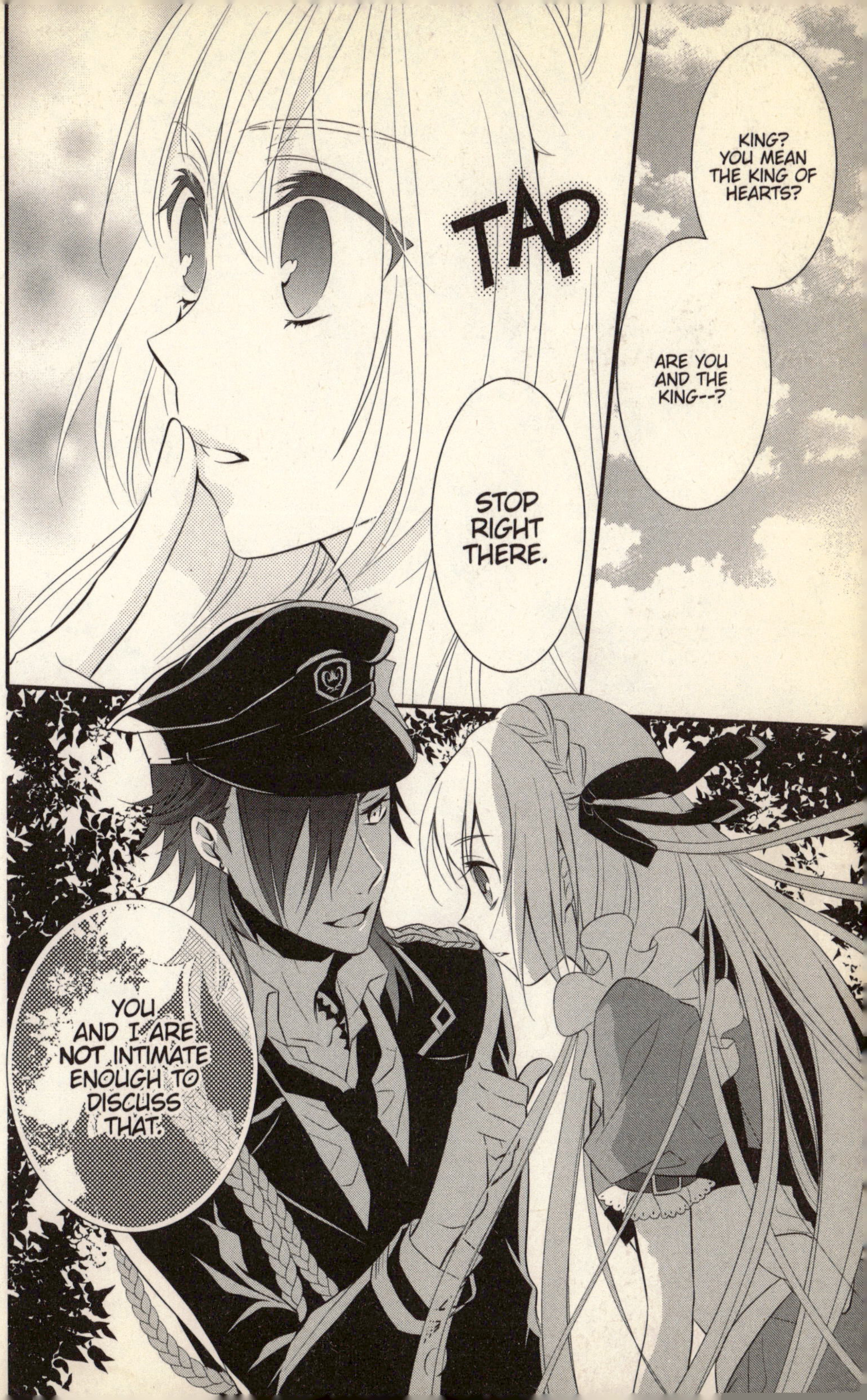
KING? YOU MEAN THE KING OF HEARTS?
ARE YOU AND THE KING--?
TAP
STOP RIGHT THERE.
YOU AND I ARE NOT INTIMATE ENOUGH TO DISCUSS THAT.

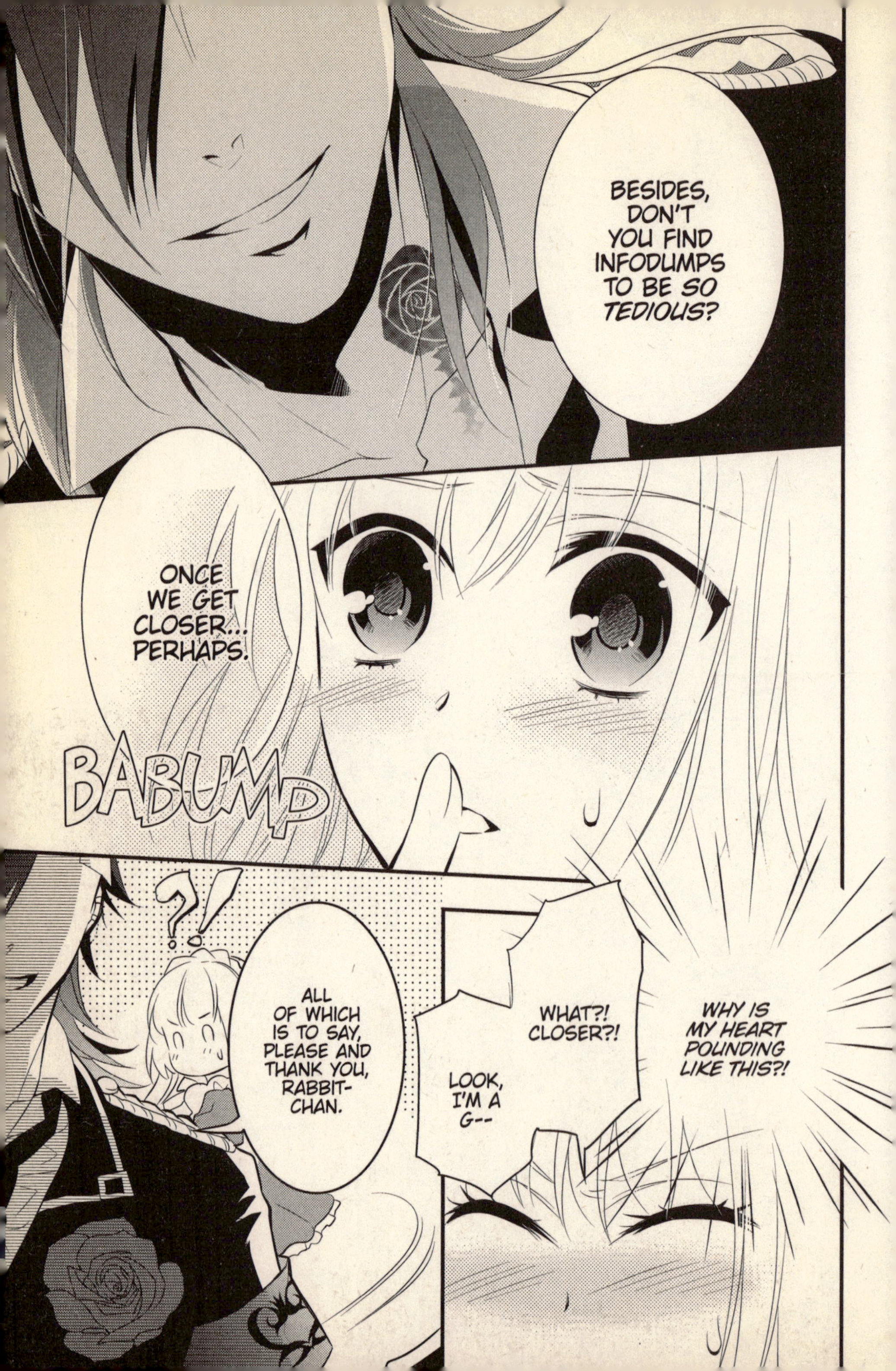
BESIDES, DON'T YOU FIND INFODUMPS TO BE SO *TEDIOUS?*
ONCE WE GET CLOSER... PERHAPS.
BABUMP
WHY IS MY HEART POUNDING LIKE THIS?!
WHAT?! CLOSER?!
LOOK, I'M A G--
?!
ALL OF WHICH IS TO SAY, PLEASE AND THANK YOU, RABBIT-CHAN.

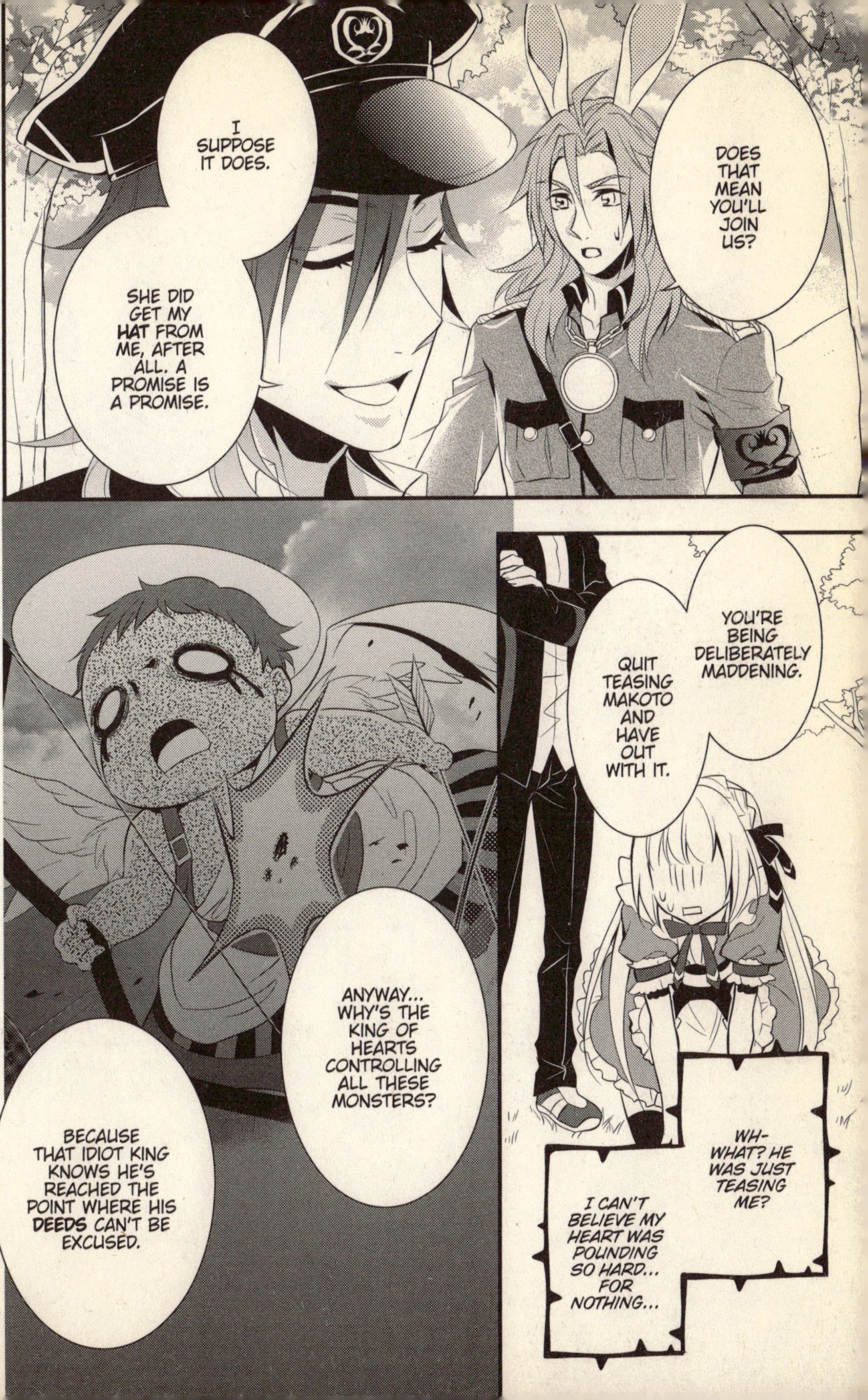
DOES THAT MEAN YOU'LL JOIN US?
I SUPPOSE IT DOES.
SHE DID GET MY **HAT** FROM ME, AFTER ALL. A PROMISE IS A PROMISE.
YOU'RE BEING DELIBERATELY MADDENING.
QUIT TEASING MAKOTO AND HAVE OUT WITH IT.
WH-WHAT? HE WAS JUST TEASING ME?
I CAN'T BELIEVE MY HEART WAS POUNDING SO HARD... FOR NOTHING...
ANYWAY... WHY'S THE KING OF HEARTS CONTROLLING ALL THESE MONSTERS?
BECAUSE THAT IDIOT KING KNOWS HE'S REACHED THE POINT WHERE HIS **DEEDS** CAN'T BE EXCUSED.

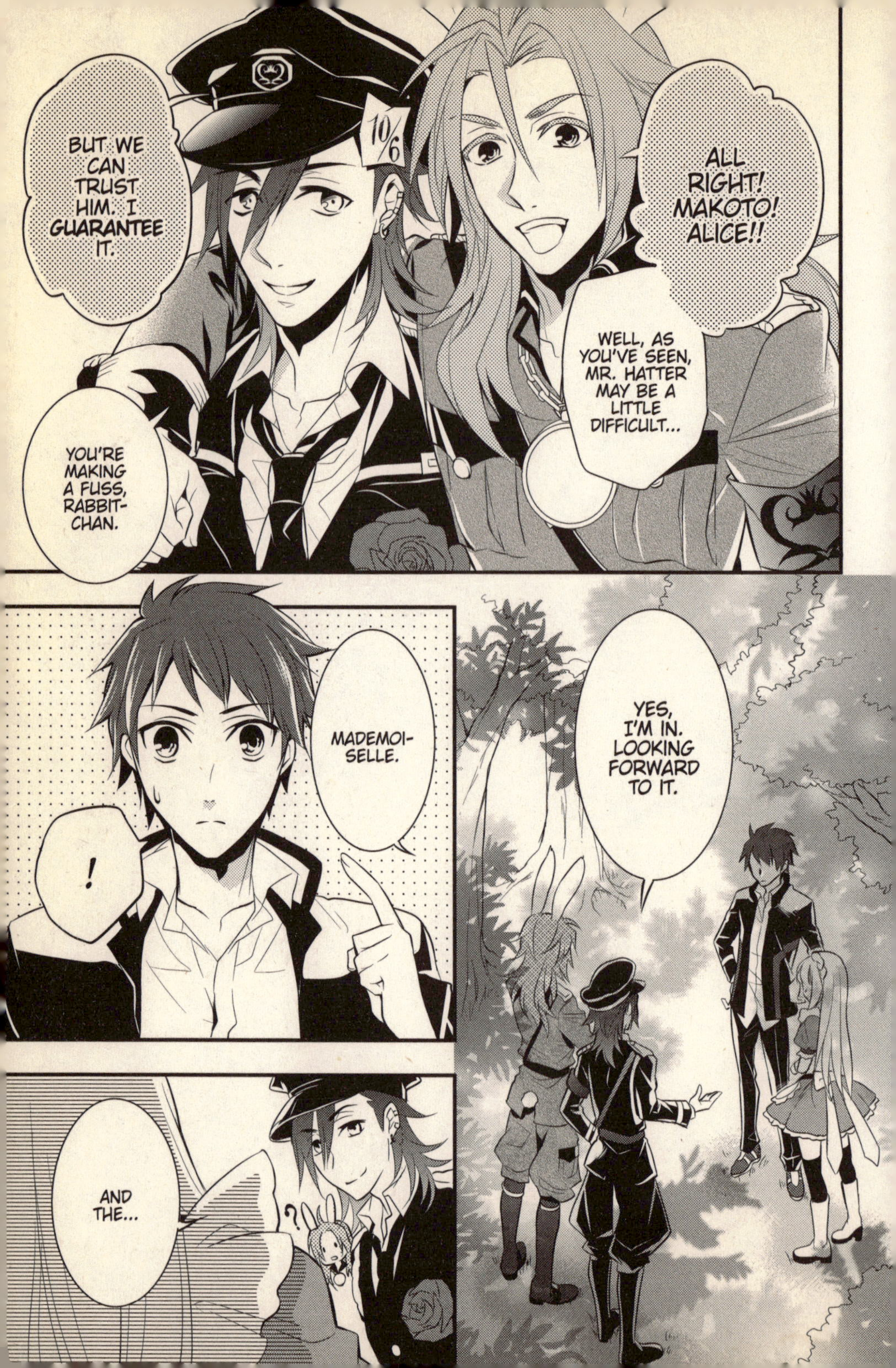
ALL RIGHT! MAKOTO! ALICE!!
WELL, AS YOU'VE SEEN, MR. HATTER MAY BE A LITTLE DIFFICULT...
BUT WE CAN TRUST HIM. I GUARANTEE IT.
YOU'RE MAKING A FUSS, RABBIT-CHAN.
YES, I'M IN. LOOKING FORWARD TO IT.
MADEMOI-SELLE.
!
AND THE...
?

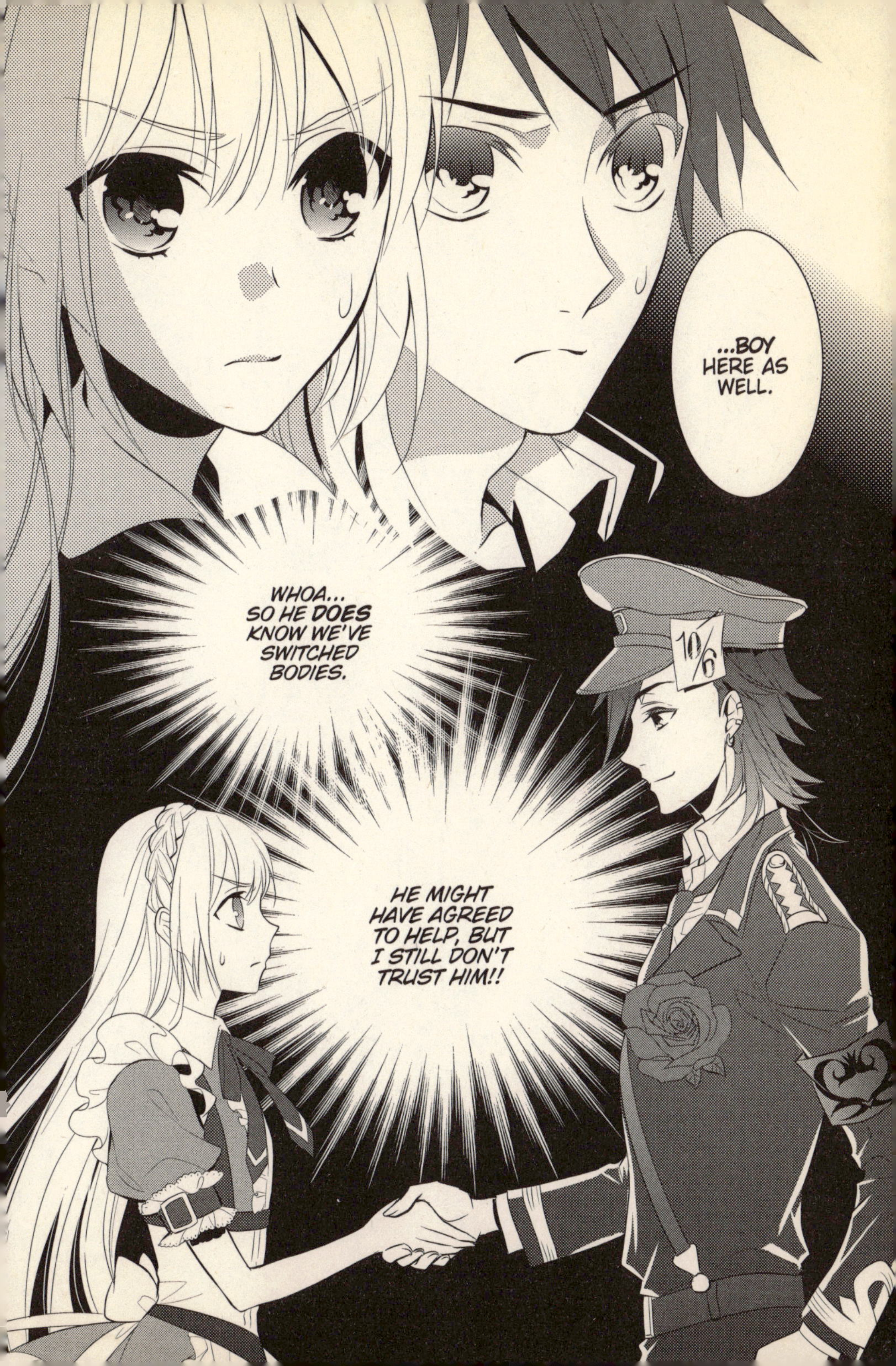
...BOY HERE AS WELL.
WHOA... SO HE DOES KNOW WE'VE SWITCHED BODIES.
HE MIGHT HAVE AGREED TO HELP, BUT I STILL DON'T TRUST HIM!!

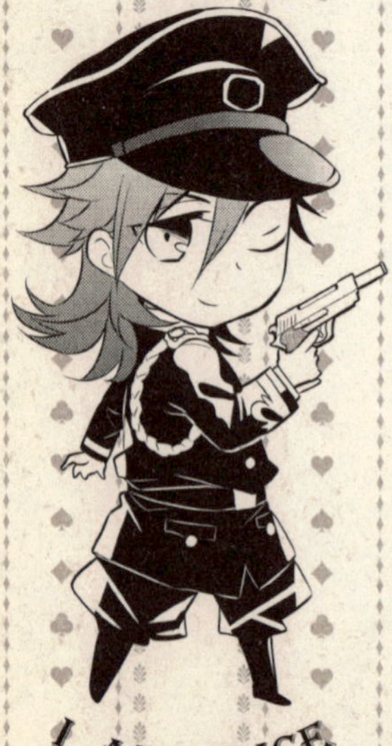
I AM ALICE

I AM ALICE

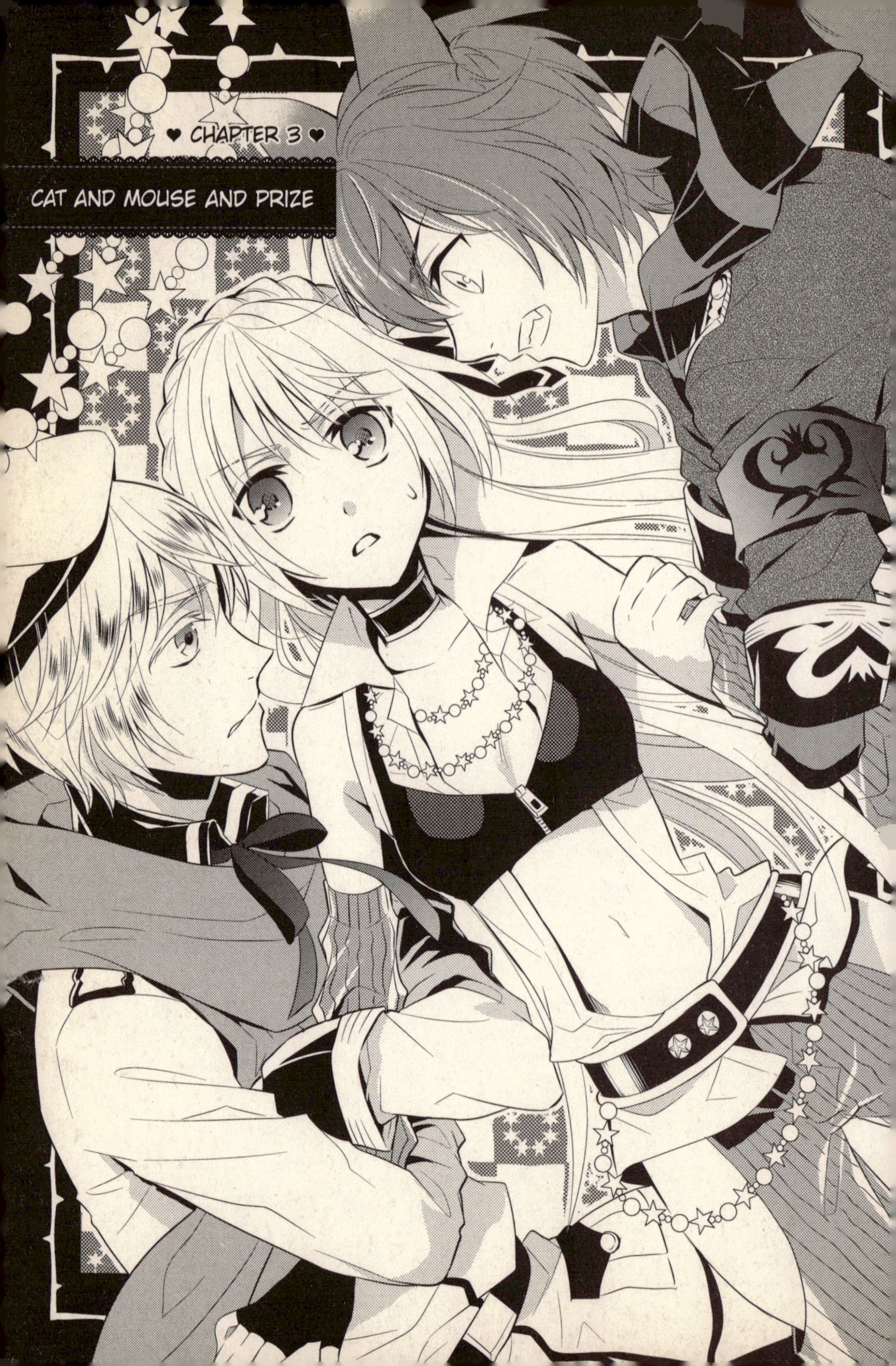
♥ CHAPTER 3 ♥
CAT AND MOUSE AND PRIZE

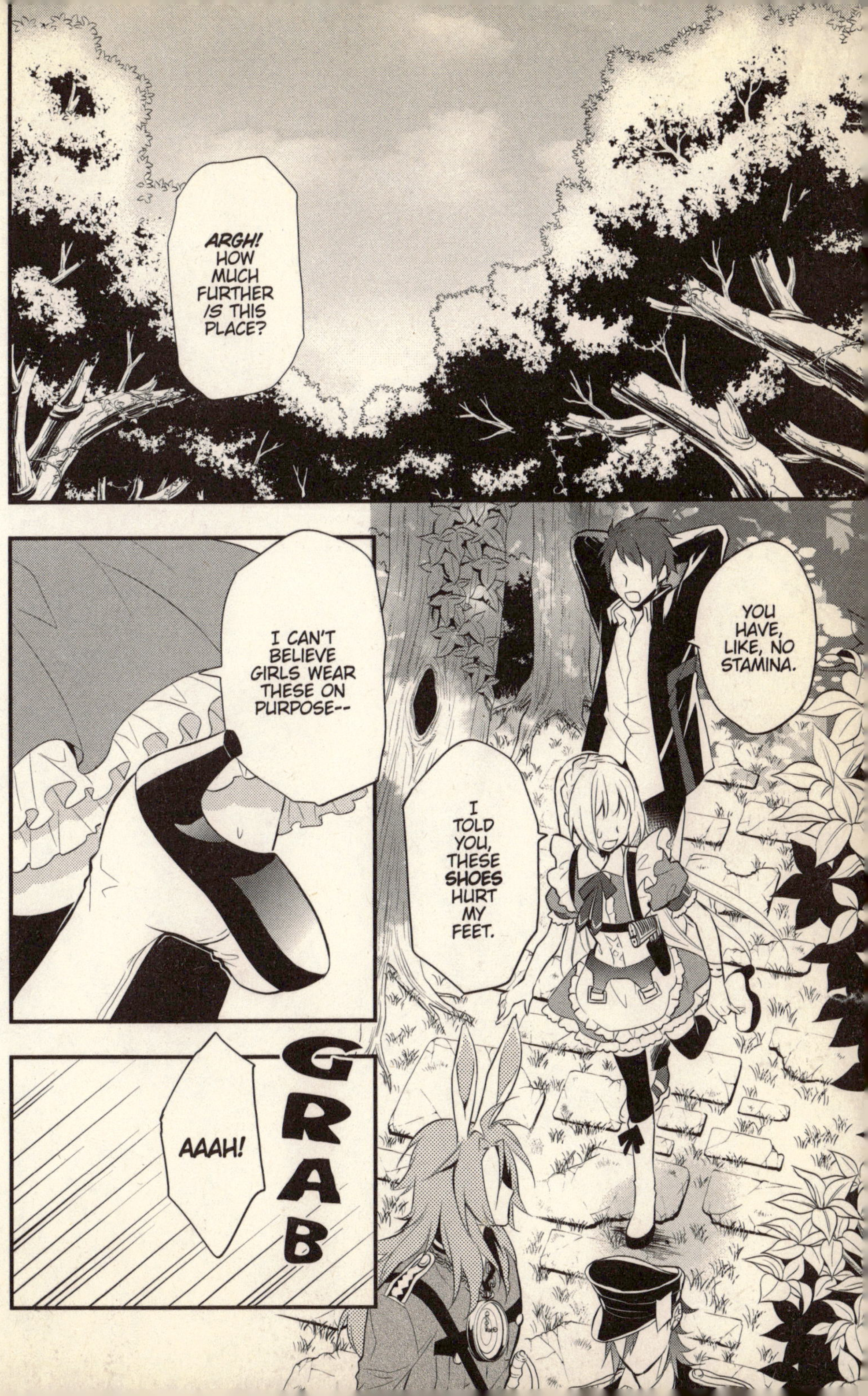
ARGH! HOW MUCH FURTHER IS THIS PLACE?
YOU HAVE, LIKE, NO STAMINA.
I TOLD YOU, THESE SHOES HURT MY FEET.
GRAB
I CAN'T BELIEVE GIRLS WEAR THESE ON PURPOSE--
AAAH!

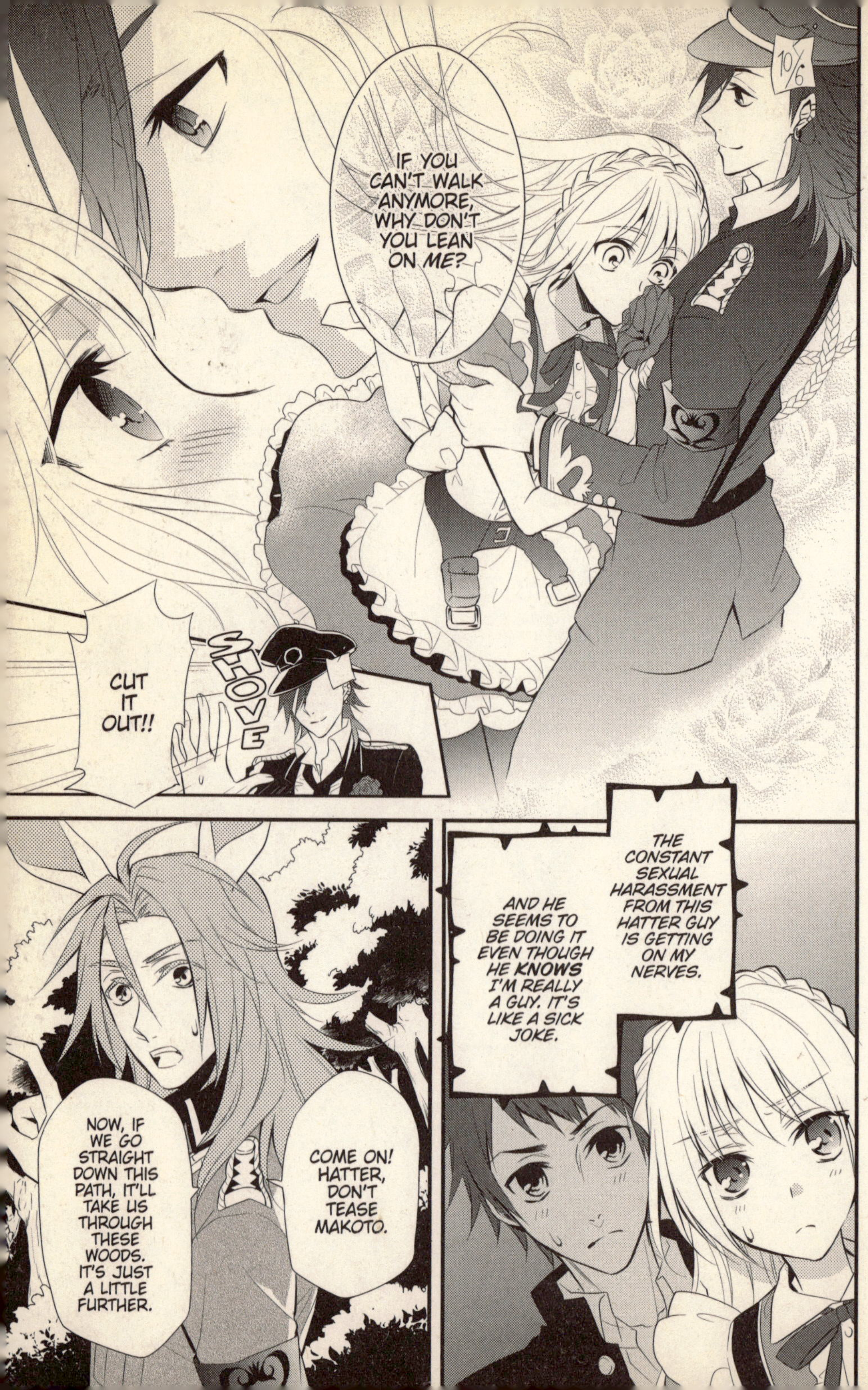
10/6
IF YOU CAN'T WALK ANYMORE, WHY DON'T YOU LEAN ON *ME*?
SHOVE
CUT IT OUT!!
THE CONSTANT SEXUAL HARASSMENT FROM THIS HATTER GUY IS GETTING ON MY NERVES.
AND HE SEEMS TO BE DOING IT EVEN THOUGH HE **KNOWS** I'M REALLY A GUY. IT'S LIKE A SICK JOKE.
COME ON! HATTER, DON'T TEASE MAKOTO.
NOW, IF WE GO STRAIGHT DOWN THIS PATH, IT'LL TAKE US THROUGH THESE WOODS. IT'S JUST A LITTLE FURTHER.

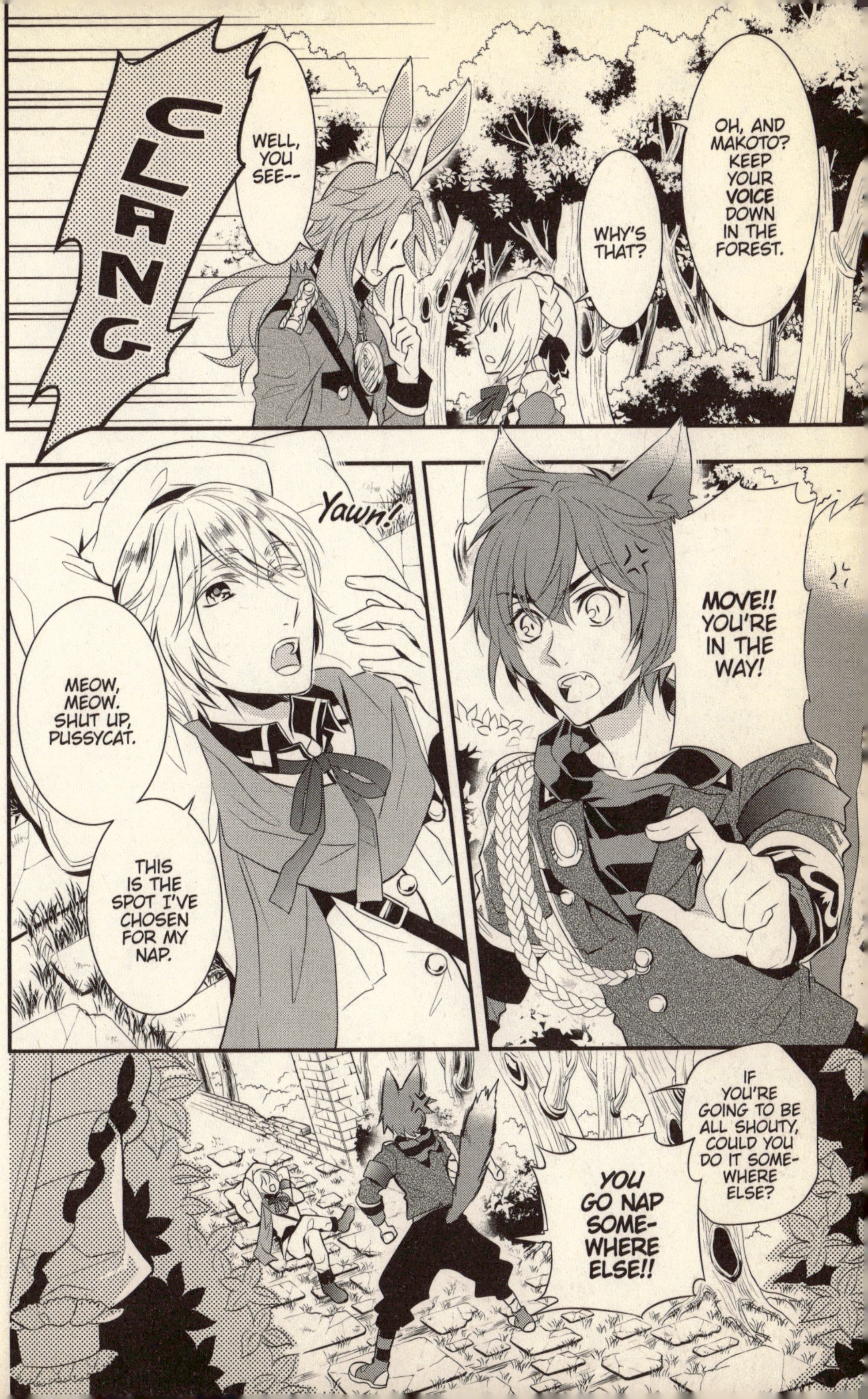
OH, AND MAKOTO? KEEP YOUR VOICE DOWN IN THE FOREST.
WHY'S THAT?
WELL, YOU SEE--
CLANG
MOVE!! YOU'RE IN THE WAY!
Yawn!
MEOW, MEOW. SHUT UP, PUSSYCAT.
THIS IS THE SPOT I'VE CHOSEN FOR MY NAP.
IF YOU'RE GOING TO BE ALL SHOUTY, COULD YOU DO IT SOME-WHERE ELSE?
YOU GO NAP SOME-WHERE ELSE!!

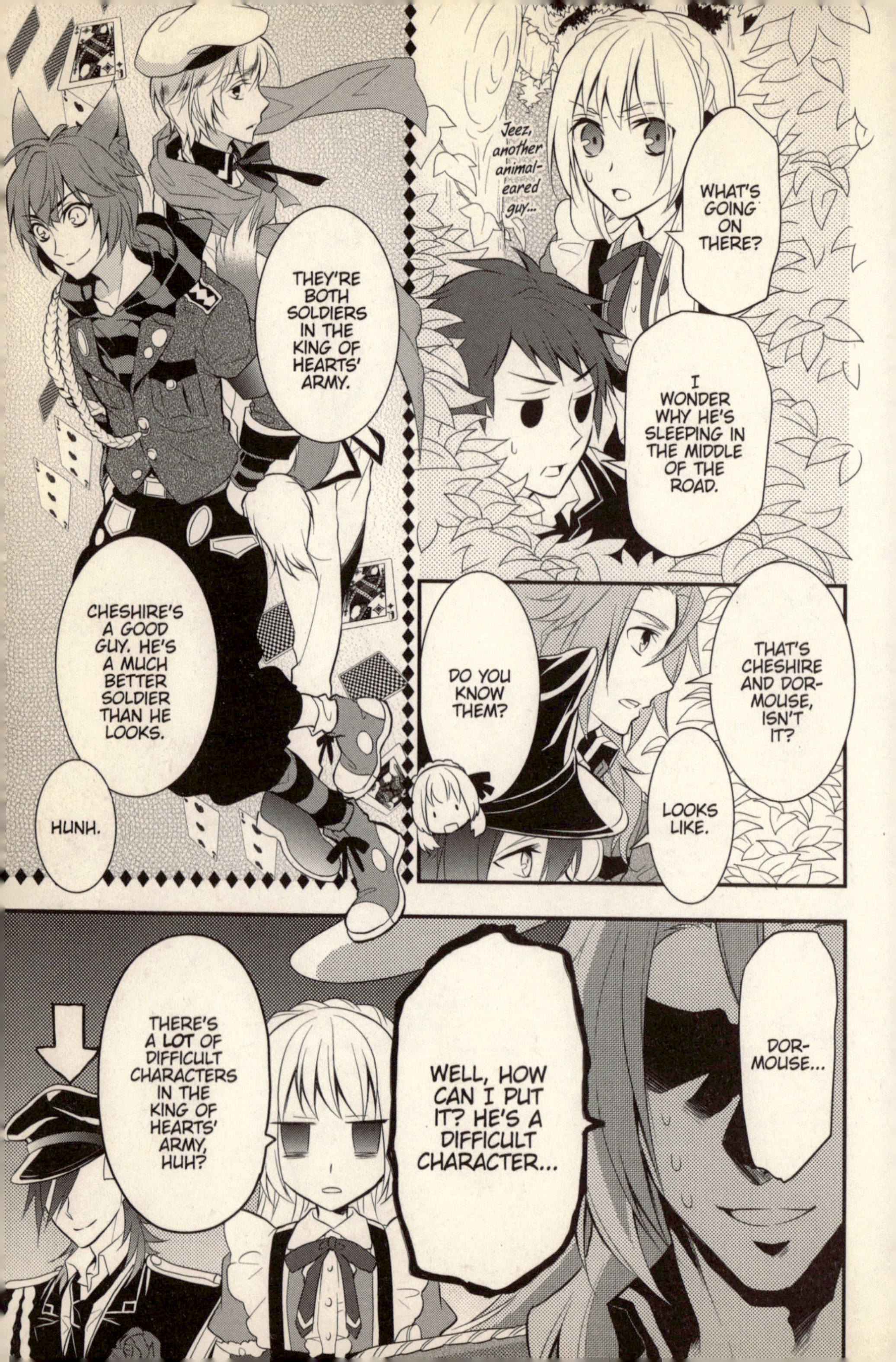
WHAT'S GOING ON THERE?
Jeez, another animal-eared guy...
I WONDER WHY HE'S SLEEPING IN THE MIDDLE OF THE ROAD.
THAT'S CHESHIRE AND DOR-MOUSE, ISN'T IT?
DO YOU KNOW THEM?
LOOKS LIKE.
THEY'RE BOTH SOLDIERS IN THE KING OF HEARTS' ARMY.
CHESHIRE'S A GOOD GUY. HE'S A MUCH BETTER SOLDIER THAN HE LOOKS.
HUNH.
DOR-MOUSE...
WELL, HOW CAN I PUT IT? HE'S A DIFFICULT CHARACTER...
THERE'S A **LOT** OF DIFFICULT CHARACTERS IN THE KING OF HEARTS' ARMY, HUH?

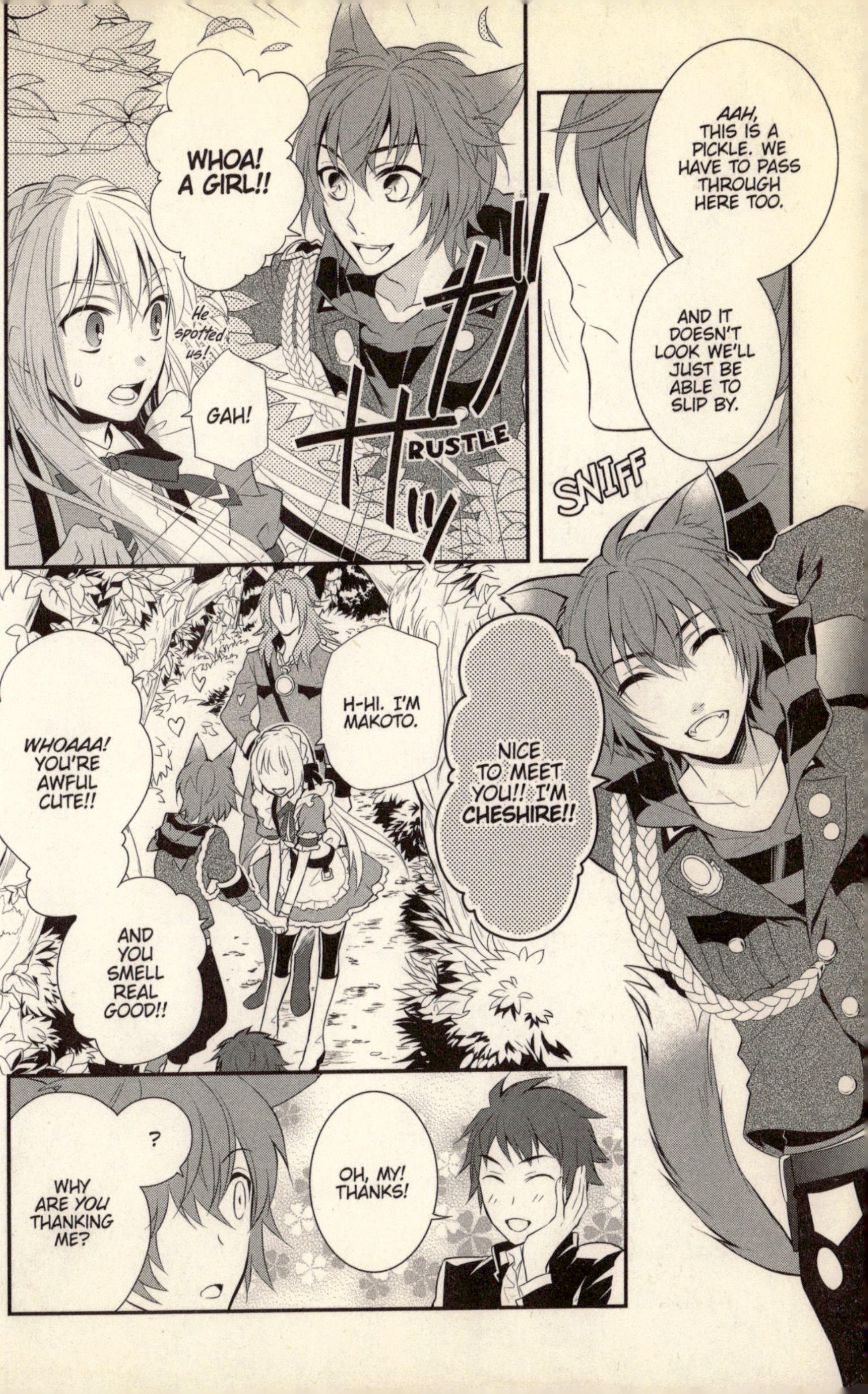
AAH, THIS IS A PICKLE. WE HAVE TO PASS THROUGH HERE TOO.
AND IT DOESN'T LOOK WE'LL JUST BE ABLE TO SLIP BY.
SNIFF
WHOA! A GIRL!!
He spotted us!
GAH!
RUSTLE
NICE TO MEET YOU!! I'M CHESHIRE!!
H-HI. I'M MAKOTO.
WHOAAA! YOU'RE AWFUL CUTE!!
AND YOU SMELL REAL GOOD!!
OH, MY! THANKS!
?
WHY ARE YOU THANKING ME?

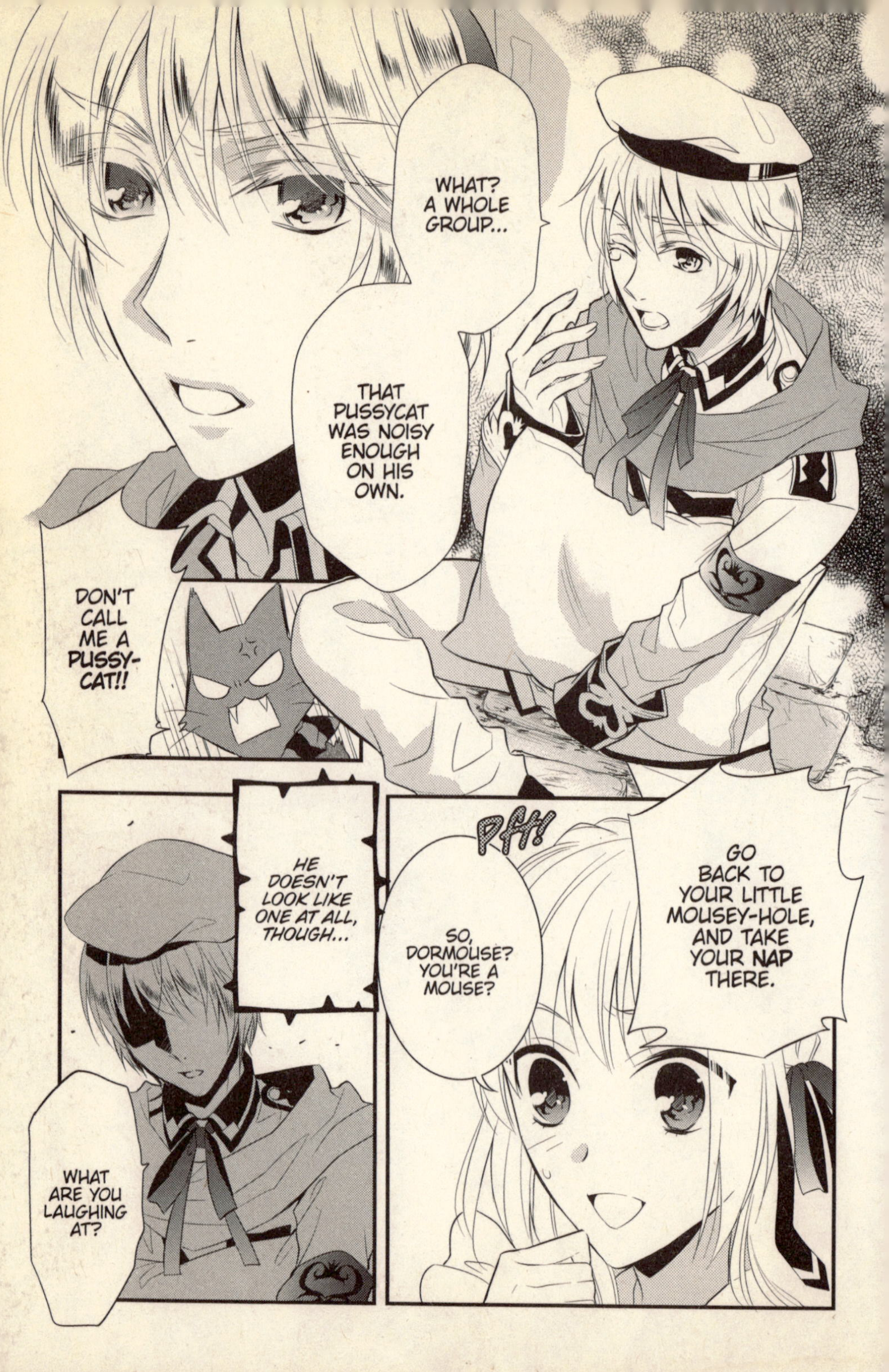
WHAT? A WHOLE GROUP...
THAT PUSSYCAT WAS NOISY ENOUGH ON HIS OWN.
DON'T CALL ME A PUSSY-CAT!!
GO BACK TO YOUR LITTLE MOUSEY-HOLE, AND TAKE YOUR NAP THERE.
PFFT!
SO, DORMOUSE? YOU'RE A MOUSE?
HE DOESN'T LOOK LIKE ONE AT ALL, THOUGH...
WHAT ARE YOU LAUGHING AT?

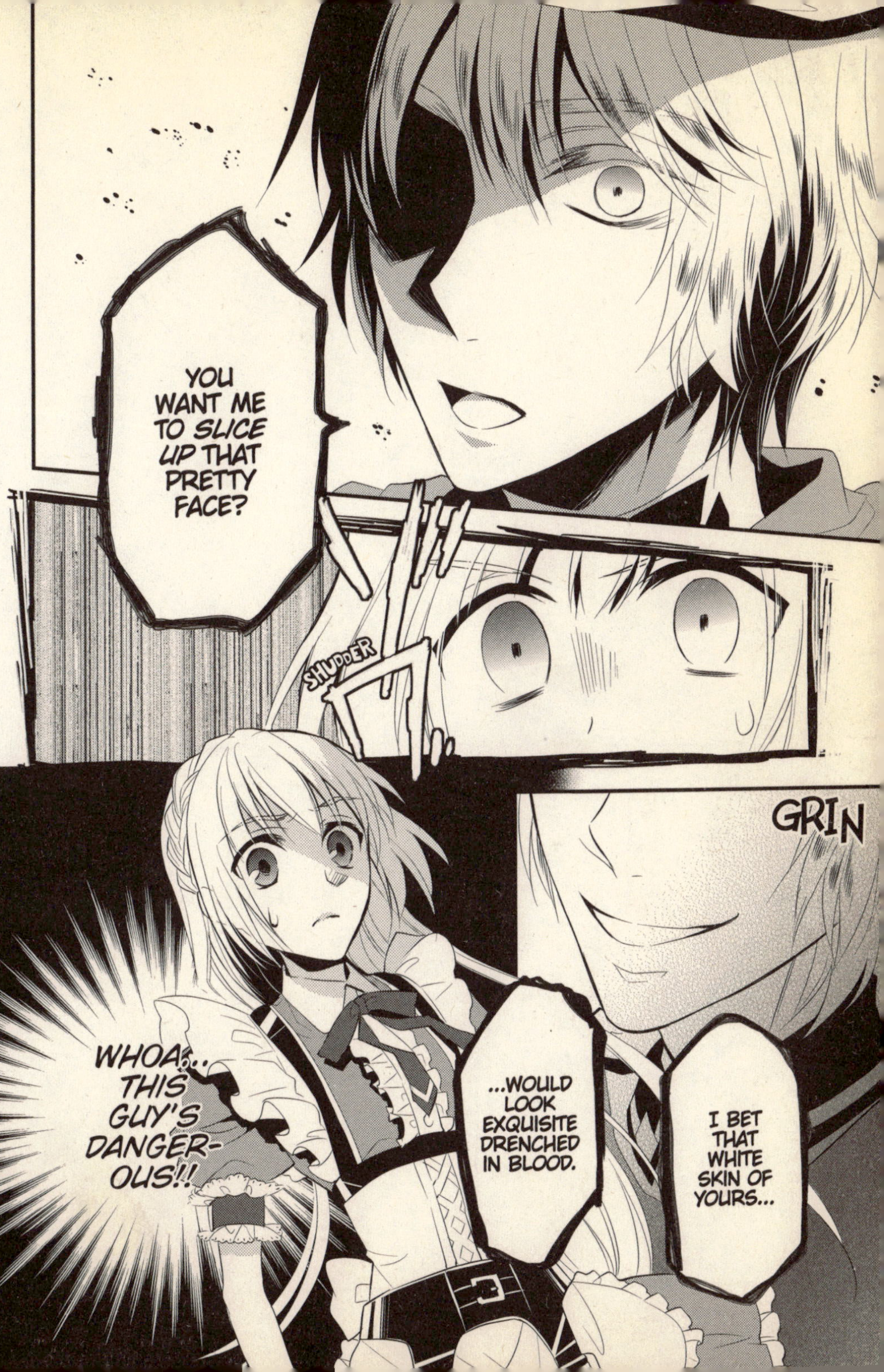
YOU WANT ME TO SLICE UP THAT PRETTY FACE?
SHUDDER
GRIN
I BET THAT WHITE SKIN OF YOURS...
...WOULD LOOK EXQUISITE DRENCHED IN BLOOD.
WHOA... THIS GUY'S DANGER-OUS!!

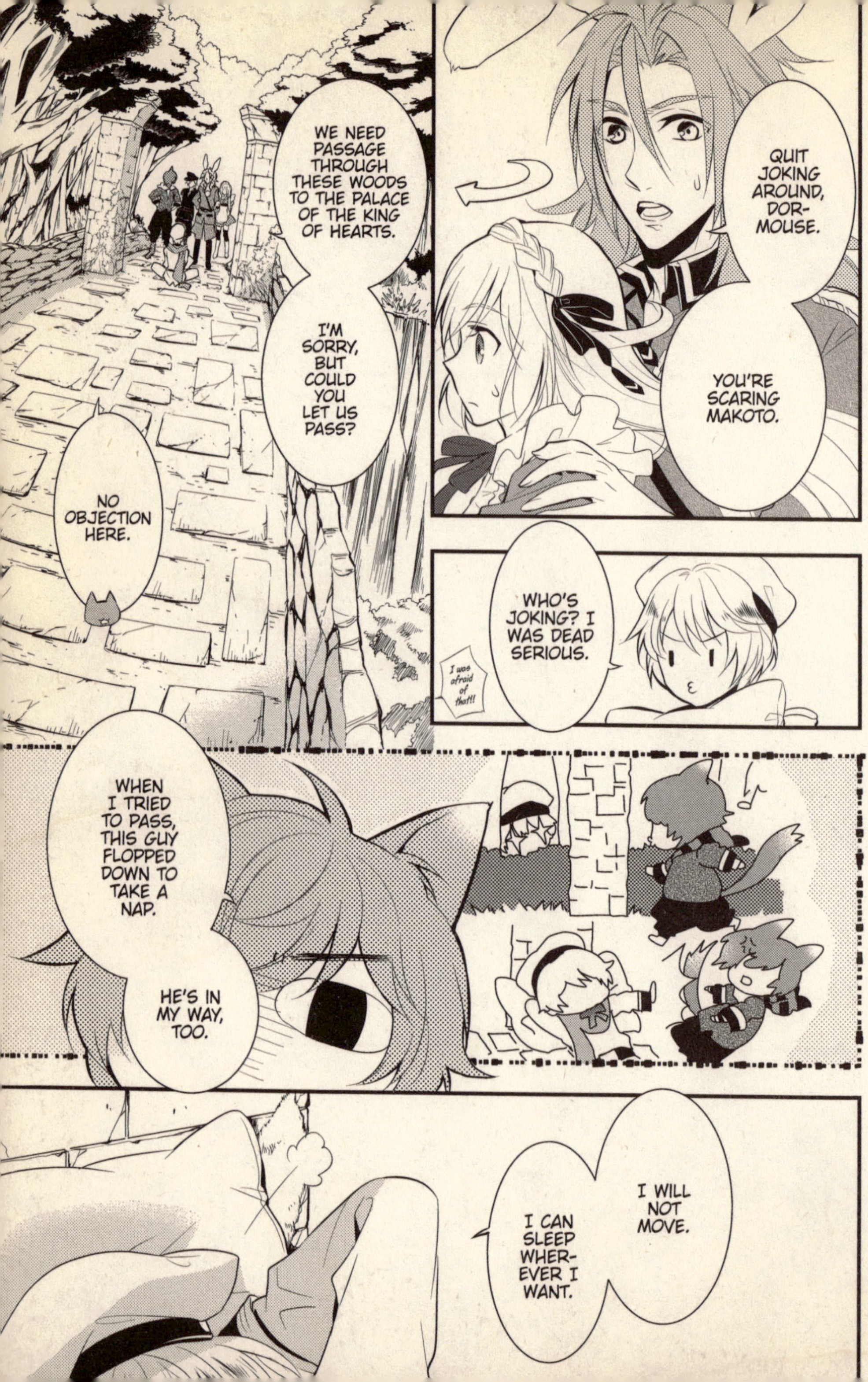
QUIT JOKING AROUND, DOR-MOUSE.
YOU'RE SCARING MAKOTO.
WHO'S JOKING? I WAS DEAD SERIOUS.
I was afraid of that!!
WE NEED PASSAGE THROUGH THESE WOODS TO THE PALACE OF THE KING OF HEARTS.
I'M SORRY, BUT COULD YOU LET US PASS?
NO OBJECTION HERE.
WHEN I TRIED TO PASS, THIS GUY FLOPPED DOWN TO TAKE A NAP.
HE'S IN MY WAY, TOO.
I WILL NOT MOVE.
I CAN SLEEP WHER-EVER I WANT.

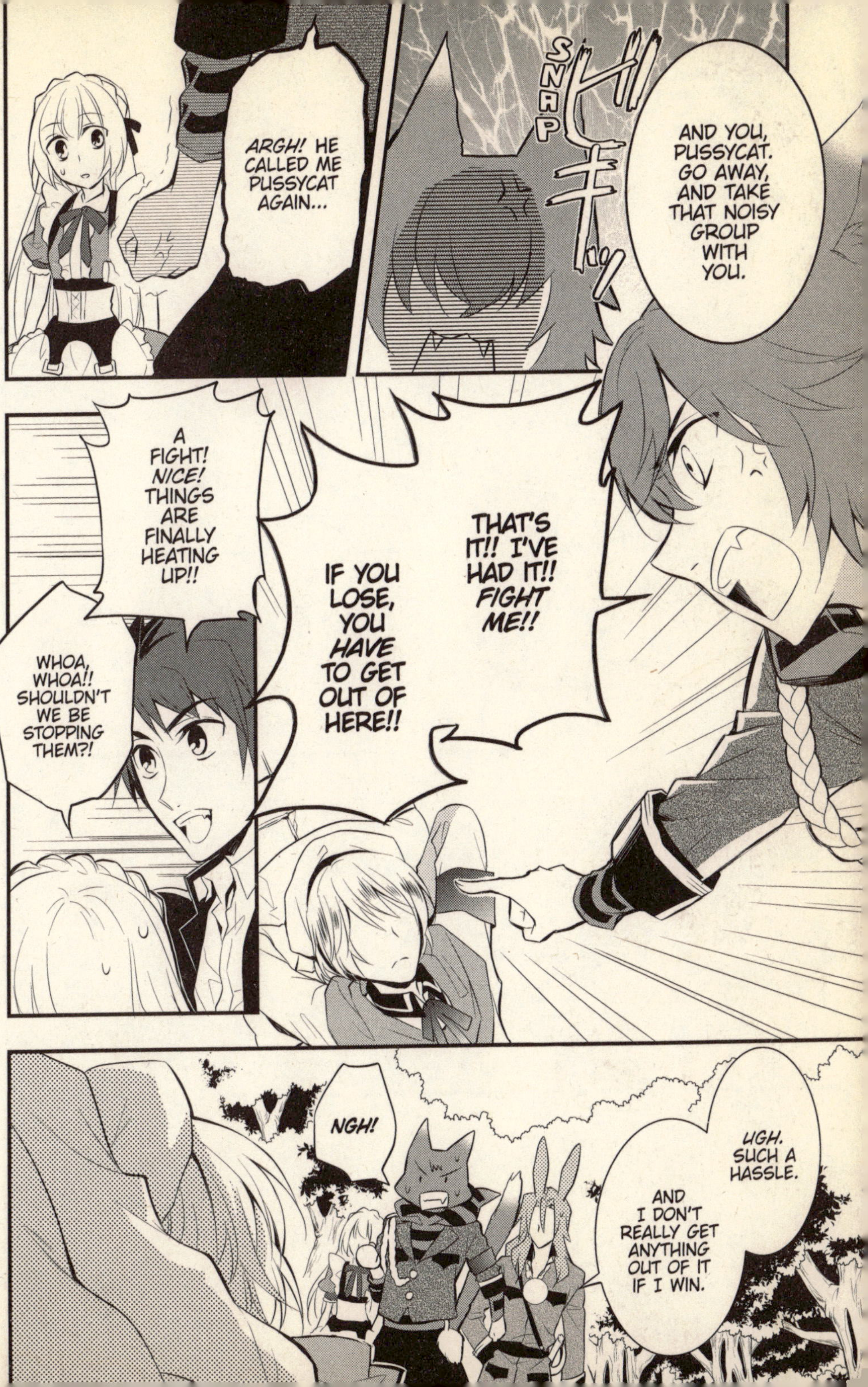
AND YOU, PUSSYCAT. GO AWAY, AND TAKE THAT NOISY GROUP WITH YOU.
SNAP
ARGH! HE CALLED ME PUSSYCAT AGAIN...
THAT'S IT!! I'VE HAD IT!! FIGHT ME!!
IF YOU LOSE, YOU HAVE TO GET OUT OF HERE!!
A FIGHT! NICE! THINGS ARE FINALLY HEATING UP!!
WHOA, WHOA!! SHOULDN'T WE BE STOPPING THEM?!
UGH. SUCH A HASSLE.
AND I DON'T REALLY GET ANYTHING OUT OF IT IF I WIN.
NGH!

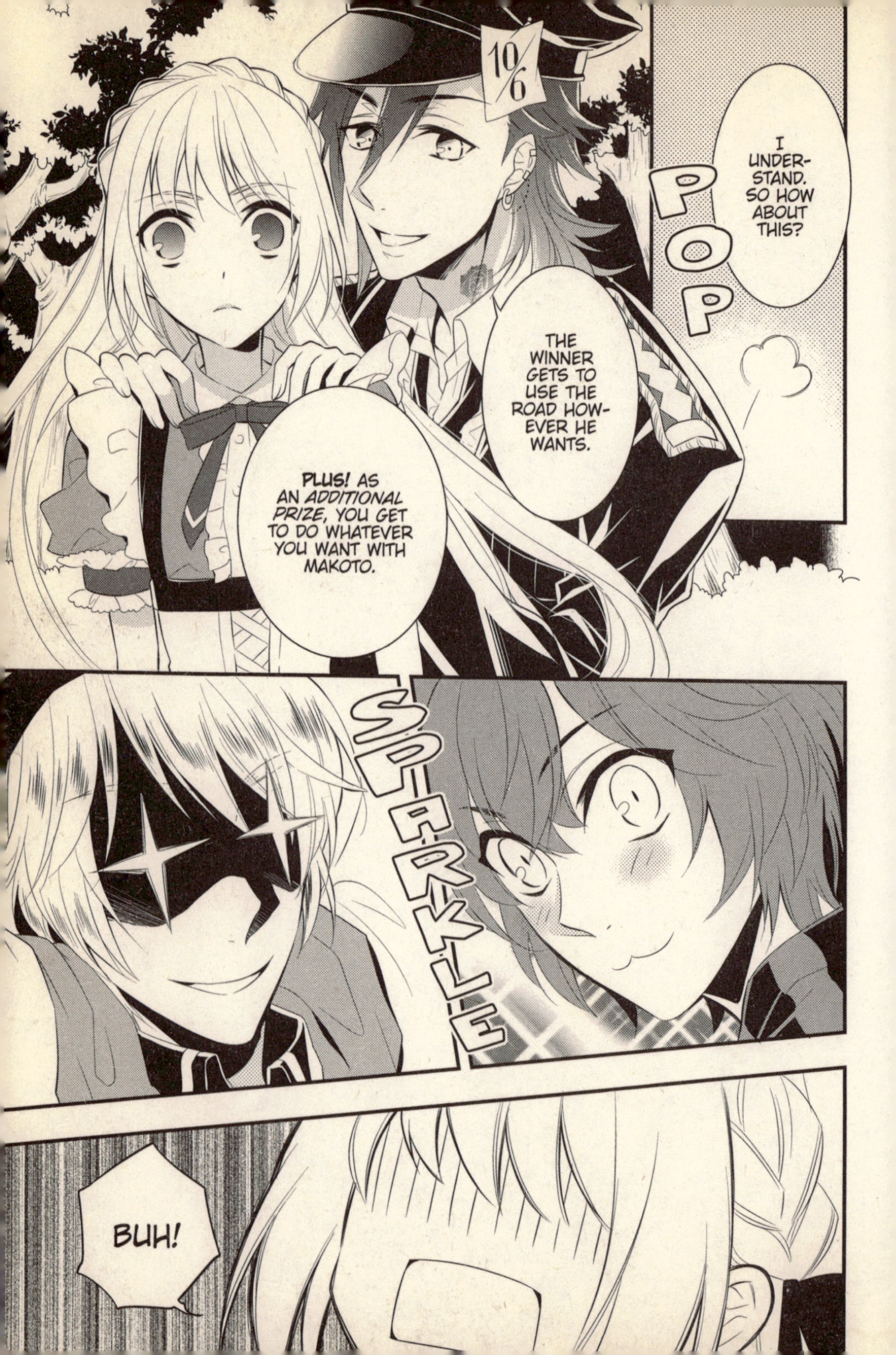
I UNDER-STAND. SO HOW ABOUT THIS?
POP
THE WINNER GETS TO USE THE ROAD HOW-EVER HE WANTS.
PLUS! AS AN ADDITIONAL PRIZE, YOU GET TO DO WHATEVER YOU WANT WITH MAKOTO.
SPARKLE
BUH!

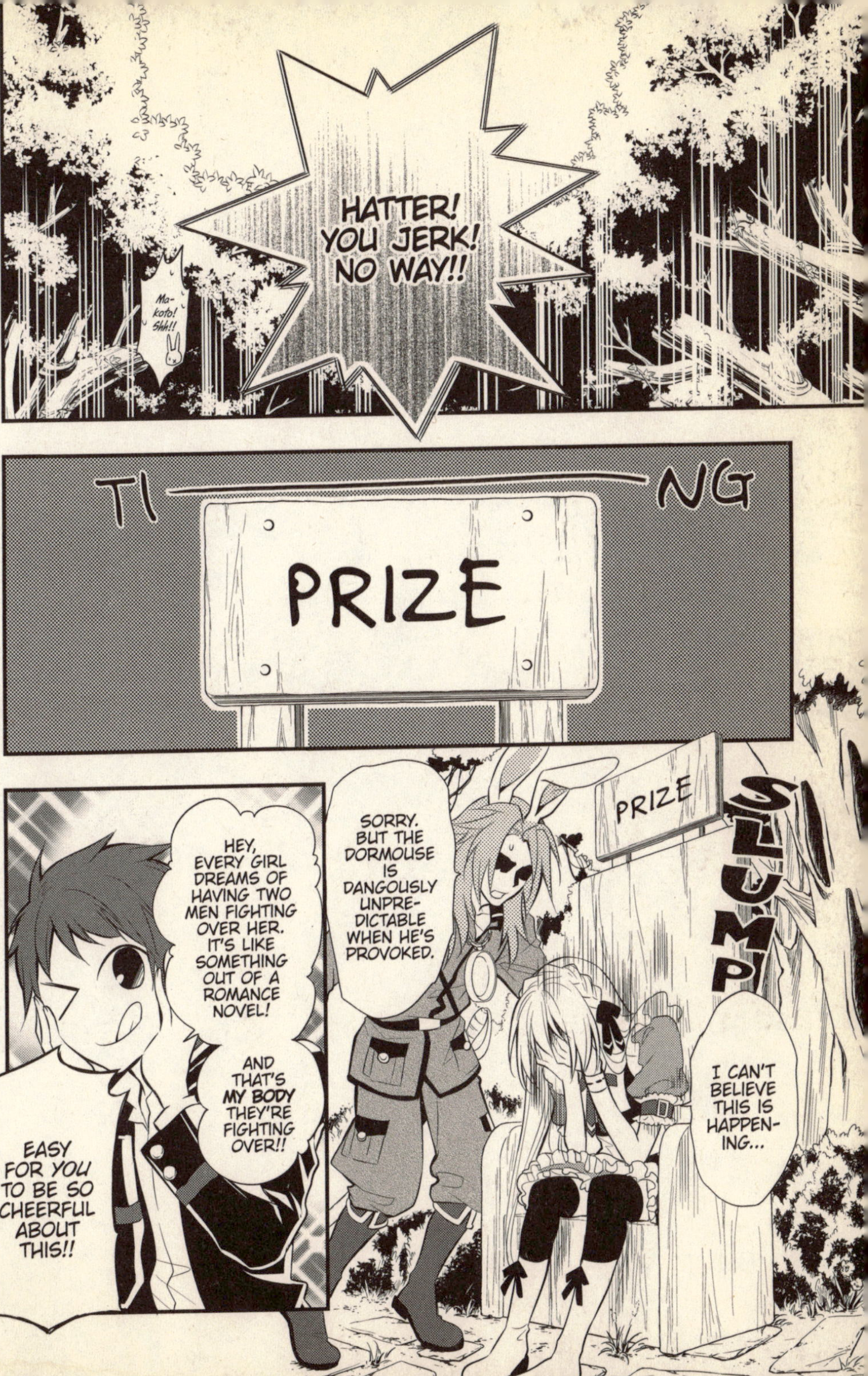
HATTER! YOU JERK! NO WAY!!
Ma-koto! Shhh!!
TI——NG
PRIZE
PRIZE
SLUMP
I CAN'T BELIEVE THIS IS HAPPEN-ING...
SORRY. BUT THE DORMOUSE IS DANGOUSLY UNPRE-DICTABLE WHEN HE'S PROVOKED.
HEY, EVERY GIRL DREAMS OF HAVING TWO MEN FIGHTING OVER HER. IT'S LIKE SOMETHING OUT OF A ROMANCE NOVEL!
AND THAT'S MY BODY THEY'RE FIGHTING OVER!!
EASY FOR YOU TO BE SO CHEERFUL ABOUT THIS!!

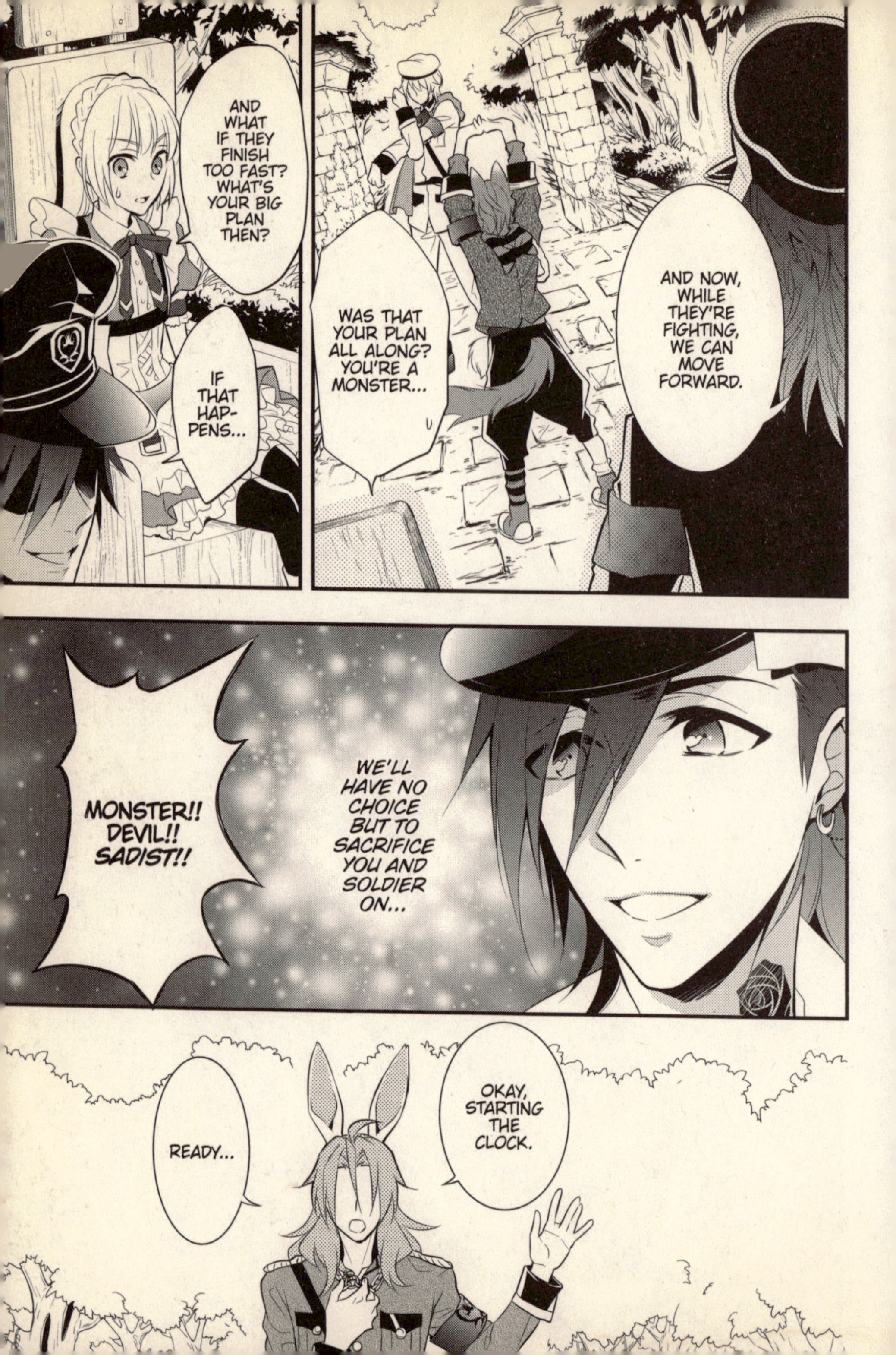
AND NOW, WHILE THEY'RE FIGHTING, WE CAN MOVE FORWARD.
WAS THAT YOUR PLAN ALL ALONG? YOU'RE A MONSTER...
AND WHAT IF THEY FINISH TOO FAST? WHAT'S YOUR BIG PLAN THEN?
IF THAT HAP-PENS...
WE'LL HAVE NO CHOICE BUT TO SACRIFICE YOU AND SOLDIER ON...
MONSTER!! DEVIL!! SADIST!!
OKAY, STARTING THE CLOCK.
READY...

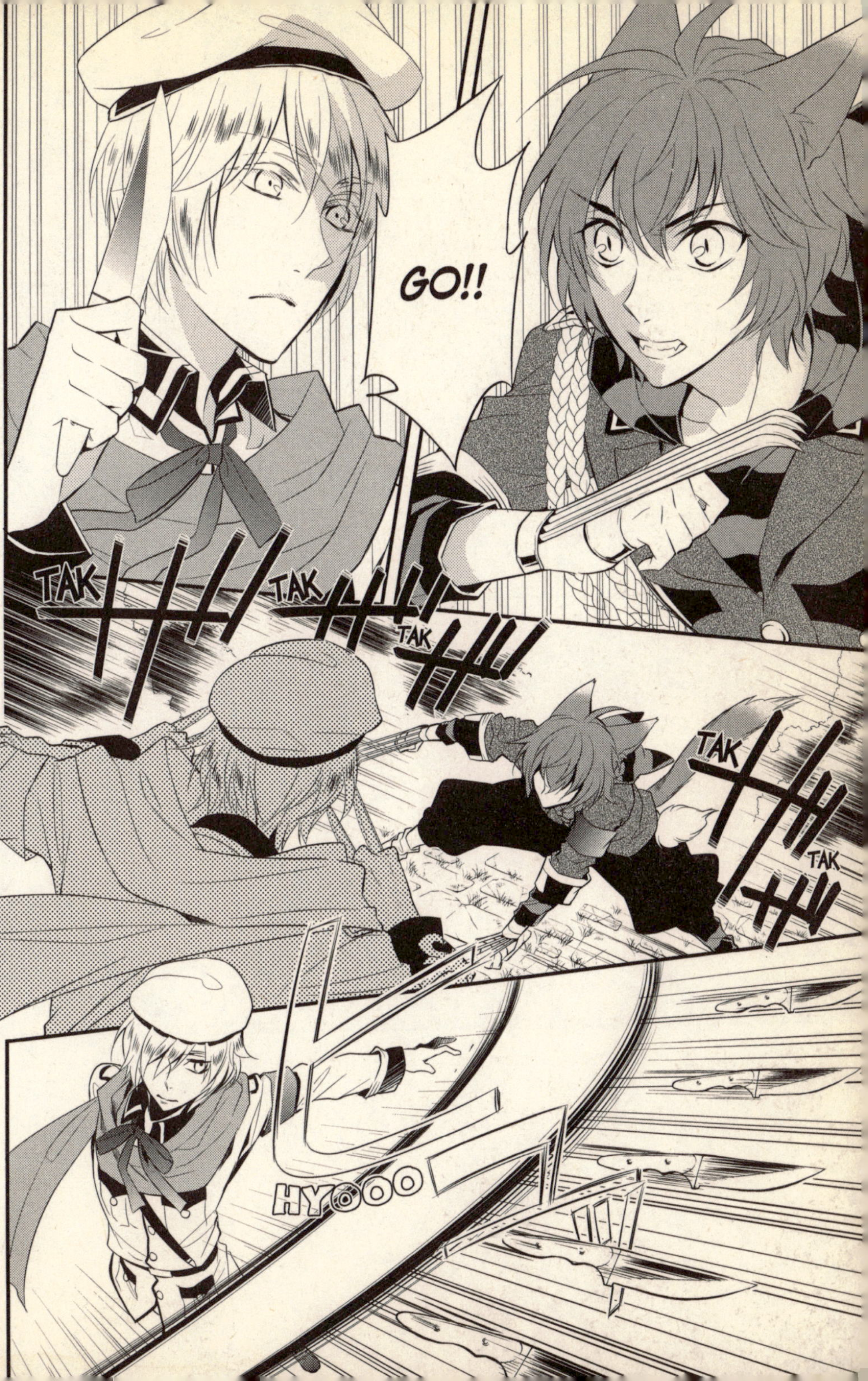
GO!!
TAK
TAK
TAK
TAK
TAK
HYOOO

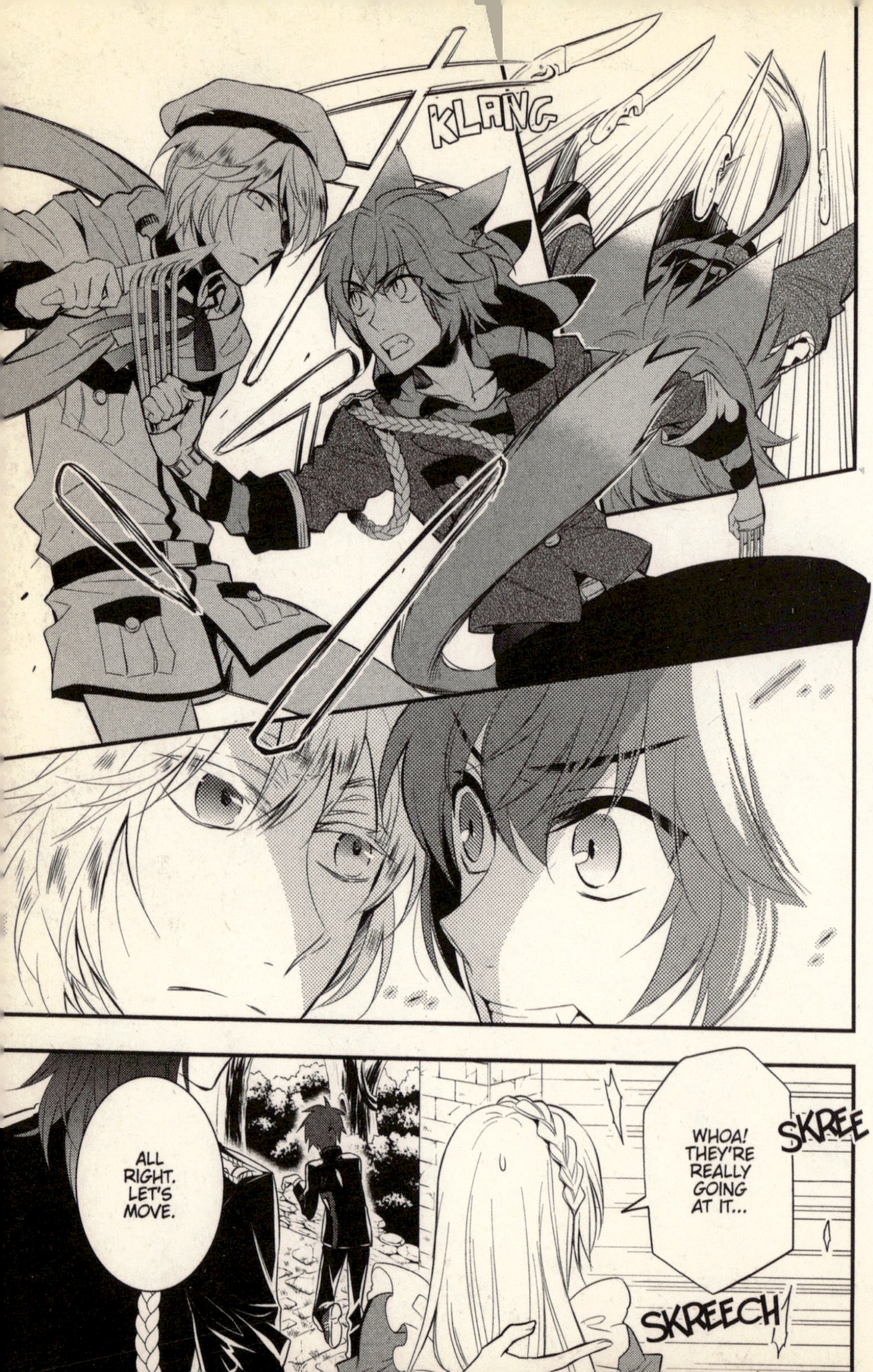
KLANG
WHOA! THEY'RE REALLY GOING AT IT...
SKREE
SKREECH
ALL RIGHT. LET'S MOVE.

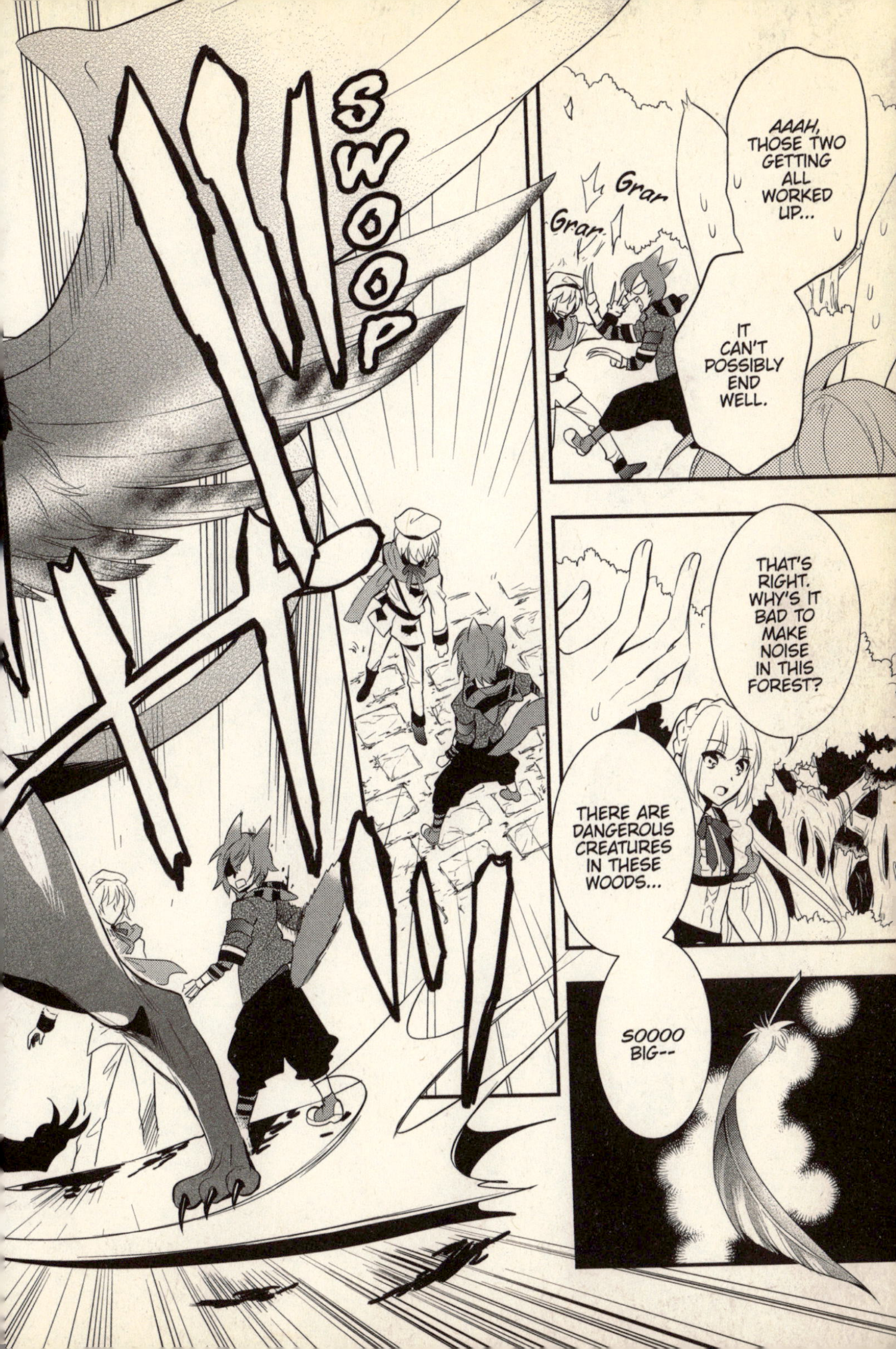
AAAH, THOSE TWO GETTING ALL WORKED UP...
Grar
Grar
IT CAN'T POSSIBLY END WELL.
THAT'S RIGHT. WHY'S IT BAD TO MAKE NOISE IN THIS FOREST?
THERE ARE DANGEROUS CREATURES IN THESE WOODS...
SOOOO BIG--
SWOOP

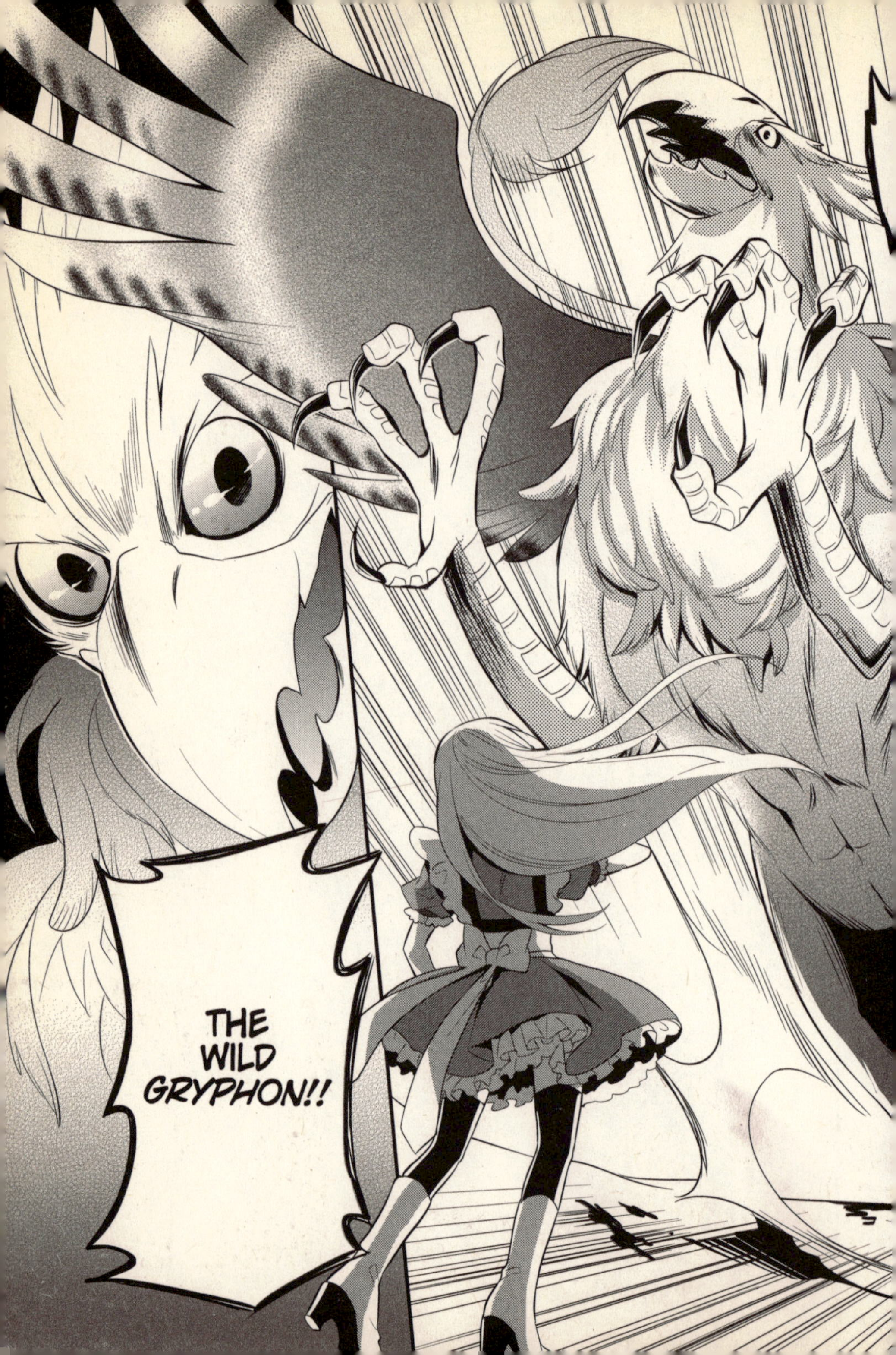
THE WILD GRYPHON!!

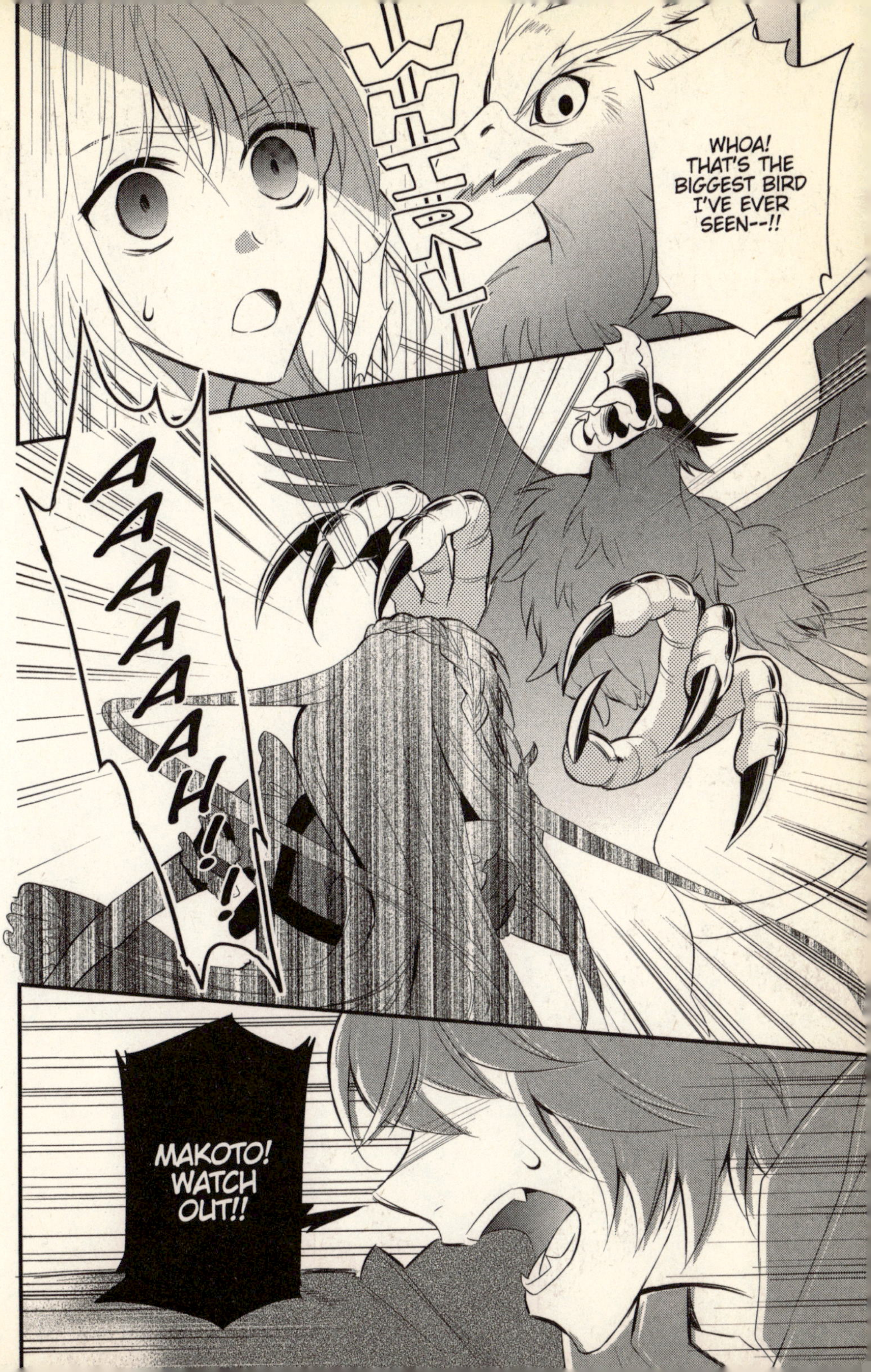
WHOA! THAT'S THE BIGGEST BIRD I'VE EVER SEEN--!!
WHIRL
AAAAAAH!!!
MAKOTO! WATCH OUT!!

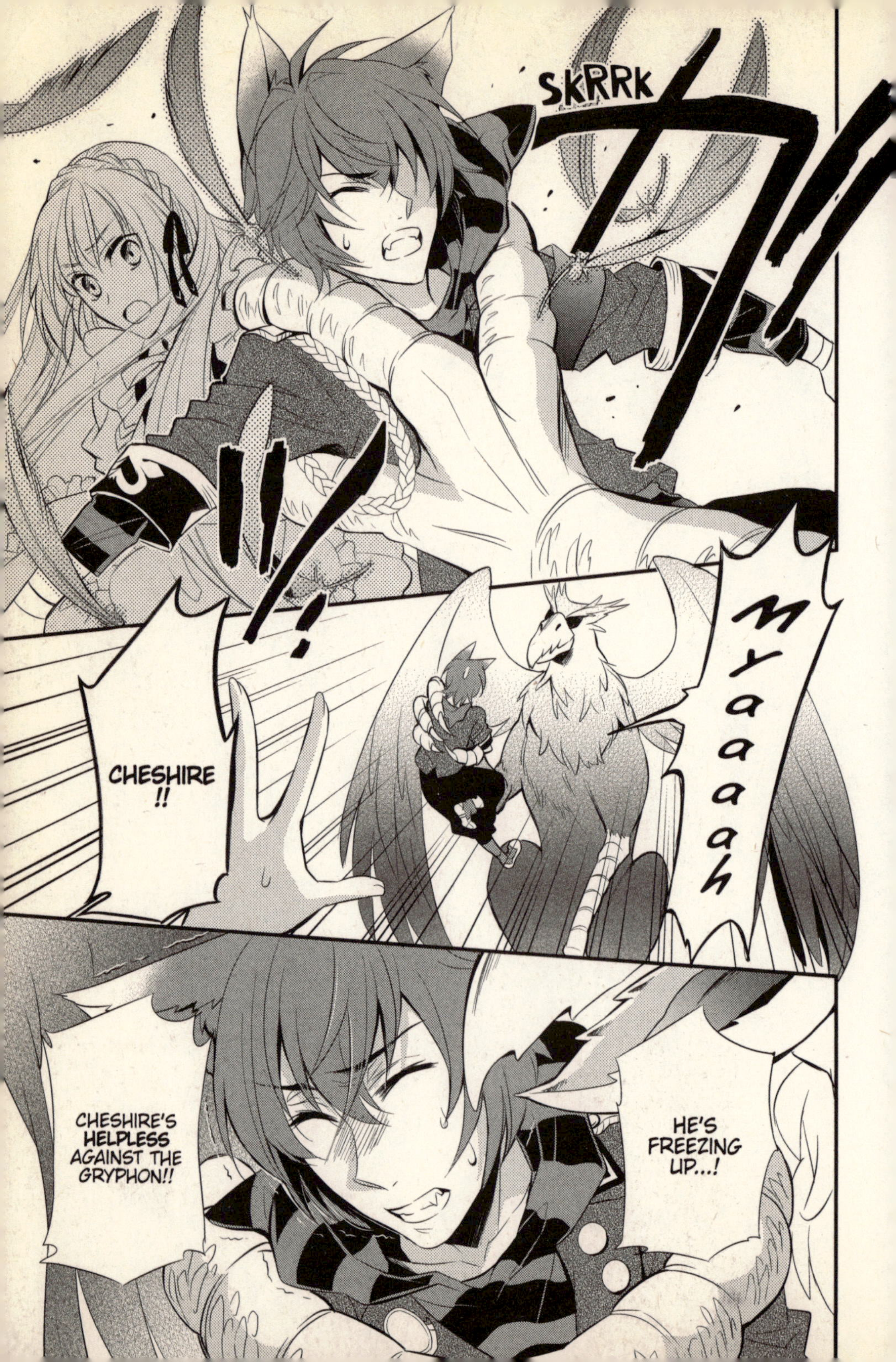
SKRRK
MYAAAAAH
CHESHIRE !!
HE'S FREEZING UP...!
CHESHIRE'S HELPLESS AGAINST THE GRYPHON!!

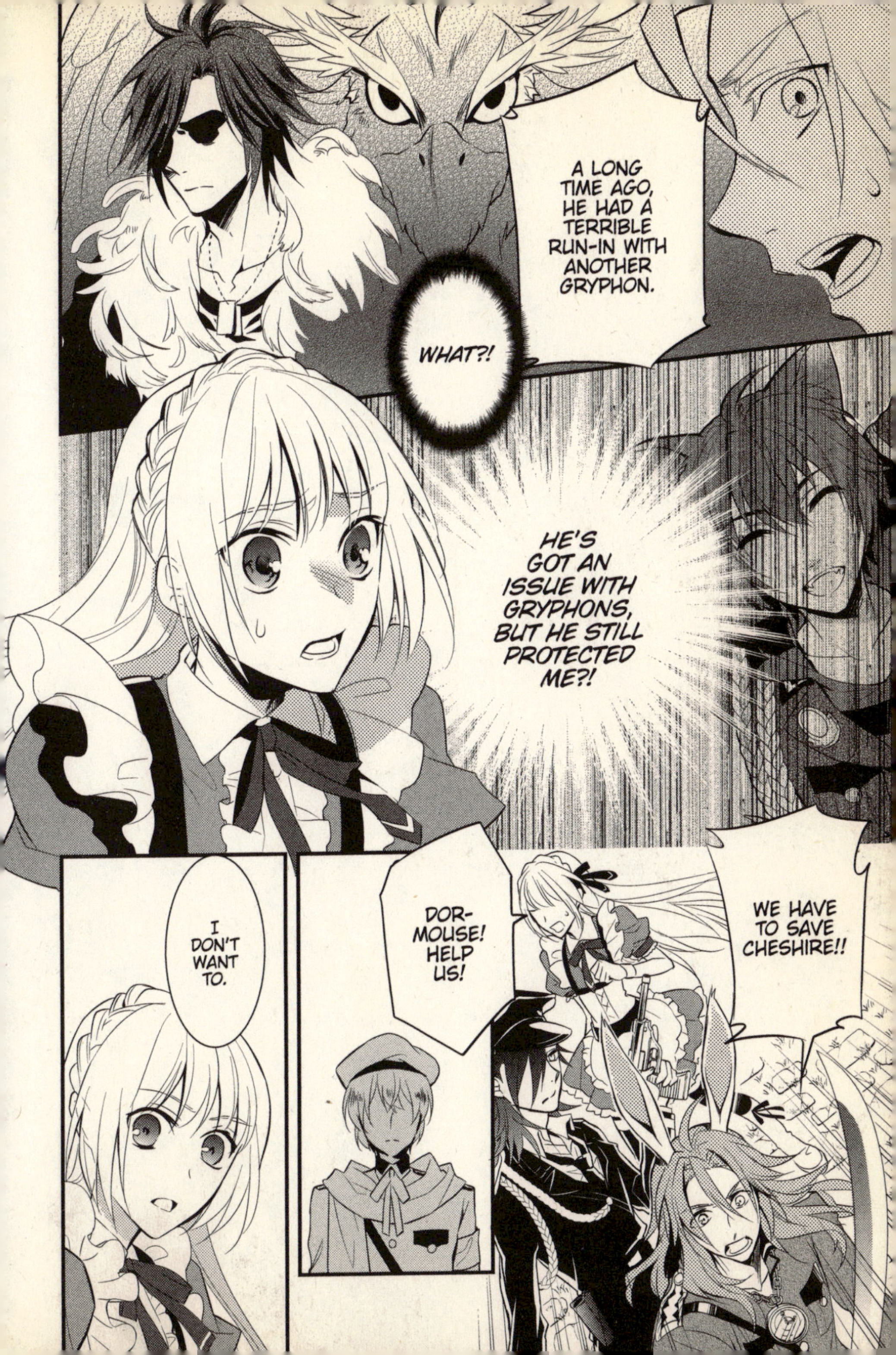
A LONG TIME AGO, HE HAD A TERRIBLE RUN-IN WITH ANOTHER GRYPHON.
WHAT?!
HE'S GOT AN ISSUE WITH GRYPHONS, BUT HE STILL PROTECTED ME?!
WE HAVE TO SAVE CHESHIRE!!
DOR-MOUSE! HELP US!
I DON'T WANT TO.

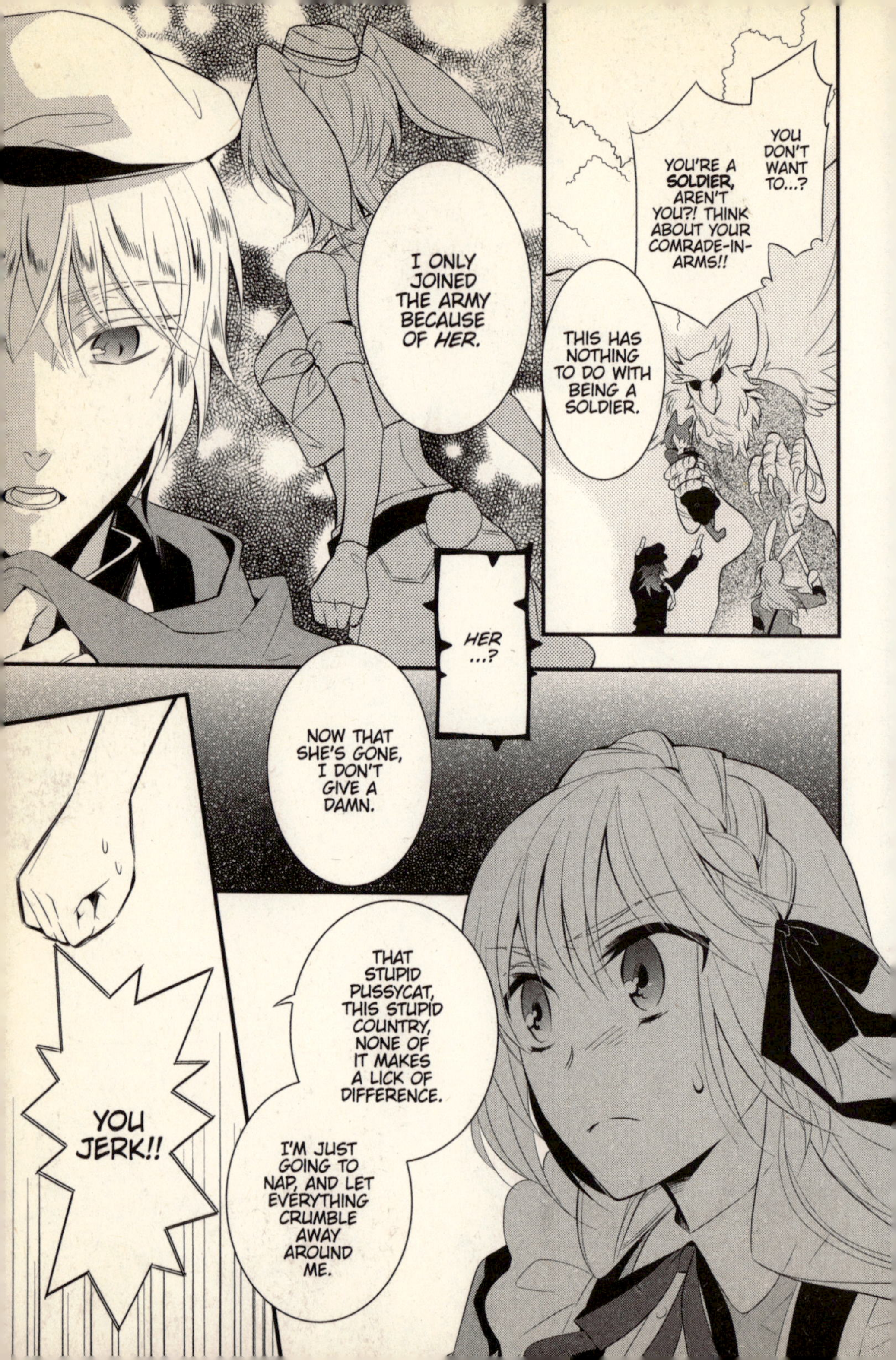
YOU DON'T WANT TO...?
YOU'RE A SOLDIER, AREN'T YOU?! THINK ABOUT YOUR COMRADE-IN-ARMS!!
THIS HAS NOTHING TO DO WITH BEING A SOLDIER.
I ONLY JOINED THE ARMY BECAUSE OF HER.
HER ...?
NOW THAT SHE'S GONE, I DON'T GIVE A DAMN.
THAT STUPID PUSSYCAT, THIS STUPID COUNTRY, NONE OF IT MAKES A LICK OF DIFFERENCE.
I'M JUST GOING TO NAP, AND LET EVERYTHING CRUMBLE AWAY AROUND ME.
YOU JERK!!

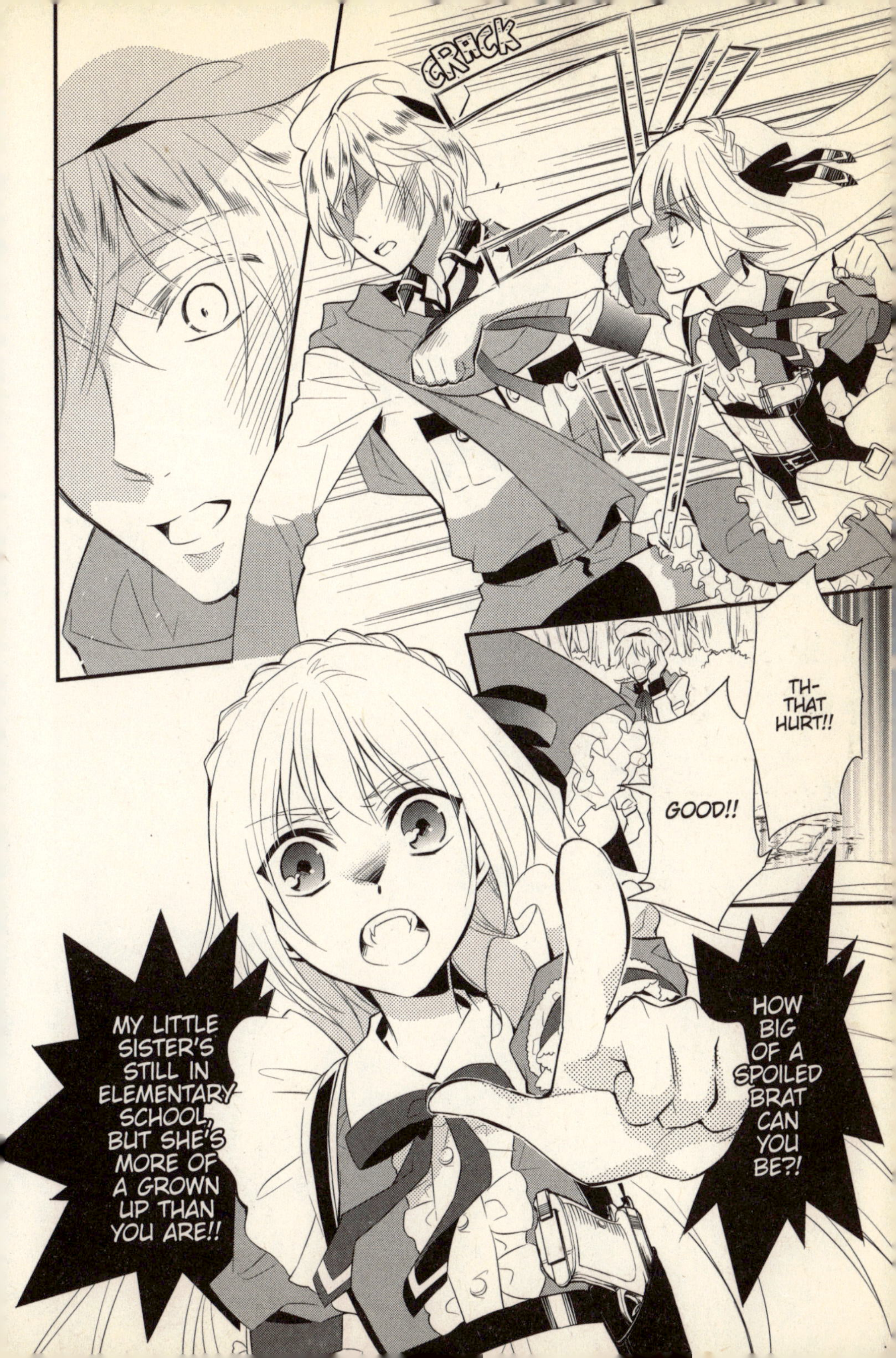
CRACK
TH-THAT HURT!!
GOOD!!
HOW BIG OF A SPOILED BRAT CAN YOU BE?!
MY LITTLE SISTER'S STILL IN ELEMENTARY SCHOOL, BUT SHE'S MORE OF A GROWN UP THAN YOU ARE!!

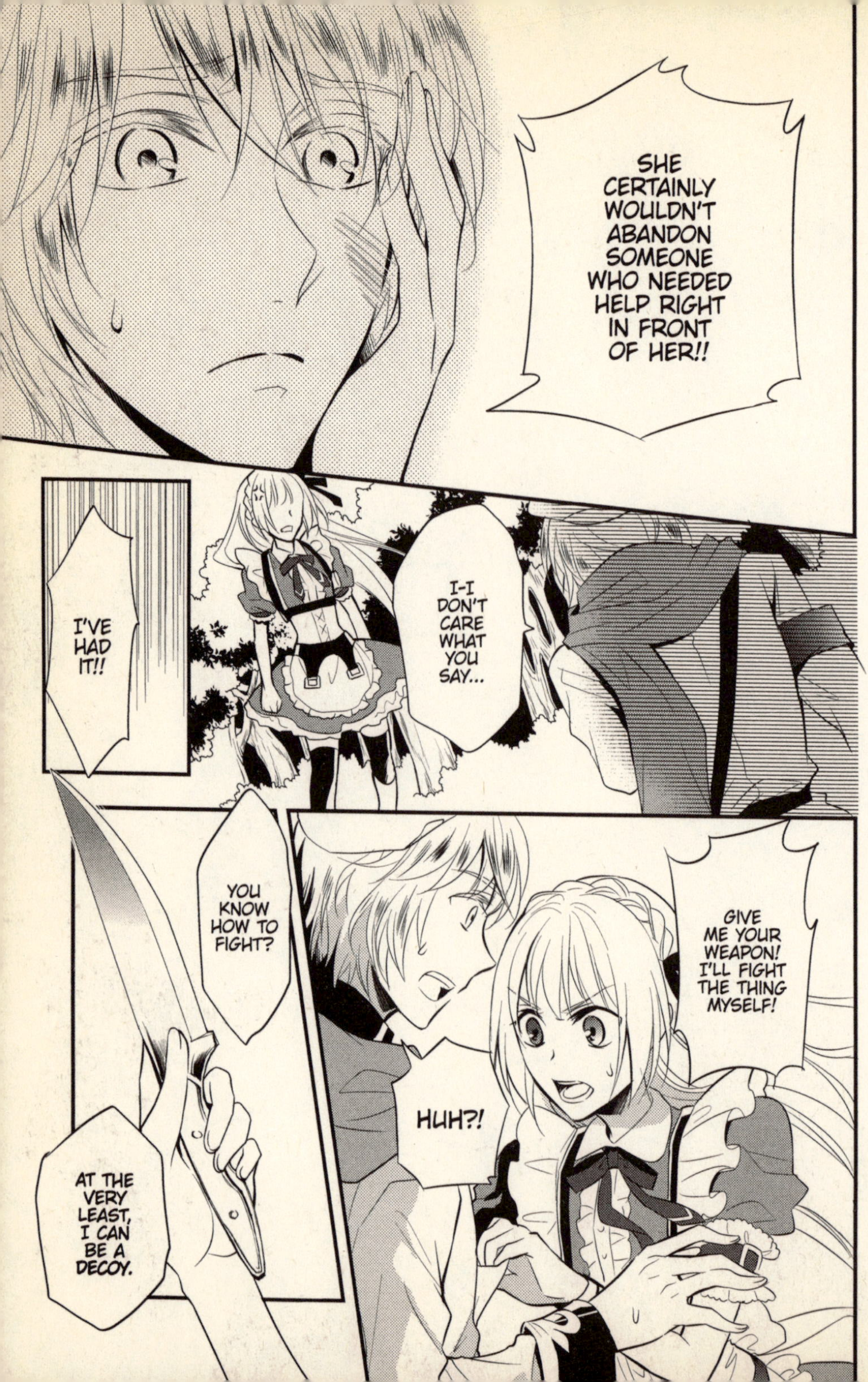
SHE CERTAINLY WOULDN'T ABANDON SOMEONE WHO NEEDED HELP RIGHT IN FRONT OF HER!!
I-I DON'T CARE WHAT YOU SAY...
I'VE HAD IT!!
GIVE ME YOUR WEAPON! I'LL FIGHT THE THING MYSELF!
HUH?!
YOU KNOW HOW TO FIGHT?
AT THE VERY LEAST, I CAN BE A DECOY.

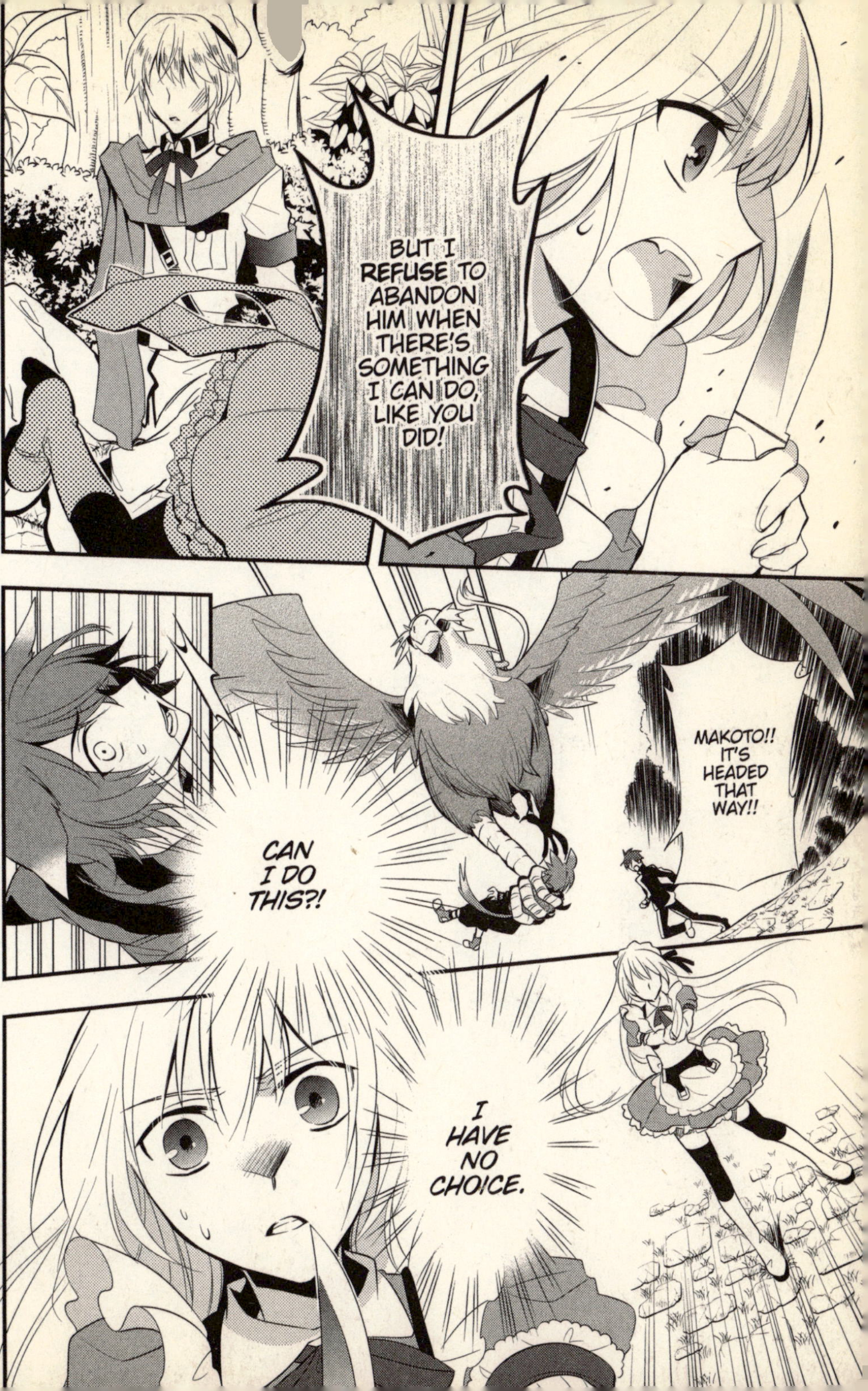
BUT I REFUSE TO ABANDON HIM WHEN THERE'S SOMETHING I CAN DO, LIKE YOU DID!
MAKOTO!! IT'S HEADED THAT WAY!!
CAN I DO THIS?!
I HAVE NO CHOICE.

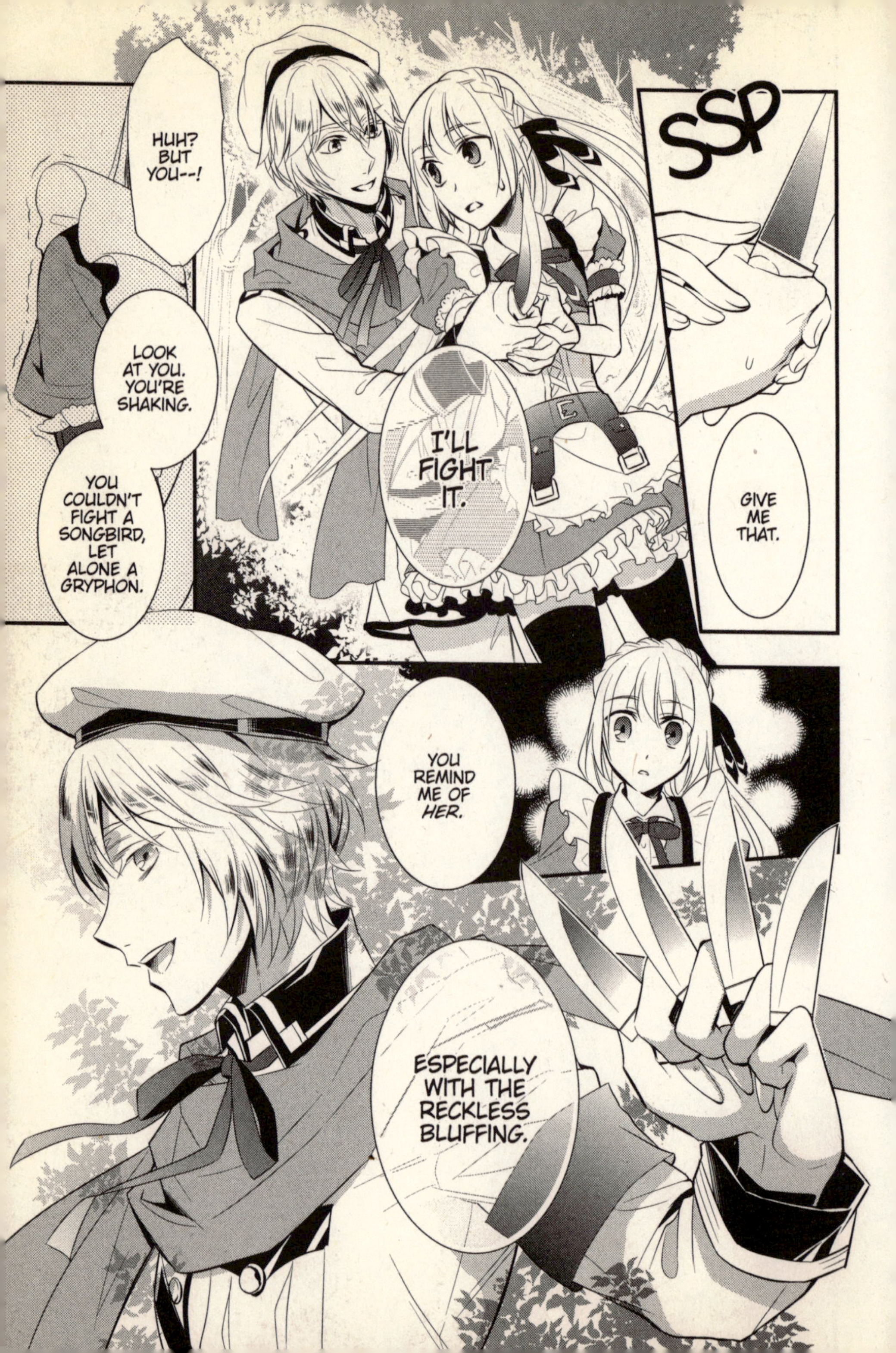
SSP
GIVE ME THAT.
I'LL FIGHT IT.
HUH? BUT YOU--!
LOOK AT YOU. YOU'RE SHAKING.
YOU COULDN'T FIGHT A SONGBIRD, LET ALONE A GRYPHON.
YOU REMIND ME OF *HER*.
ESPECIALLY WITH THE RECKLESS BLUFFING.

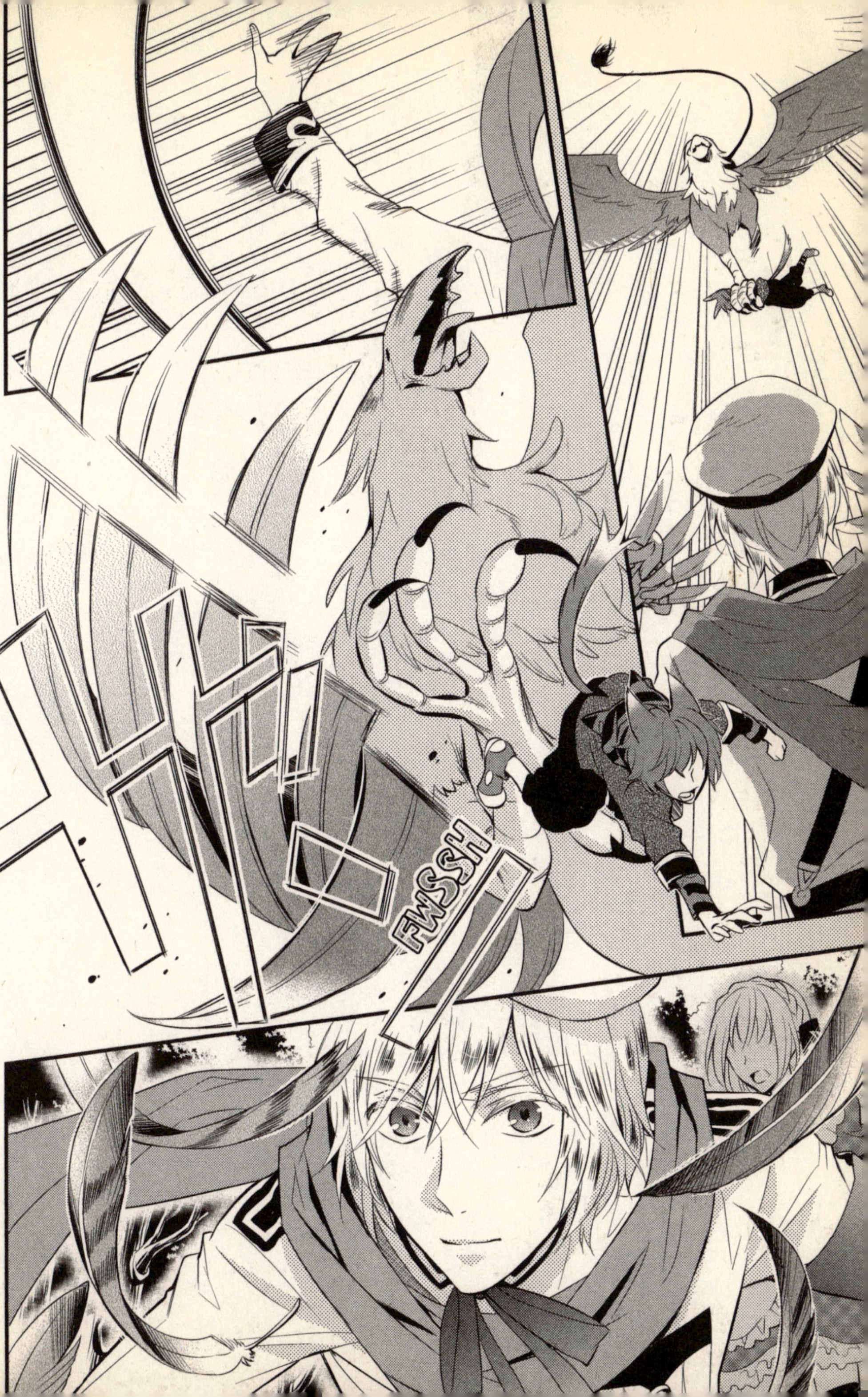
FWSSH

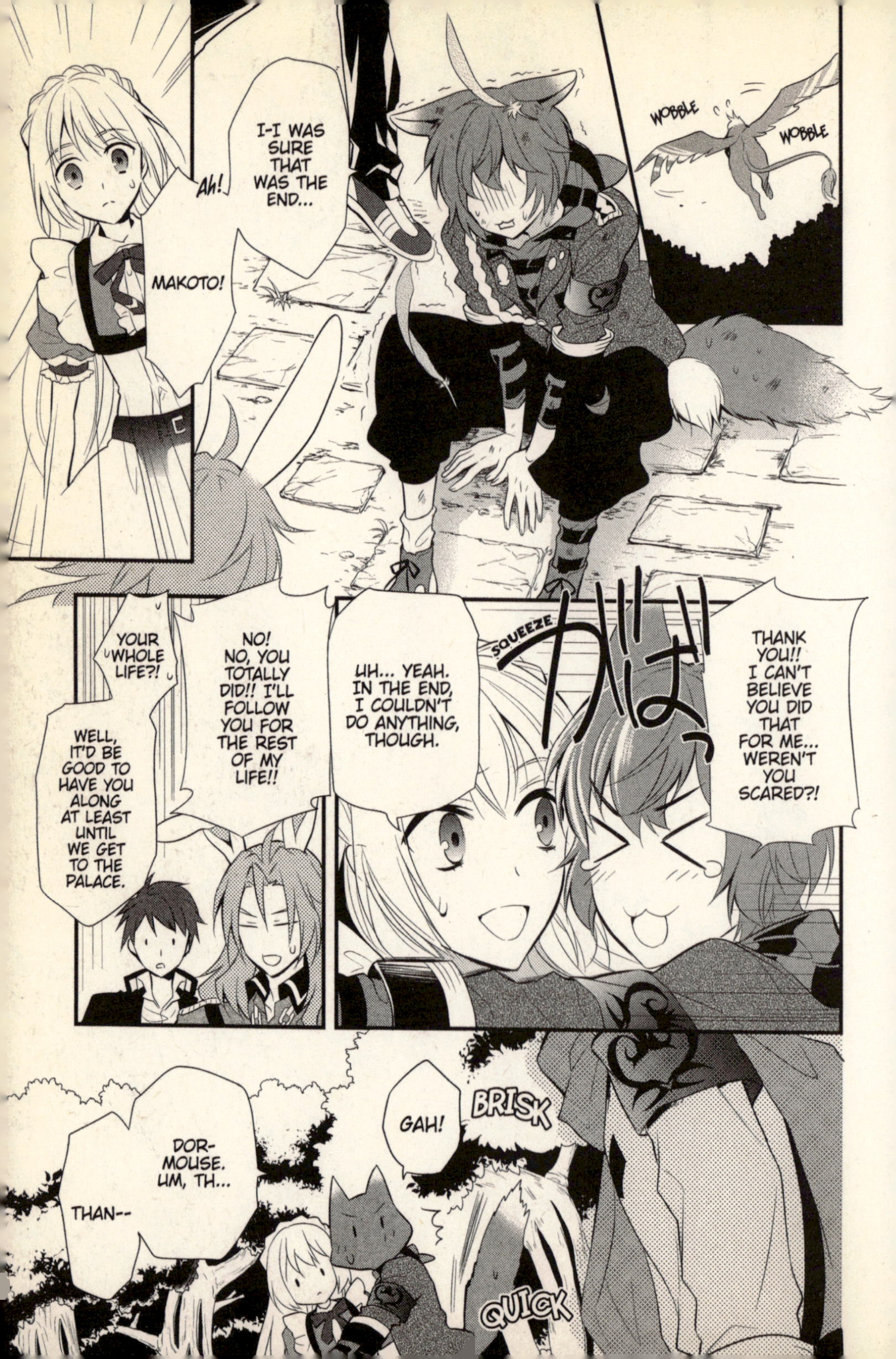
WOBBLE
WOBBLE
I-I WAS SURE THAT WAS THE END...
Ah!
MAKOTO!
THANK YOU!! I CAN'T BELIEVE YOU DID THAT FOR ME... WEREN'T YOU SCARED?!
SQUEEZE
かばっ
UH... YEAH. IN THE END, I COULDN'T DO ANYTHING, THOUGH.
NO! NO, YOU TOTALLY DID!! I'LL FOLLOW YOU FOR THE REST OF MY LIFE!!
YOUR WHOLE LIFE?!
WELL, IT'D BE GOOD TO HAVE YOU ALONG AT LEAST UNTIL WE GET TO THE PALACE.
GAH!
BRISK
DOR-MOUSE. UM, TH...
THAN--
QUICK

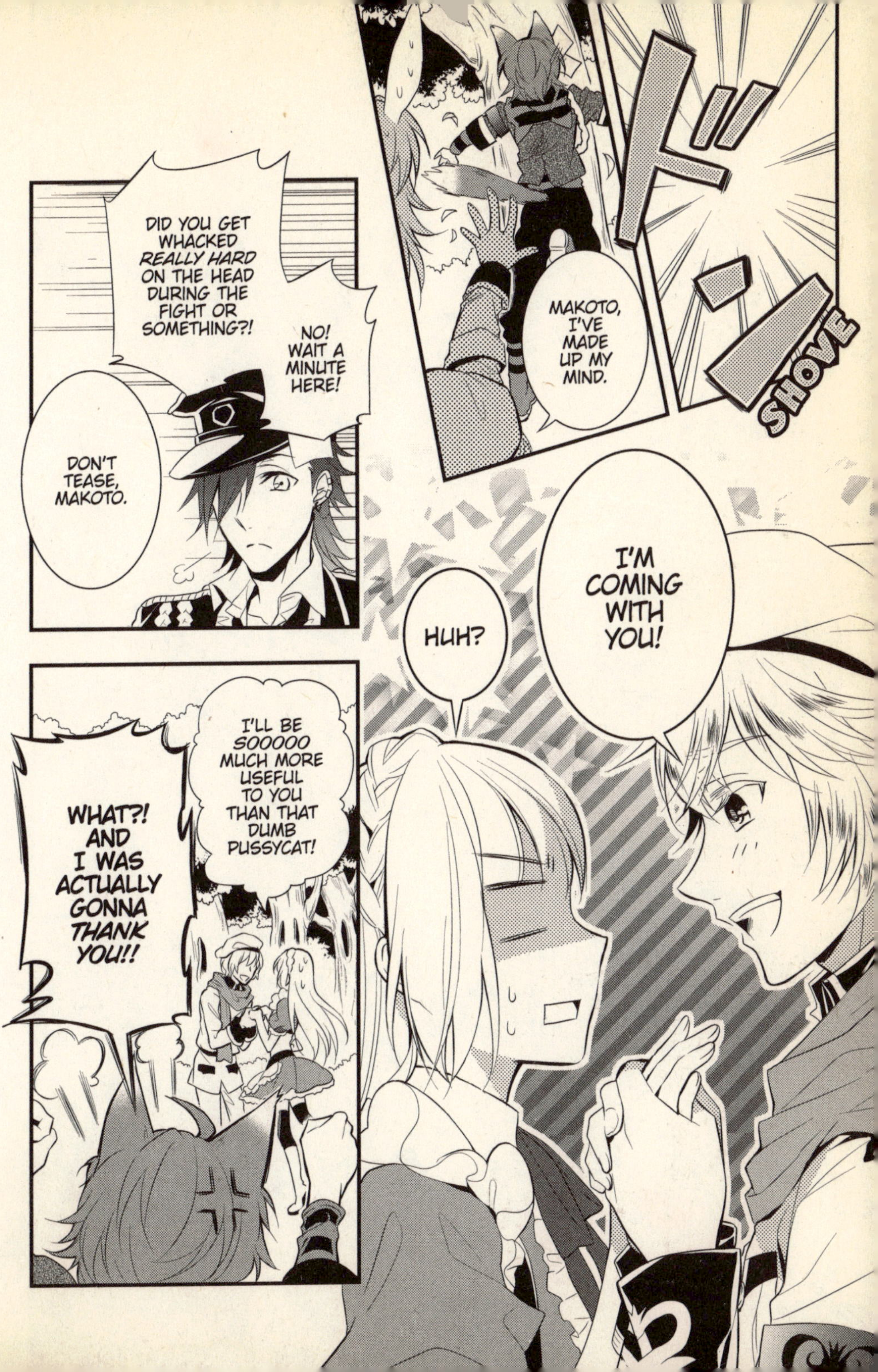
SHOVE
MAKOTO, I'VE MADE UP MY MIND.
DID YOU GET WHACKED *REALLY HARD* ON THE HEAD DURING THE FIGHT OR SOMETHING?!
NO! WAIT A MINUTE HERE!
DON'T TEASE, MAKOTO.
I'M COMING WITH YOU!
HUH?
I'LL BE SOOOOO MUCH MORE USEFUL TO YOU THAN THAT DUMB PUSSYCAT!
WHAT?! AND I WAS ACTUALLY GONNA *THANK YOU!!*

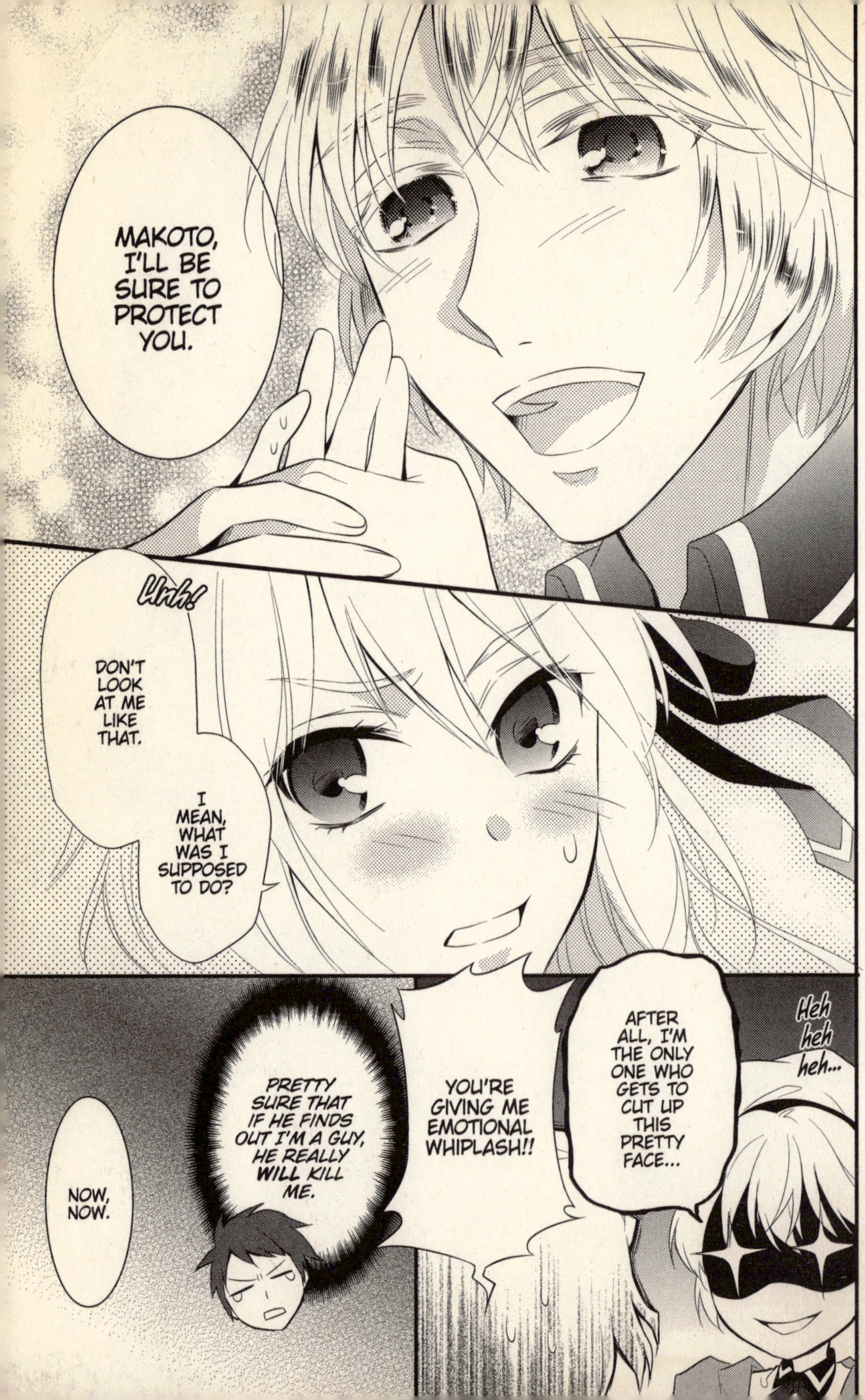
MAKOTO, I'LL BE SURE TO PROTECT YOU.
Unh!
DON'T LOOK AT ME LIKE THAT.
I MEAN, WHAT WAS I SUPPOSED TO DO?
Heh heh heh...
AFTER ALL, I'M THE ONLY ONE WHO GETS TO CUT UP THIS PRETTY FACE...
YOU'RE GIVING ME EMOTIONAL WHIPLASH!!
PRETTY SURE THAT IF HE FINDS OUT I'M A GUY, HE REALLY WILL KILL ME.
NOW, NOW.

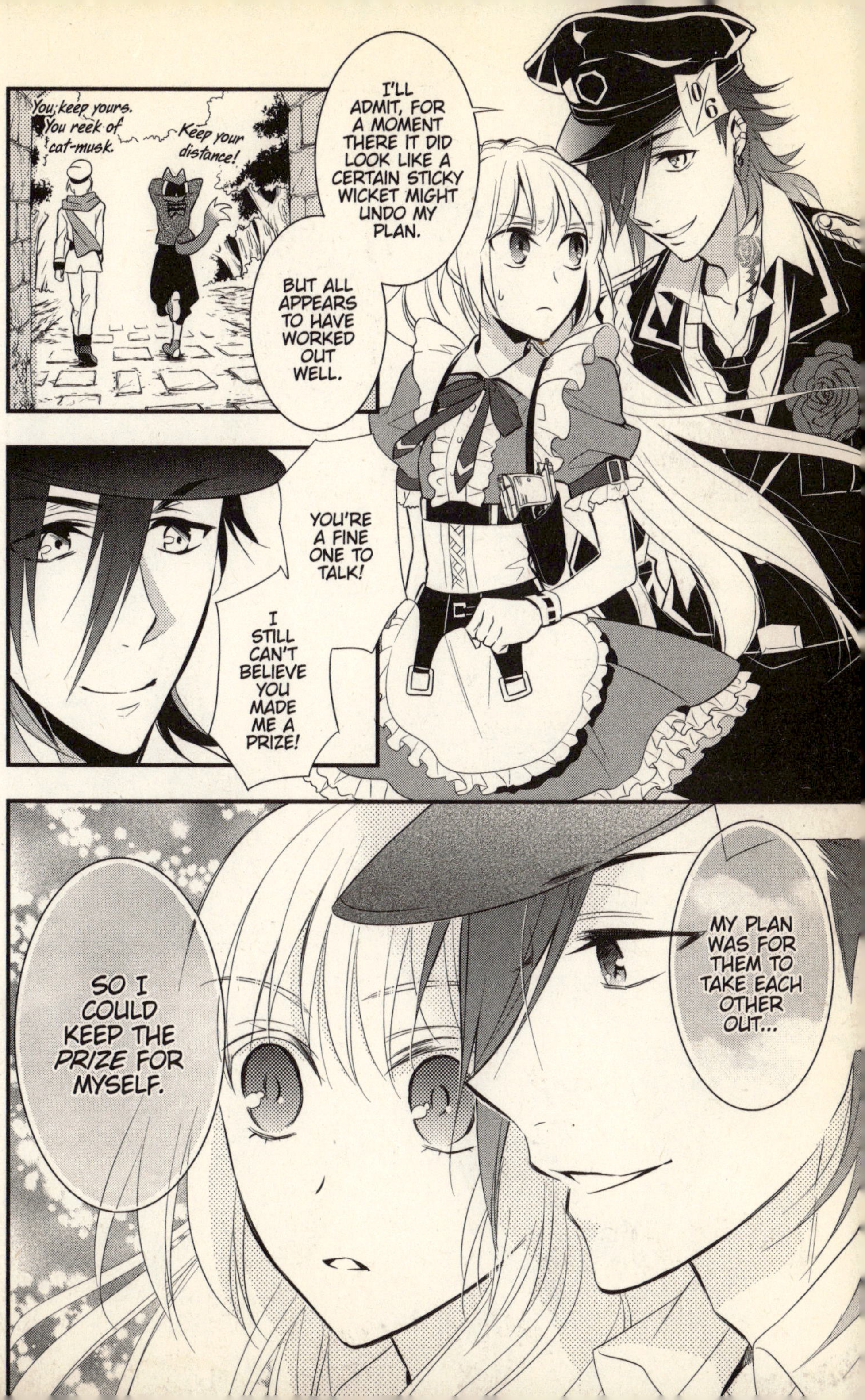
I'LL ADMIT, FOR A MOMENT THERE IT DID LOOK LIKE A CERTAIN STICKY WICKET MIGHT UNDO MY PLAN.
BUT ALL APPEARS TO HAVE WORKED OUT WELL.
Keep your distance!
You, keep yours. You reek of cat-musk.
YOU'RE A FINE ONE TO TALK!
I STILL CAN'T BELIEVE YOU MADE ME A PRIZE!
MY PLAN WAS FOR THEM TO TAKE EACH OTHER OUT...
SO I COULD KEEP THE *PRIZE* FOR MYSELF.

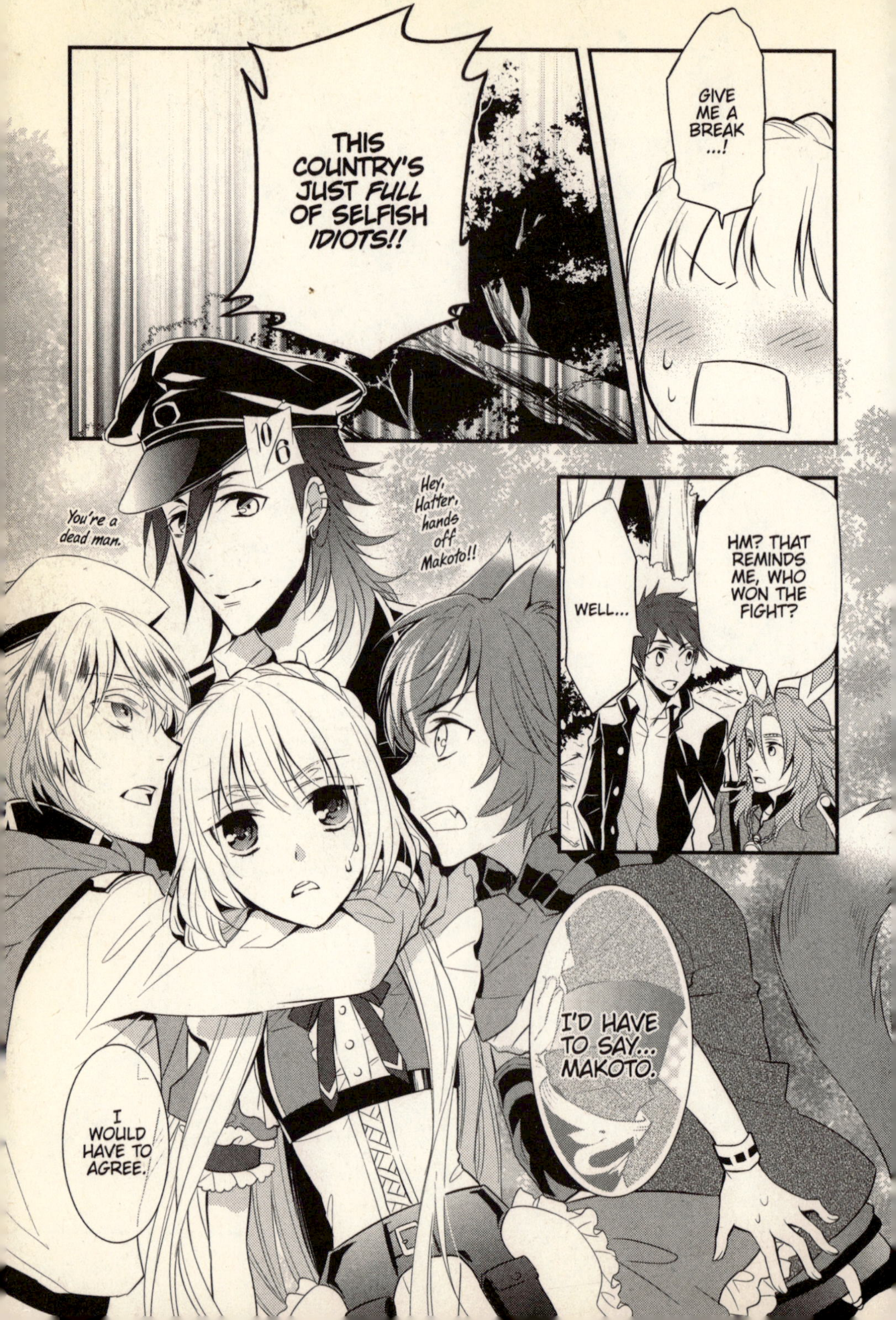
GIVE ME A BREAK ...!
THIS COUNTRY'S JUST FULL OF SELFISH IDIOTS!!
HM? THAT REMINDS ME, WHO WON THE FIGHT?
WELL...
Hey, Hatter, hands off Makoto!!
You're a dead man.
I'D HAVE TO SAY... MAKOTO.
I WOULD HAVE TO AGREE.

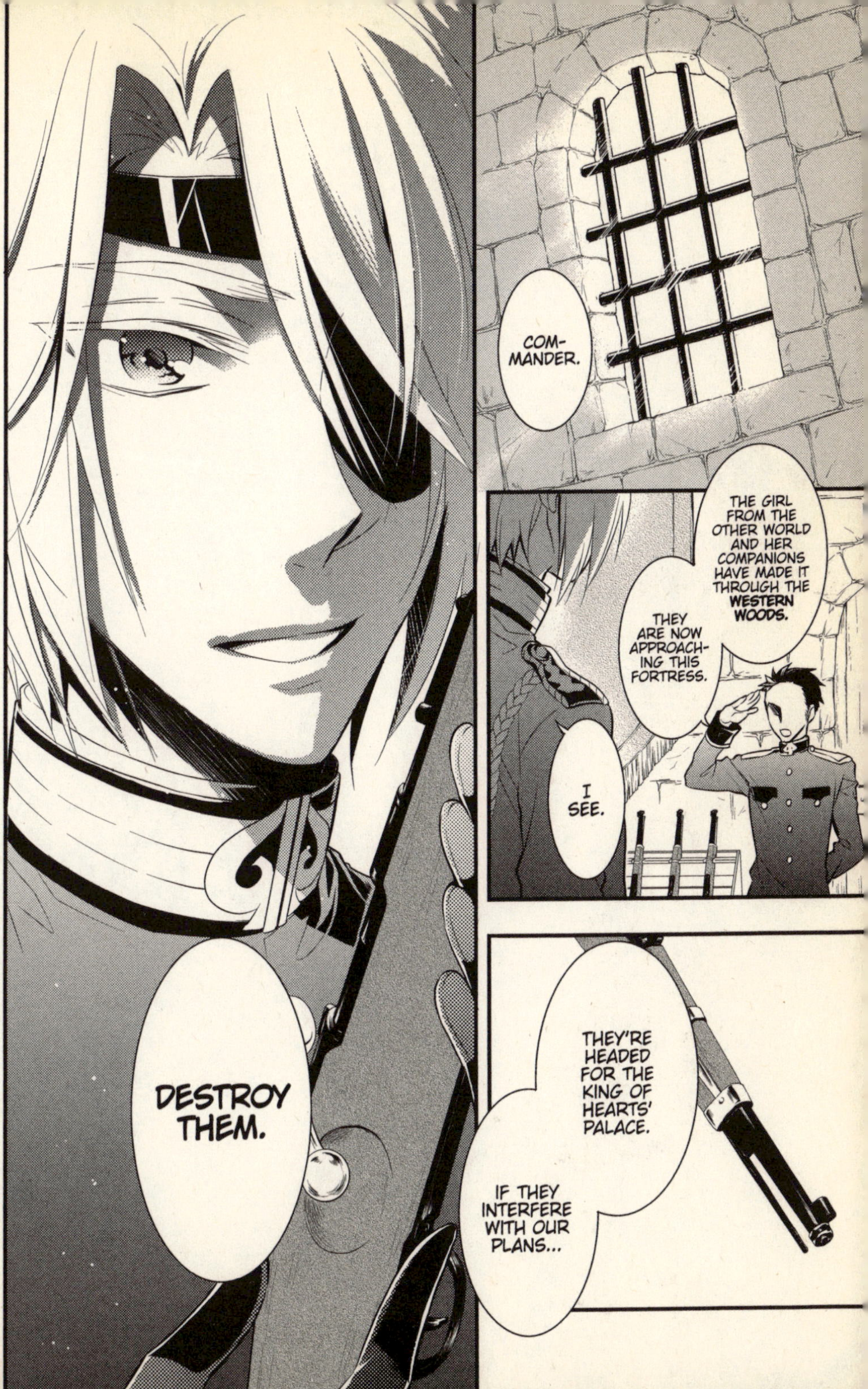
COM-MANDER.
THE GIRL FROM THE OTHER WORLD AND HER COMPANIONS HAVE MADE IT THROUGH THE **WESTERN WOODS.**
THEY ARE NOW APPROACHING THIS FORTRESS.
I SEE.
THEY'RE HEADED FOR THE KING OF HEARTS' PALACE.
IF THEY INTERFERE WITH OUR PLANS...
DESTROY THEM.

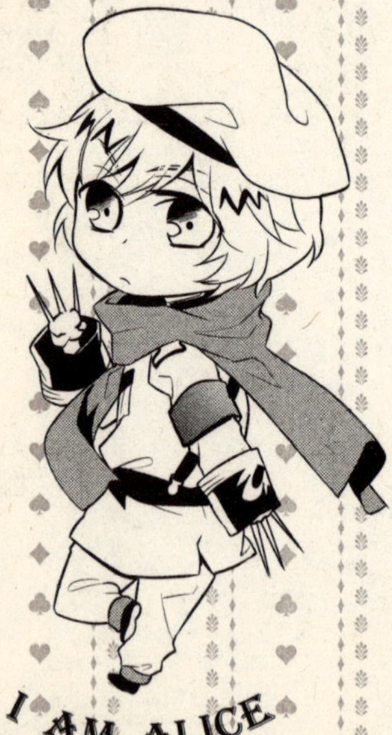
I AM ALICE

I AM ALICE

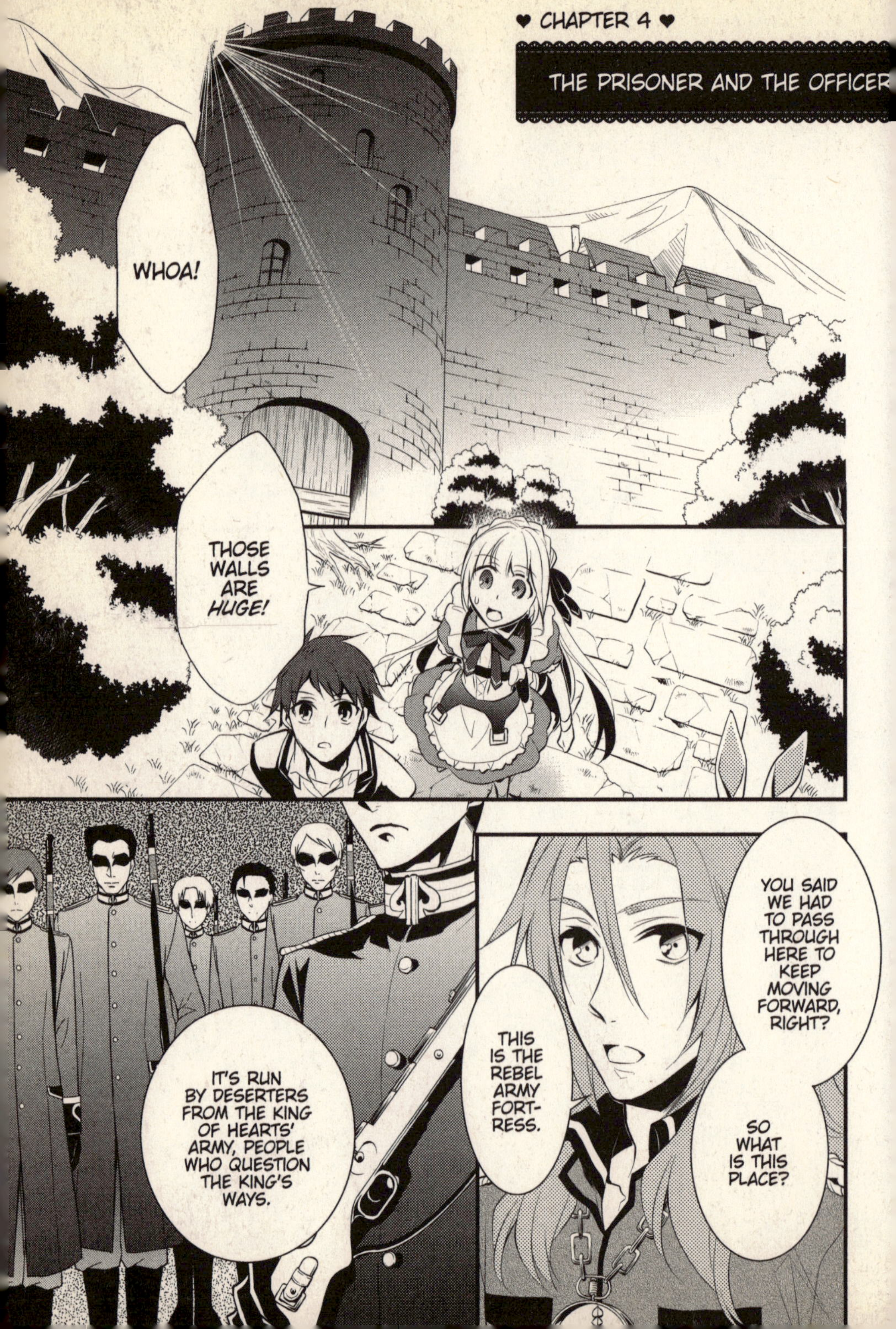
CHAPTER 4
THE PRISONER AND THE OFFICER
WHOA!
THOSE WALLS ARE *HUGE!*
YOU SAID WE HAD TO PASS THROUGH HERE TO KEEP MOVING FORWARD, RIGHT?
SO WHAT IS THIS PLACE?
THIS IS THE REBEL ARMY FORTRESS.
IT'S RUN BY DESERTERS FROM THE KING OF HEARTS' ARMY, PEOPLE WHO QUESTION THE KING'S WAYS.

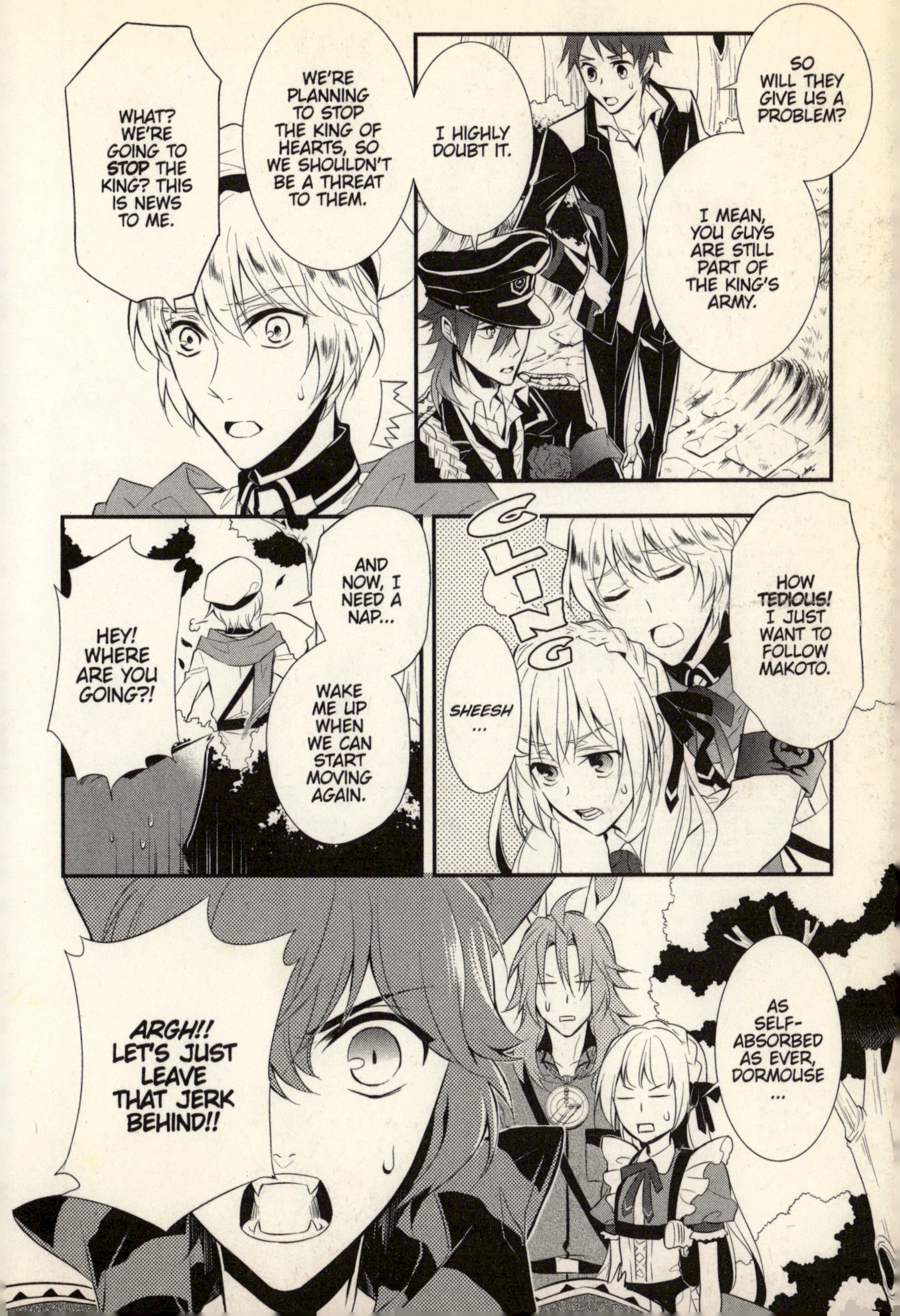
SO WILL THEY GIVE US A PROBLEM?
I MEAN, YOU GUYS ARE STILL PART OF THE KING'S ARMY.
I HIGHLY DOUBT IT.
WE'RE PLANNING TO STOP THE KING OF HEARTS, SO WE SHOULDN'T BE A THREAT TO THEM.
WHAT? WE'RE GOING TO **STOP** THE KING? THIS IS NEWS TO ME.
GLING
HOW **TEDIOUS!** I JUST WANT TO FOLLOW MAKOTO.
SHEESH...
AND NOW, I NEED A NAP...
WAKE ME UP WHEN WE CAN START MOVING AGAIN.
HEY! WHERE ARE YOU GOING?!
AS SELF-ABSORBED AS EVER, DORMOUSE...
ARGH!! LET'S JUST LEAVE THAT JERK BEHIND!!

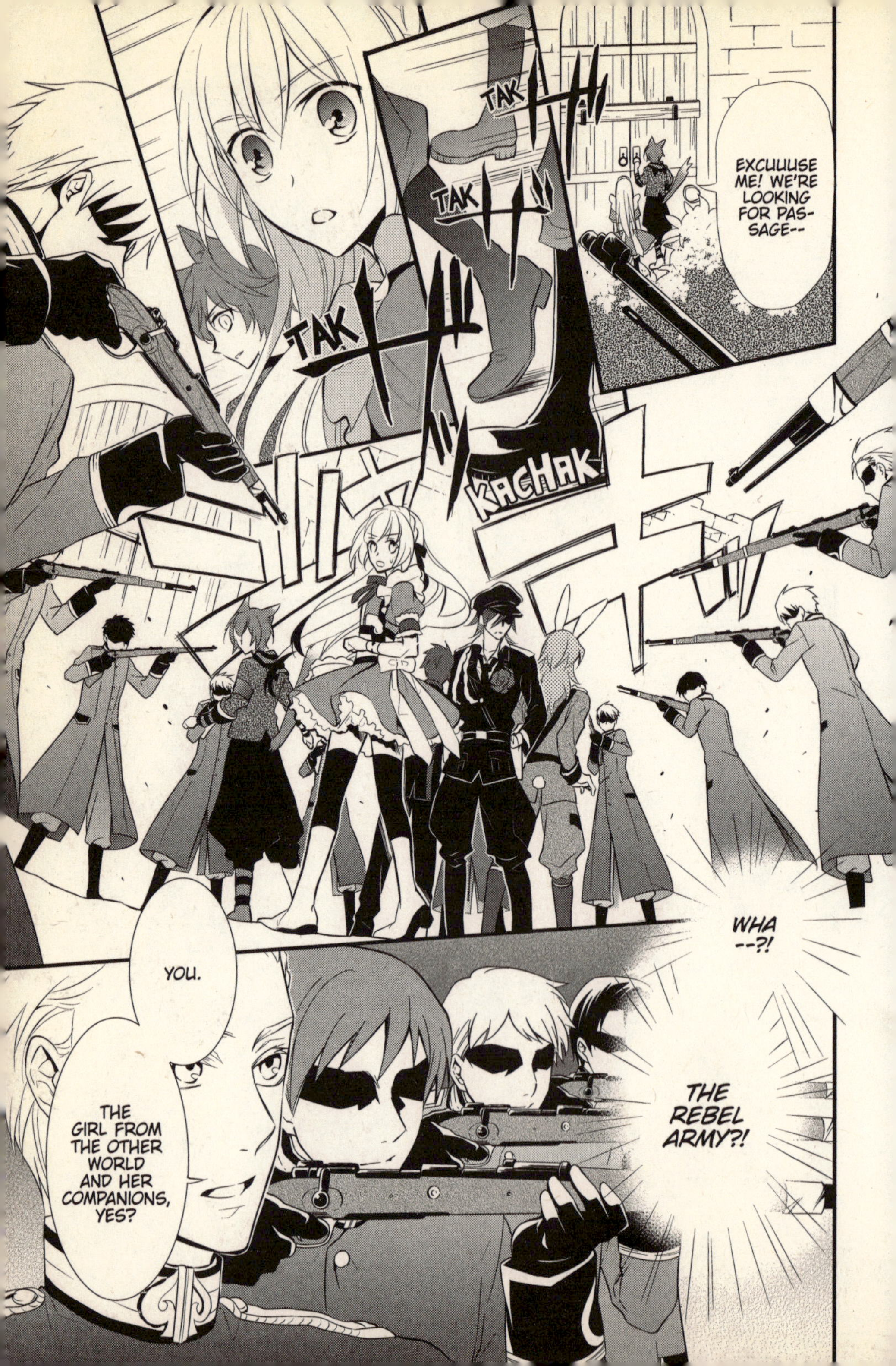
EXCUUUSE ME! WE'RE LOOKING FOR PAS- SAGE--
TAK
TAK
TAK
KACHAK
WHA --?!
THE REBEL ARMY?!
YOU.
THE GIRL FROM THE OTHER WORLD AND HER COMPANIONS, YES?

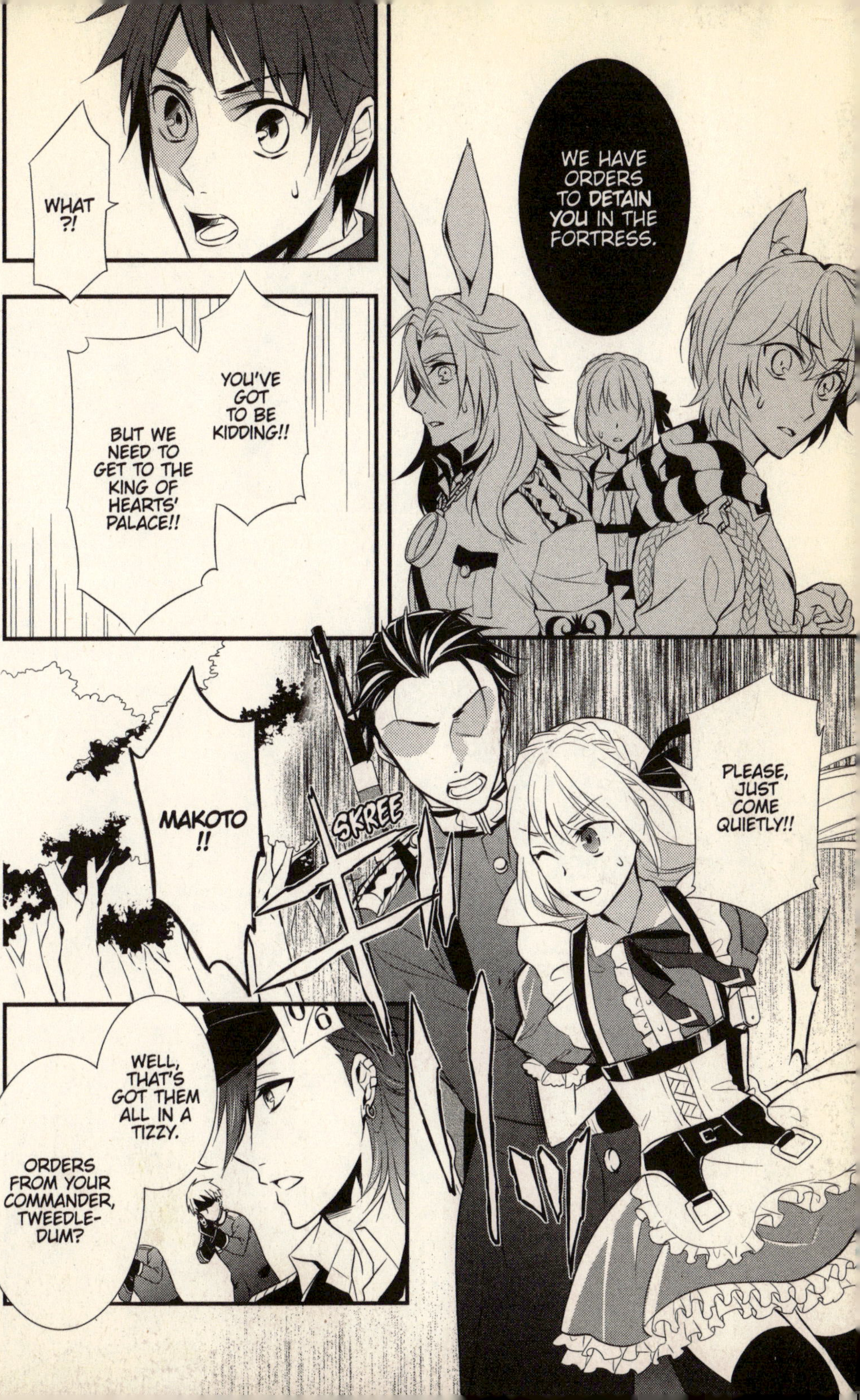
WE HAVE ORDERS TO DETAIN YOU IN THE FORTRESS.
WHAT ?!
YOU'VE GOT TO BE KIDDING!!
BUT WE NEED TO GET TO THE KING OF HEARTS' PALACE!!
PLEASE, JUST COME QUIETLY!!
SKREE
MAKOTO !!
WELL, THAT'S GOT THEM ALL IN A TIZZY.
ORDERS FROM YOUR COMMANDER, TWEEDLE-DUM?

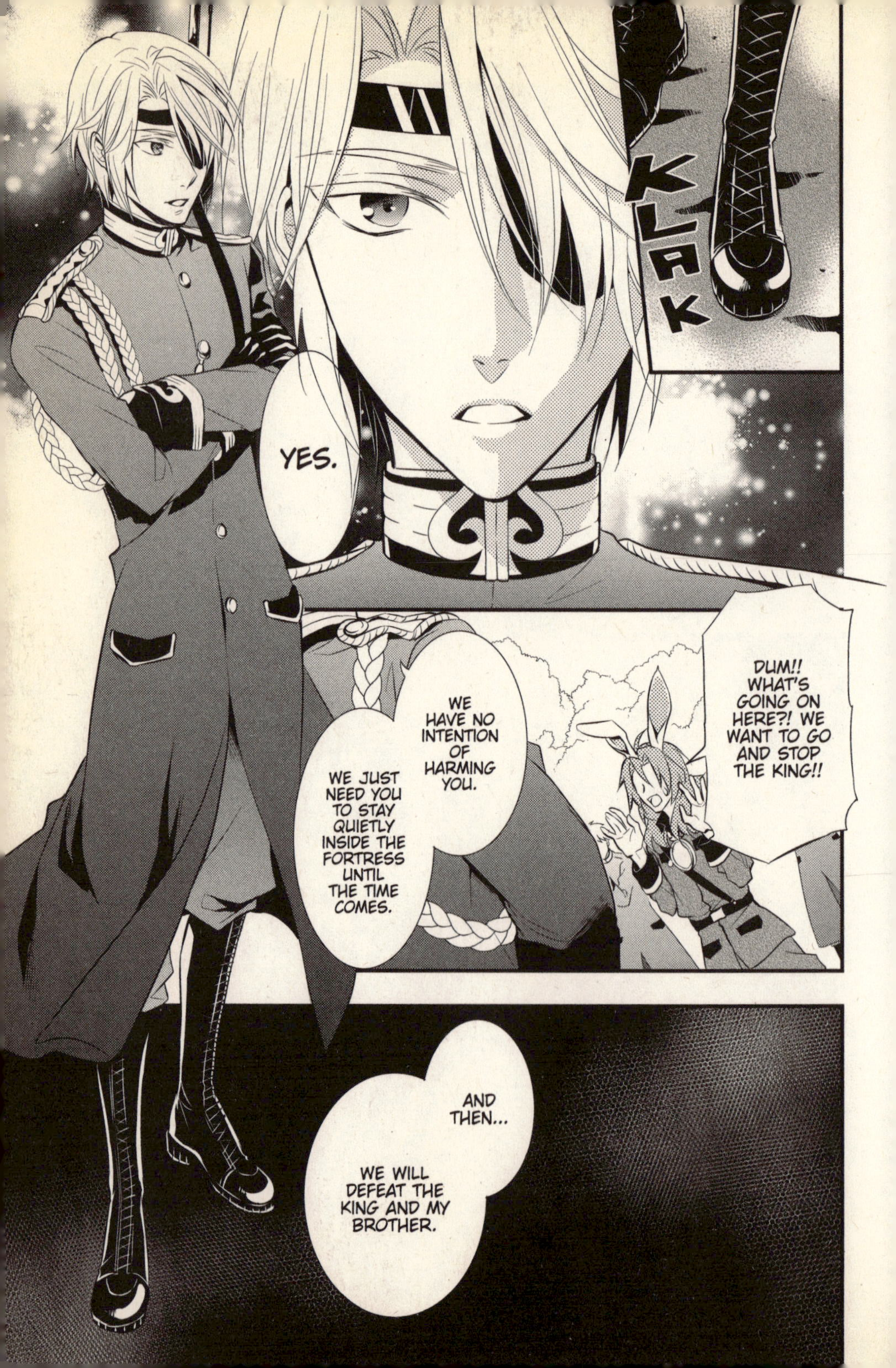
KLAK
YES.
DUM!! WHAT'S GOING ON HERE?! WE WANT TO GO AND STOP THE KING!!
WE HAVE NO INTENTION OF HARMING YOU.
WE JUST NEED YOU TO STAY QUIETLY INSIDE THE FORTRESS UNTIL THE TIME COMES.
AND THEN...
WE WILL DEFEAT THE KING AND MY BROTHER.

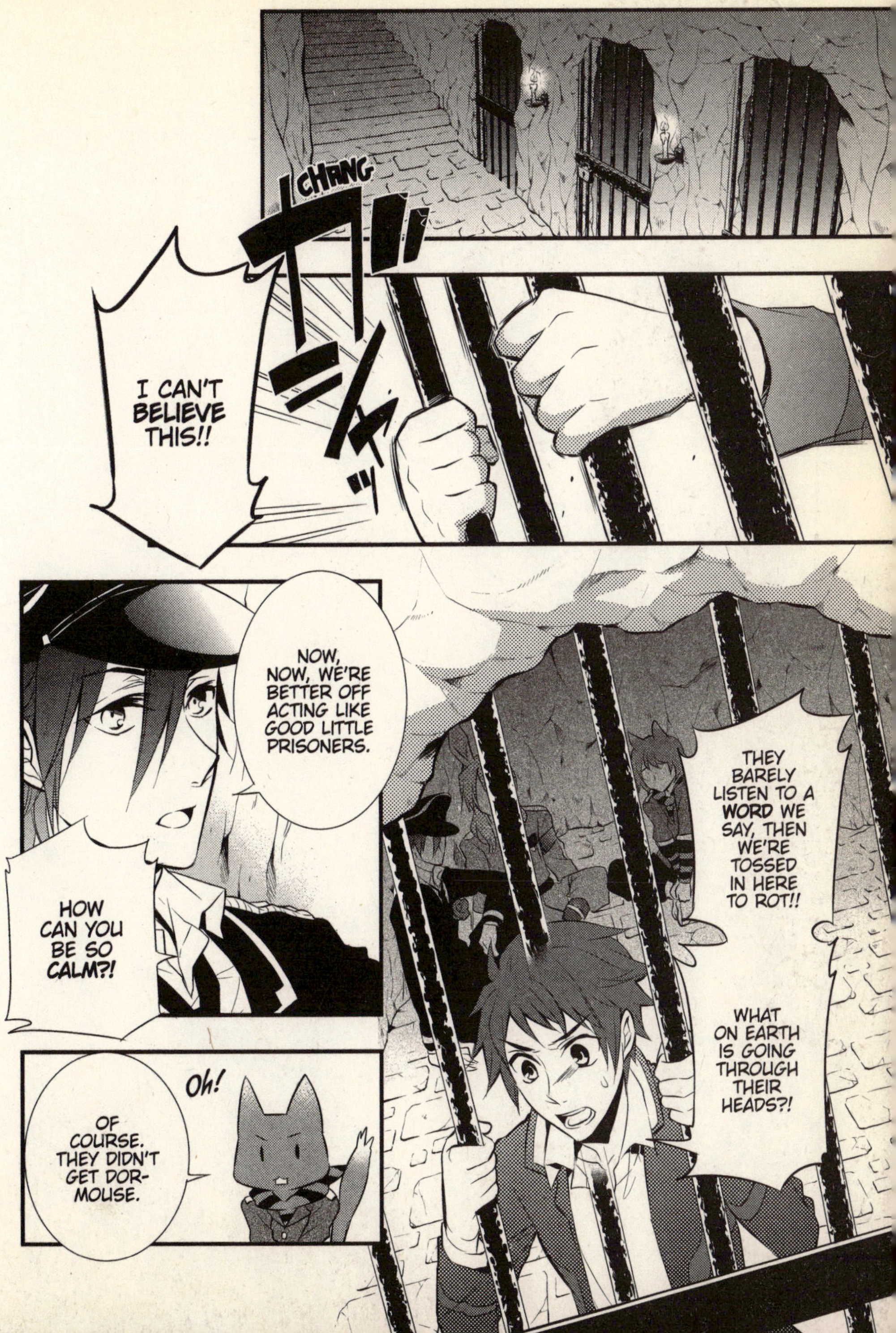
CHANG
I CAN'T BELIEVE THIS!!
THEY BARELY LISTEN TO A WORD WE SAY, THEN WE'RE TOSSED IN HERE TO ROT!!
WHAT ON EARTH IS GOING THROUGH THEIR HEADS?!
NOW, NOW, WE'RE BETTER OFF ACTING LIKE GOOD LITTLE PRISONERS.
HOW CAN YOU BE SO CALM?!
Oh!
OF COURSE. THEY DIDN'T GET DOR-MOUSE.

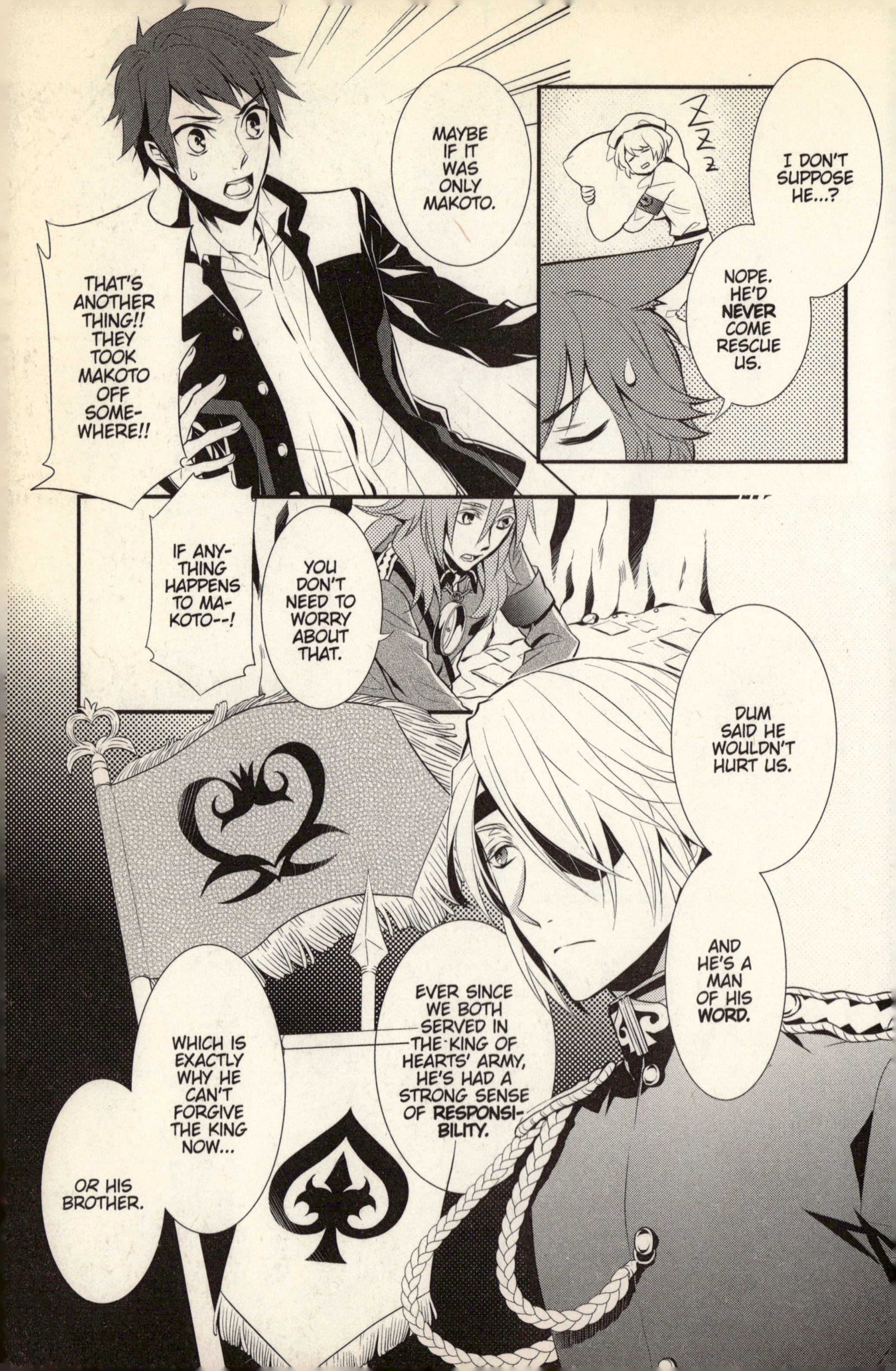

I DON'T SUPPOSE HE...?
Z Z Z
NOPE. HE'D NEVER COME RESCUE US.
MAYBE IF IT WAS ONLY MAKOTO.
THAT'S ANOTHER THING!! THEY TOOK MAKOTO OFF SOME-WHERE!!
IF ANY-THING HAPPENS TO MA-KOTO--!
YOU DON'T NEED TO WORRY ABOUT THAT.
DUM SAID HE WOULDN'T HURT US.
AND HE'S A MAN OF HIS WORD.
EVER SINCE WE BOTH SERVED IN THE KING OF HEARTS' ARMY, HE'S HAD A STRONG SENSE OF RESPONSI-BILITY.
WHICH IS EXACTLY WHY HE CAN'T FORGIVE THE KING NOW...
OR HIS BROTHER.

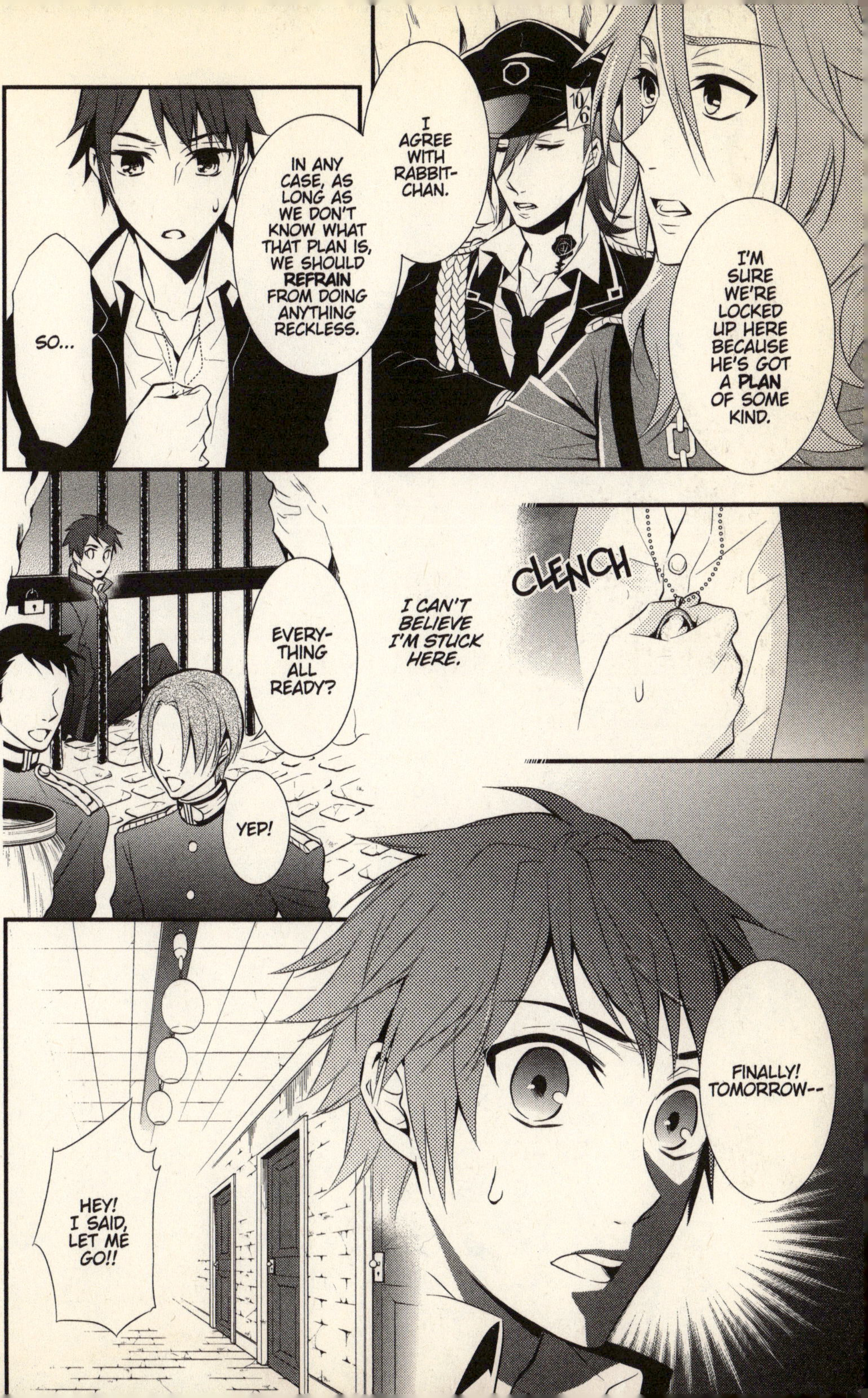
I'M SURE WE'RE LOCKED UP HERE BECAUSE HE'S GOT A **PLAN** OF SOME KIND.
I AGREE WITH RABBIT-CHAN.
IN ANY CASE, AS LONG AS WE DON'T KNOW WHAT THAT PLAN IS, WE SHOULD **REFRAIN** FROM DOING ANYTHING RECKLESS.
SO...
CLENCH
I CAN'T BELIEVE I'M STUCK HERE.
EVERY-THING ALL READY?
YEP!
FINALLY! TOMORROW--
HEY! I SAID, LET ME GO!!

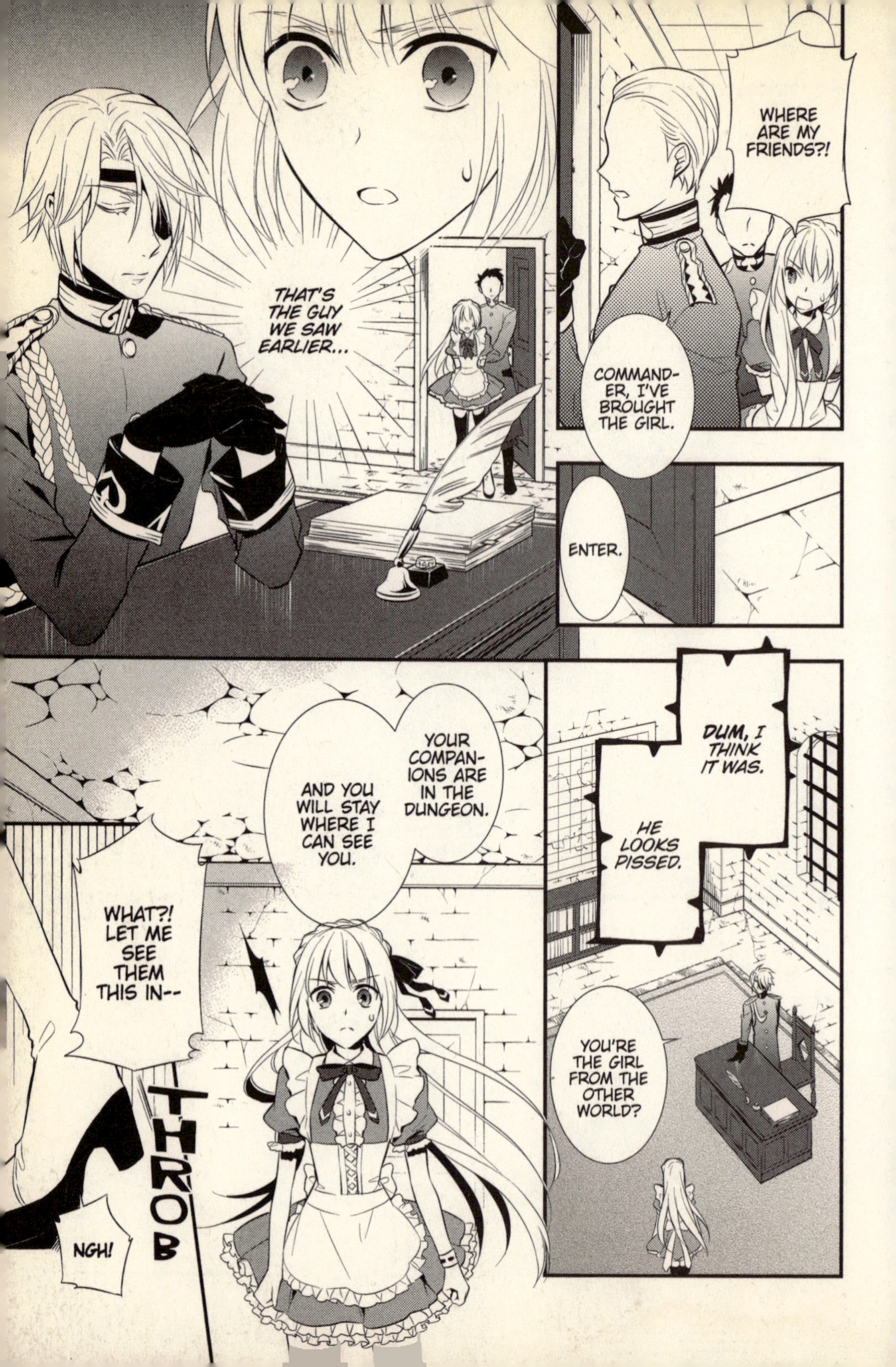
WHERE ARE MY FRIENDS?!
COMMANDER, I'VE BROUGHT THE GIRL.
ENTER.
THAT'S THE GUY WE SAW EARLIER...
DUM, I THINK IT WAS.
HE LOOKS PISSED.
YOU'RE THE GIRL FROM THE OTHER WORLD?
YOUR COMPANIONS ARE IN THE DUNGEON.
AND YOU WILL STAY WHERE I CAN SEE YOU.
WHAT?! LET ME SEE THEM THIS IN--
THROB
NGH!

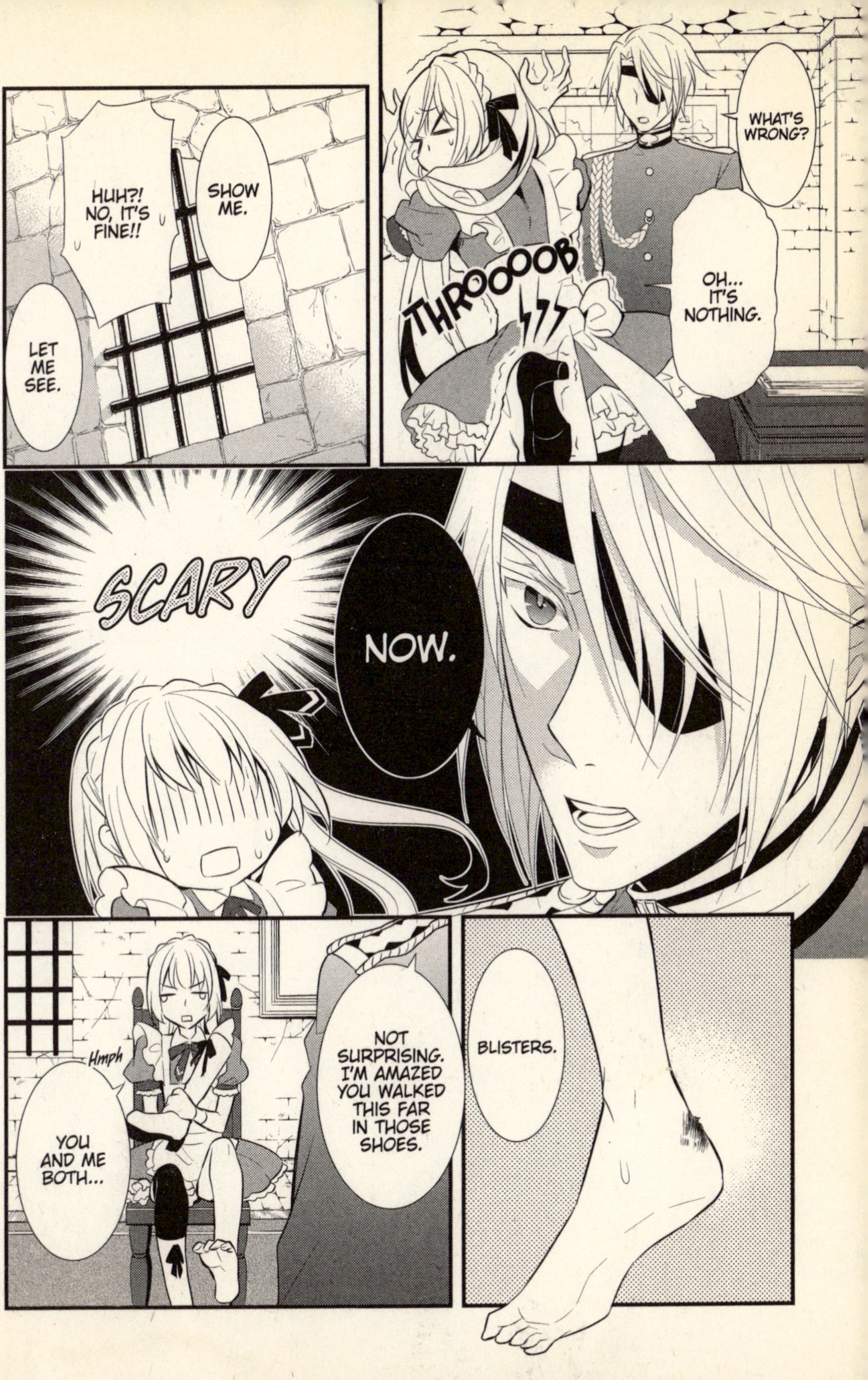
WHAT'S WRONG?
THROOOOB
OH... IT'S NOTHING.
SHOW ME.
HUH?! NO, IT'S FINE!!
LET ME SEE.
NOW.
SCARY
BLISTERS.
NOT SURPRISING. I'M AMAZED YOU WALKED THIS FAR IN THOSE SHOES.
Hmph
YOU AND ME BOTH...

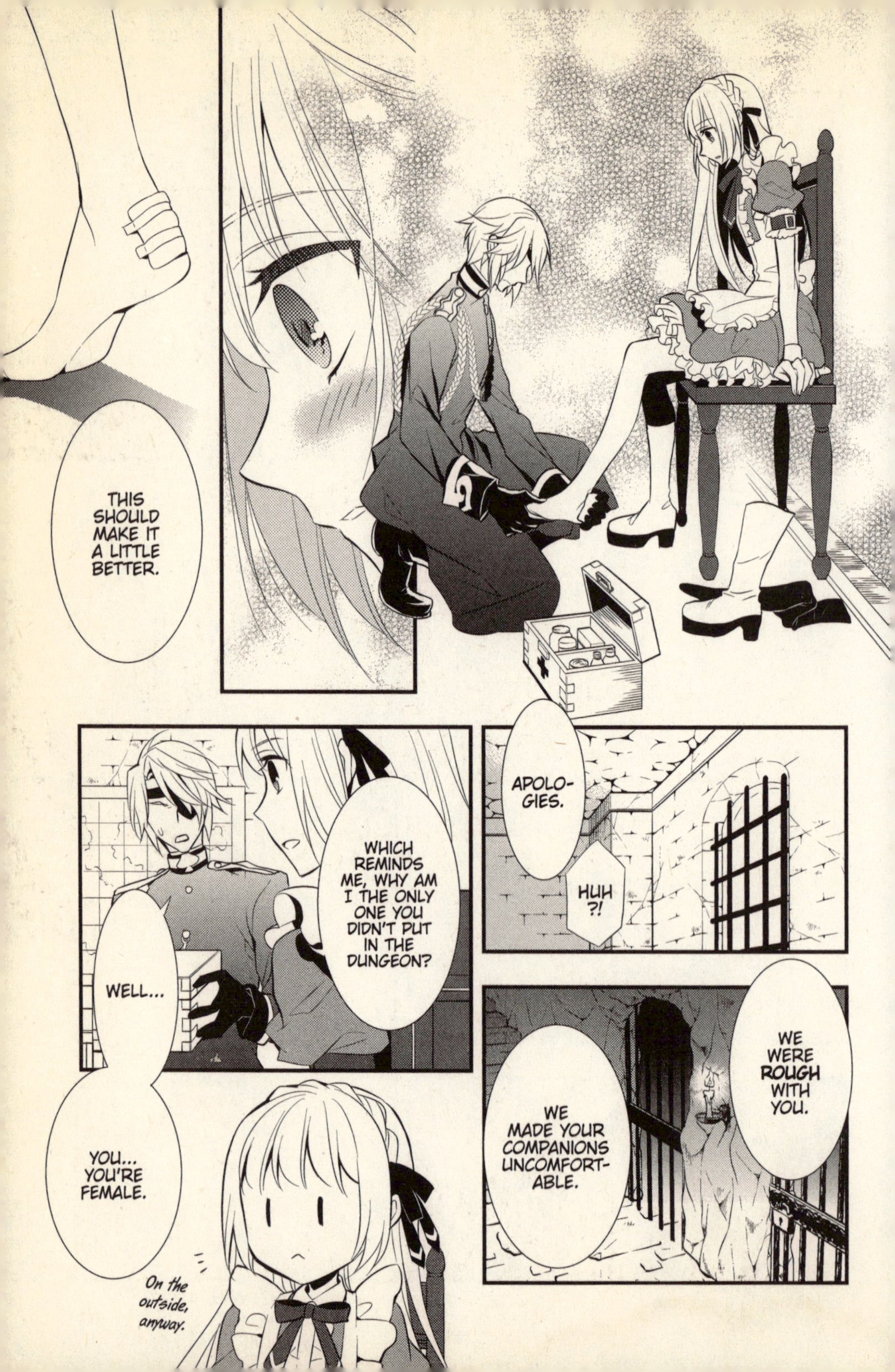
THIS SHOULD MAKE IT A LITTLE BETTER.
APOLO-GIES.
HUH?!
WE WERE **ROUGH** WITH YOU.
WE MADE YOUR COMPANIONS UNCOMFORT-ABLE.
WHICH REMINDS ME, WHY AM I THE ONLY ONE YOU DIDN'T PUT IN THE DUNGEON?
WELL...
YOU... YOU'RE FEMALE.
On the outside, anyway.

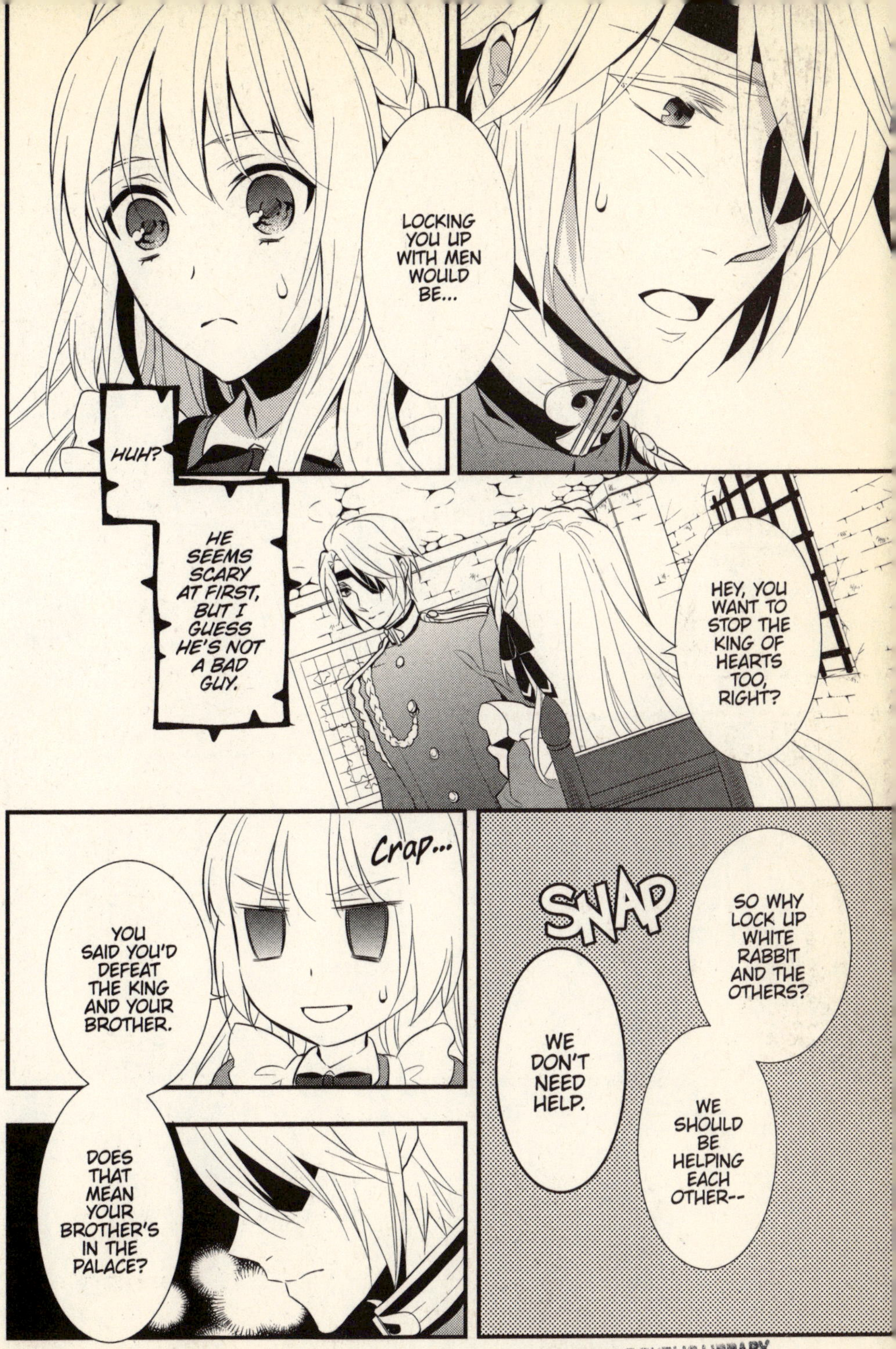
LOCKING YOU UP WITH MEN WOULD BE...
HUH?
HE SEEMS SCARY AT FIRST, BUT I GUESS HE'S NOT A BAD GUY.
HEY, YOU WANT TO STOP THE KING OF HEARTS TOO, RIGHT?
SO WHY LOCK UP WHITE RABBIT AND THE OTHERS?
WE SHOULD BE HELPING EACH OTHER--
SNAP
WE DON'T NEED HELP.
Crap...
YOU SAID YOU'D DEFEAT THE KING AND YOUR BROTHER.
DOES THAT MEAN YOUR BROTHER'S IN THE PALACE?

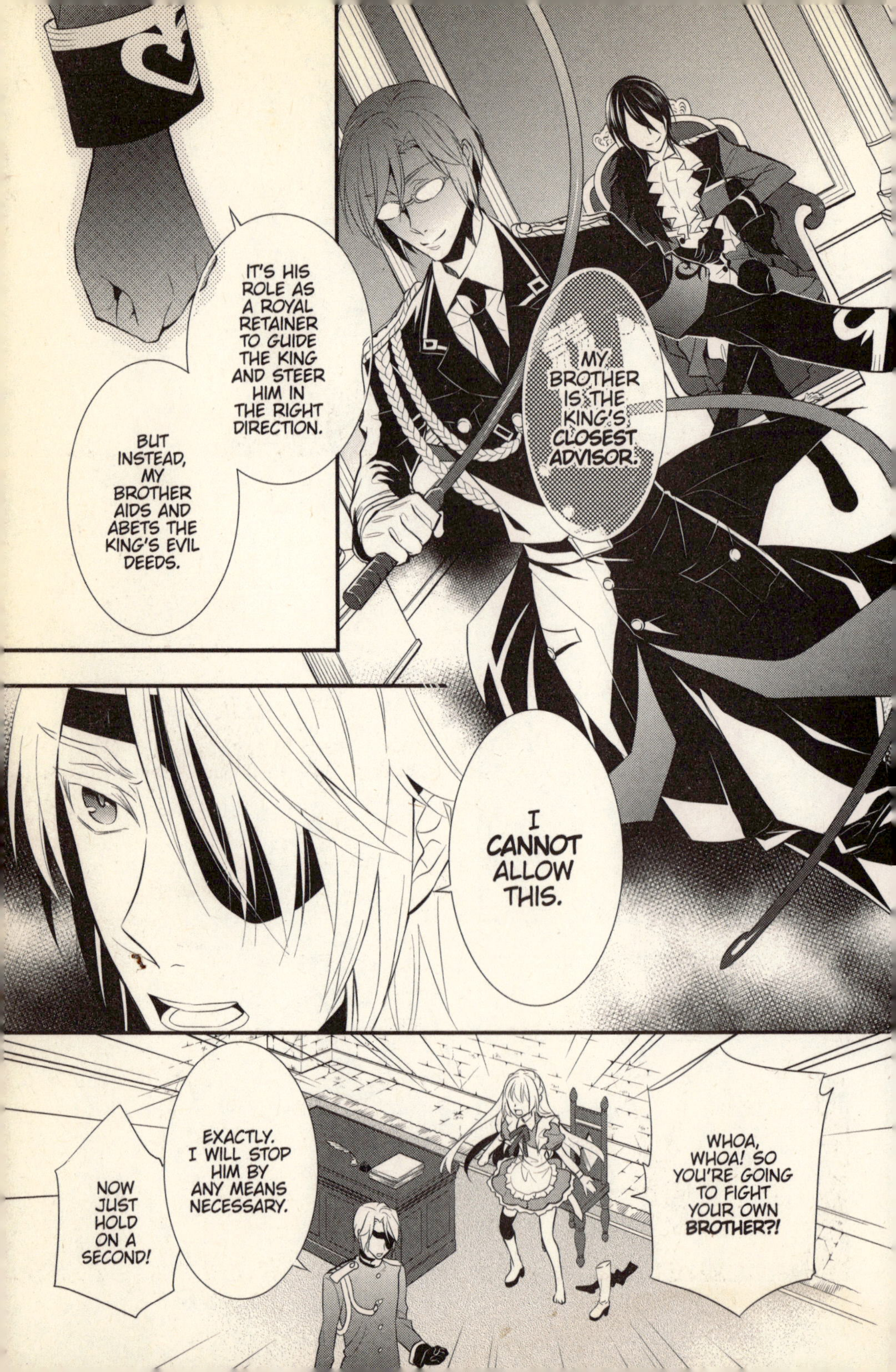
MY BROTHER IS THE KING'S CLOSEST ADVISOR.
IT'S HIS ROLE AS A ROYAL RETAINER TO GUIDE THE KING AND STEER HIM IN THE RIGHT DIRECTION.
BUT INSTEAD, MY BROTHER AIDS AND ABETS THE KING'S EVIL DEEDS.
I CANNOT ALLOW THIS.
WHOA, WHOA! SO YOU'RE GOING TO FIGHT YOUR OWN BROTHER?!
EXACTLY. I WILL STOP HIM BY ANY MEANS NECESSARY.
NOW JUST HOLD ON A SECOND!

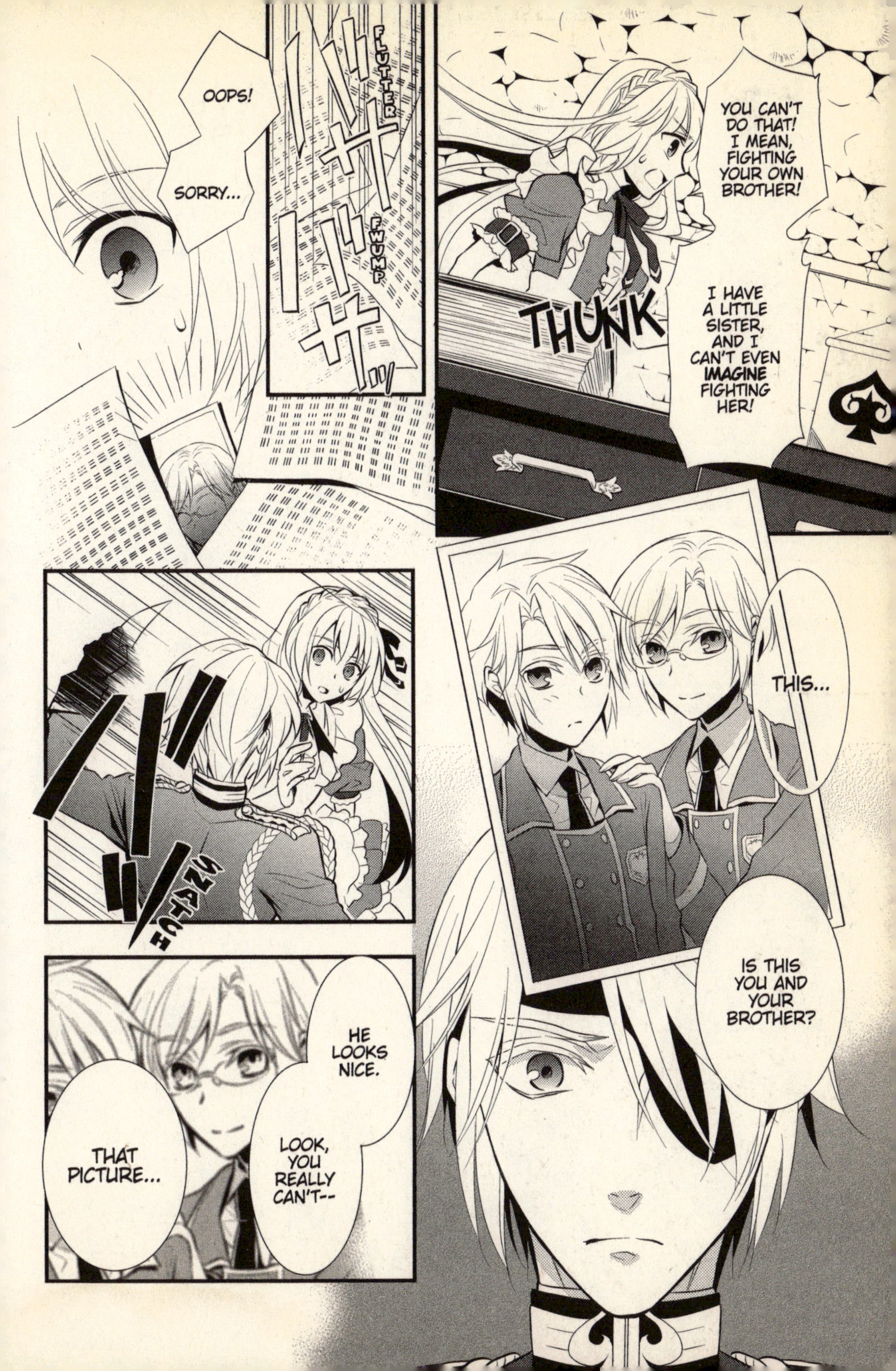
YOU CAN'T DO THAT! I MEAN, FIGHTING YOUR OWN BROTHER!
THUNK
I HAVE A LITTLE SISTER, AND I CAN'T EVEN IMAGINE FIGHTING HER!
FLUTTER
FWUMP
OOPS!
SORRY...
THIS...
IS THIS YOU AND YOUR BROTHER?
SNATCH
HE LOOKS NICE.
LOOK, YOU REALLY CAN'T--
THAT PICTURE...

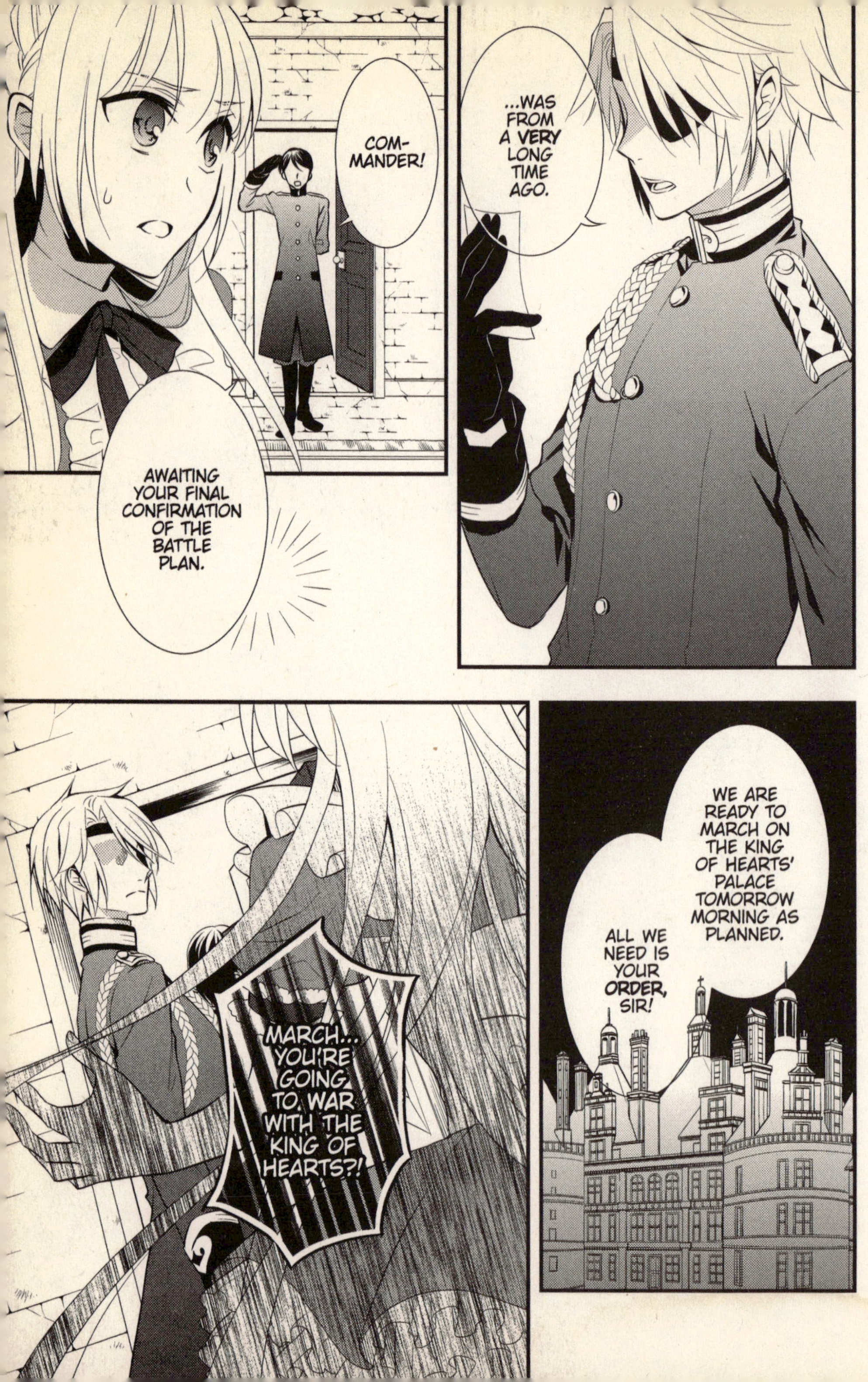
...WAS FROM A VERY LONG TIME AGO.
COM-MANDER!
AWAITING YOUR FINAL CONFIRMATION OF THE BATTLE PLAN.
WE ARE READY TO MARCH ON THE KING OF HEARTS' PALACE TOMORROW MORNING AS PLANNED.
ALL WE NEED IS YOUR ORDER, SIR!
MARCH... YOU'RE GOING TO WAR WITH THE KING OF HEARTS?!

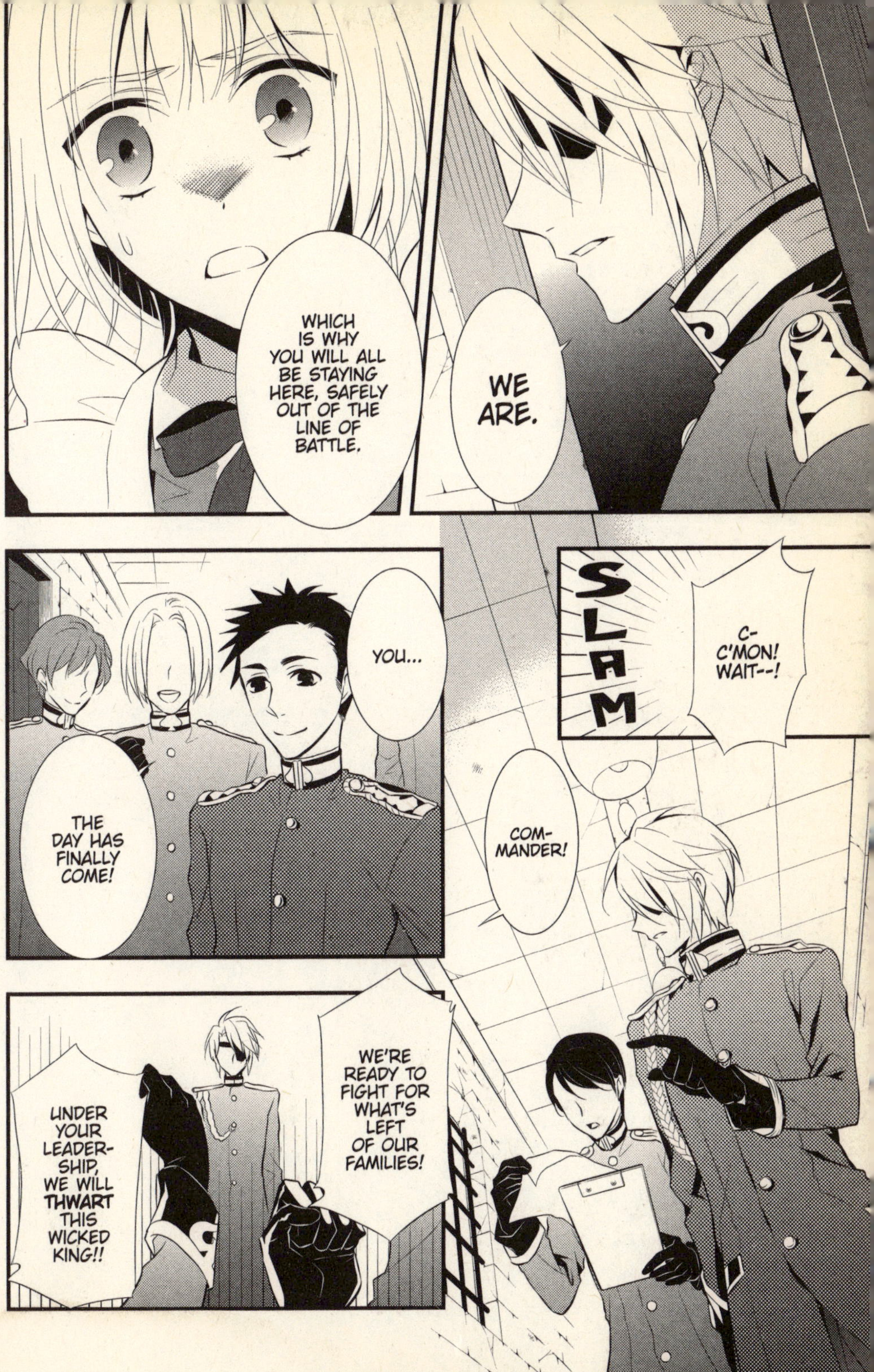
WE ARE.
WHICH IS WHY YOU WILL ALL BE STAYING HERE, SAFELY OUT OF THE LINE OF BATTLE.
SLAM
C-C'MON! WAIT--!
COM-MANDER!
YOU...
THE DAY HAS FINALLY COME!
WE'RE READY TO FIGHT FOR WHAT'S LEFT OF OUR FAMILIES!
UNDER YOUR LEADER-SHIP, WE WILL THWART THIS WICKED KING!!

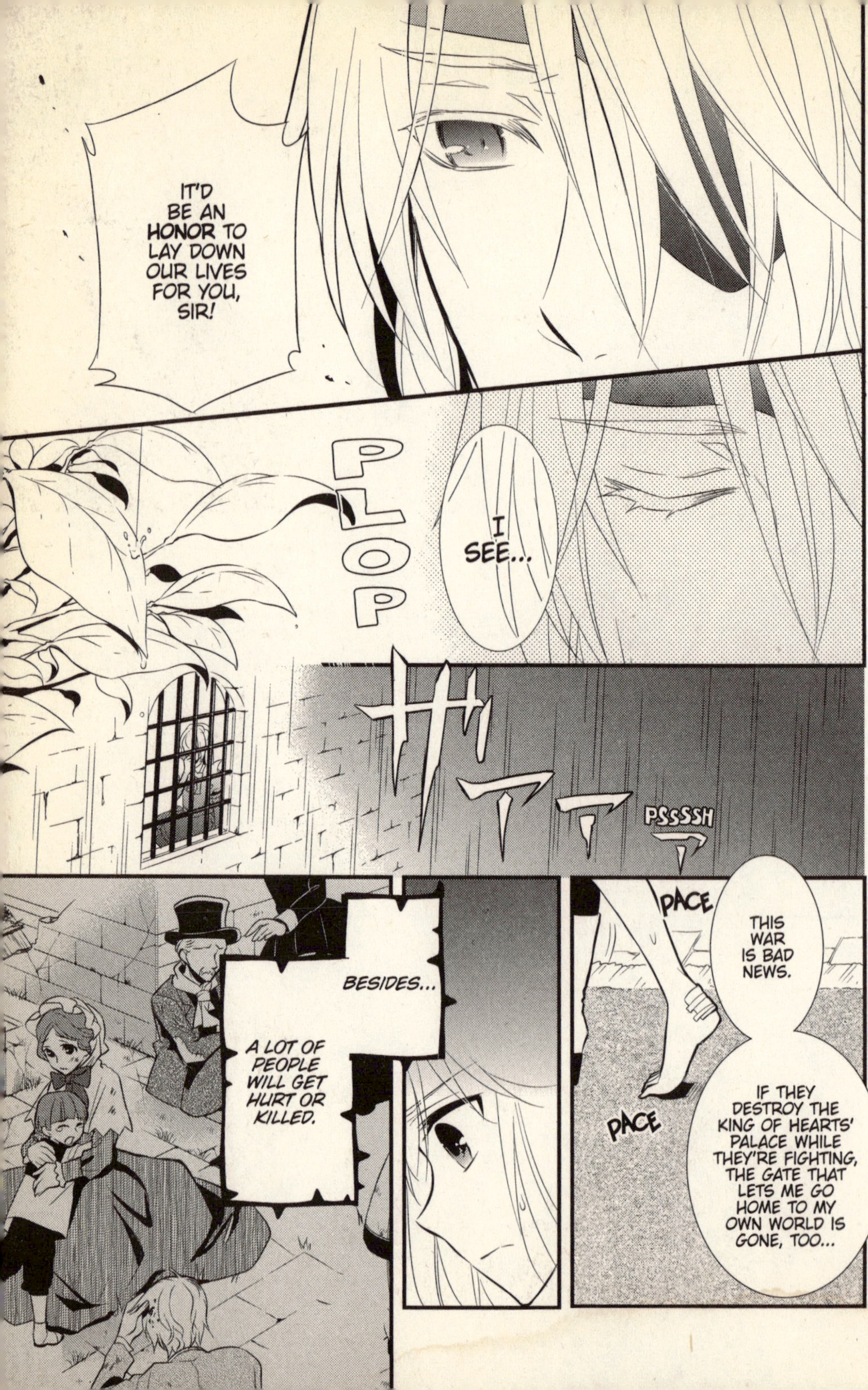
IT'D BE AN HONOR TO LAY DOWN OUR LIVES FOR YOU, SIR!
I SEE...
PLOP
ザァァ
PSSSSH
PACE
THIS WAR IS BAD NEWS.
PACE
IF THEY DESTROY THE KING OF HEARTS' PALACE WHILE THEY'RE FIGHTING, THE GATE THAT LETS ME GO HOME TO MY OWN WORLD IS GONE, TOO...
BESIDES...
A LOT OF PEOPLE WILL GET HURT OR KILLED.

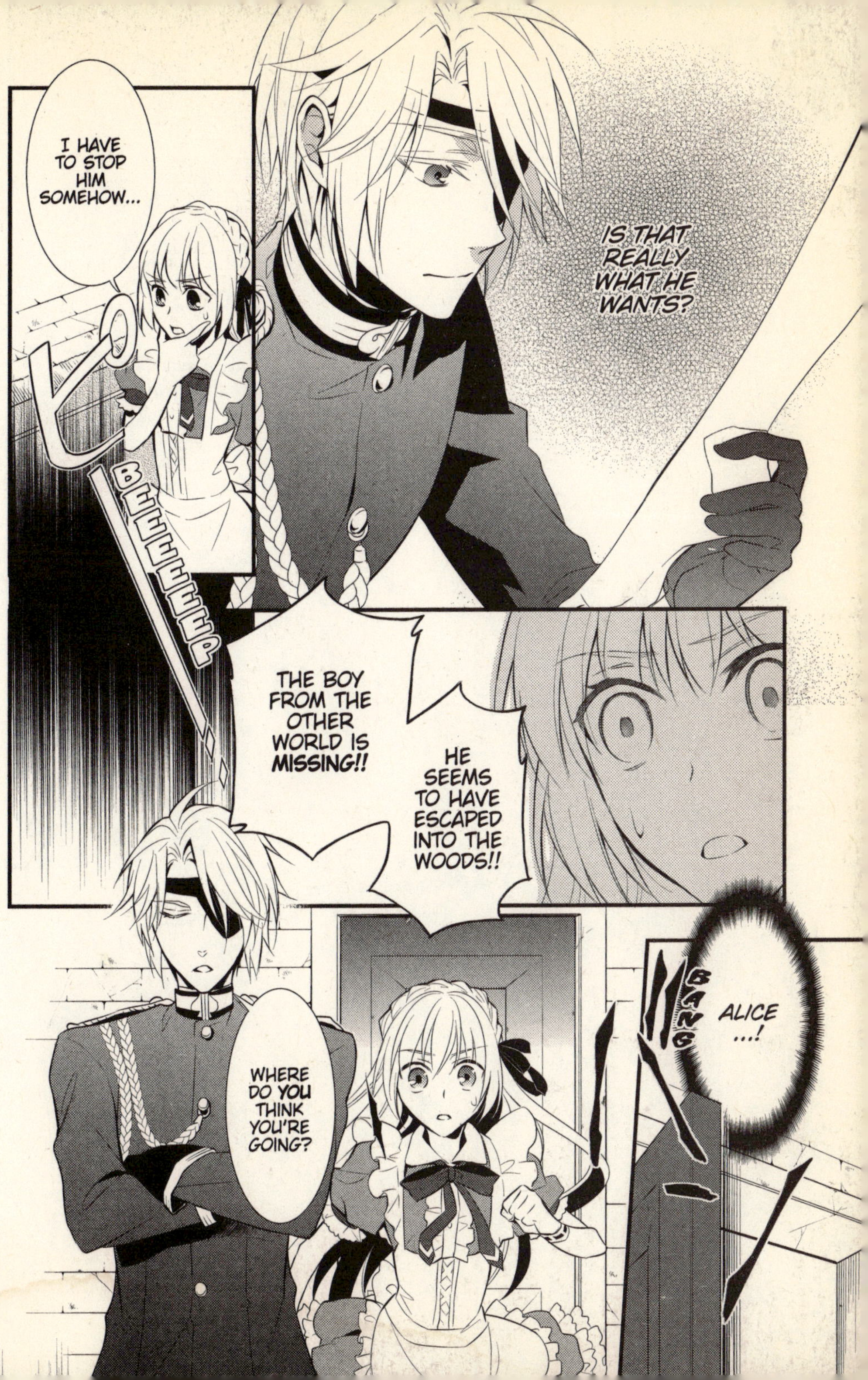
IS THAT REALLY WHAT HE WANTS?
I HAVE TO STOP HIM SOMEHOW...
BEEEEEEEP
THE BOY FROM THE OTHER WORLD IS **MISSING!!**
HE SEEMS TO HAVE ESCAPED INTO THE WOODS!!
BANG
ALICE ...!
WHERE DO **YOU** THINK YOU'RE GOING?

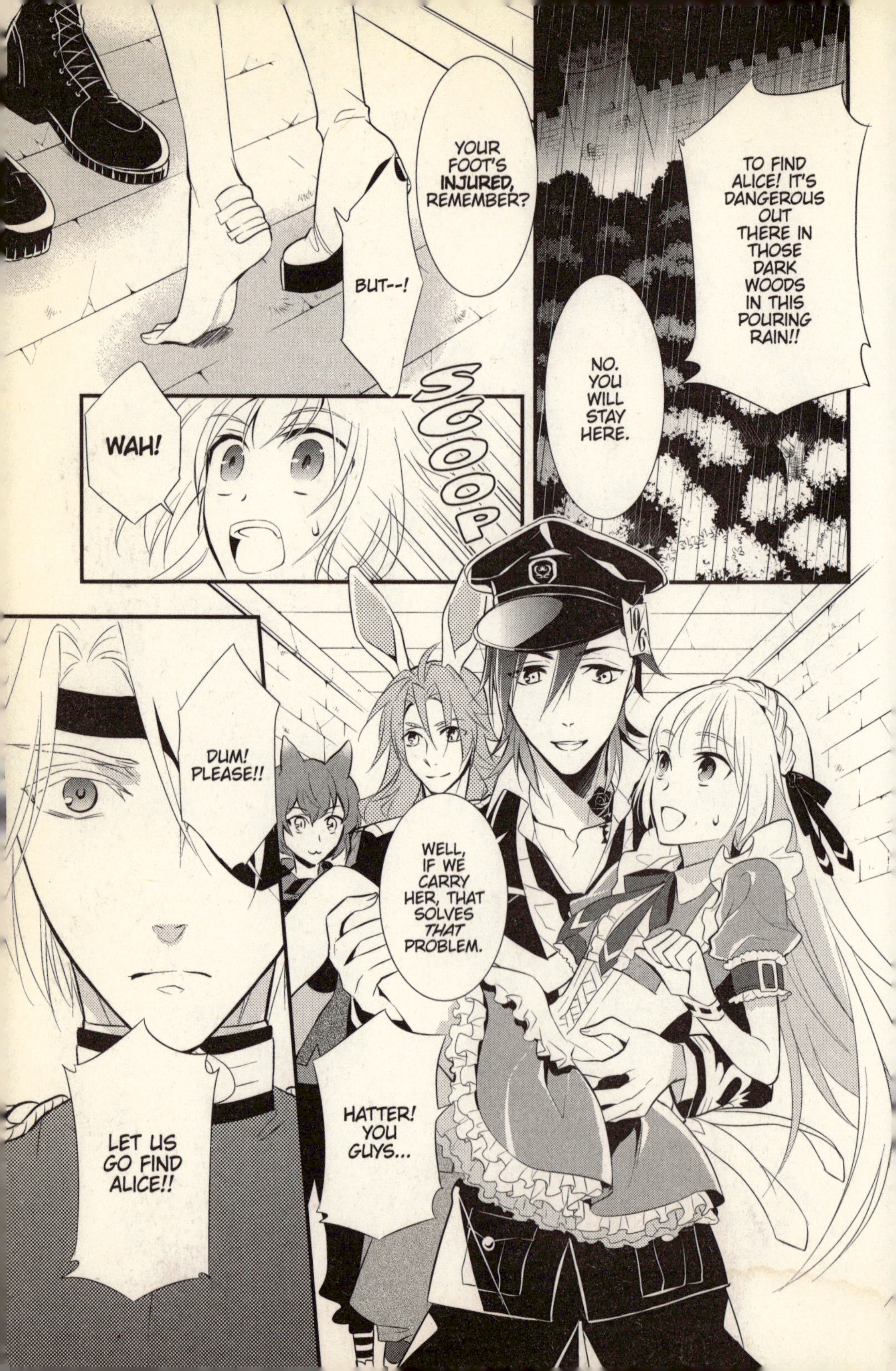
TO FIND ALICE! IT'S DANGEROUS OUT THERE IN THOSE DARK WOODS IN THIS POURING RAIN!!
NO. YOU WILL STAY HERE.
YOUR FOOT'S INJURED, REMEMBER?
BUT--!
SCOOP
WAH!
WELL, IF WE CARRY HER, THAT SOLVES *THAT* PROBLEM.
HATTER! YOU GUYS...
DUM! PLEASE!!
LET US GO FIND ALICE!!

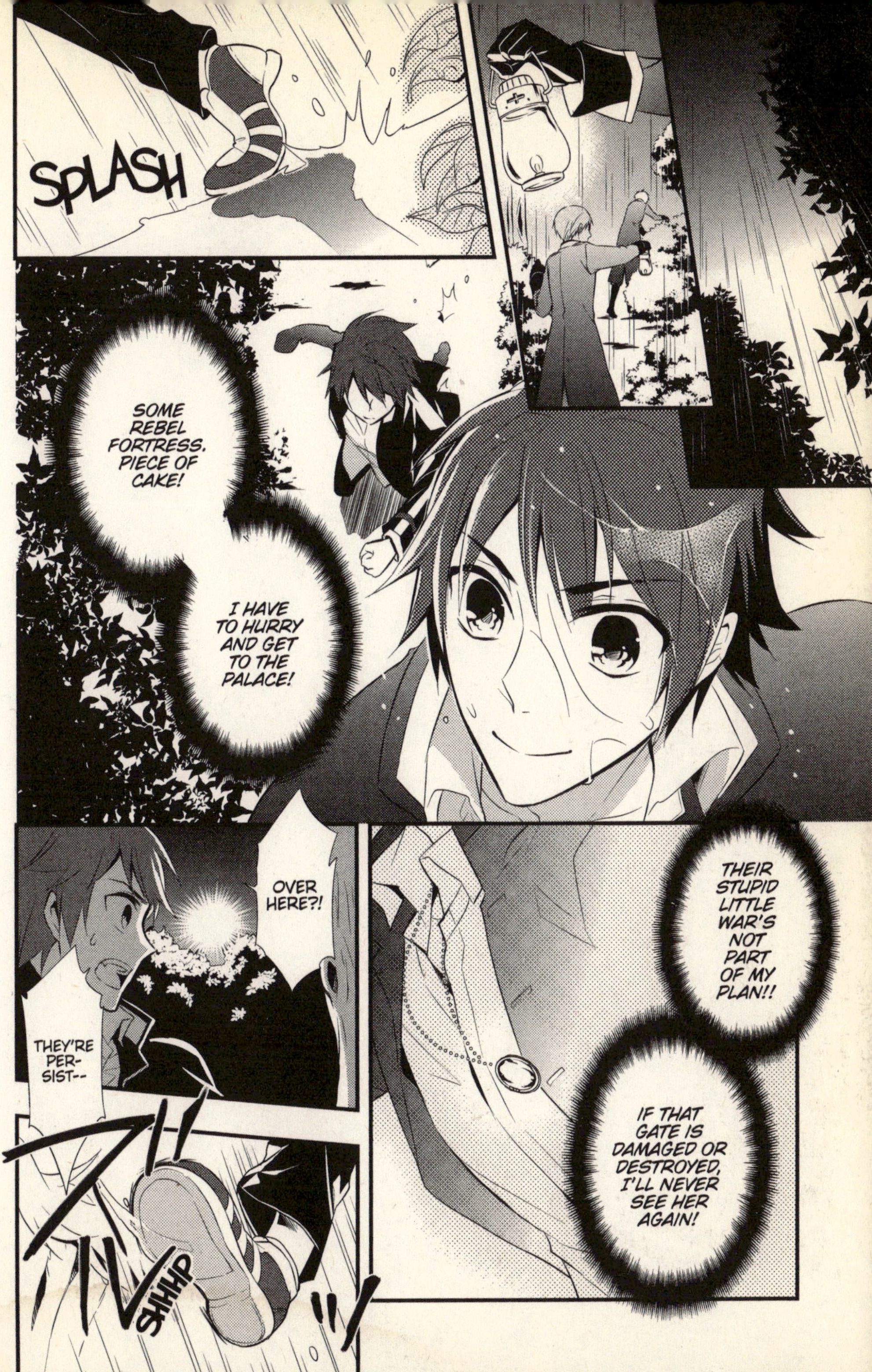
SPLASH
SOME REBEL FORTRESS. PIECE OF CAKE!
I HAVE TO HURRY AND GET TO THE PALACE!
THEIR STUPID LITTLE WAR'S NOT PART OF MY PLAN!!
IF THAT GATE IS DAMAGED OR DESTROYED, I'LL NEVER SEE HER AGAIN!
OVER HERE?!
THEY'RE PERSIST--
SHHHP

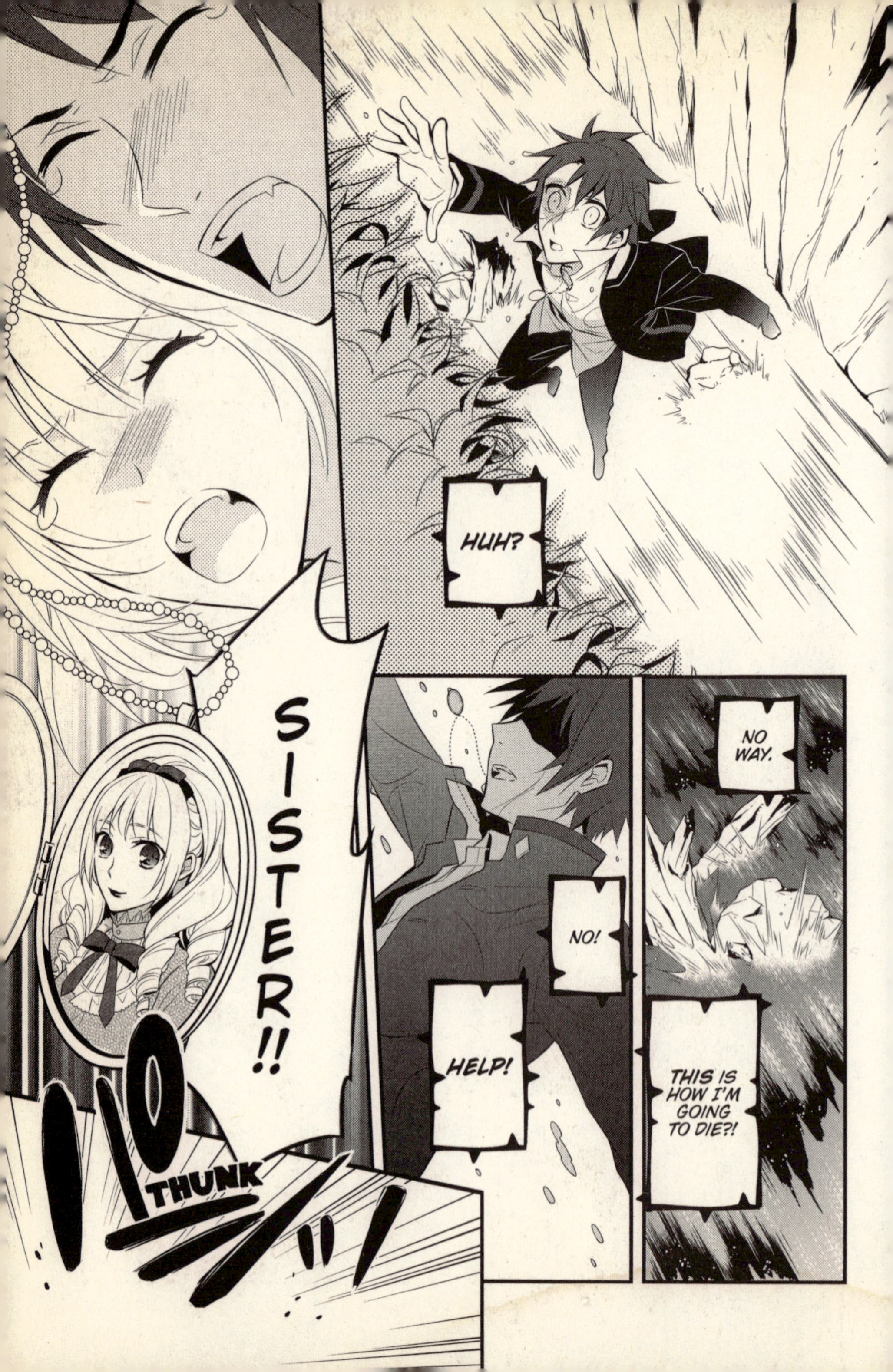
HUH?
NO WAY.
THIS IS HOW I'M GOING TO DIE?!
NO!
HELP!
SISTER!!
THUNK

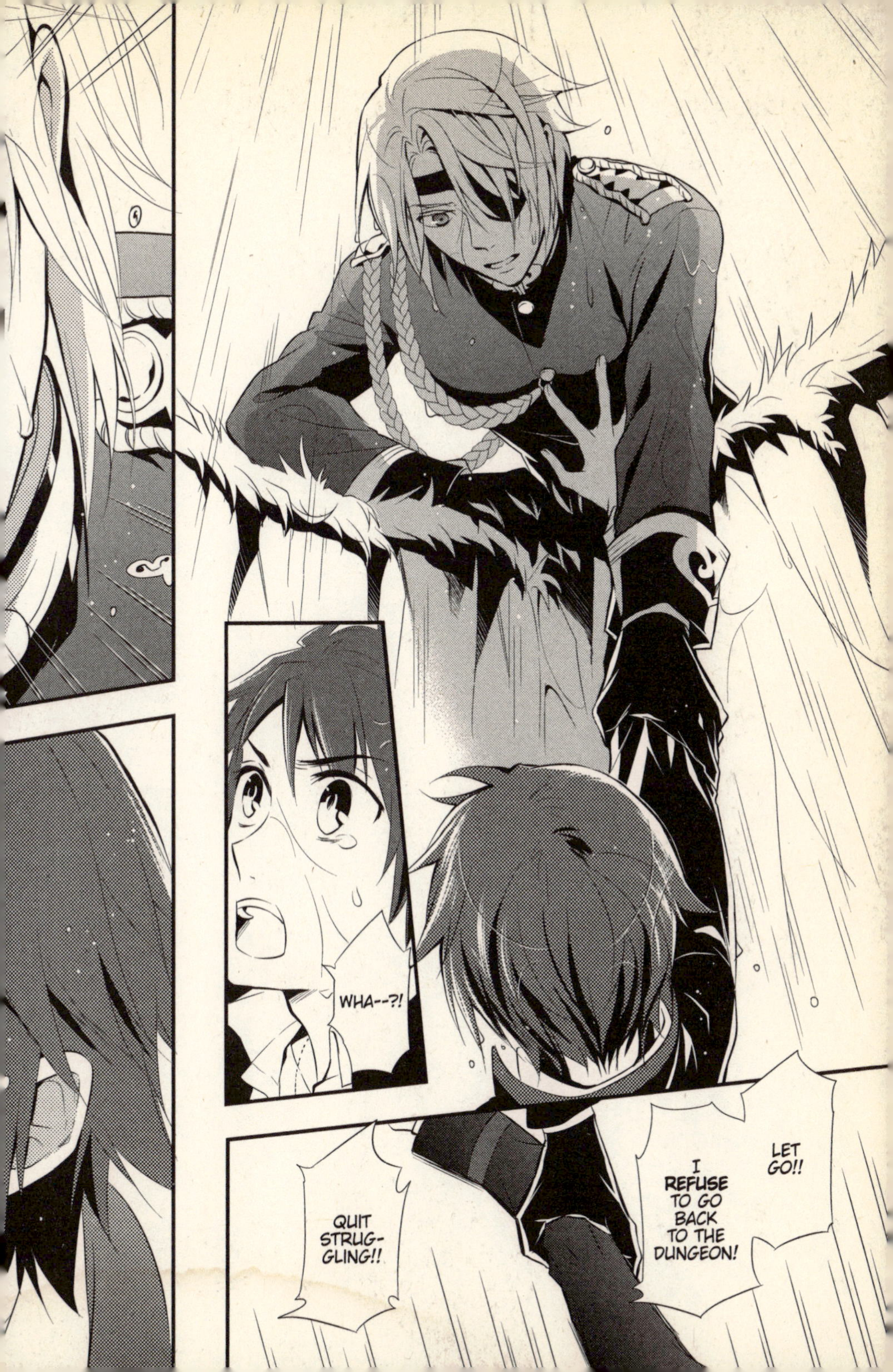
WHA--?!
LET GO!!
I REFUSE TO GO BACK TO THE DUNGEON!
QUIT STRUG-GLING!!

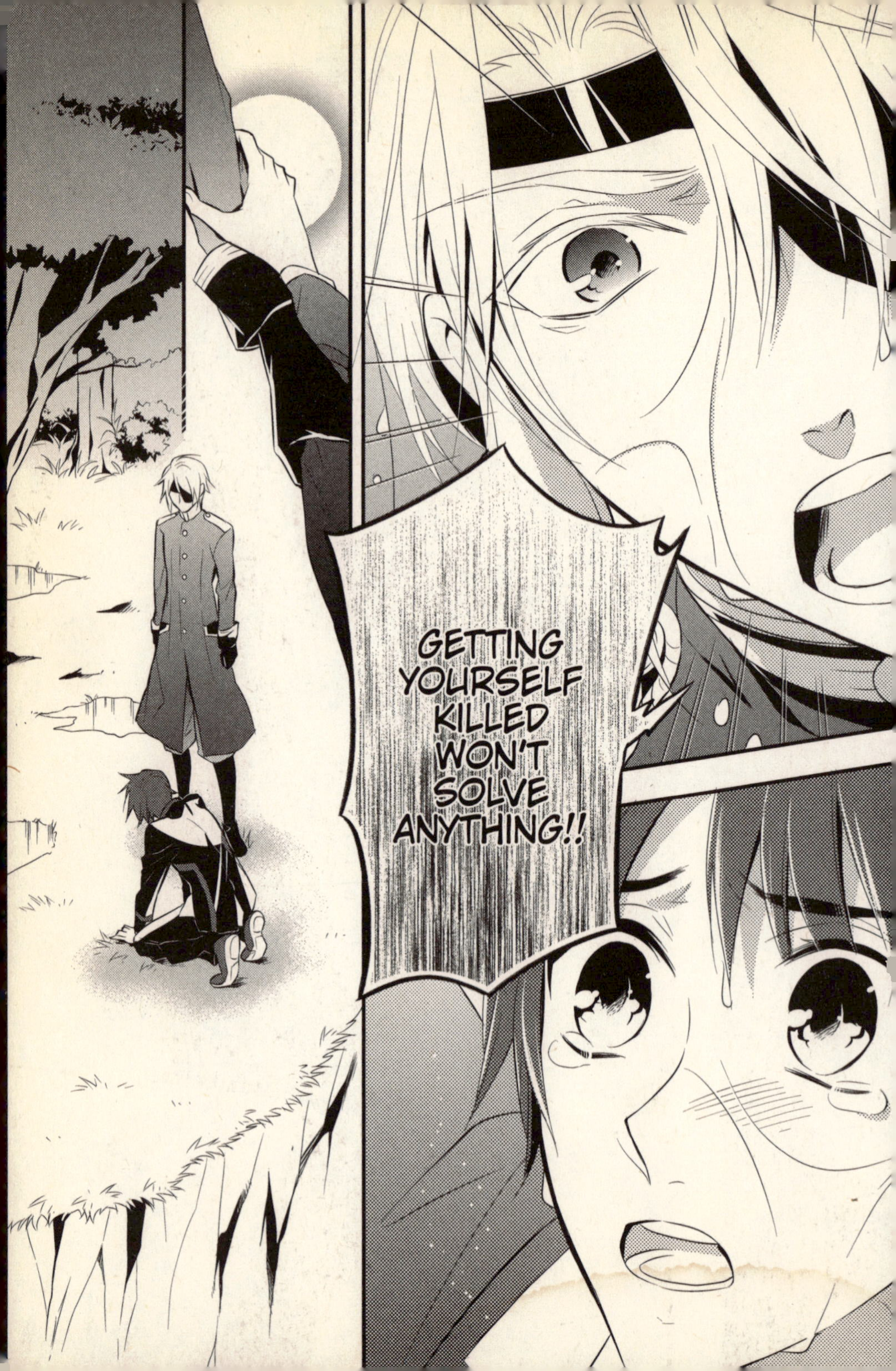
GETTING YOURSELF KILLED WON'T SOLVE ANYTHING!!

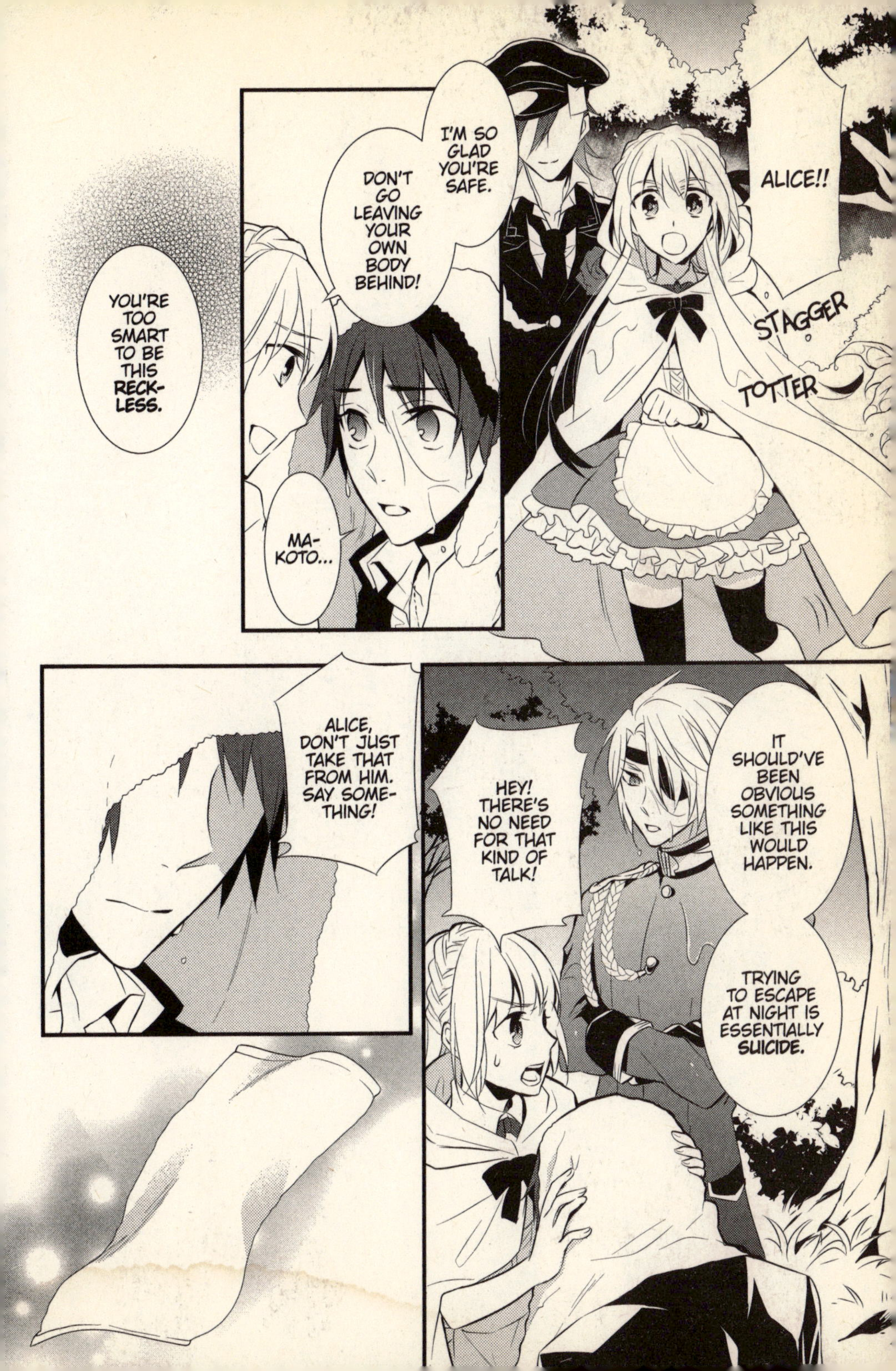

ALICE!!
STAGGER
TOTTER
I'M SO GLAD YOU'RE SAFE.
DON'T GO LEAVING YOUR OWN BODY BEHIND!
MA-KOTO...
YOU'RE TOO SMART TO BE THIS RECK-LESS.
IT SHOULD'VE BEEN OBVIOUS SOMETHING LIKE THIS WOULD HAPPEN.
TRYING TO ESCAPE AT NIGHT IS ESSENTIALLY SUICIDE.
HEY! THERE'S NO NEED FOR THAT KIND OF TALK!
ALICE, DON'T JUST TAKE THAT FROM HIM. SAY SOME-THING!

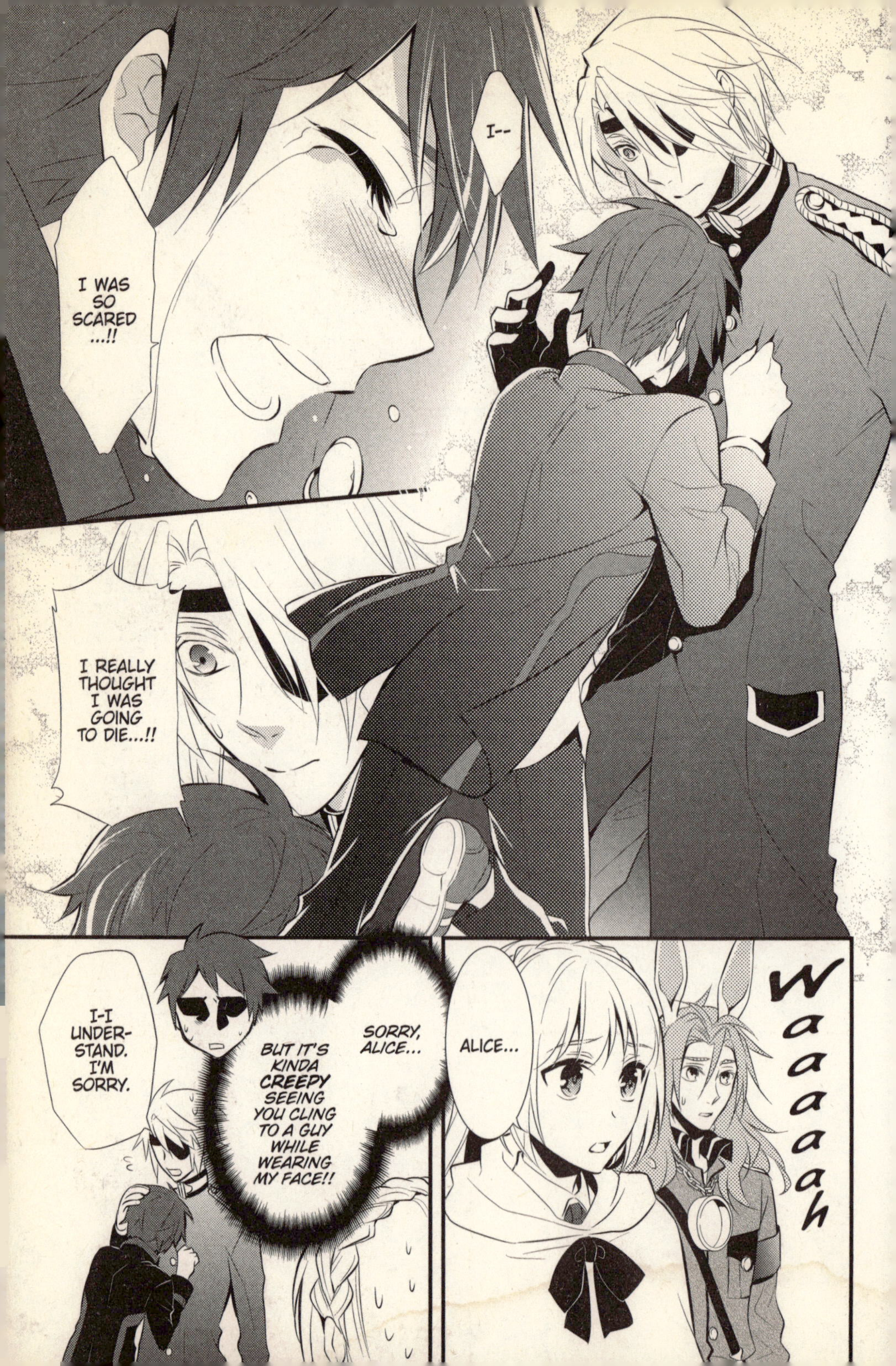
I--
I WAS SO SCARED ...!!
I REALLY THOUGHT I WAS GOING TO DIE...!!
Waaaaah
ALICE...
SORRY, ALICE...
BUT IT'S KINDA CREEPY SEEING YOU CLING TO A GUY WHILE WEARING MY FACE!!
I-I UNDER-STAND. I'M SORRY.

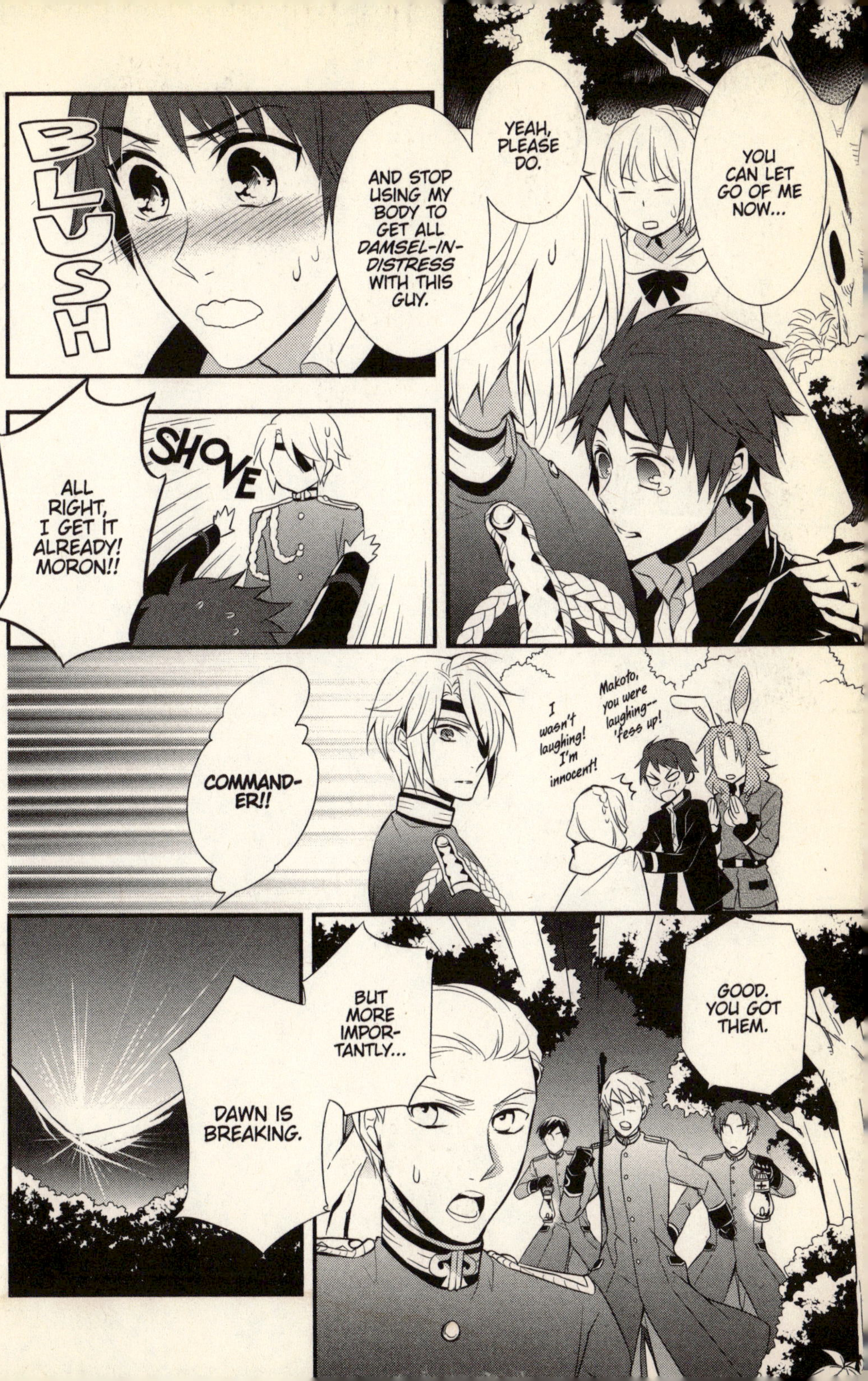
YOU CAN LET GO OF ME NOW...
YEAH, PLEASE DO.
AND STOP USING MY BODY TO GET ALL DAMSEL-IN-DISTRESS WITH THIS GUY.
BLUSH
SHOVE
ALL RIGHT, I GET IT ALREADY! MORON!!
Makoto, you were laughing-- 'fess up!
I wasn't laughing! I'm innocent!
COMMANDER!!
GOOD. YOU GOT THEM.
BUT MORE IMPORTANTLY...
DAWN IS BREAKING.

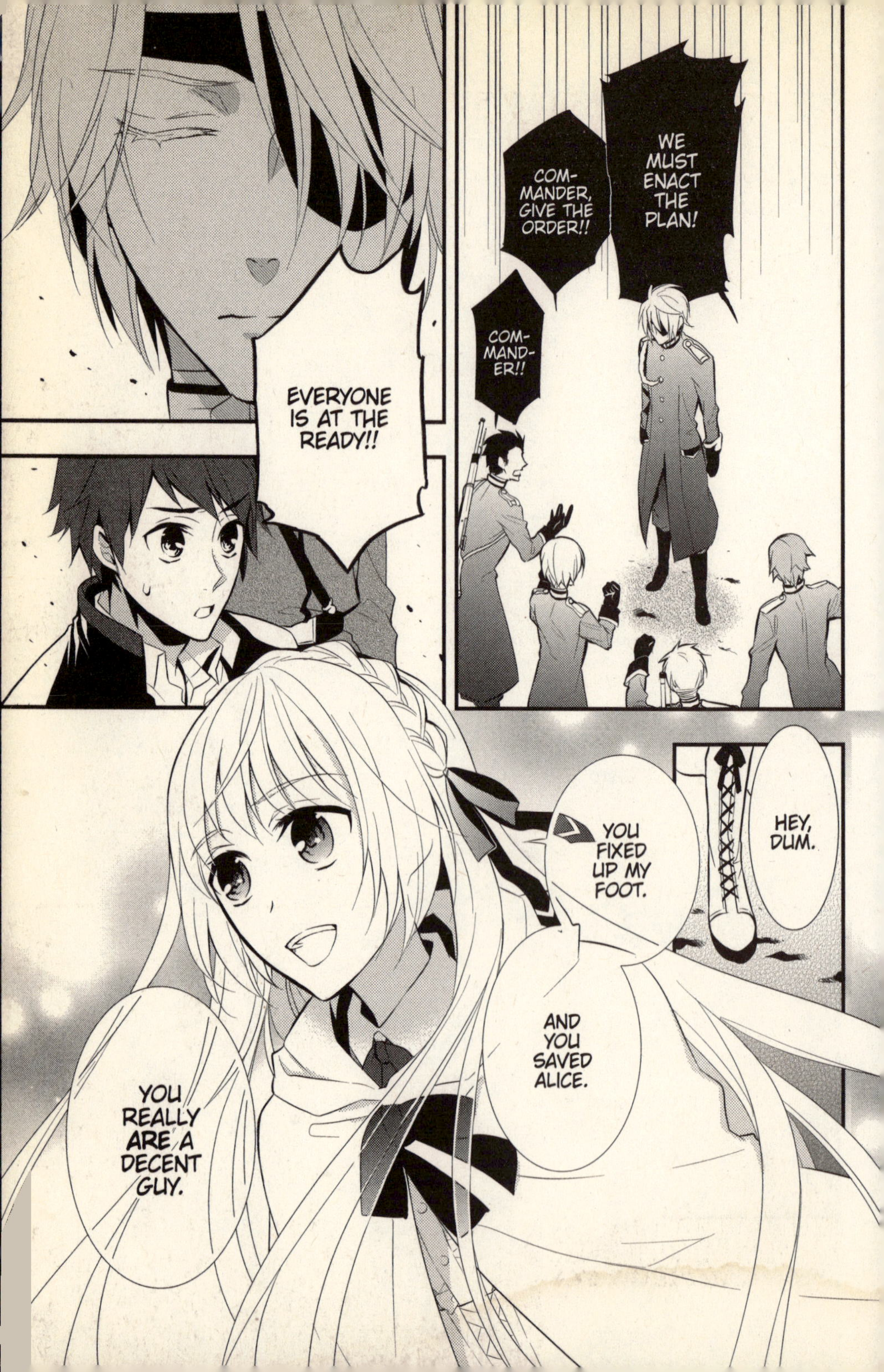
WE MUST ENACT THE PLAN!
COM-MANDER, GIVE THE ORDER!!
COM-MAND-ER!!
EVERYONE IS AT THE READY!!
HEY, DUM.
YOU FIXED UP MY FOOT.
AND YOU SAVED ALICE.
YOU REALLY ARE A DECENT GUY.

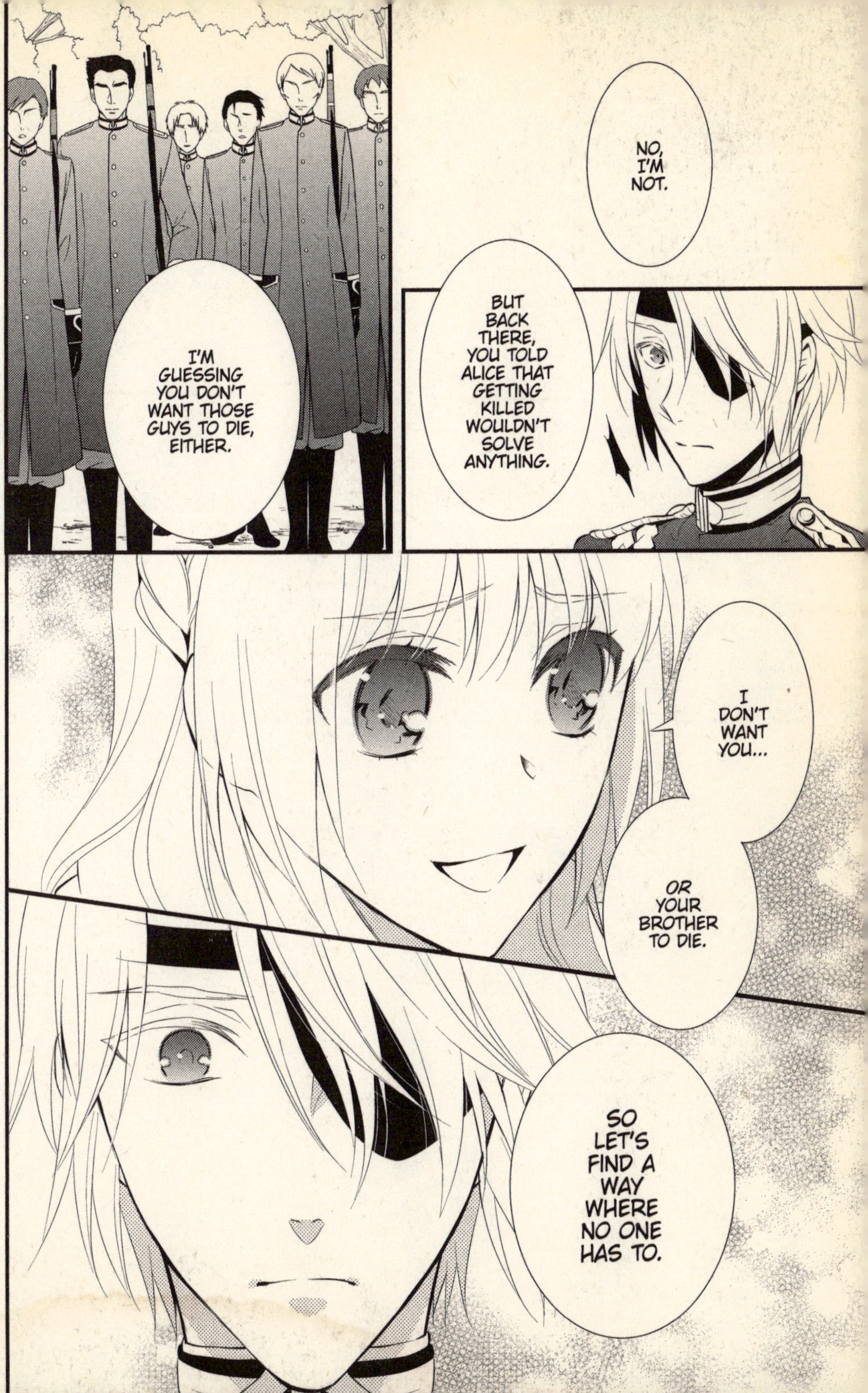
NO, I'M NOT.
BUT BACK THERE, YOU TOLD ALICE THAT GETTING KILLED WOULDN'T SOLVE ANYTHING.
I'M GUESSING YOU DON'T WANT THOSE GUYS TO DIE, EITHER.
I DON'T WANT YOU...
OR YOUR BROTHER TO DIE.
SO LET'S FIND A WAY WHERE NO ONE HAS TO.

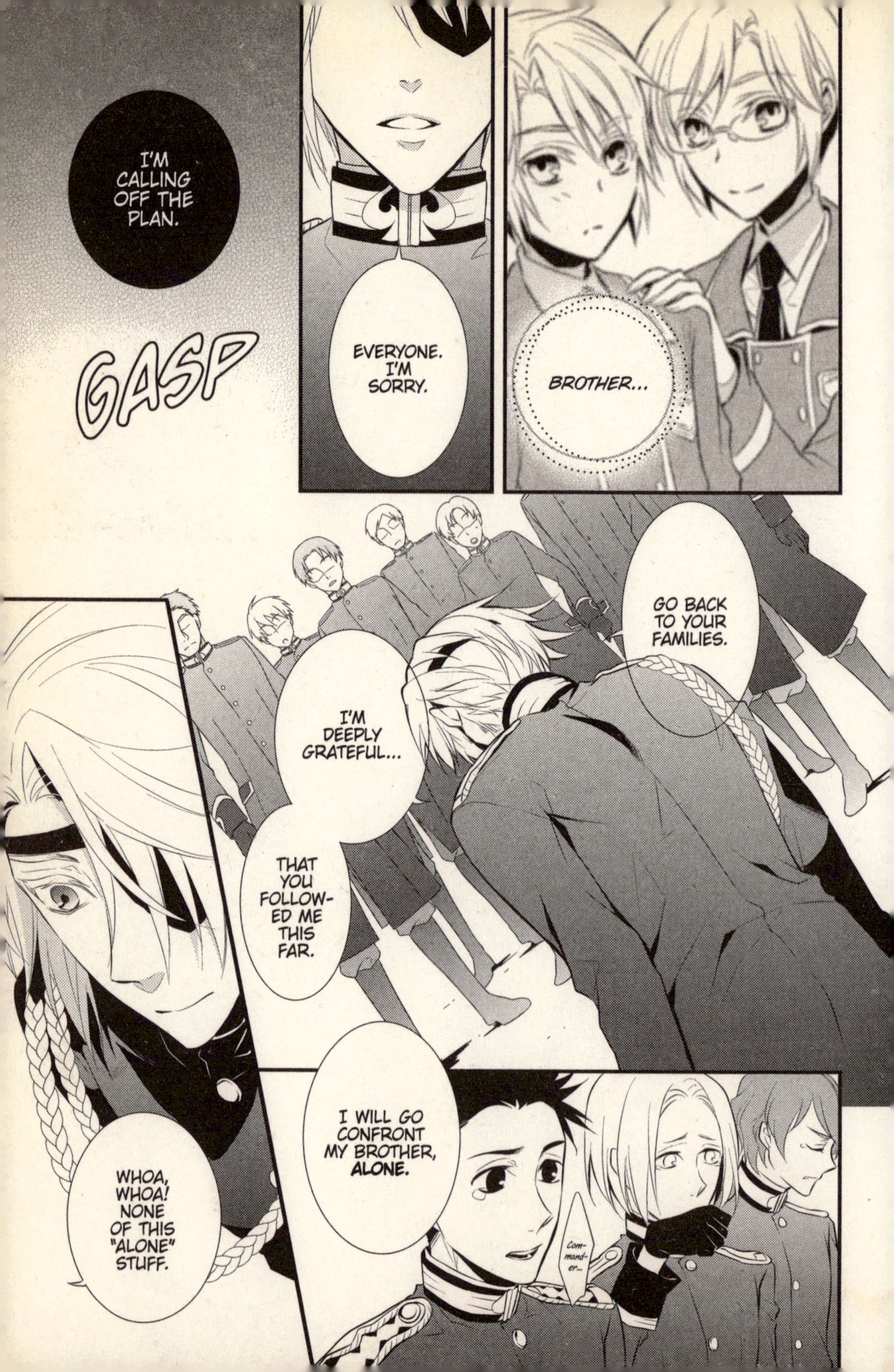
BROTHER...
EVERYONE. I'M SORRY.
I'M CALLING OFF THE PLAN.
GASP
GO BACK TO YOUR FAMILIES.
I'M DEEPLY GRATEFUL...
THAT YOU FOLLOWED ME THIS FAR.
I WILL GO CONFRONT MY BROTHER, **ALONE.**
Commander...
WHOA, WHOA! NONE OF THIS "ALONE" STUFF.

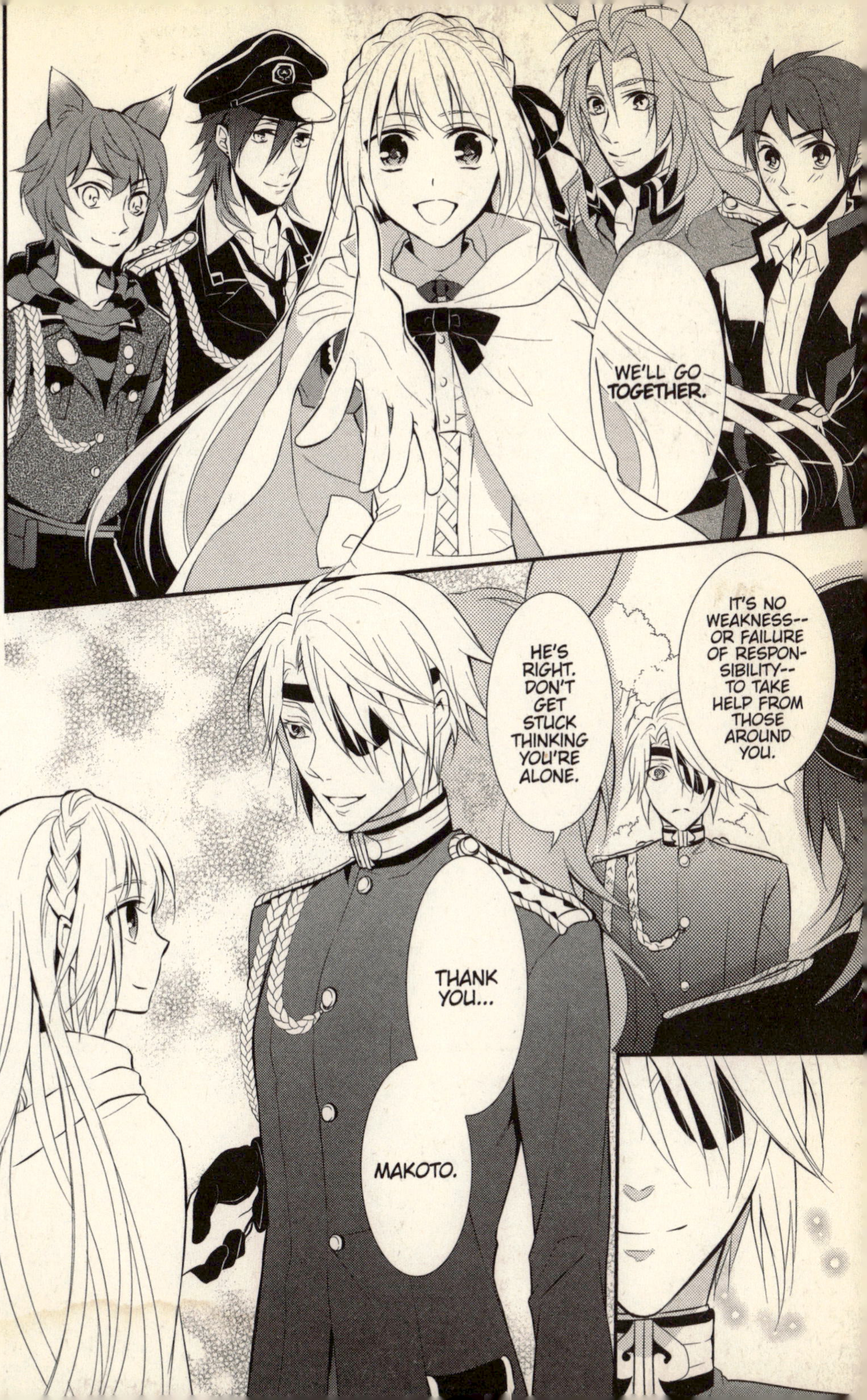
WE'LL GO TOGETHER.
IT'S NO WEAKNESS--OR FAILURE OF RESPONSIBILITY--TO TAKE HELP FROM THOSE AROUND YOU.
HE'S RIGHT. DON'T GET STUCK THINKING YOU'RE ALONE.
THANK YOU...
MAKOTO.

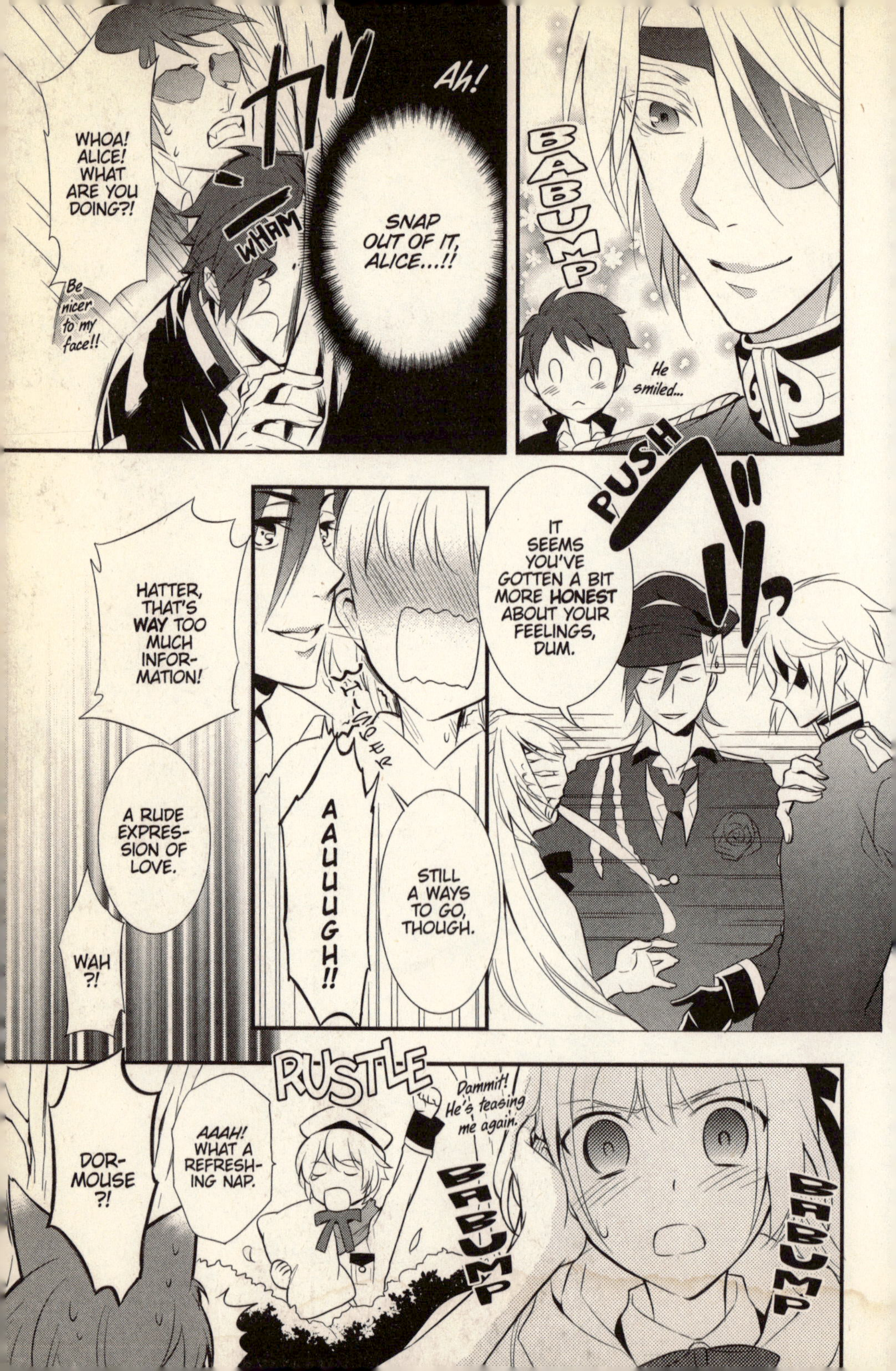
BABUMP
He smiled...
Ah!
SNAP OUT OF IT, ALICE...!!
WHAM
WHOA! ALICE! WHAT ARE YOU DOING?!
Be nicer to my face!!
PUSH
IT SEEMS YOU'VE GOTTEN A BIT MORE **HONEST** ABOUT YOUR FEELINGS, DUM.
STILL A WAYS TO GO, THOUGH.
AAUUUGH!!
HATTER, THAT'S **WAY** TOO MUCH INFORMATION!
A RUDE EXPRESSION OF LOVE.
WAH?!
BABUMP
Dammit! He's teasing me again.
BABUMP
RUSTLE
AAAH! WHAT A REFRESHING NAP.
DORMOUSE?!

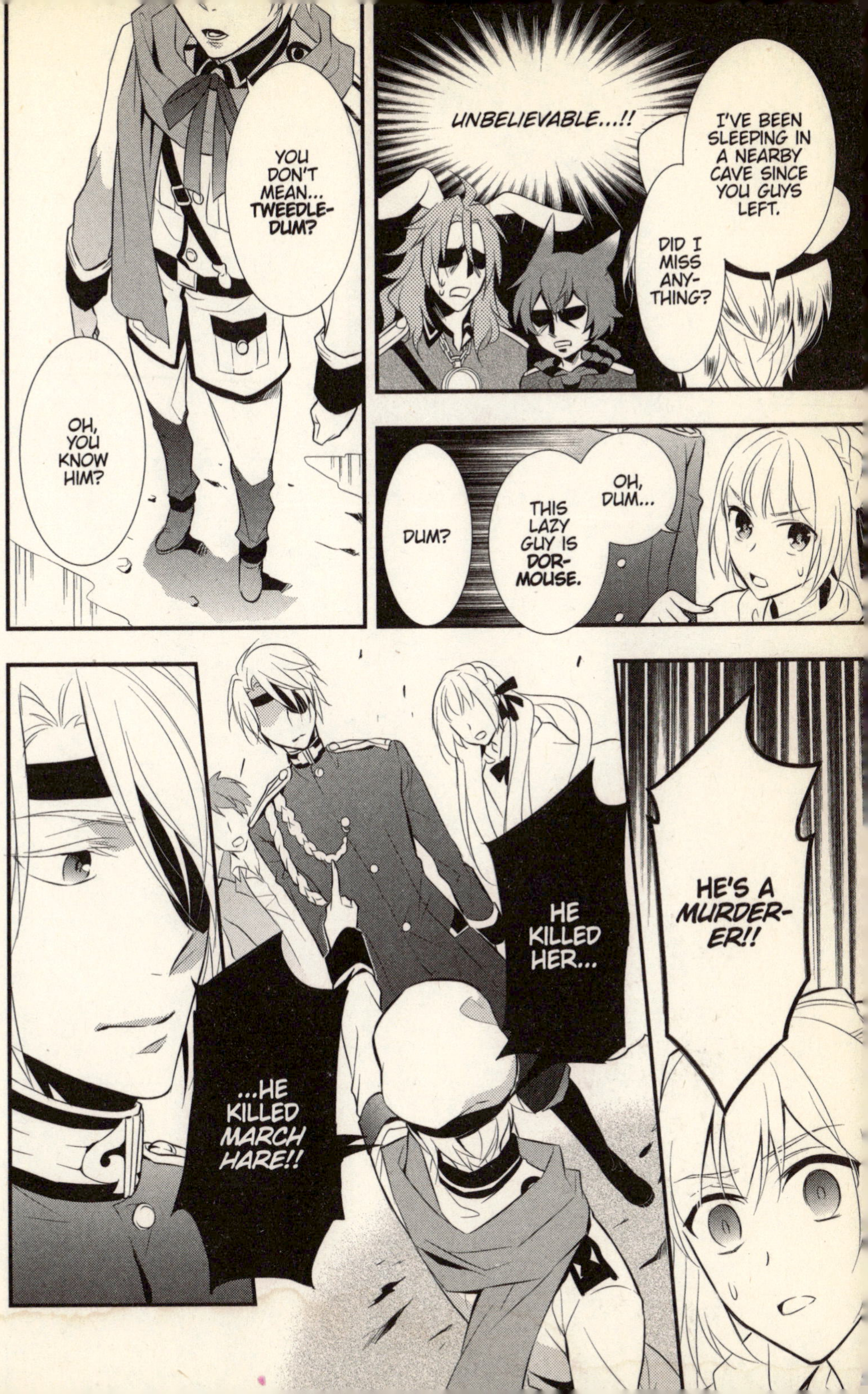

I'VE BEEN SLEEPING IN A NEARBY CAVE SINCE YOU GUYS LEFT.
DID I MISS ANYTHING?
UNBELIEVABLE...!!
OH, DUM...
THIS LAZY GUY IS DORMOUSE.
DUM?
YOU DON'T MEAN... TWEEDLE-DUM?
OH, YOU KNOW HIM?
HE'S A MURDERER!!
HE KILLED HER...
...HE KILLED MARCH HARE!!

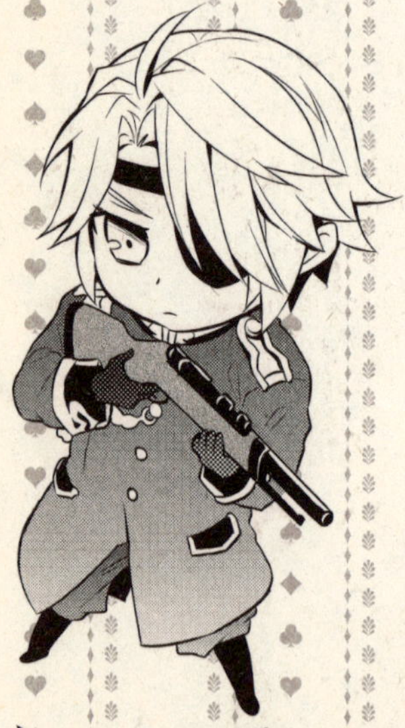
I AM ALICE

I AM ALICE

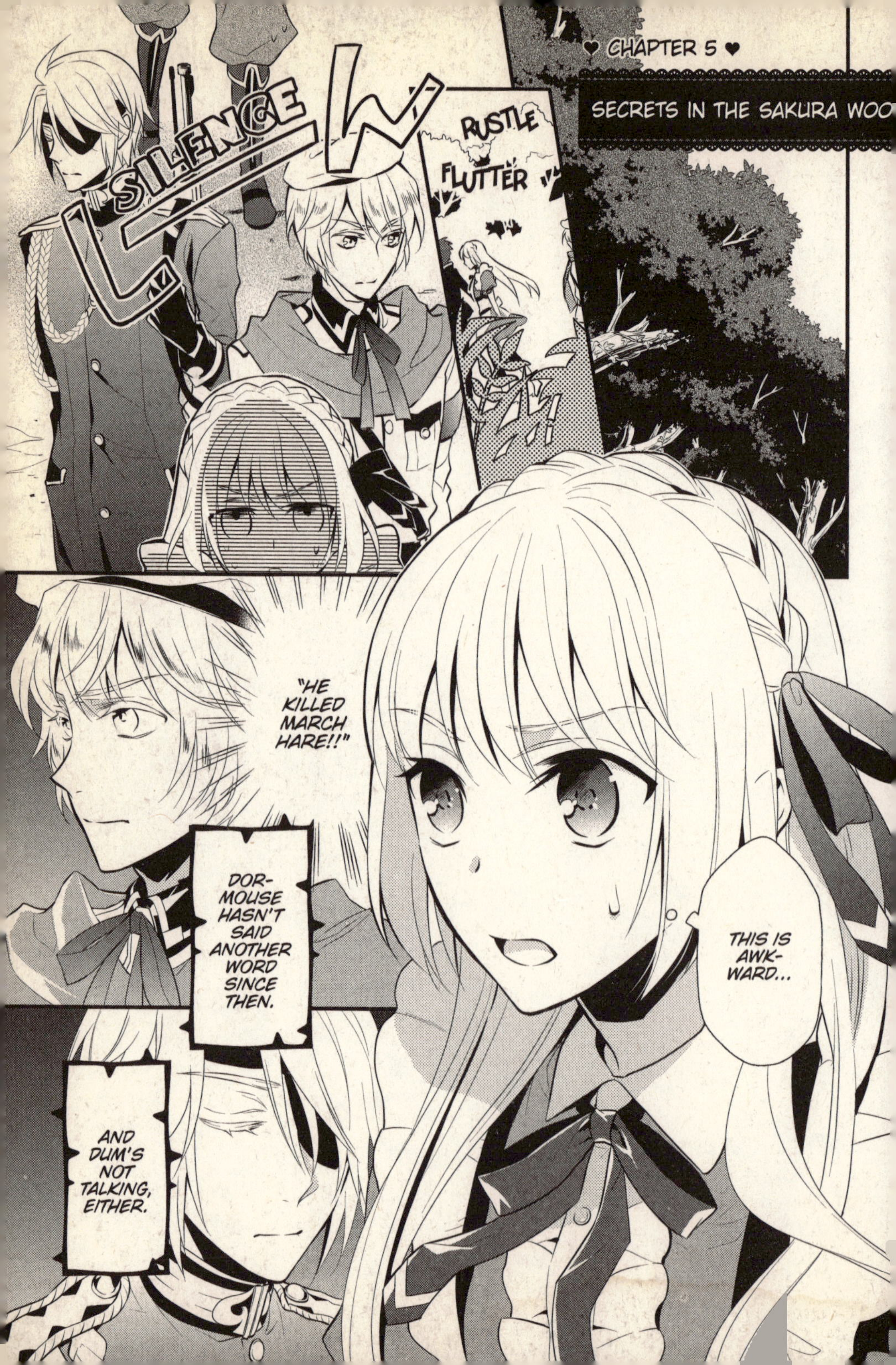
♥ CHAPTER 5 ♥
SECRETS IN THE SAKURA WOO
RUSTLE
FLUTTER
SILENCE
THIS IS AWK-WARD...
"HE KILLED MARCH HARE!!"
DOR-MOUSE HASN'T SAID ANOTHER WORD SINCE THEN.
AND DUM'S NOT TALKING, EITHER.

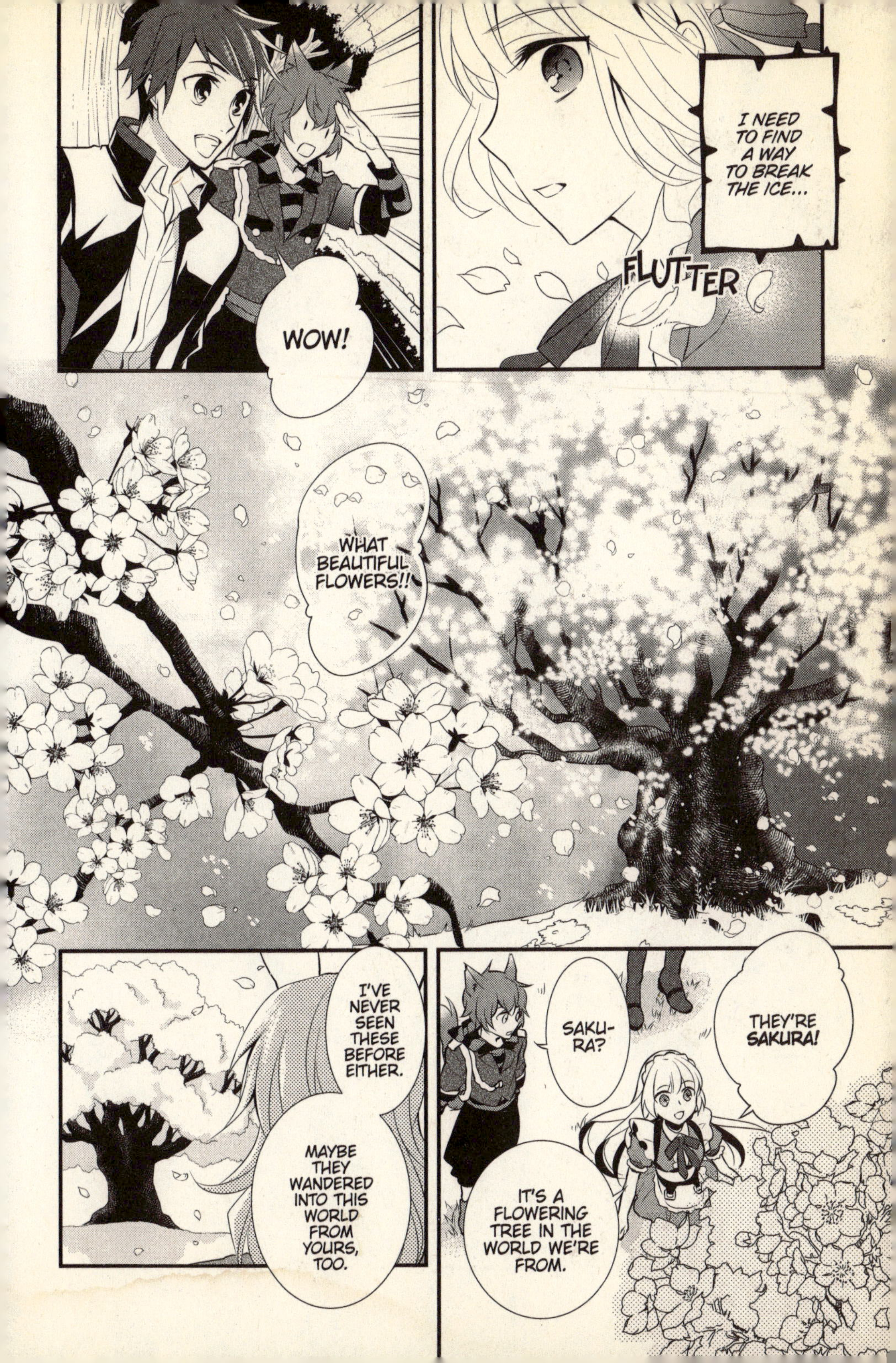
I NEED TO FIND A WAY TO BREAK THE ICE...
FLUTTER
WOW!
WHAT BEAUTIFUL FLOWERS!!
THEY'RE SAKURA!
SAKU-RA?
IT'S A FLOWERING TREE IN THE WORLD WE'RE FROM.
I'VE NEVER SEEN THESE BEFORE EITHER.
MAYBE THEY WANDERED INTO THIS WORLD FROM YOURS, TOO.

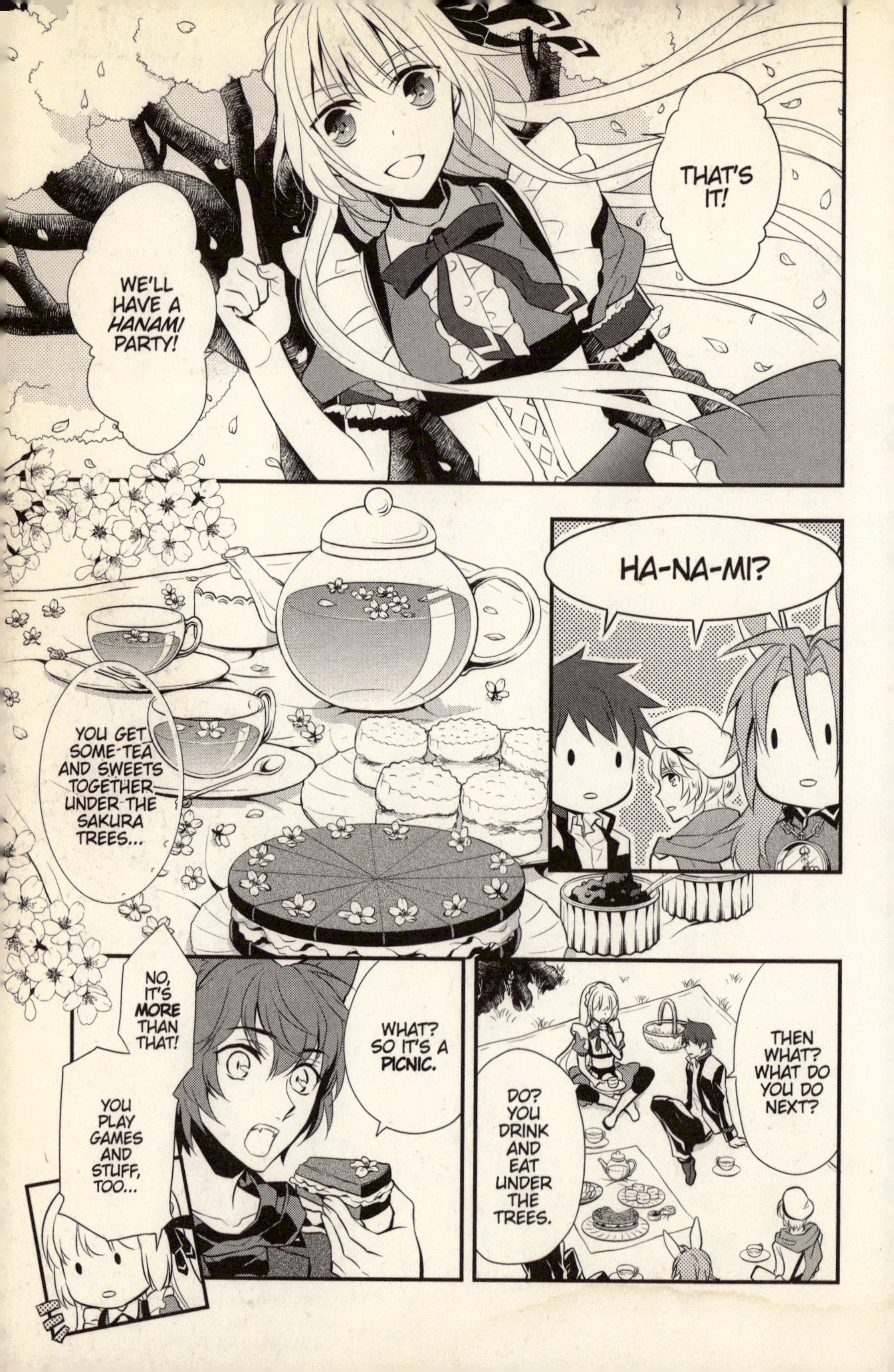
THAT'S IT!
WE'LL HAVE A *HANAMI* PARTY!
HA-NA-MI?
YOU GET SOME TEA AND SWEETS TOGETHER UNDER THE SAKURA TREES...
THEN WHAT? WHAT DO YOU DO NEXT?
DO? YOU DRINK AND EAT UNDER THE TREES.
WHAT? SO IT'S A **PICNIC.**
NO, IT'S **MORE** THAN THAT!
YOU PLAY GAMES AND STUFF, TOO...

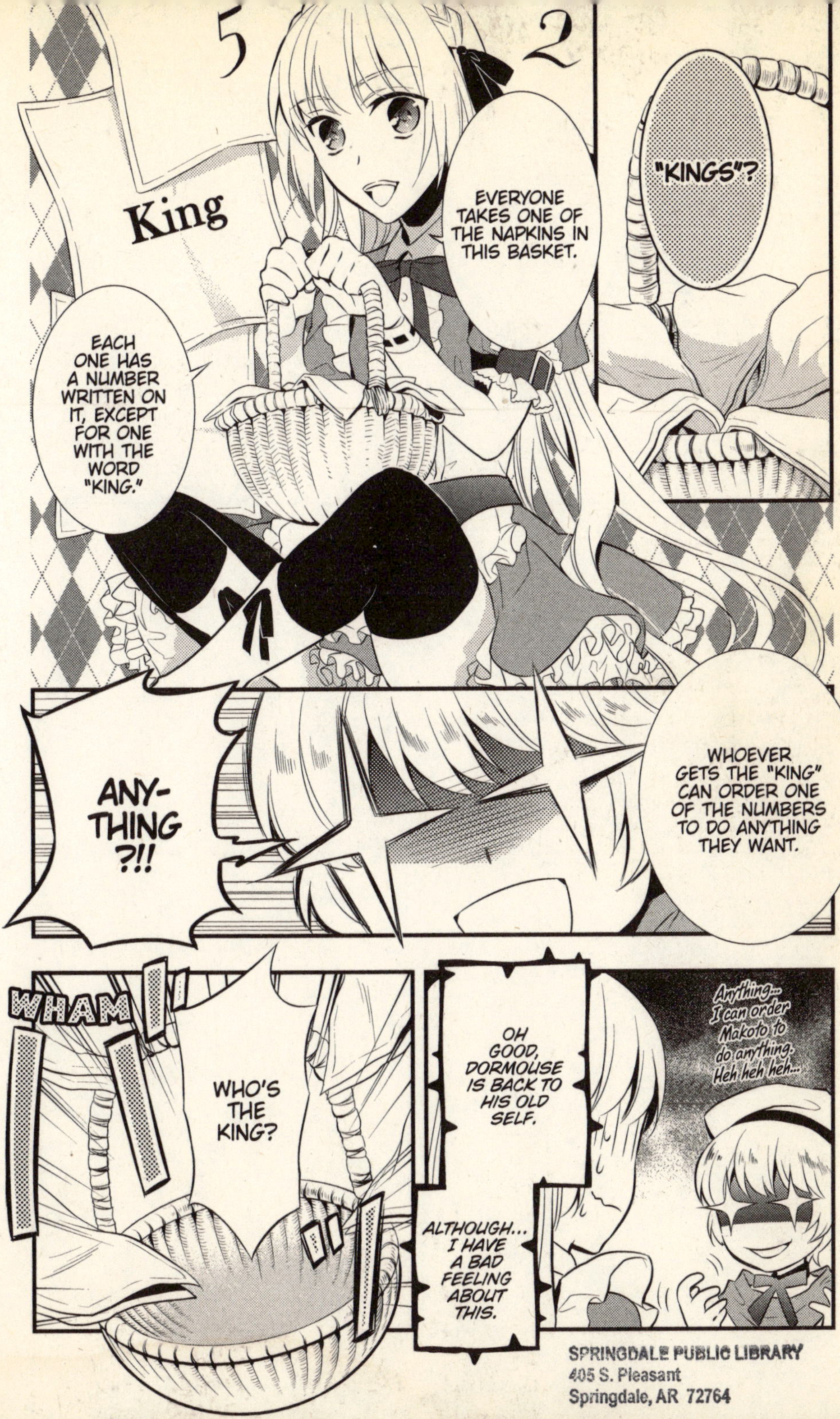
"KINGS"?
5
2
King
EVERYONE TAKES ONE OF THE NAPKINS IN THIS BASKET.
EACH ONE HAS A NUMBER WRITTEN ON IT, EXCEPT FOR ONE WITH THE WORD "KING."
WHOEVER GETS THE "KING" CAN ORDER ONE OF THE NUMBERS TO DO ANYTHING THEY WANT.
ANY-THING ?!!
Anything... I can order Makoto to do anything. Heh heh heh...
OH GOOD, DORMOUSE IS BACK TO HIS OLD SELF.
ALTHOUGH... I HAVE A BAD FEELING ABOUT THIS.
WHAM
WHO'S THE KING?

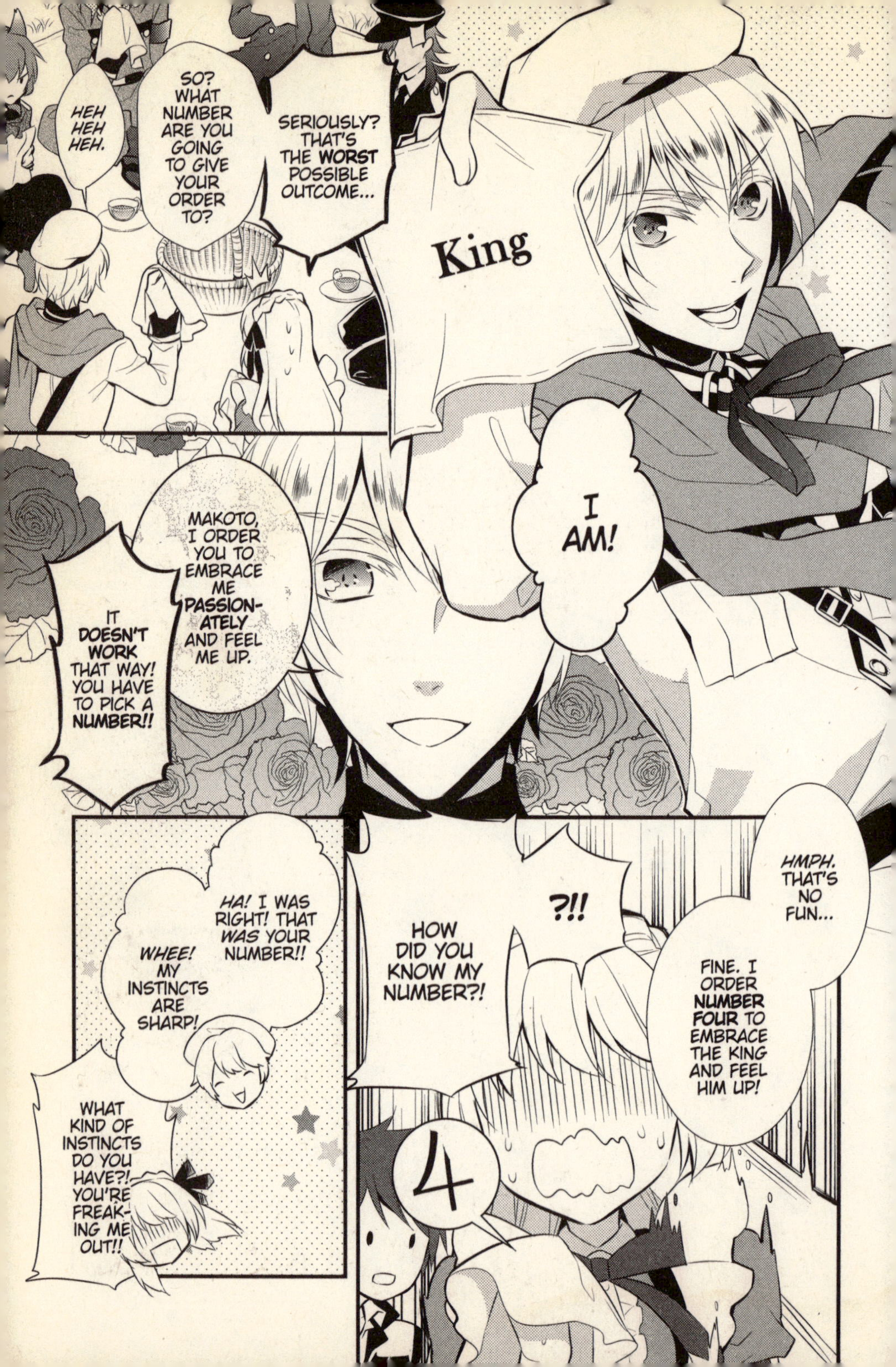
King
I AM!
SERIOUSLY? THAT'S THE **WORST** POSSIBLE OUTCOME...
SO? WHAT NUMBER ARE YOU GOING TO GIVE YOUR ORDER TO?
HEH HEH HEH.
MAKOTO, I ORDER YOU TO EMBRACE ME **PASSION-ATELY** AND FEEL ME UP.
IT **DOESN'T WORK** THAT WAY! YOU HAVE TO PICK A **NUMBER!!**
HMPH. THAT'S NO FUN...
FINE. I ORDER **NUMBER FOUR** TO EMBRACE THE KING AND FEEL HIM UP!
?!!
HOW DID YOU KNOW MY NUMBER?!
4
HA! I WAS RIGHT! THAT *WAS* YOUR NUMBER!!
WHEE! MY INSTINCTS ARE SHARP!
WHAT KIND OF INSTINCTS DO YOU HAVE?! YOU'RE FREAK-ING ME OUT!!

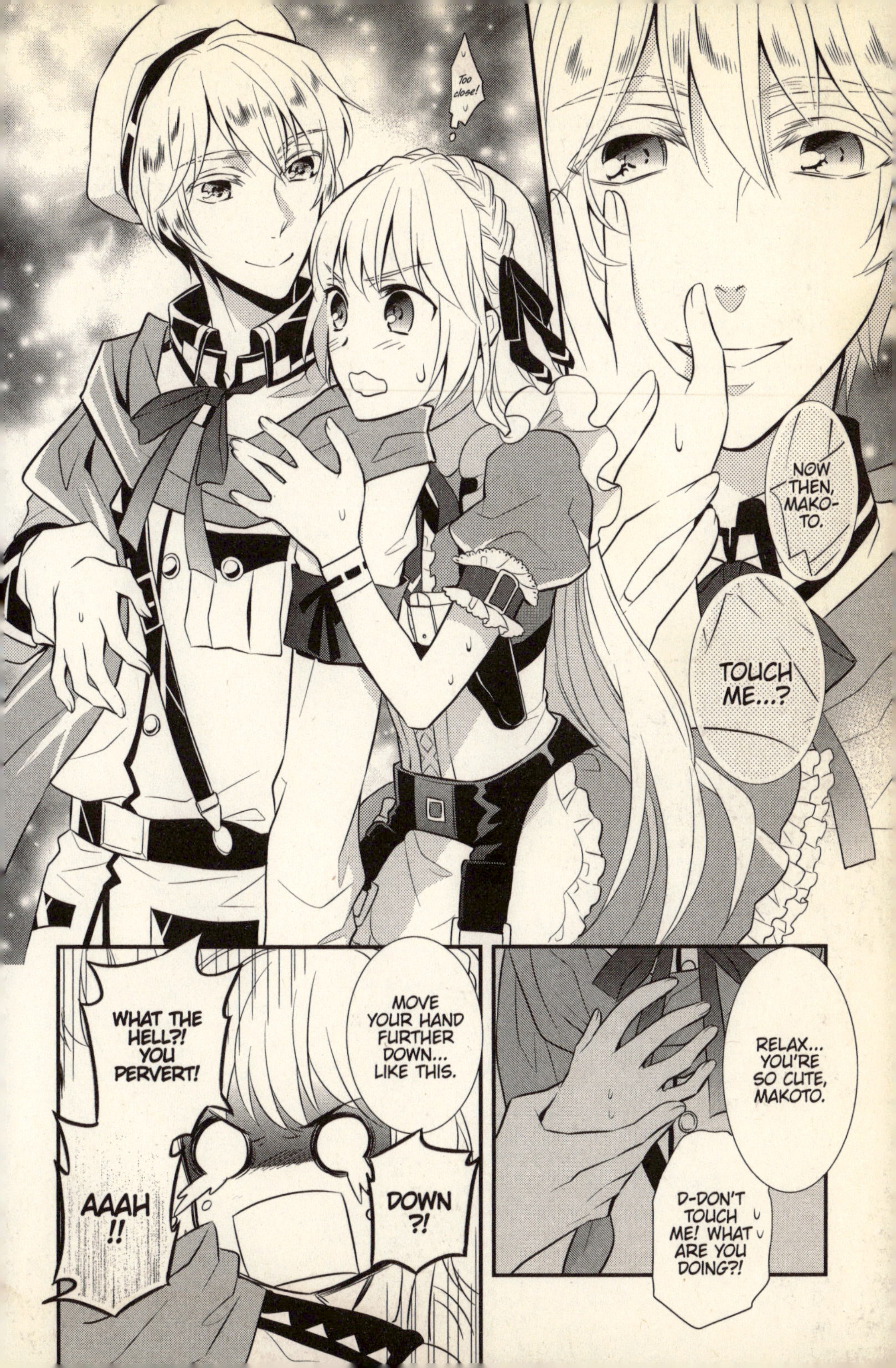
NOW THEN, MAKO-TO.
TOUCH ME...?
Too close!
RELAX... YOU'RE SO CUTE, MAKOTO.
D-DON'T TOUCH ME! WHAT ARE YOU DOING?!
MOVE YOUR HAND FURTHER DOWN... LIKE THIS.
DOWN ?!
WHAT THE HELL?! YOU PERVERT!
AAAH !!

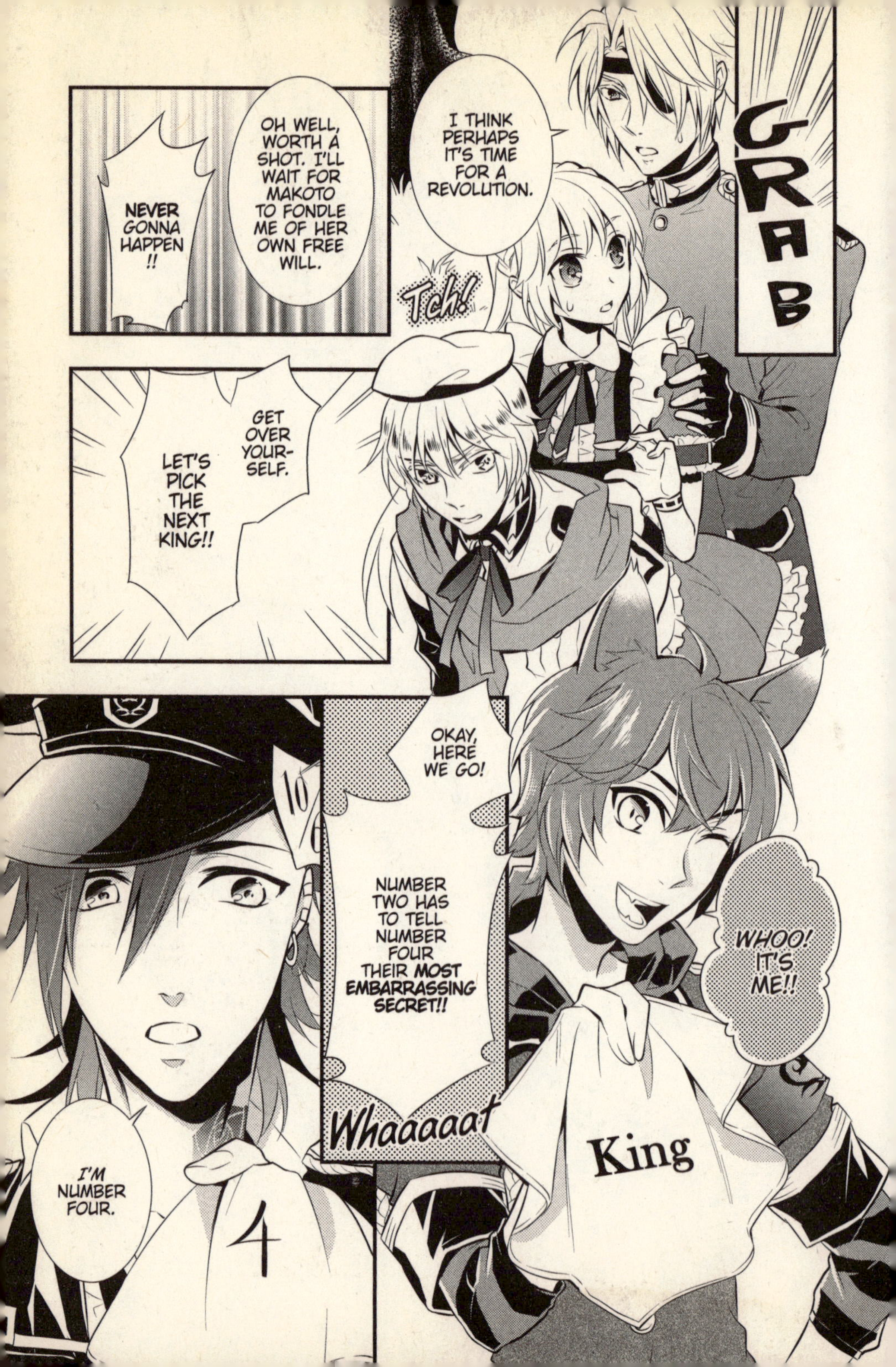

GRAB
I THINK PERHAPS IT'S TIME FOR A REVOLUTION.
Tch!
OH WELL, WORTH A SHOT. I'LL WAIT FOR MAKOTO TO FONDLE ME OF HER OWN FREE WILL.
NEVER GONNA HAPPEN !!
GET OVER YOUR-SELF.
LET'S PICK THE NEXT KING!!
WHOO! IT'S ME!!
King
OKAY, HERE WE GO!
NUMBER TWO HAS TO TELL NUMBER FOUR THEIR MOST EMBARRASSING SECRET!!
Whaaaaat
I'M NUMBER FOUR.
4

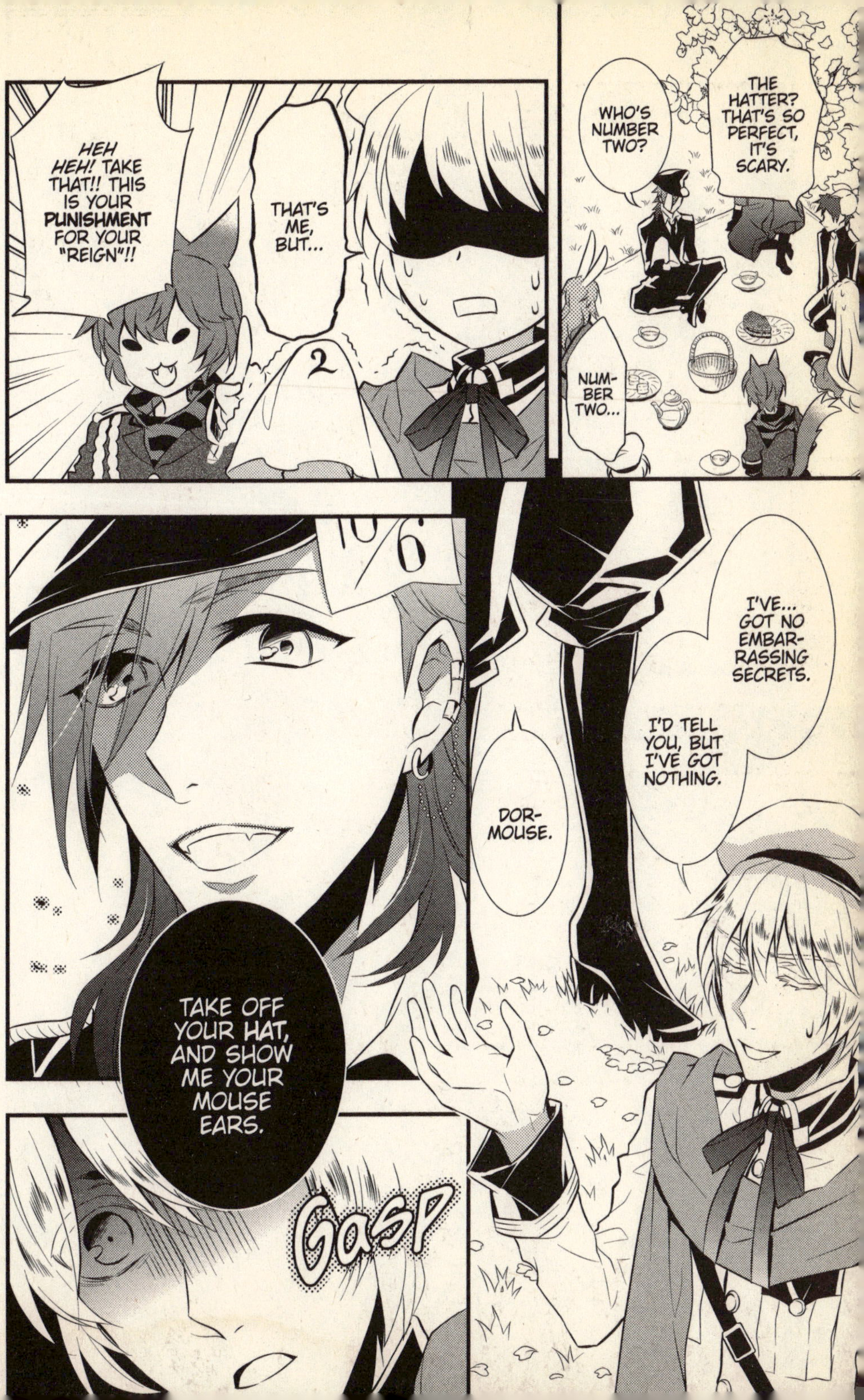
THE HATTER? THAT'S SO PERFECT, IT'S SCARY.
WHO'S NUMBER TWO?
NUM-BER TWO...
THAT'S ME, BUT...
HEH HEH! TAKE THAT!! THIS IS YOUR **PUNISHMENT** FOR YOUR "REIGN"!!
2
I'VE... GOT NO EMBAR-RASSING SECRETS.
I'D TELL YOU, BUT I'VE GOT NOTHING.
DOR-MOUSE.
10/6
TAKE OFF YOUR HAT, AND SHOW ME YOUR MOUSE EARS.
Gasp

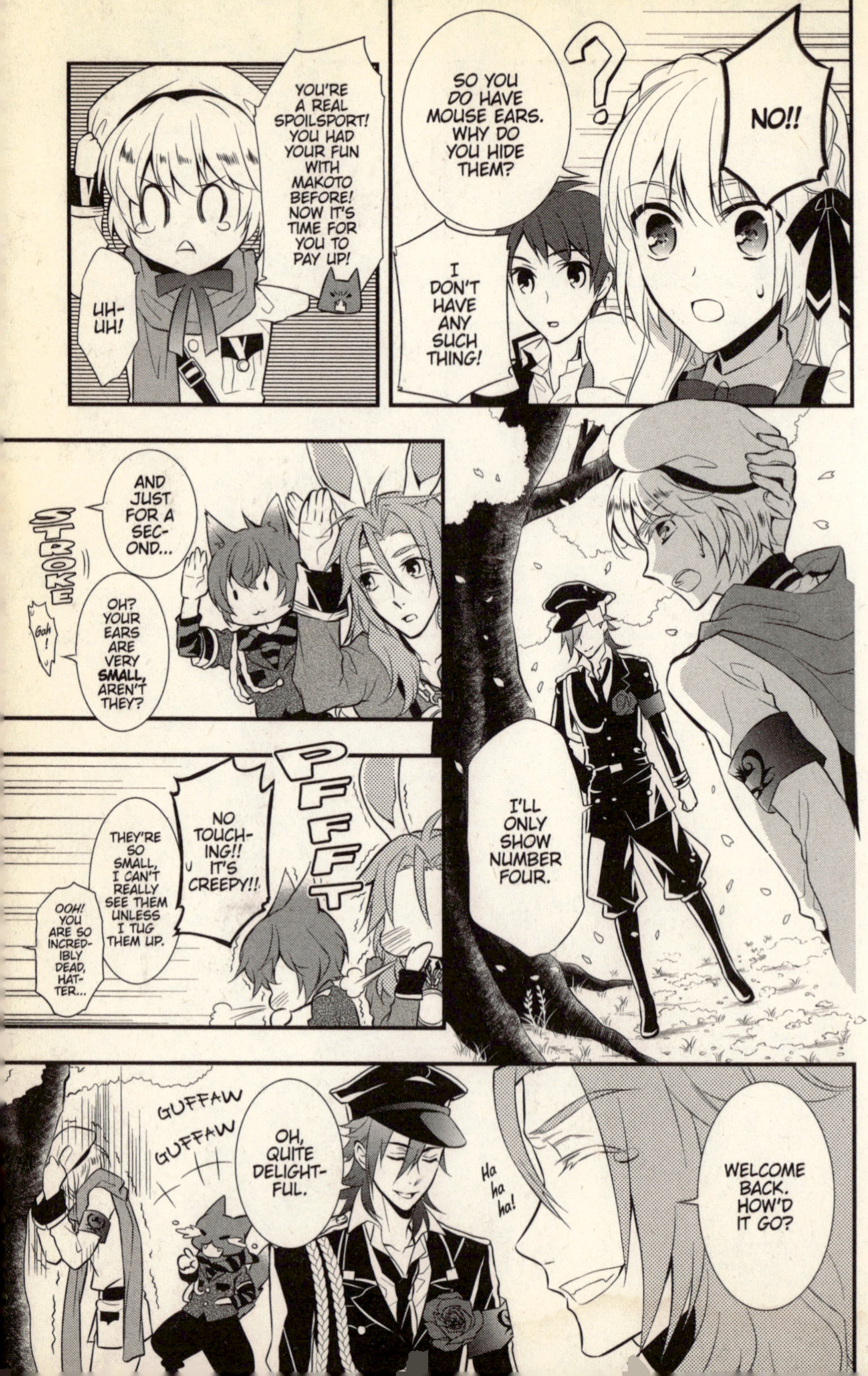
NO!!
SO YOU DO HAVE MOUSE EARS. WHY DO YOU HIDE THEM?
I DON'T HAVE ANY SUCH THING!
YOU'RE A REAL SPOILSPORT! YOU HAD YOUR FUN WITH MAKOTO BEFORE! NOW IT'S TIME FOR YOU TO PAY UP!
UH-UH!
I'LL ONLY SHOW NUMBER FOUR.
AND JUST FOR A SEC-OND...
STROKE
Gah!
OH? YOUR EARS ARE VERY SMALL, AREN'T THEY?
PFFFT
NO TOUCH-ING!! IT'S CREEPY!!
THEY'RE SO SMALL, I CAN'T REALLY SEE THEM UNLESS I TUG THEM UP.
OOH! YOU ARE SO INCRED-IBLY DEAD, HAT-TER...
WELCOME BACK. HOW'D IT GO?
Ha ha ha!
OH, QUITE DELIGHT-FUL.
GUFFAW
GUFFAW

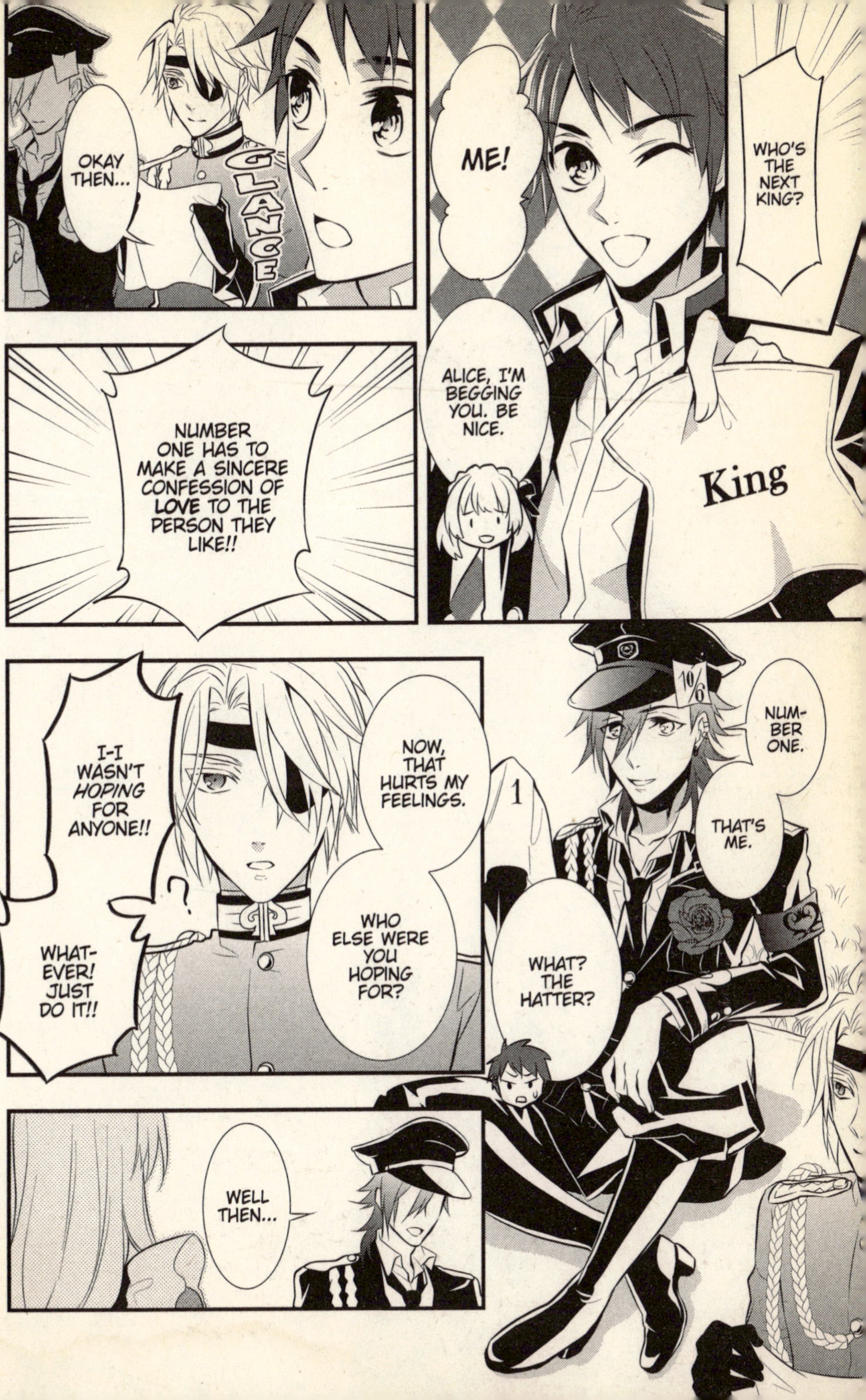

WHO'S THE NEXT KING?
ME!
ALICE, I'M BEGGING YOU. BE NICE.
King
OKAY THEN...
GLANCE
NUMBER ONE HAS TO MAKE A SINCERE CONFESSION OF **LOVE** TO THE PERSON THEY LIKE!!
10/6
NUM-BER ONE.
THAT'S ME.
1
WHAT? THE HATTER?
NOW, THAT HURTS MY FEELINGS.
WHO ELSE WERE YOU HOPING FOR?
I-I WASN'T *HOPING* FOR ANYONE!!
?
WHAT-EVER! JUST DO IT!!
WELL THEN...

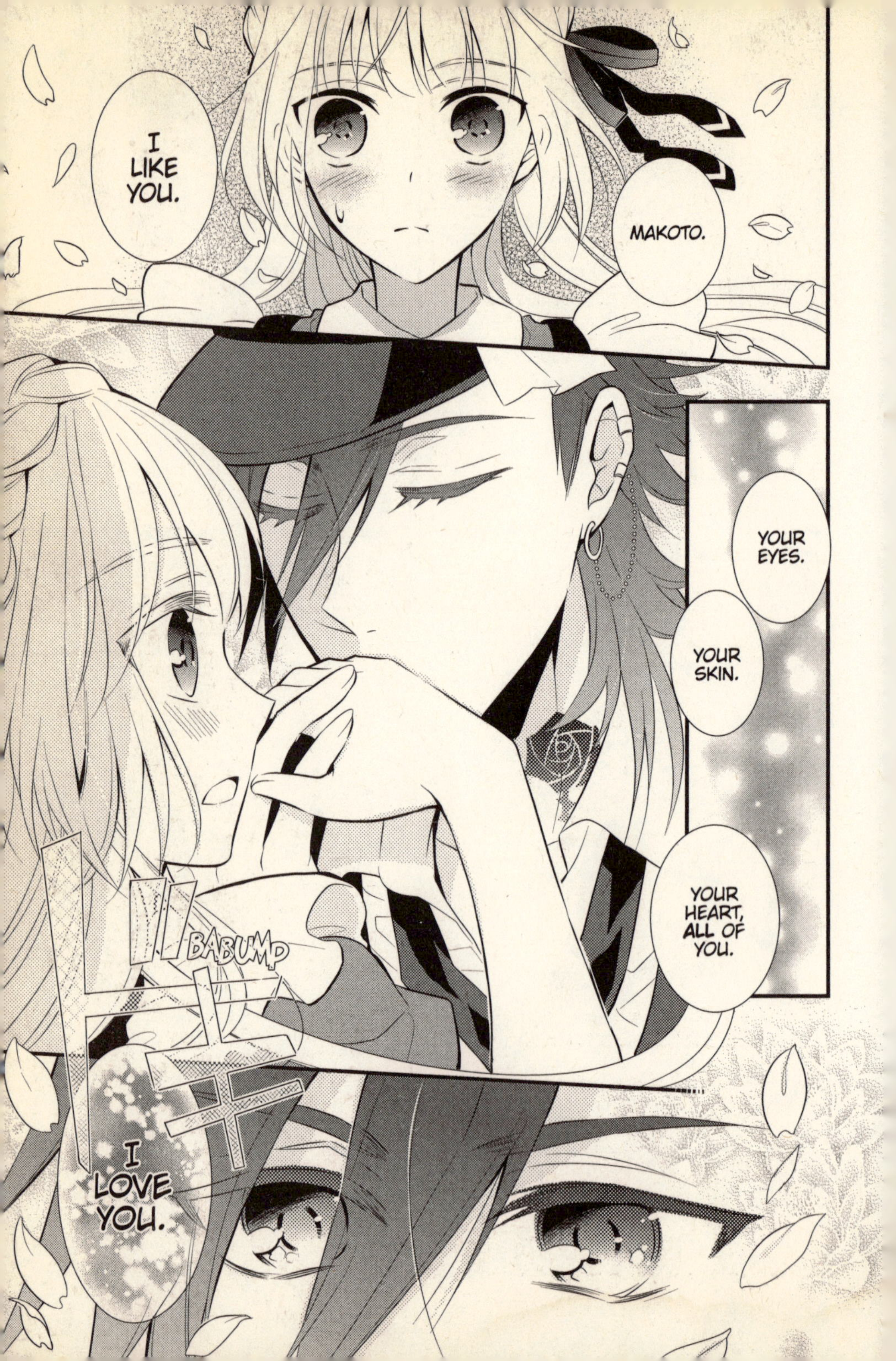
MAKOTO.
I LIKE YOU.
YOUR EYES.
YOUR SKIN.
YOUR HEART, ALL OF YOU.
BABUMP
I LOVE YOU.

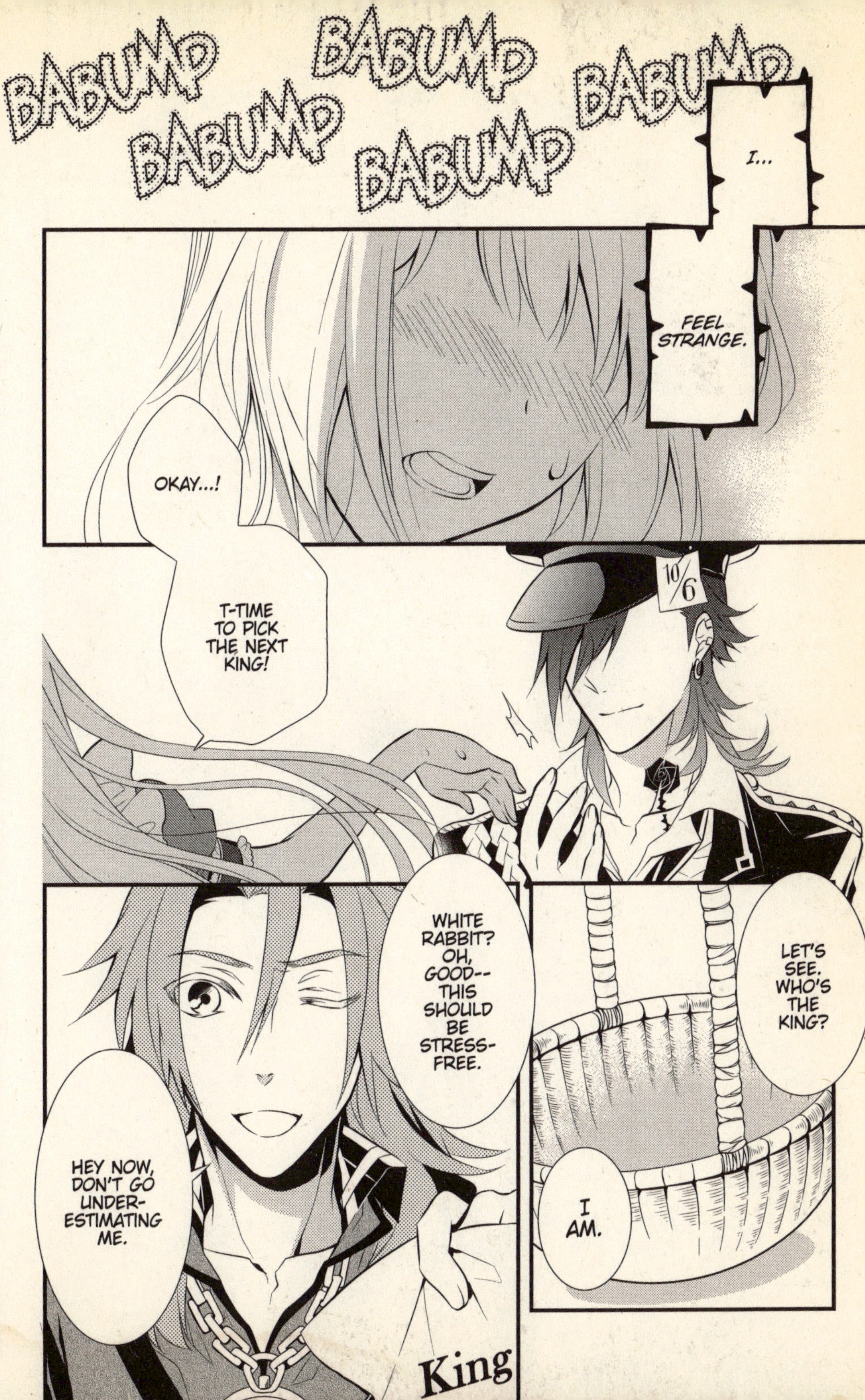
BABUMP
BABUMP
BABUMP
BABUMP
BABUMP
I...
FEEL STRANGE.
OKAY...!
10/6
T-TIME TO PICK THE NEXT KING!
LET'S SEE. WHO'S THE KING?
I AM.
WHITE RABBIT? OH, GOOD-- THIS SHOULD BE STRESS-FREE.
HEY NOW, DON'T GO UNDER-ESTIMATING ME.
King

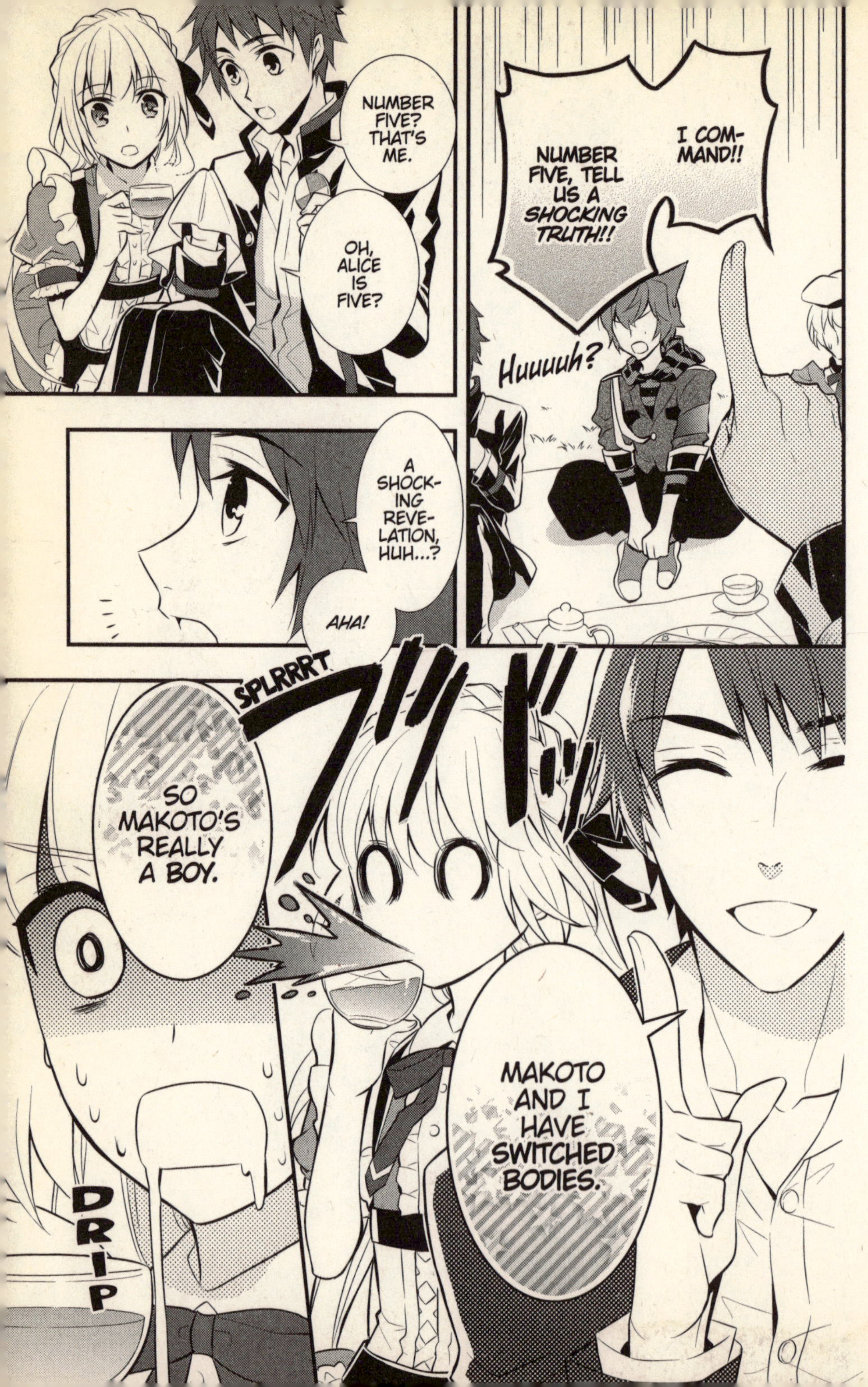
NUMBER FIVE, TELL US A SHOCKING TRUTH!!
I COMMAND!!
Huuuuh?
NUMBER FIVE? THAT'S ME.
OH, ALICE IS FIVE?
A SHOCKING REVELATION, HUH...?
AHA!
MAKOTO AND I HAVE SWITCHED BODIES.
SPLRRRT
SO MAKOTO'S REALLY A BOY.
DRIP

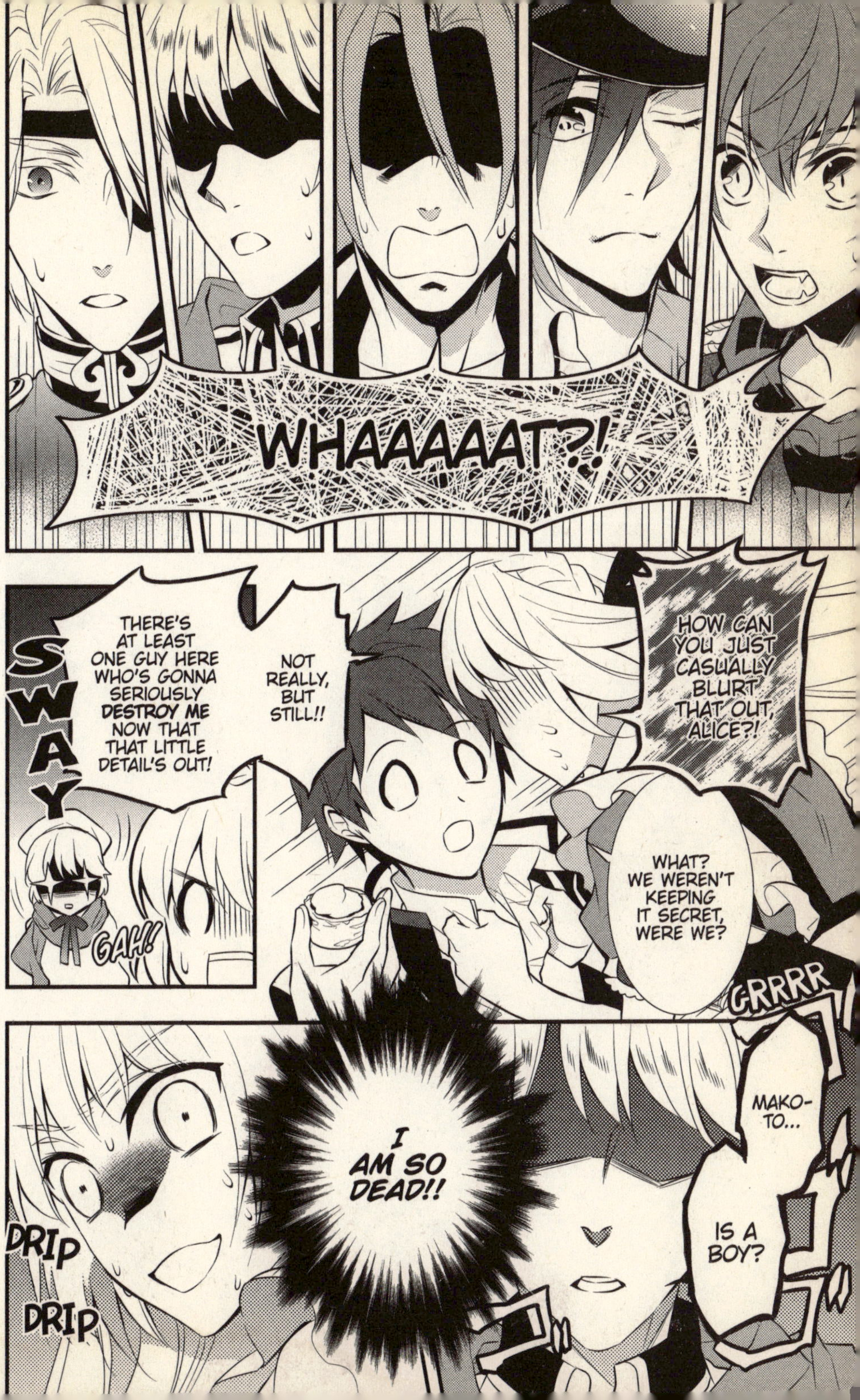
WHAAAAAT?!
HOW CAN YOU JUST CASUALLY BLURT THAT OUT, ALICE?!
WHAT? WE WEREN'T KEEPING IT SECRET, WERE WE?
NOT REALLY, BUT STILL!!
THERE'S AT LEAST ONE GUY HERE WHO'S GONNA SERIOUSLY **DESTROY ME** NOW THAT THAT LITTLE DETAIL'S OUT!
SWAY
GAH!
GRRRR
MAKO-TO...
IS A BOY?
I AM SO DEAD!!
DRIP
DRIP

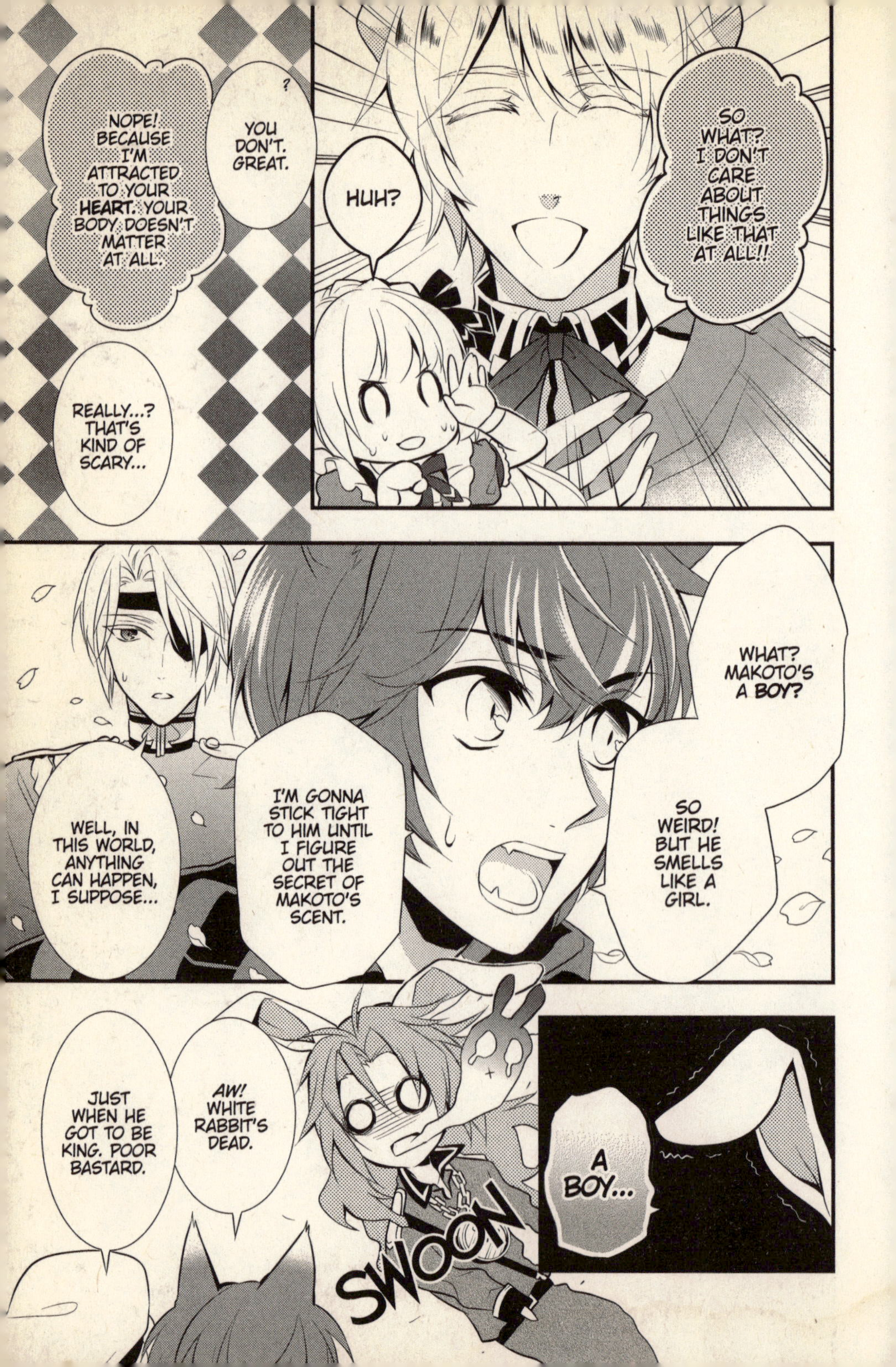
SO WHAT? I DON'T CARE ABOUT THINGS LIKE THAT AT ALL!!
HUH?
?
YOU DON'T. GREAT.
NOPE! BECAUSE I'M ATTRACTED TO YOUR **HEART**. YOUR BODY DOESN'T MATTER AT ALL.
REALLY...? THAT'S KIND OF SCARY...
WHAT? MAKOTO'S A **BOY**?
SO WEIRD! BUT HE SMELLS LIKE A GIRL.
I'M GONNA STICK TIGHT TO HIM UNTIL I FIGURE OUT THE SECRET OF MAKOTO'S SCENT.
WELL, IN THIS WORLD, ANYTHING CAN HAPPEN, I SUPPOSE...
A BOY...
SWOON
AW! WHITE RABBIT'S DEAD.
JUST WHEN HE GOT TO BE KING. POOR BASTARD.

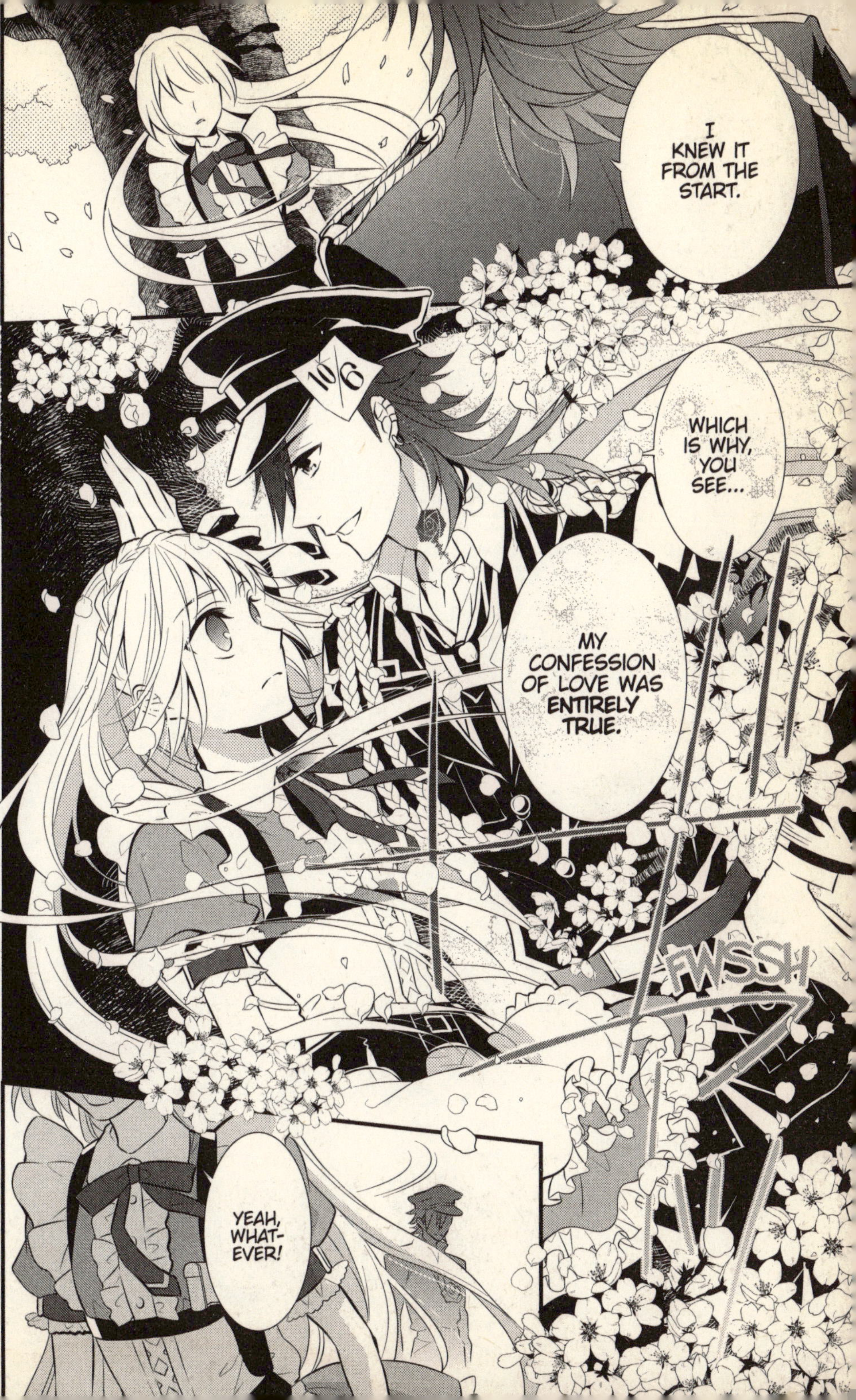
I KNEW IT FROM THE START.
WHICH IS WHY, YOU SEE...
MY CONFESSION OF LOVE WAS ENTIRELY TRUE.
FWSSH
YEAH, WHAT-EVER!

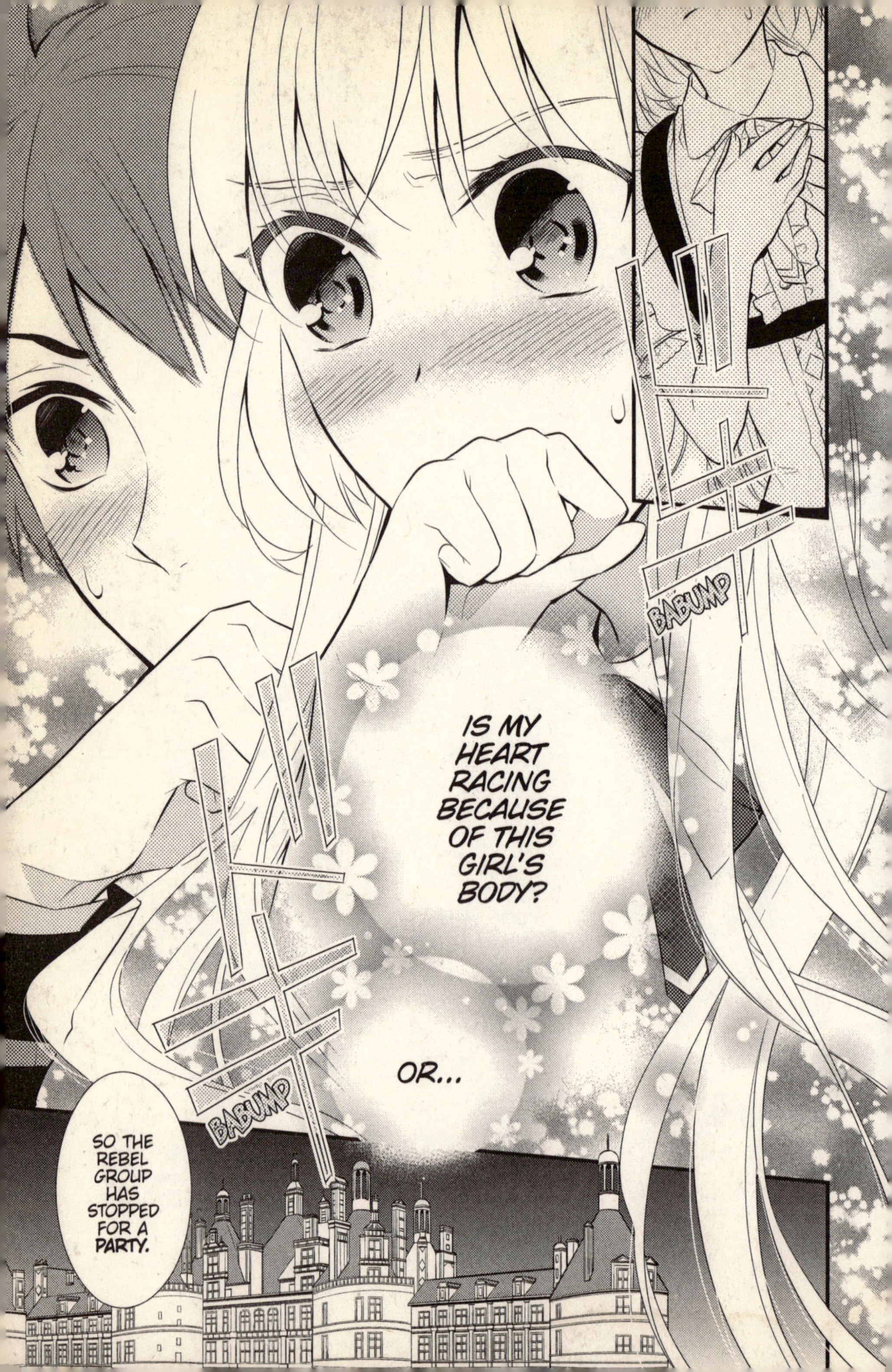
BABUMP
IS MY HEART RACING BECAUSE OF THIS GIRL'S BODY?
OR...
BABUMP
SO THE REBEL GROUP HAS STOPPED FOR A **PARTY**.

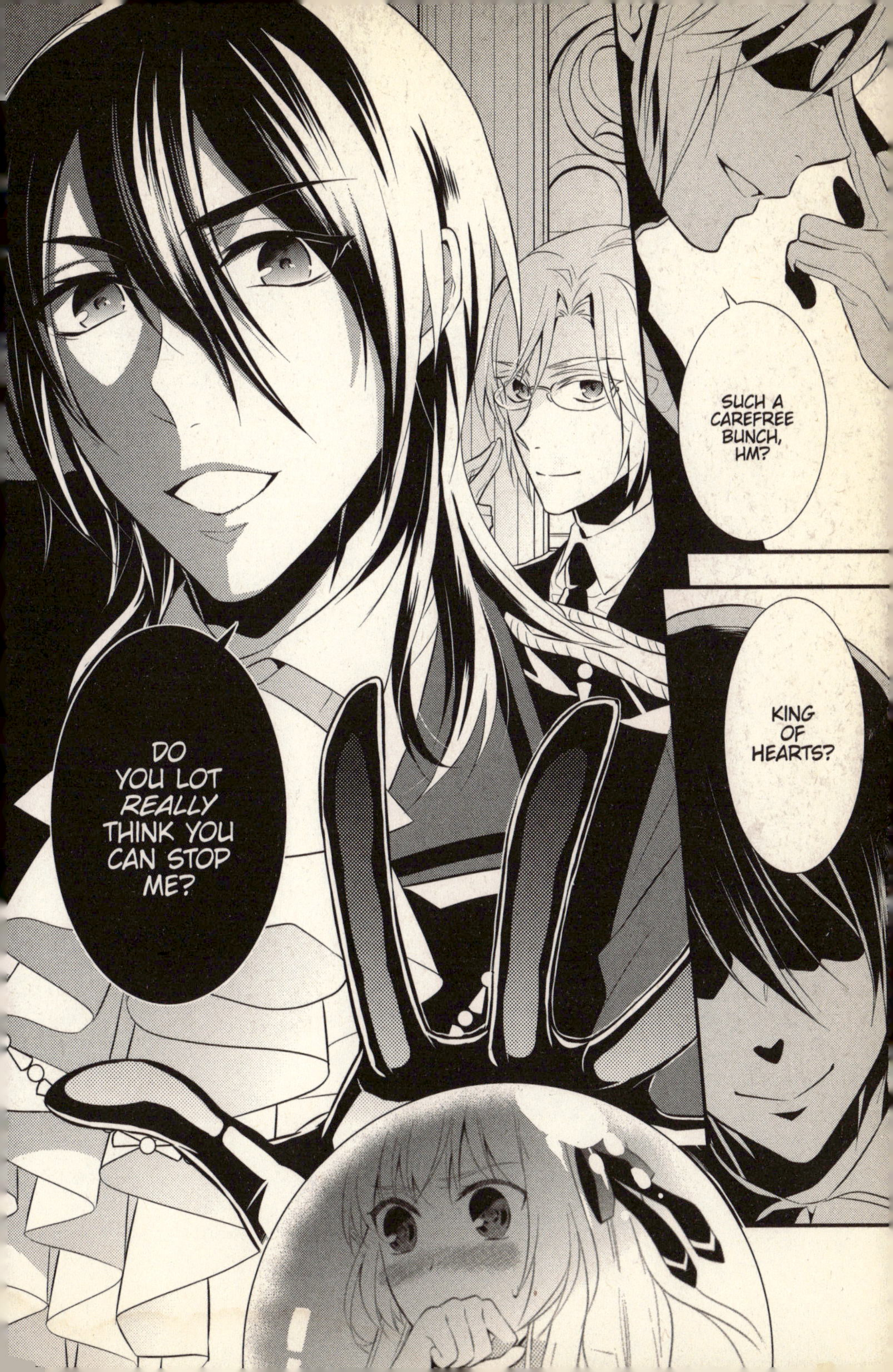
SUCH A CAREFREE BUNCH, HM?
KING OF HEARTS?
DO YOU LOT *REALLY* THINK YOU CAN STOP ME?

TO BE CONTINUED...

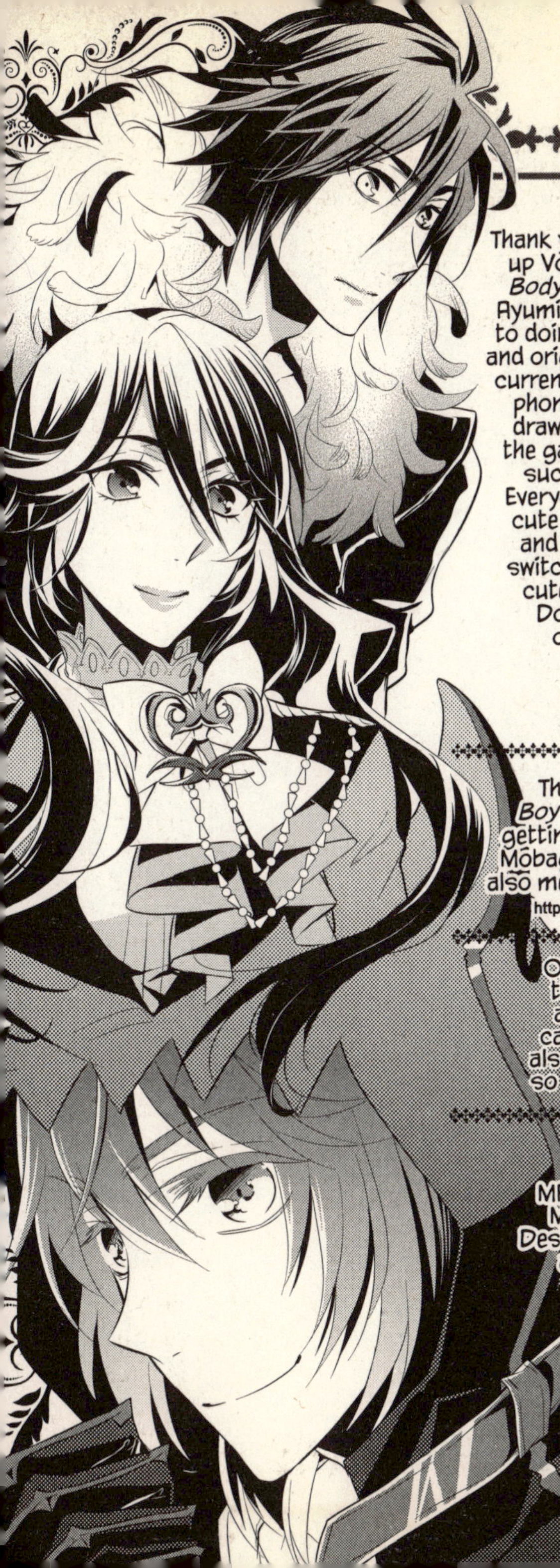

Thank you so much for picking up Volume 1 of *I Am Alice: Body Swap in Wonderland*. Ayumi Kanou here. in addition to doing the character design and original art for *I Am Alice*, currently available as a mobile phone game, I also got to draw the manga version of the game, which fills me with such incredible emotion. Everyone's personality is so cute in this love adventure, and there's girl-boy body switching, too! I hope their cuteness comes across. Don't forget to check out the game, too!

January 2013
Ayumi Kanou

The series *I Am Alice: Boy x Boy* is available and getting rave reviews at GREE, Mobage, and BLobby. You can also meet some new characters.
http://pro-page.jp/fpp/alice02/index

Open the QR code on the next page to get an avatar dress you can use in the game. I also designed the dress, so grab it while you can.

SPECIAL THANKS
Visual Works
MF Gene Editorial Dept
My supervisor, Y-san
Designer, Morohashi-sama
ai-san, Yukina-san,
K-yama-san
My family

~OMAKE~

I Am Alice: Body Swap in Wonderland Volume 1 First Edition Game Dress

For the initial Japanese release of volume 1 of the *I Am Alice: Body Swap in Wonderland* manga, Kanou Ayumi designed a super cute avatar dress that could be used in the *I Am Alice: Boy x Boy* game. While the dress is no longer available, we're including the artist's designs here as a special extra.

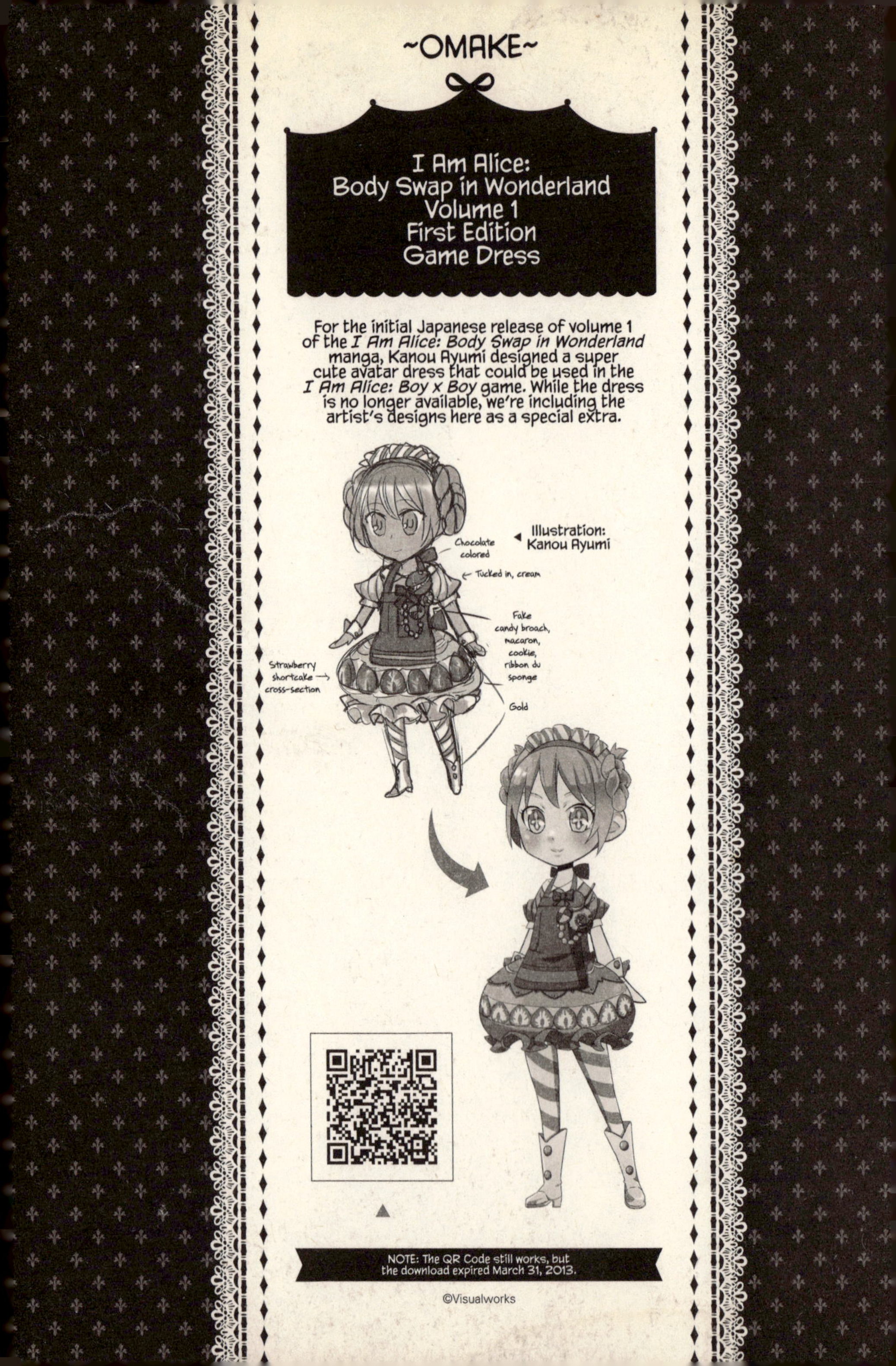
Chocolate colored
Tucked in, cream
Fake candy broach, macaron, cookie, ribbon du sponge
Strawberry shortcake cross-section
Gold

Illustration: Kanou Ayumi

NOTE: The QR Code still works, but the download expired March 31, 2013.

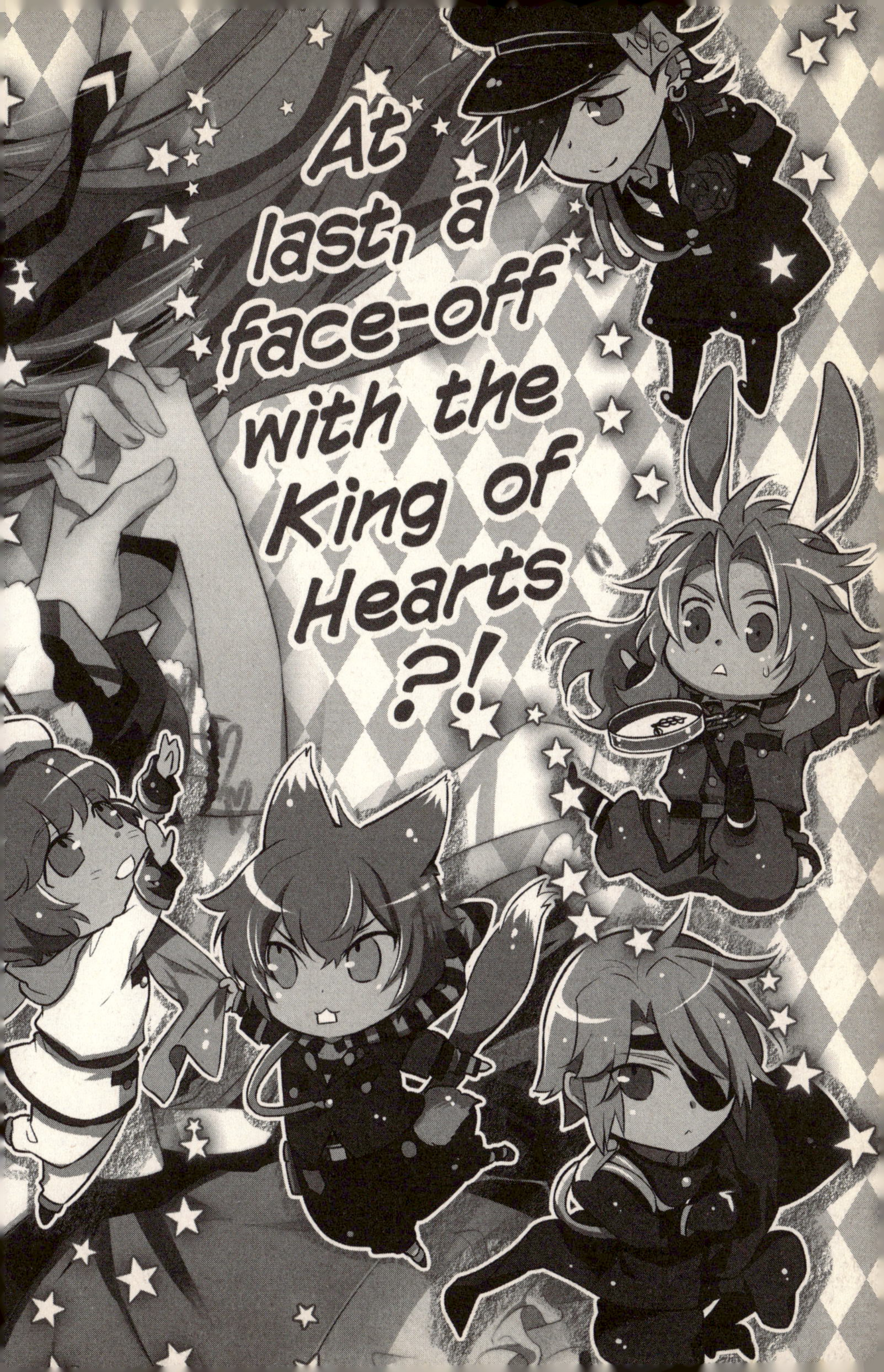
At last, a face-off with the King of Hearts ?!

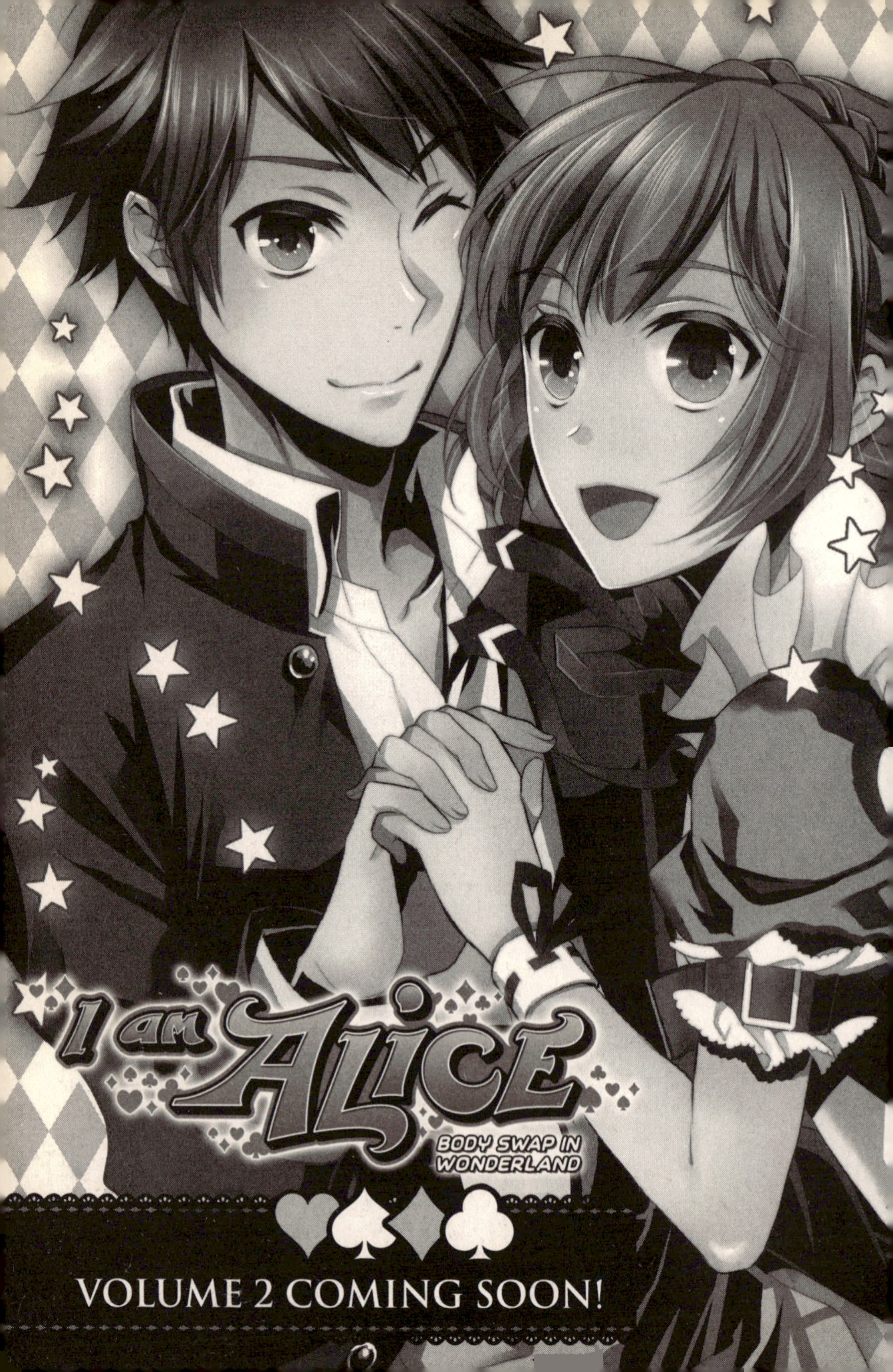
I am ALICE
BODY SWAP IN WONDERLAND
VOLUME 2 COMING SOON!

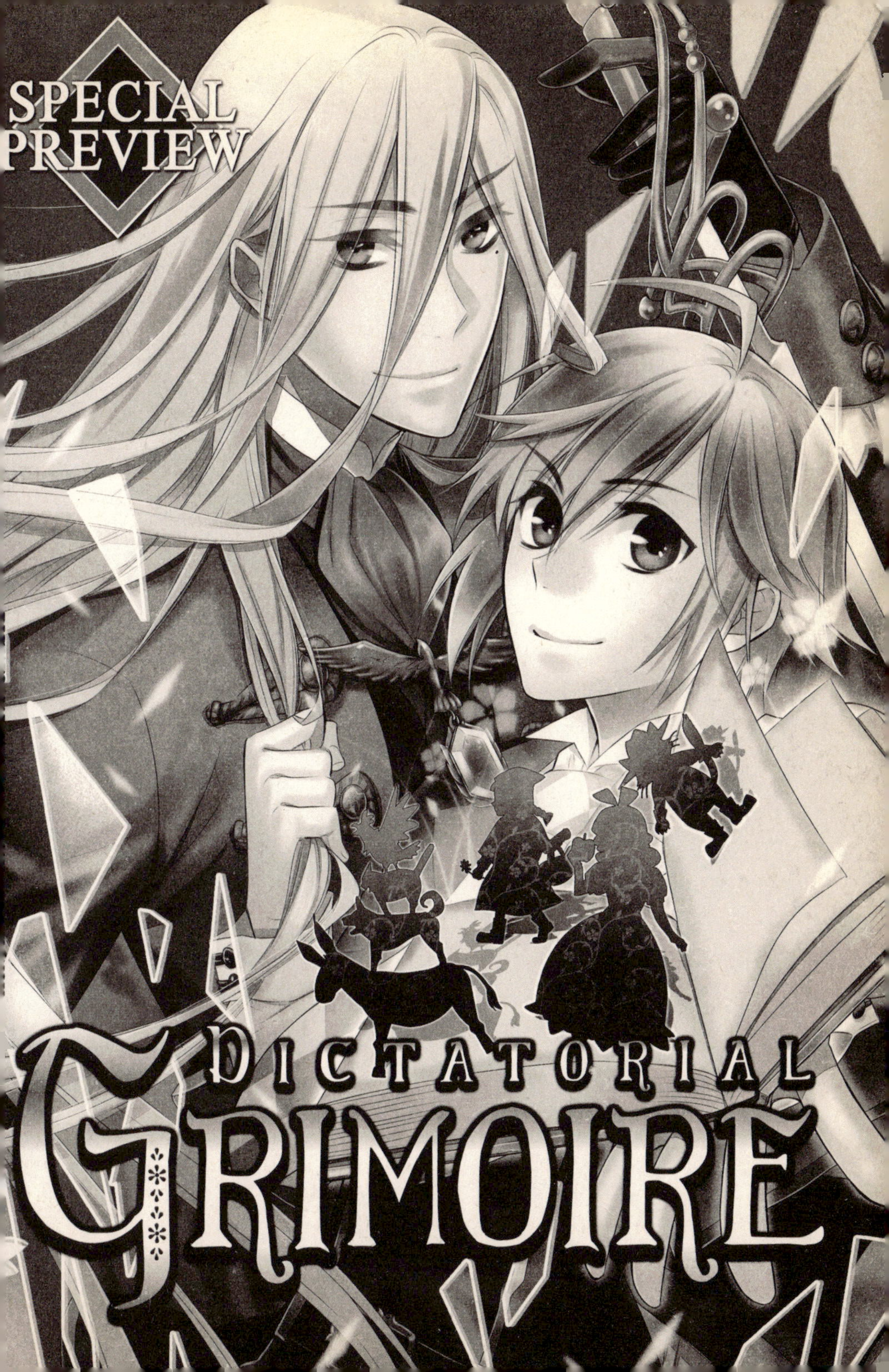
SPECIAL PREVIEW
DICTATORIAL GRIMOIRE

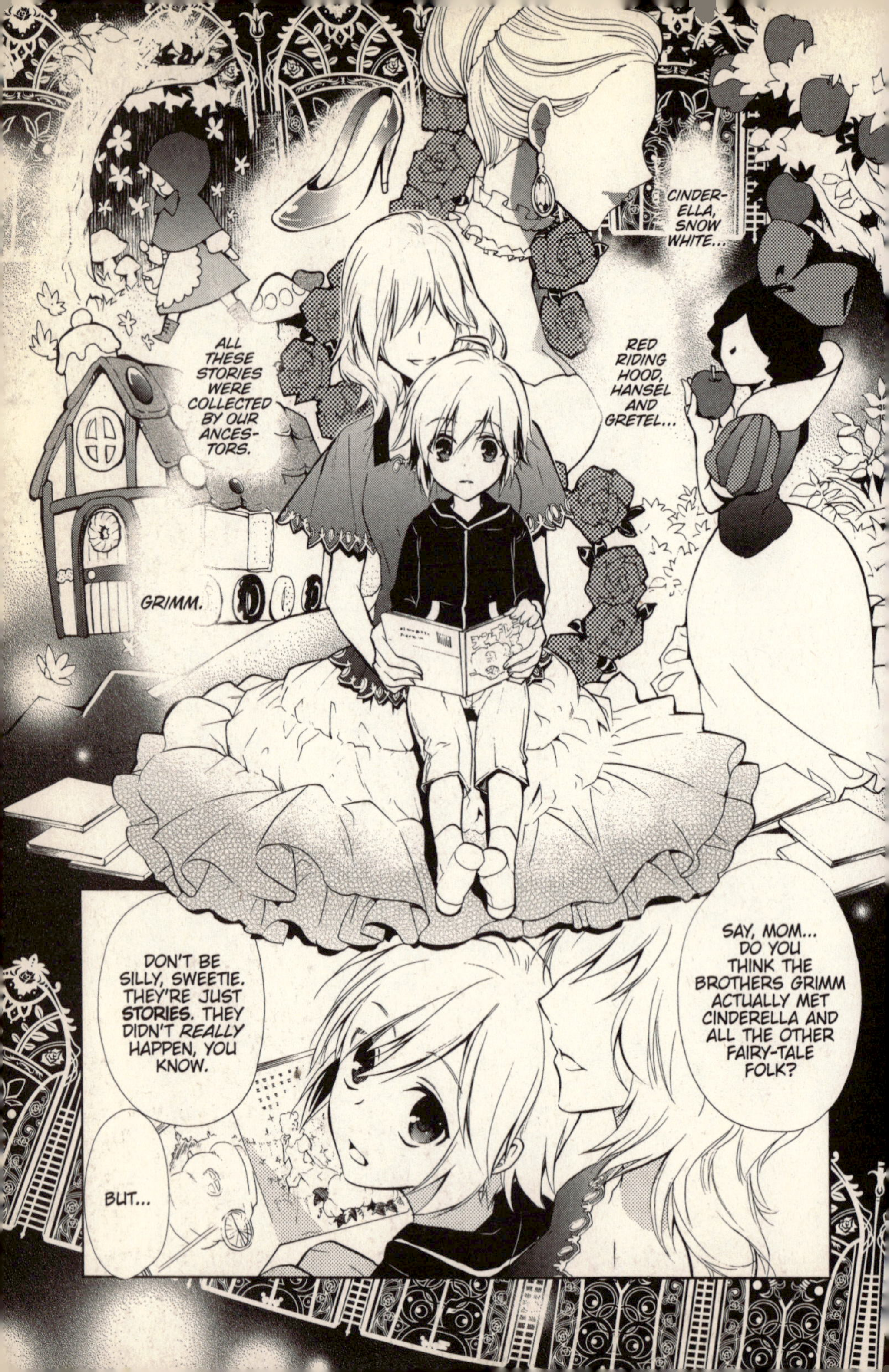
CINDERELLA, SNOW WHITE...
RED RIDING HOOD, HANSEL AND GRETEL...
ALL THESE STORIES WERE COLLECTED BY OUR ANCESTORS.
GRIMM.
SAY, MOM... DO YOU THINK THE BROTHERS GRIMM ACTUALLY MET CINDERELLA AND ALL THE OTHER FAIRY-TALE FOLK?
DON'T BE SILLY, SWEETIE. THEY'RE JUST **STORIES**. THEY DIDN'T *REALLY* HAPPEN, YOU KNOW.
BUT...

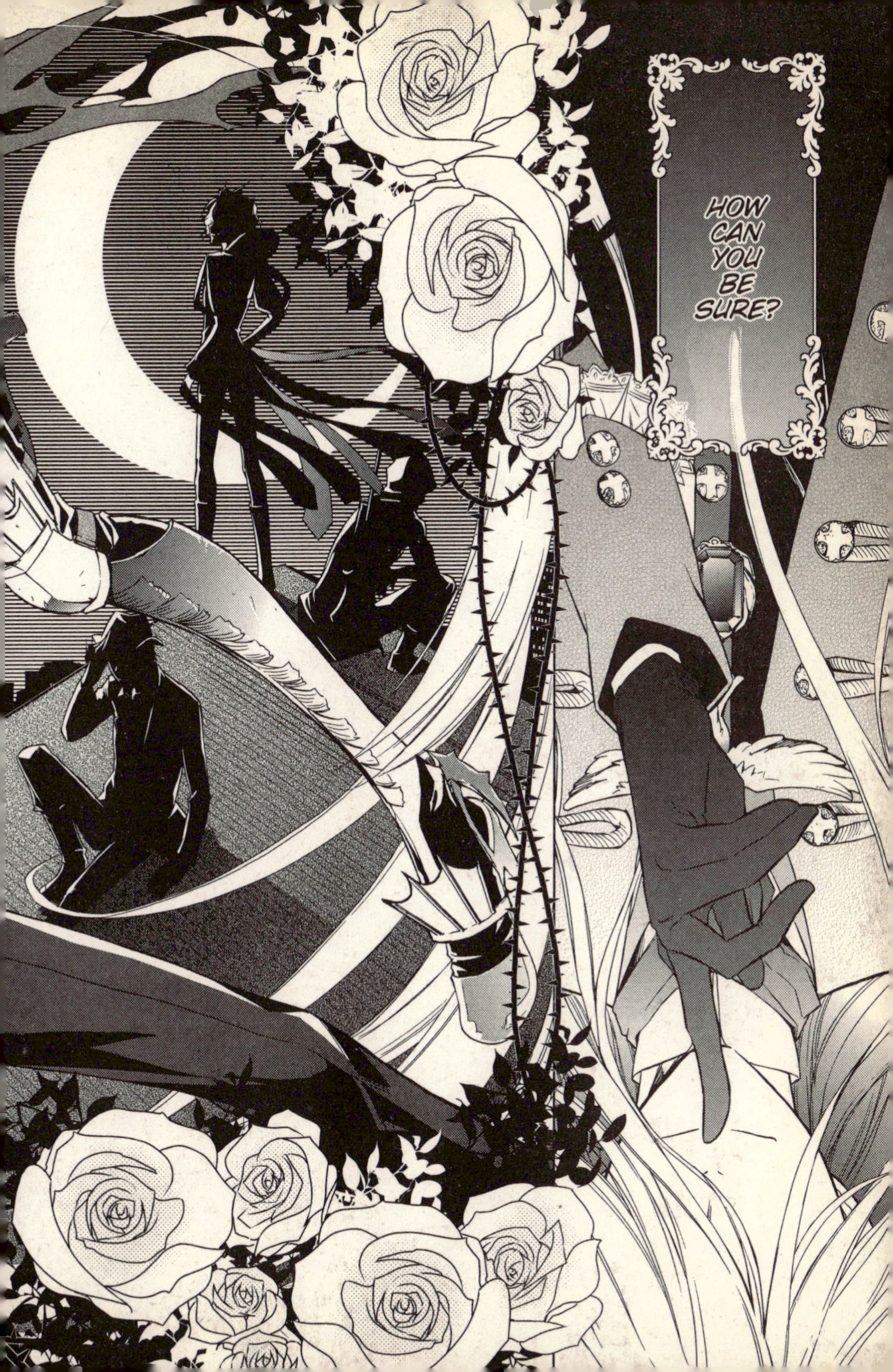
HOW CAN YOU BE SURE?

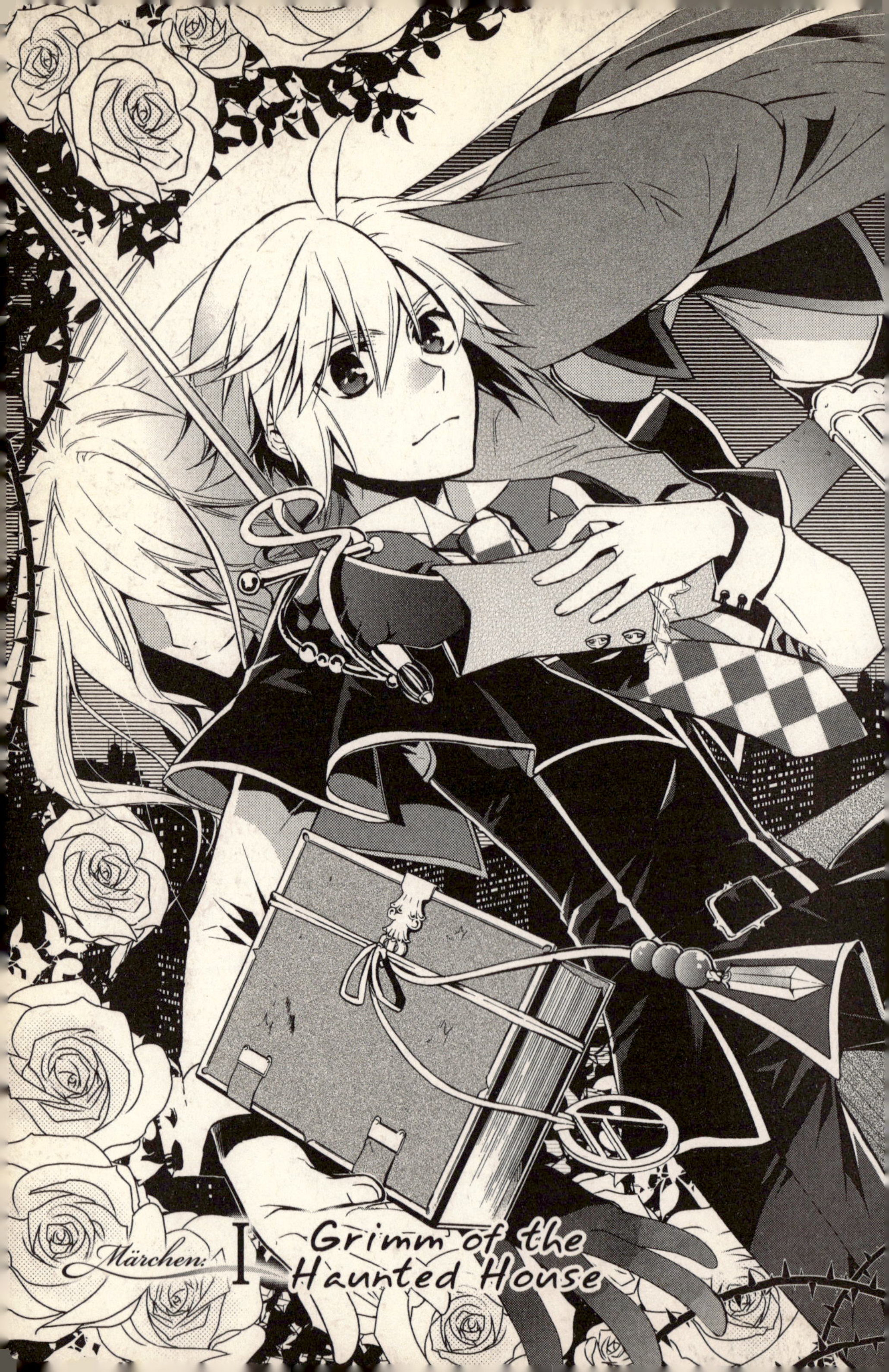
Märchen: I
Grimm of the Haunted House

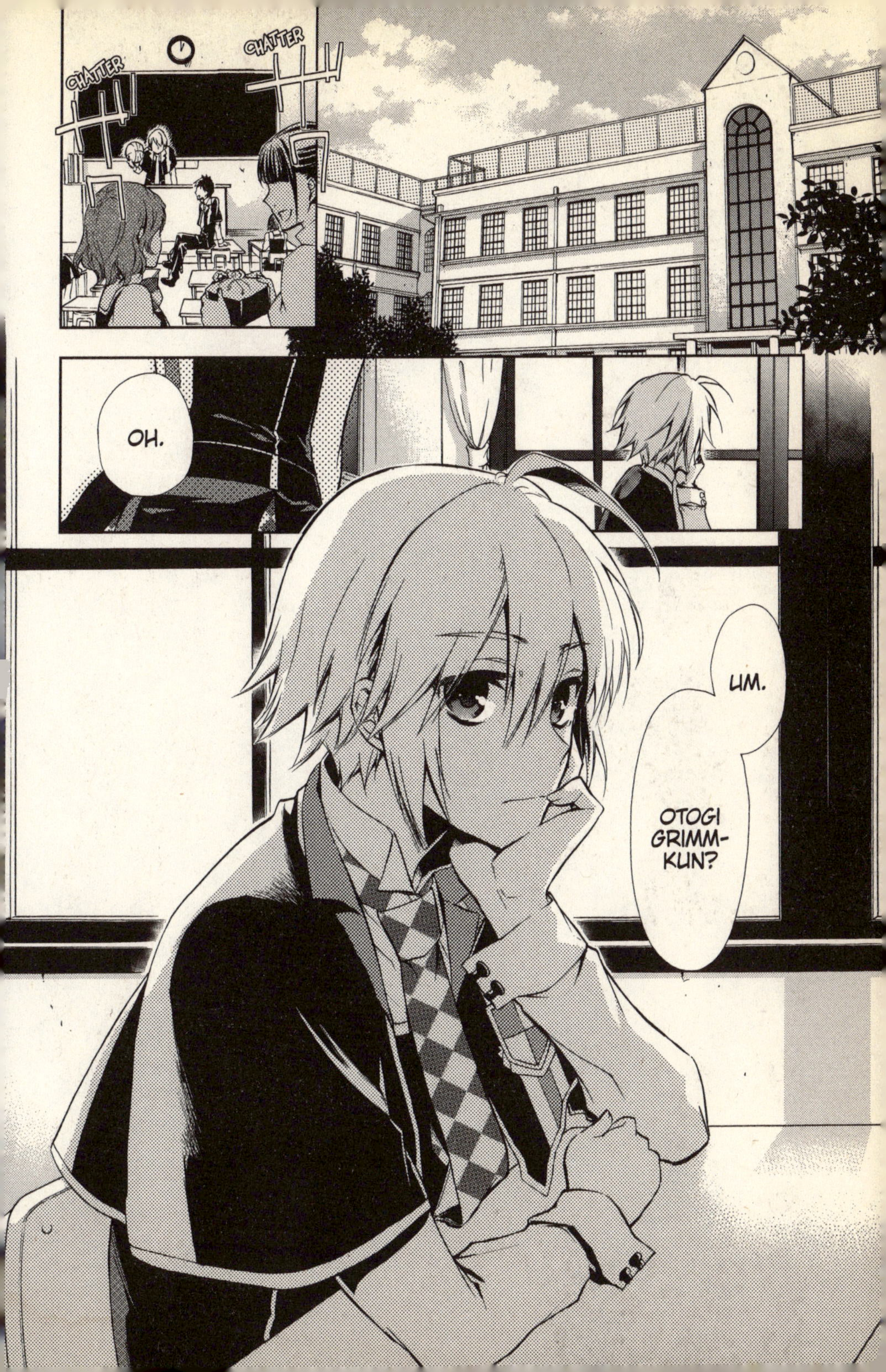
CHATTER
CHATTER
OH.
UM.
OTOGI GRIMM-KUN?

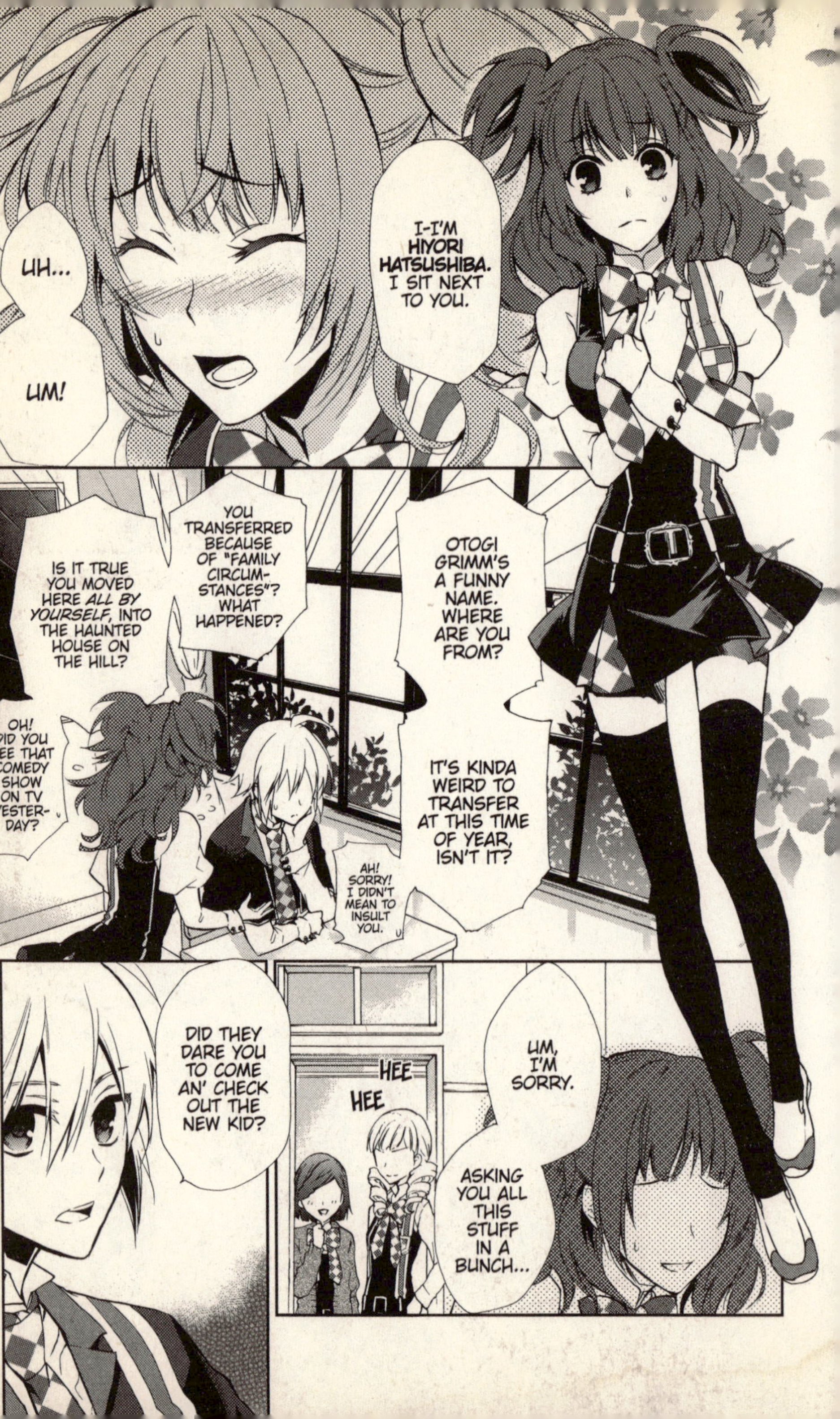
I-I'M HIYORI HATSUSHIBA. I SIT NEXT TO YOU.
UH...
UM!
OTOGI GRIMM'S A FUNNY NAME. WHERE ARE YOU FROM?
YOU TRANSFERRED BECAUSE OF "FAMILY CIRCUM-STANCES"? WHAT HAPPENED?
IS IT TRUE YOU MOVED HERE *ALL BY YOURSELF*, INTO THE HAUNTED HOUSE ON THE HILL?
IT'S KINDA WEIRD TO TRANSFER AT THIS TIME OF YEAR, ISN'T IT?
OH! DID YOU SEE THAT COMEDY SHOW ON TV YESTER-DAY?
AH! SORRY! I DIDN'T MEAN TO INSULT YOU.
UM, I'M SORRY.
ASKING YOU ALL THIS STUFF IN A BUNCH...
HEE
HEE
DID THEY DARE YOU TO COME AN' CHECK OUT THE NEW KID?

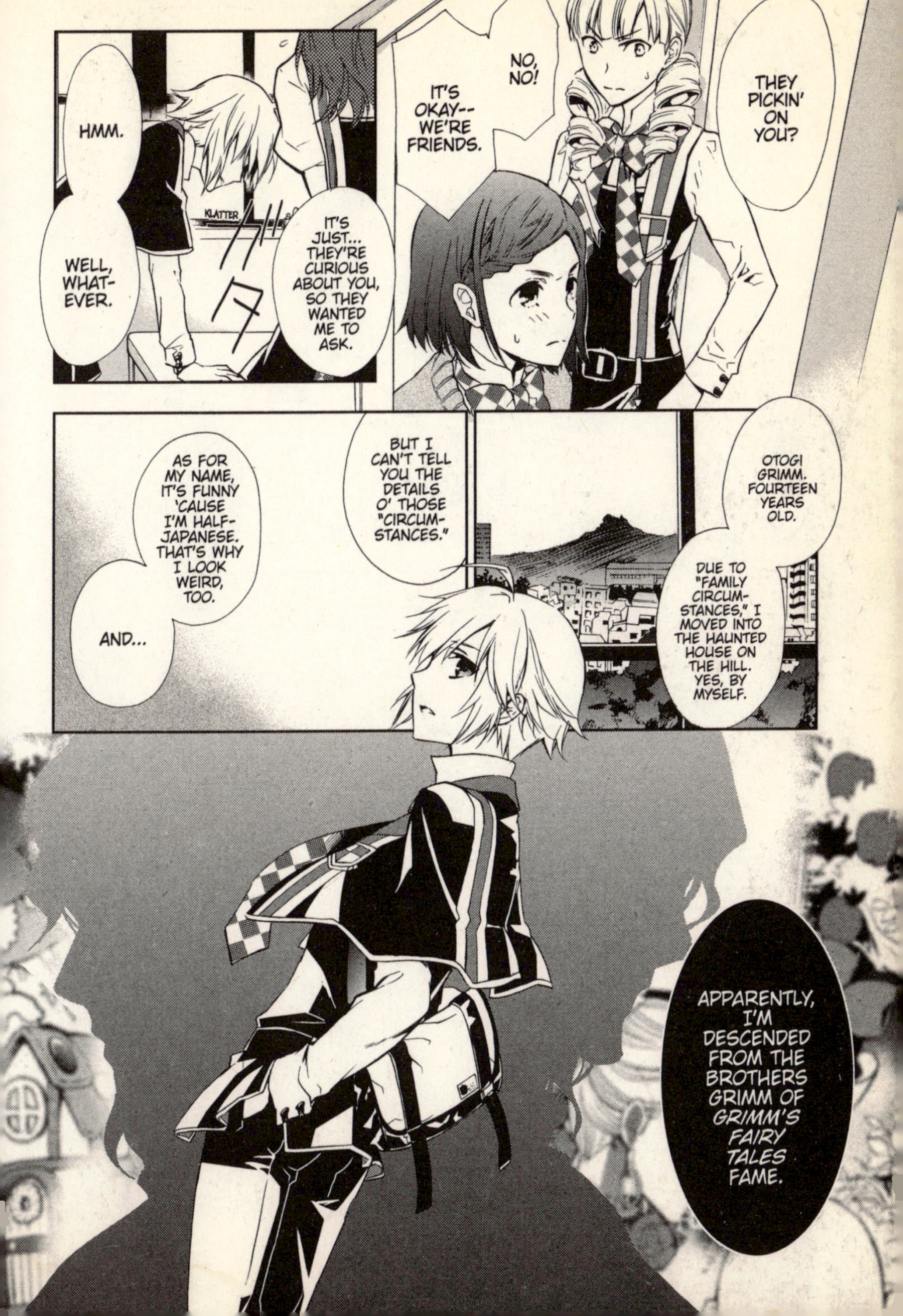
THEY PICKIN' ON YOU?
NO, NO!
IT'S OKAY-- WE'RE FRIENDS.
IT'S JUST... THEY'RE CURIOUS ABOUT YOU, SO THEY WANTED ME TO ASK.
HMM.
KLATTER
WELL, WHAT-EVER.
OTOGI GRIMM. FOURTEEN YEARS OLD.
DUE TO "FAMILY CIRCUM-STANCES," I MOVED INTO THE HAUNTED HOUSE ON THE HILL. YES, BY MYSELF.
BUT I CAN'T TELL YOU THE DETAILS O' THOSE "CIRCUM-STANCES."
AS FOR MY NAME, IT'S FUNNY 'CAUSE I'M HALF-JAPANESE. THAT'S WHY I LOOK WEIRD, TOO.
AND...
APPARENTLY, I'M DESCENDED FROM THE BROTHERS GRIMM OF *GRIMM'S FAIRY TALES* FAME.

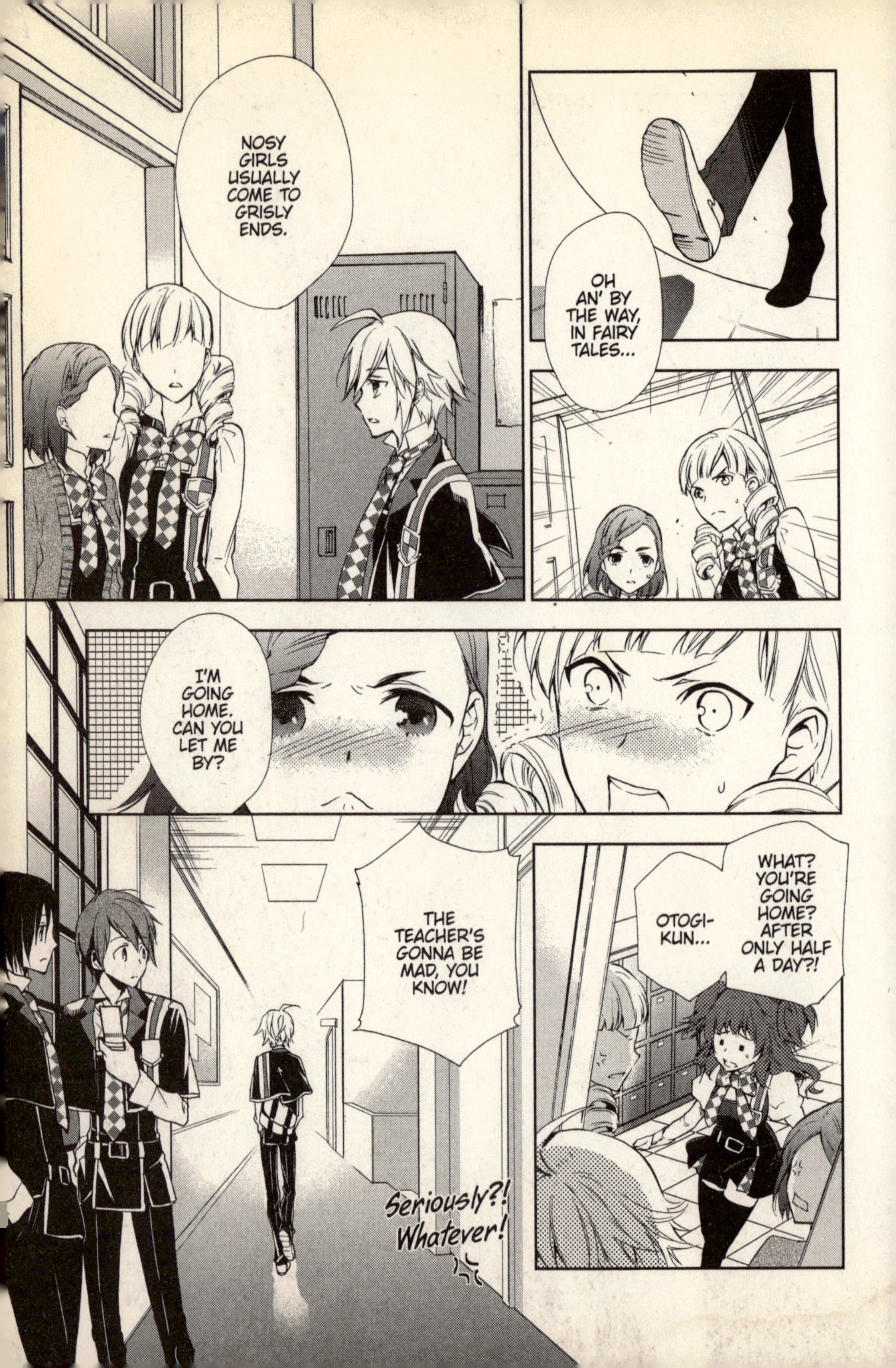
OH AN' BY THE WAY, IN FAIRY TALES...
NOSY GIRLS USUALLY COME TO GRISLY ENDS.
I'M GOING HOME. CAN YOU LET ME BY?
WHAT? YOU'RE GOING HOME? AFTER ONLY HALF A DAY?!
OTOGI-KUN...
THE TEACHER'S GONNA BE MAD, YOU KNOW!
Seriously?! Whatever!

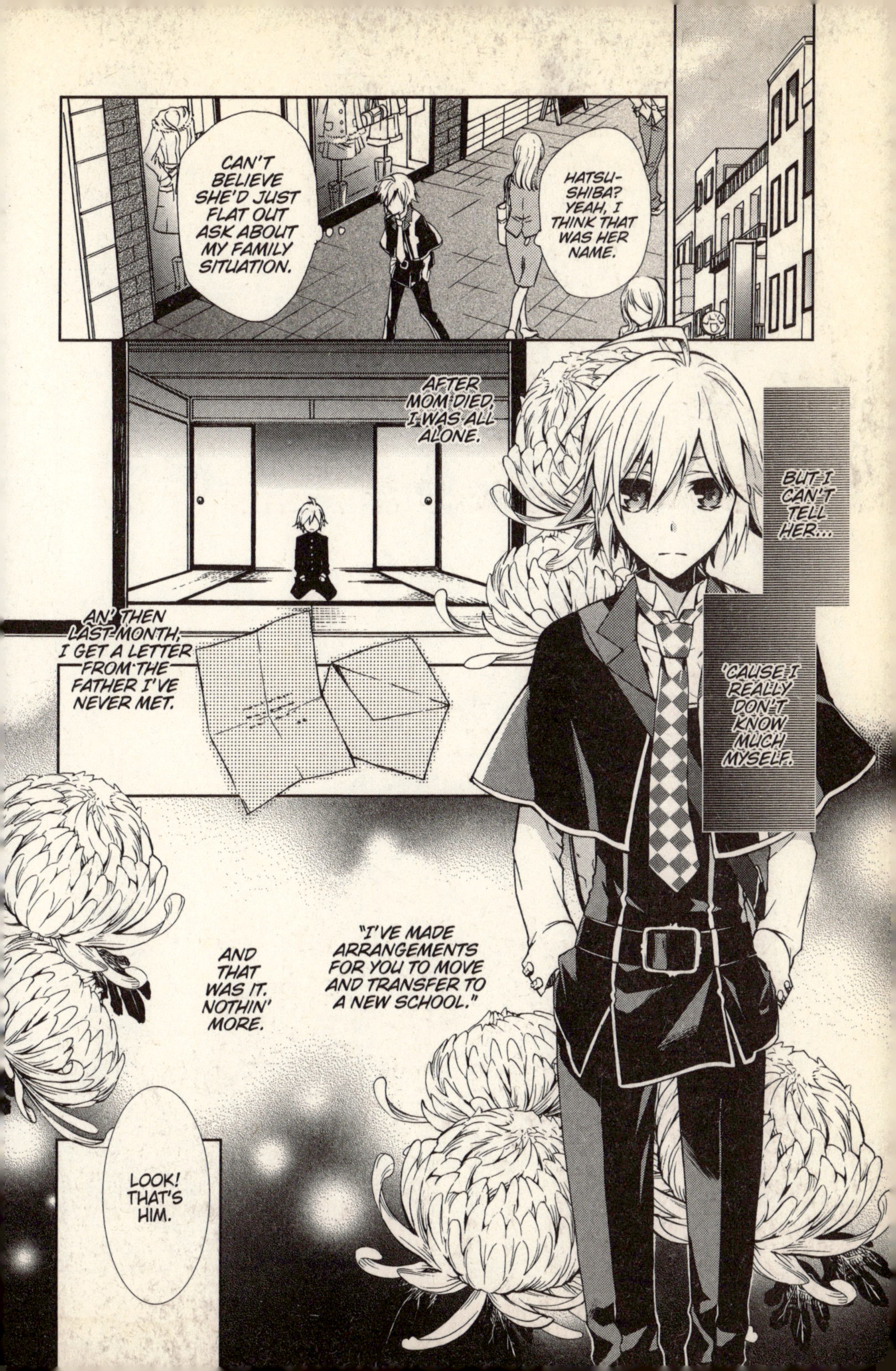
HATSU-SHIBA? YEAH, I THINK THAT WAS HER NAME.
CAN'T BELIEVE SHE'D JUST FLAT OUT ASK ABOUT MY FAMILY SITUATION.
BUT I CAN'T TELL HER...
'CAUSE I REALLY DON'T KNOW MUCH MYSELF.
AFTER MOM DIED, I WAS ALL ALONE.
AN' THEN LAST MONTH, I GET A LETTER FROM THE FATHER I'VE NEVER MET.
"I'VE MADE ARRANGEMENTS FOR YOU TO MOVE AND TRANSFER TO A NEW SCHOOL."
AND THAT WAS IT. NOTHIN' MORE.
LOOK! THAT'S HIM.

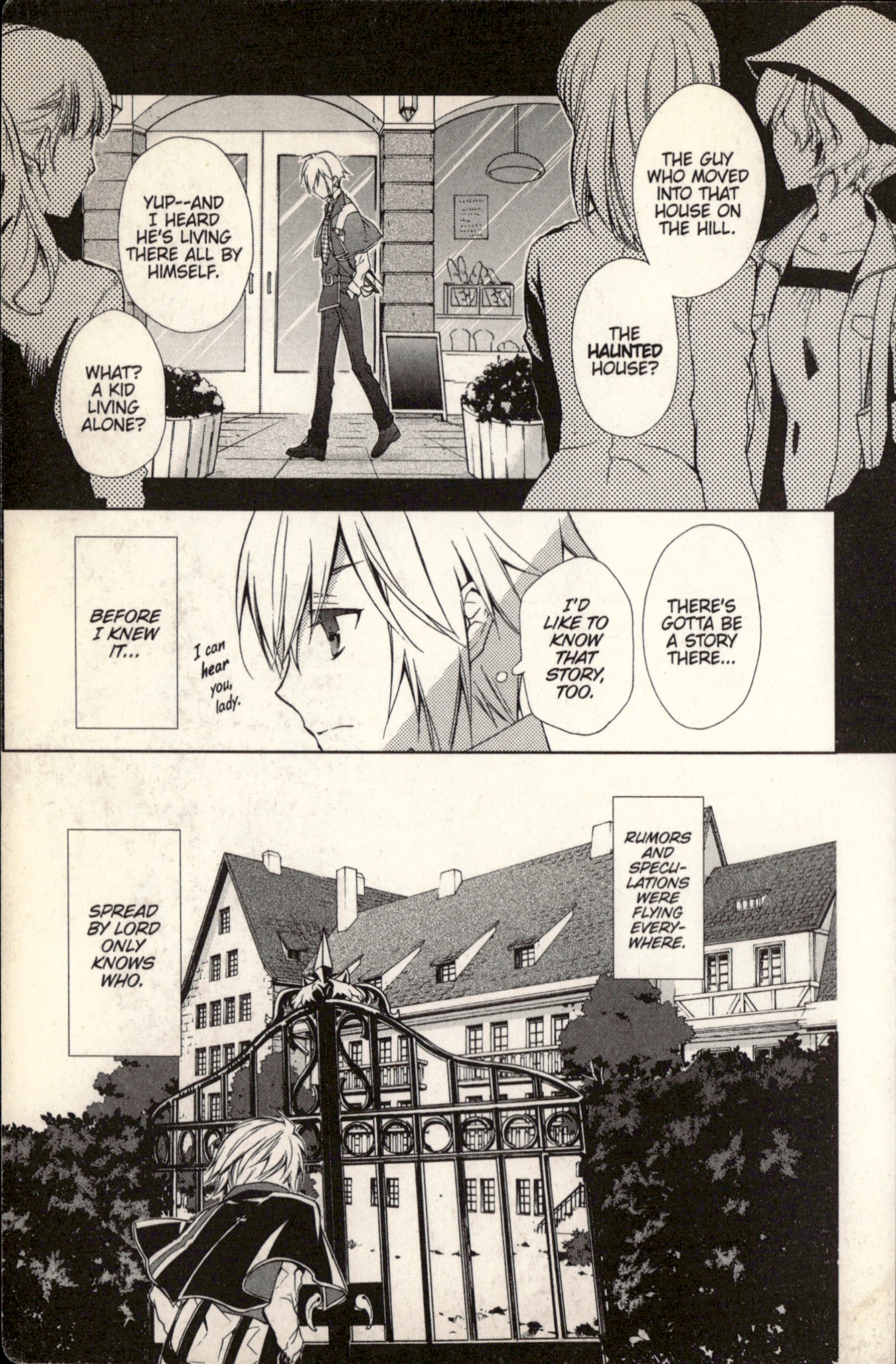
THE GUY WHO MOVED INTO THAT HOUSE ON THE HILL.
THE HAUNTED HOUSE?
YUP--AND I HEARD HE'S LIVING THERE ALL BY HIMSELF.
WHAT? A KID LIVING ALONE?
THERE'S GOTTA BE A STORY THERE...
I'D LIKE TO KNOW THAT STORY, TOO.
I can hear you, lady.
BEFORE I KNEW IT...
RUMORS AND SPECULATIONS WERE FLYING EVERYWHERE.
SPREAD BY LORD ONLY KNOWS WHO.

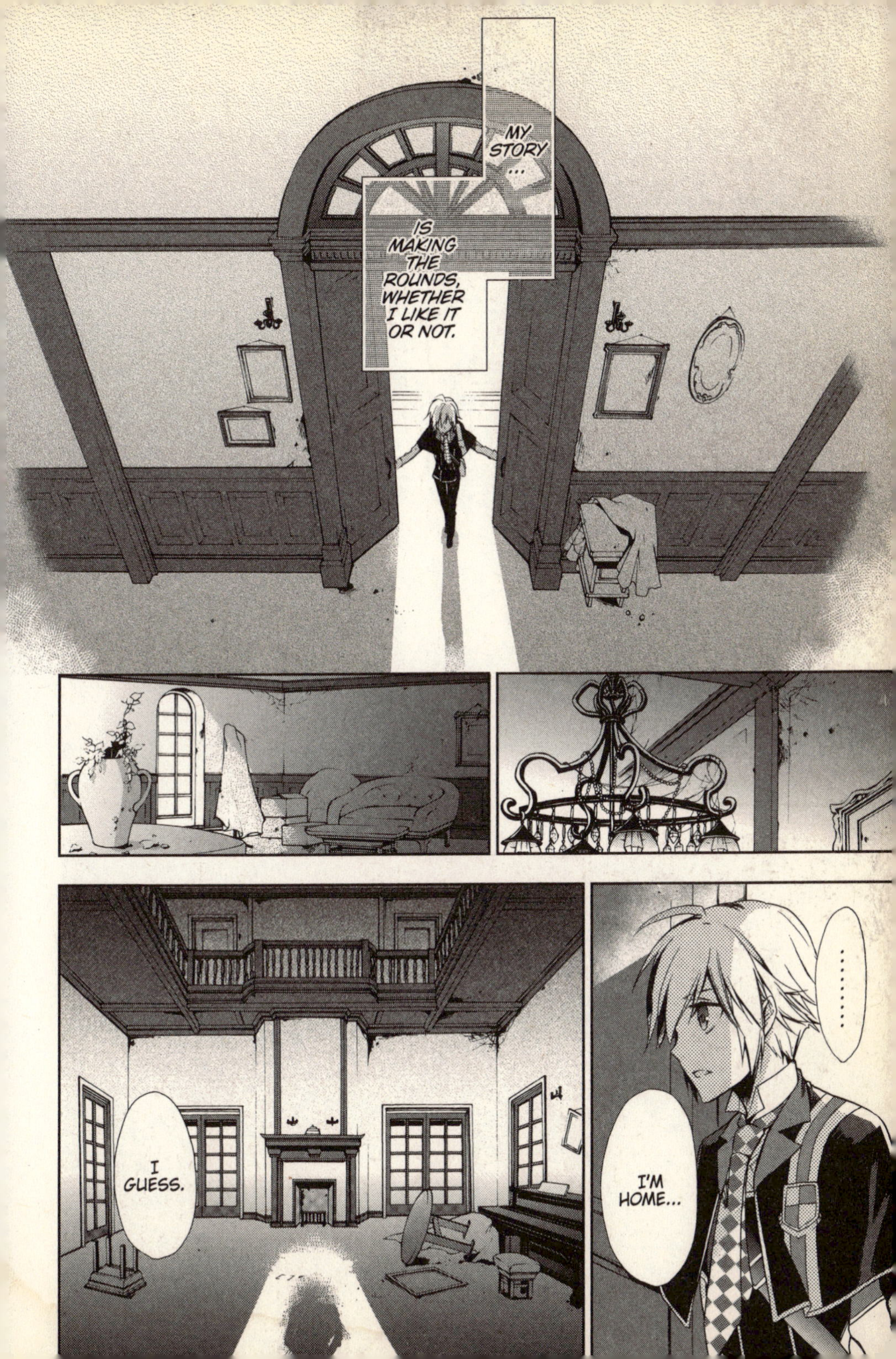
MY STORY...
IS MAKING THE ROUNDS, WHETHER I LIKE IT OR NOT.
......
I'M HOME...
I GUESS.

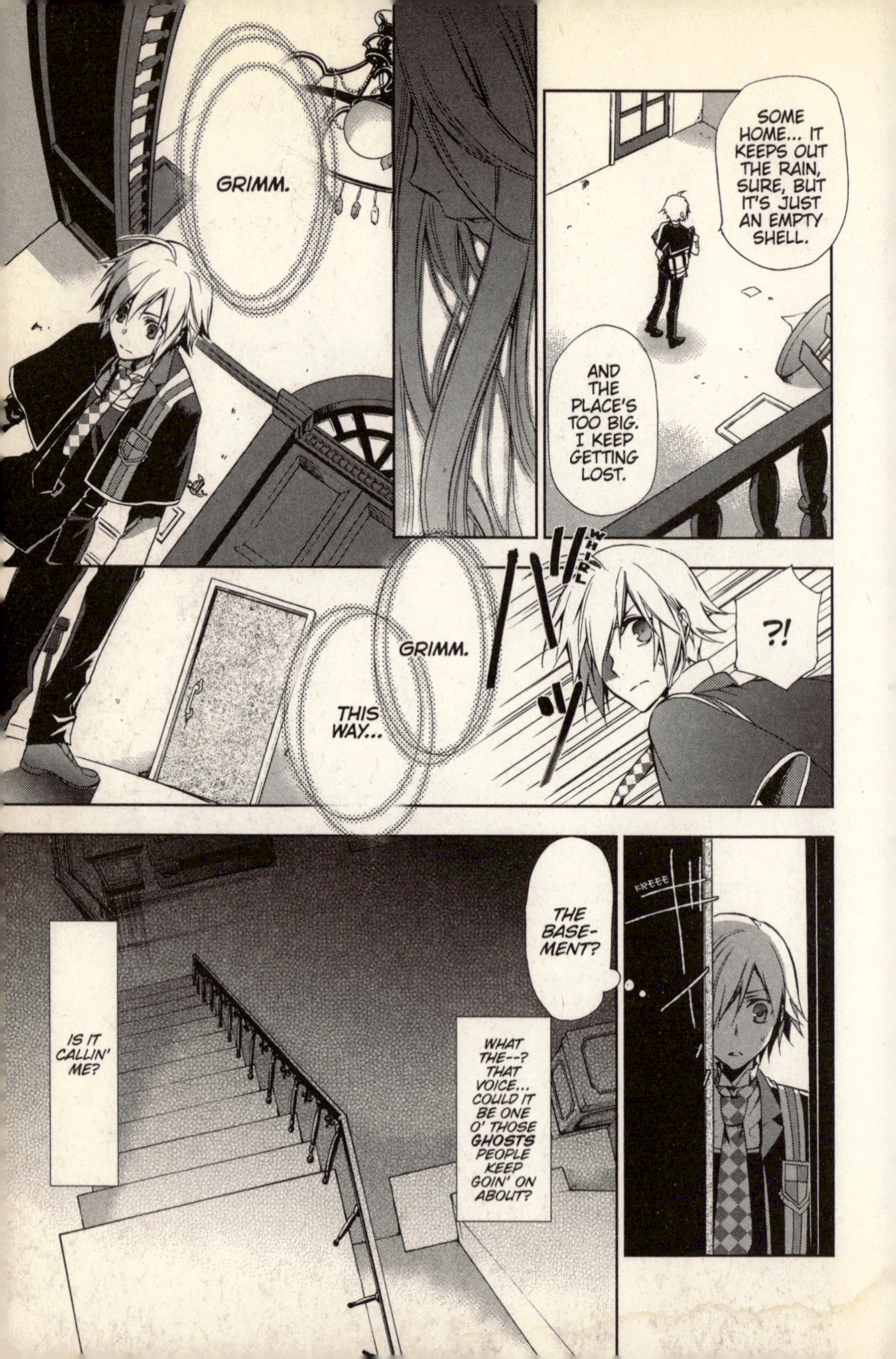
SOME HOME... IT KEEPS OUT THE RAIN, SURE, BUT IT'S JUST AN EMPTY SHELL.
AND THE PLACE'S TOO BIG. I KEEP GETTING LOST.
GRIMM.
WHIRL
?!
GRIMM.
THIS WAY...
THE BASE-MENT?
WHAT THE--? THAT VOICE... COULD IT BE ONE O' THOSE GHOSTS PEOPLE KEEP GOIN' ON ABOUT?
IS IT CALLIN' ME?

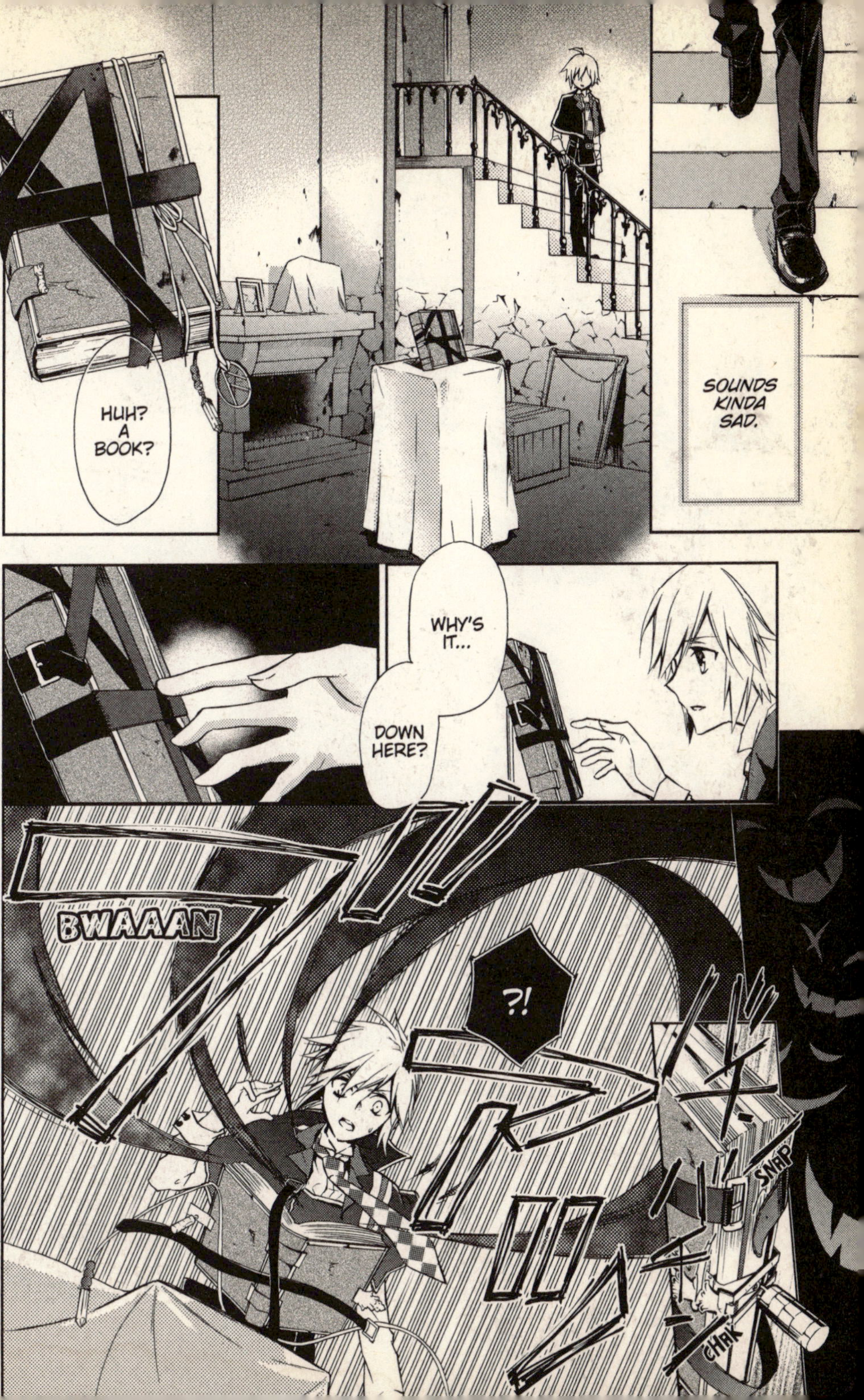
SOUNDS KINDA SAD.
HUH? A BOOK?
WHY'S IT...
DOWN HERE?
BWAAAN
?!
SNAP
CHAK

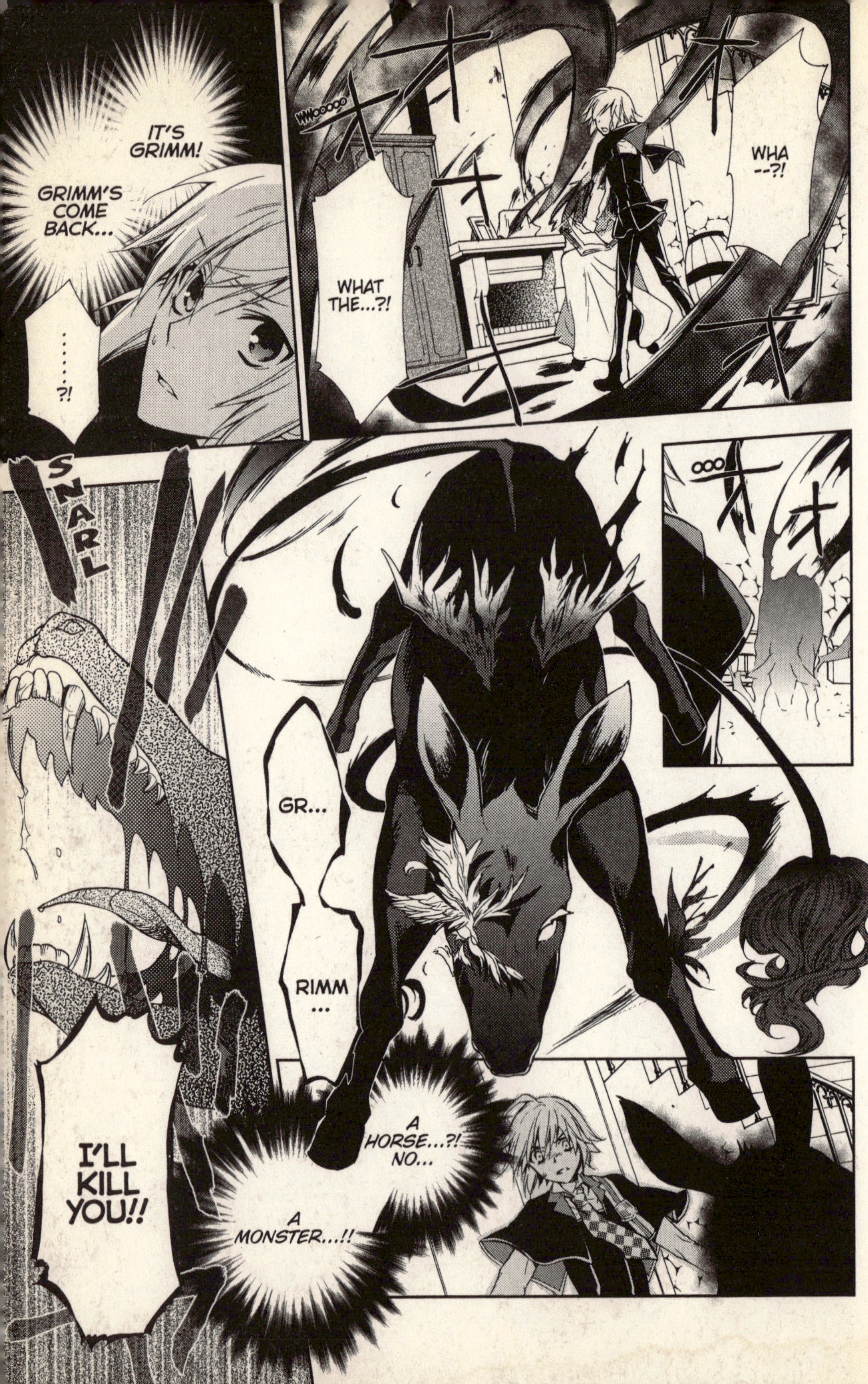
WHA --?!
WHOOOOO
WHAT THE...?!
IT'S GRIMM!
GRIMM'S COME BACK...
......?!
OOO
A HORSE...?! NO...
A MONSTER...!!
GR...
RIMM...
SNARL
I'LL KILL YOU!!

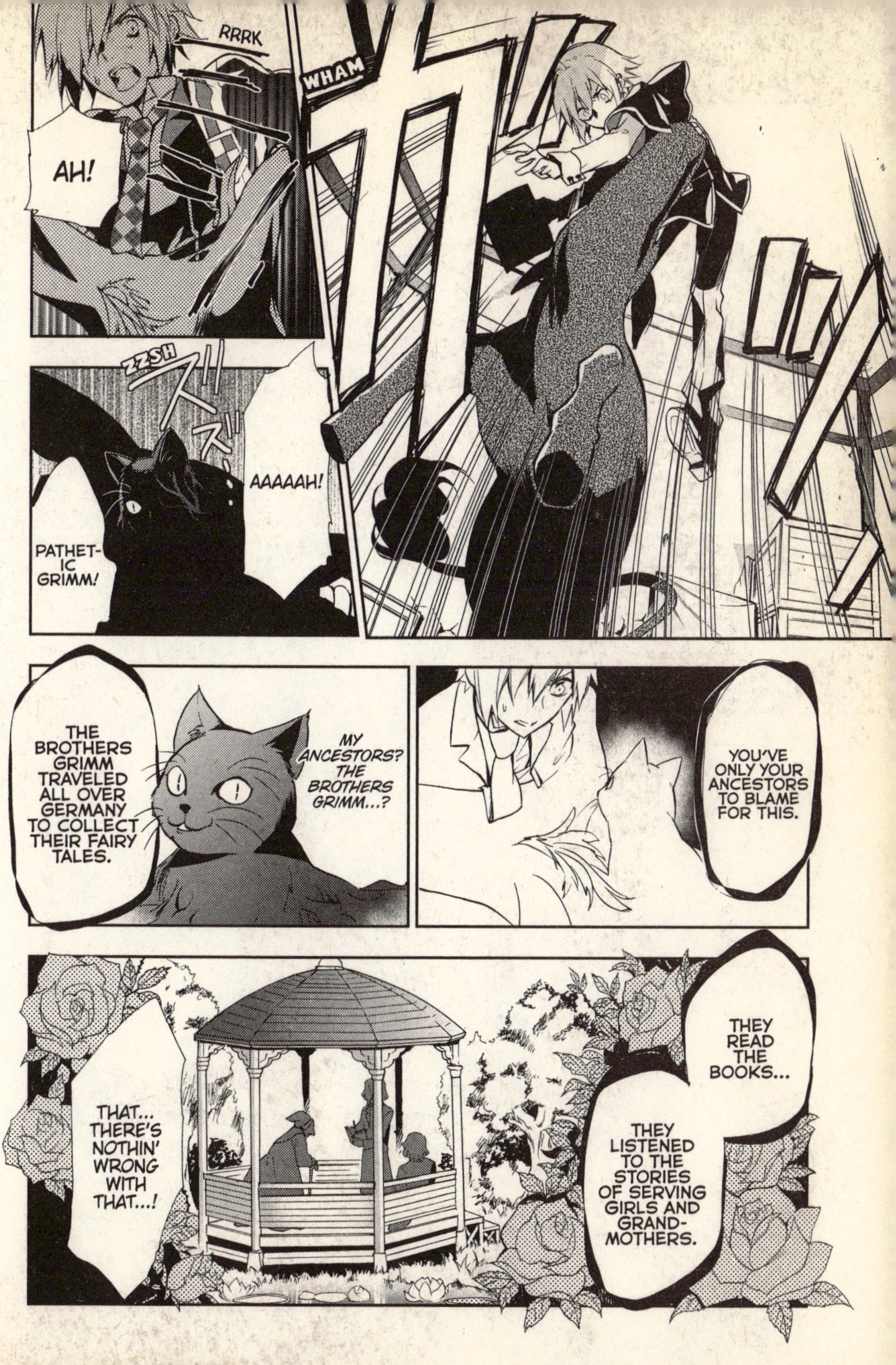
WHAM
RRRK
AH!
ZZSH
AAAAAH!
PATHET-IC GRIMM!
YOU'VE ONLY YOUR ANCESTORS TO BLAME FOR THIS.
MY ANCESTORS? THE BROTHERS GRIMM...?
THE BROTHERS GRIMM TRAVELED ALL OVER GERMANY TO COLLECT THEIR FAIRY TALES.
THEY READ THE BOOKS...
THEY LISTENED TO THE STORIES OF SERVING GIRLS AND GRAND-MOTHERS.
THAT... THERE'S NOTHIN' WRONG WITH THAT...!

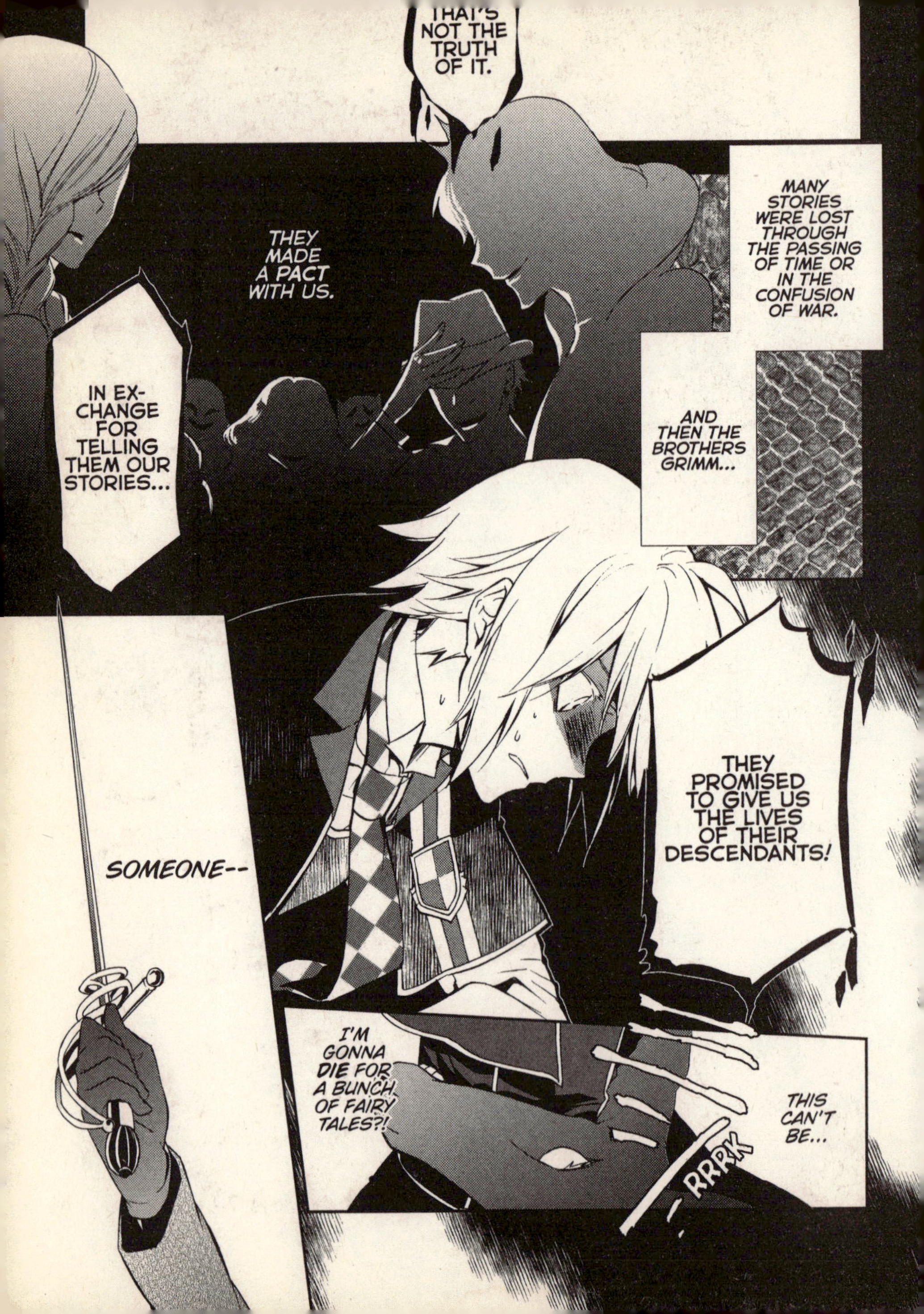
THAT'S NOT THE TRUTH OF IT.
MANY STORIES WERE LOST THROUGH THE PASSING OF TIME OR IN THE CONFUSION OF WAR.
AND THEN THE BROTHERS GRIMM...
THEY MADE A PACT WITH US.
IN EX-CHANGE FOR TELLING THEM OUR STORIES...
THEY PROMISED TO GIVE US THE LIVES OF THEIR DESCENDANTS!
THIS CAN'T BE...
RRRK
I'M GONNA DIE FOR A BUNCH OF FAIRY TALES?!
SOMEONE--

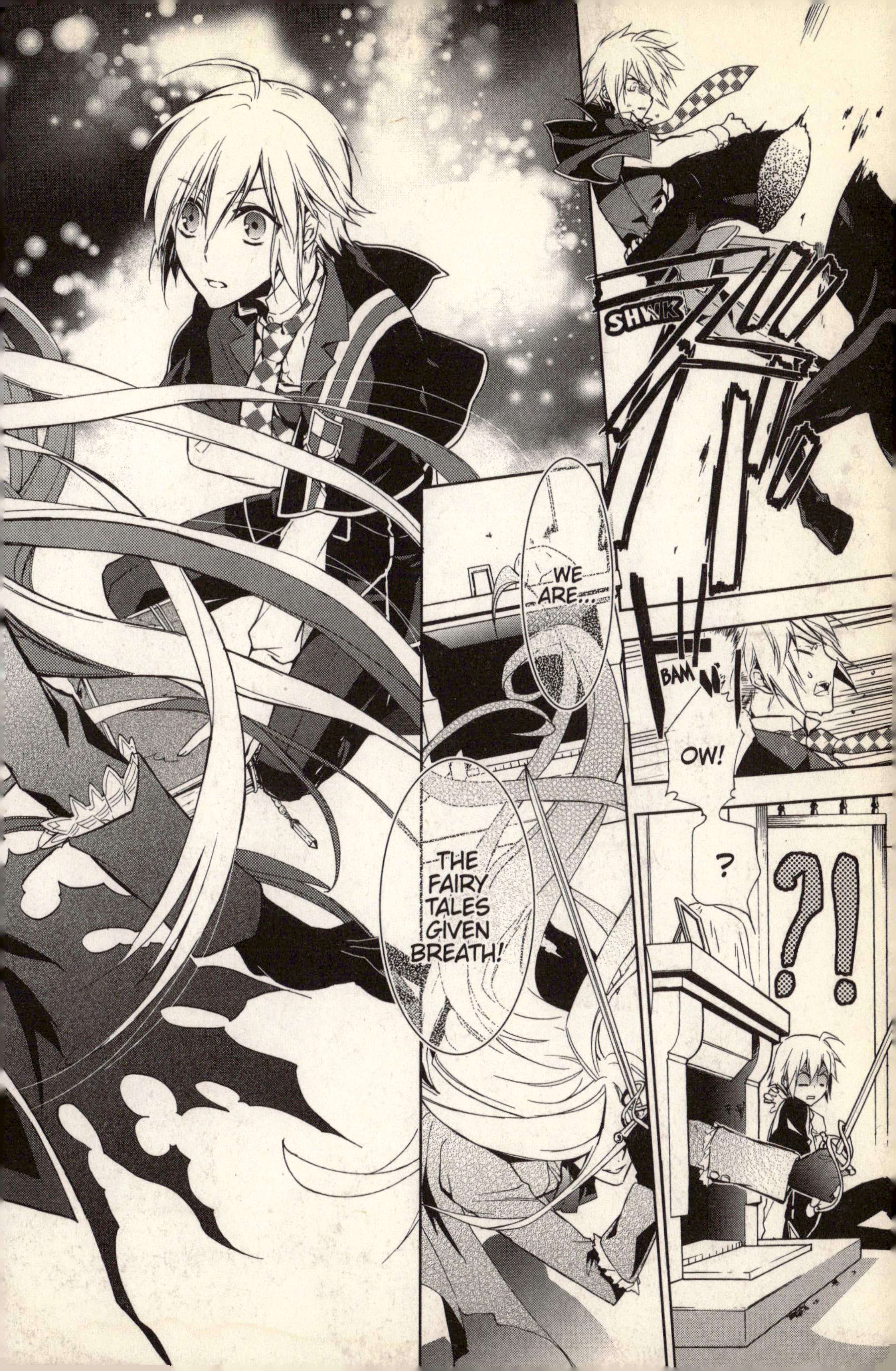
SHWK
BAM
OW!
?
?!
WE ARE...
THE FAIRY TALES GIVEN BREATH!

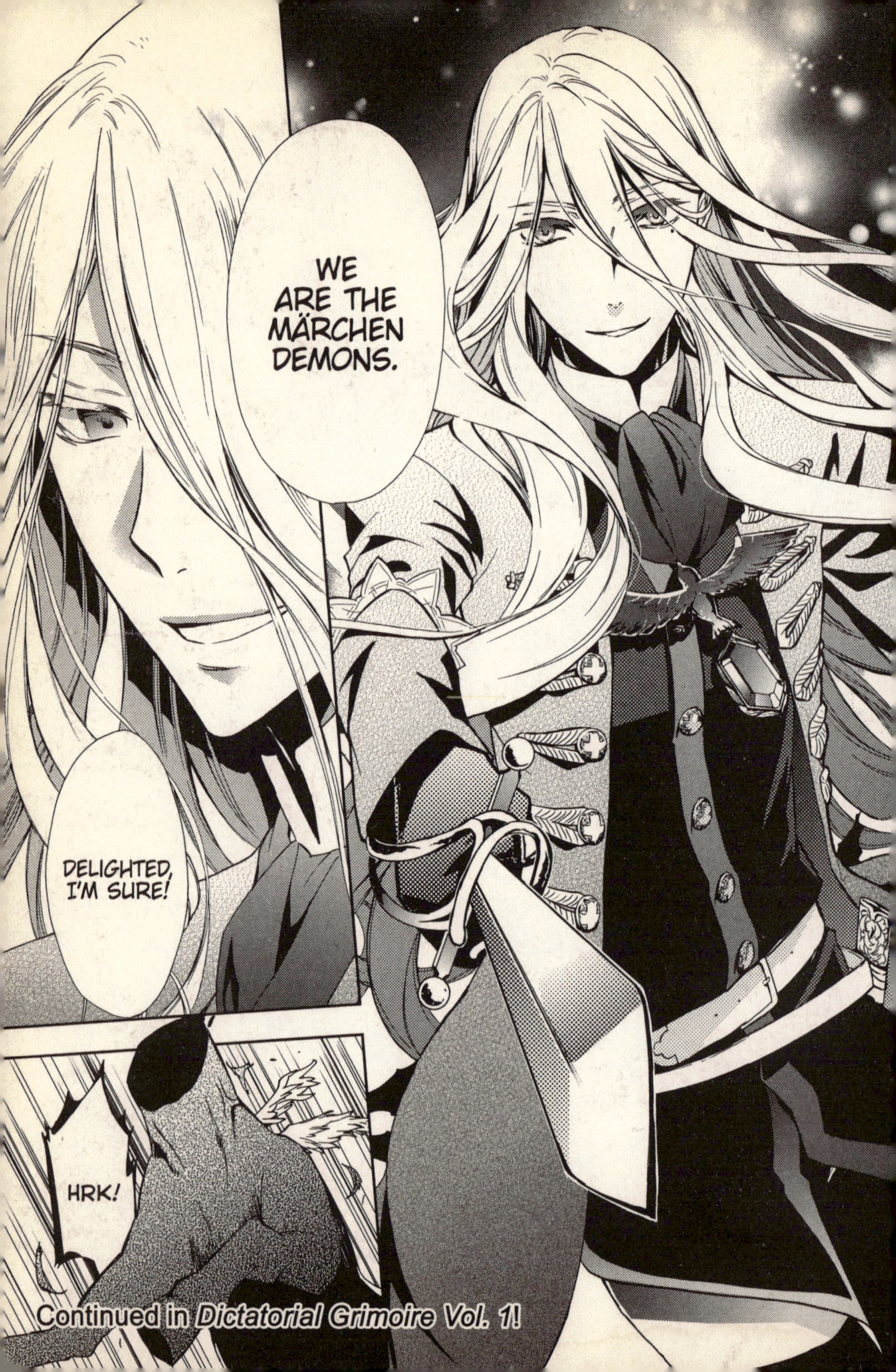
WE ARE THE MÄRCHEN DEMONS.
DELIGHTED, I'M SURE!
HRK!
Continued in *Dictatorial Grimoire Vol. 1!*

SEVEN SEAS ENTERTAINM

P9-DNO-079

MAY 1 2 2015

I am ALICE
BODY SWAP IN WONDERLAND

art by **AYUMI KANOU** / story by **VISUALWORKS**   **VOLUME 1**

TRANSLATION
Jocelyne Allen

ADAPTATION
Shanti Whitesides

LETTERING AND LAYOUT
Jennifer Skarupa

LOGO DESIGN
Phil Balsman

COVER DESIGN
Nicky Lim

PROOFREADER
Katherine Bell

MANAGING EDITOR
Adam Arnold

PUBLISHER
Jason DeAngelis

I AM ALICE: BODY SWAP IN WONDERLAND VOL. 1
© Kanou Ayumi 2013, © Visualworks 2013
Edited by MEDIA FACTORY.
First published in Japan in 2013 by KADOKAWA CORPORATION, Tokyo.
English translation rights reserved by Seven Seas Entertainment, LLC.
Under the license from KADOKAWA CORPORATION, Tokyo.

Seven Seas books may be purchased in bulk for educational, business, or promotional use. For information on bulk purchases, please contact Macmillan Corporate & Premium Sales Department at 1-800-221-7945 (ext 5442) or write specialmarkets@macmillan.com.

ISBN: 978-1-626920-65-1

Printed in Canada

First Printing: September 2014

10 9 8 7 6 5 4 3 2 1

FOLLOW US ONLINE: **www.gomanga.com**

READING DIRECTIONS

This book reads from *right to left*, Japanese style. If this is your first time reading manga, you start reading from the top right panel on each page and take it from there. If you get lost, just follow the numbered diagram here. It may seem backwards at first, but you□ll get the hang of it! Have fun!!

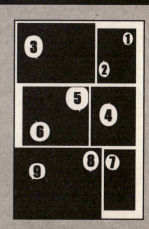